Hell's Paradise

JIGOKURAKU

STORY AND ART BY
YUJI KAKU

Hell's Paradise: Cast of Characters

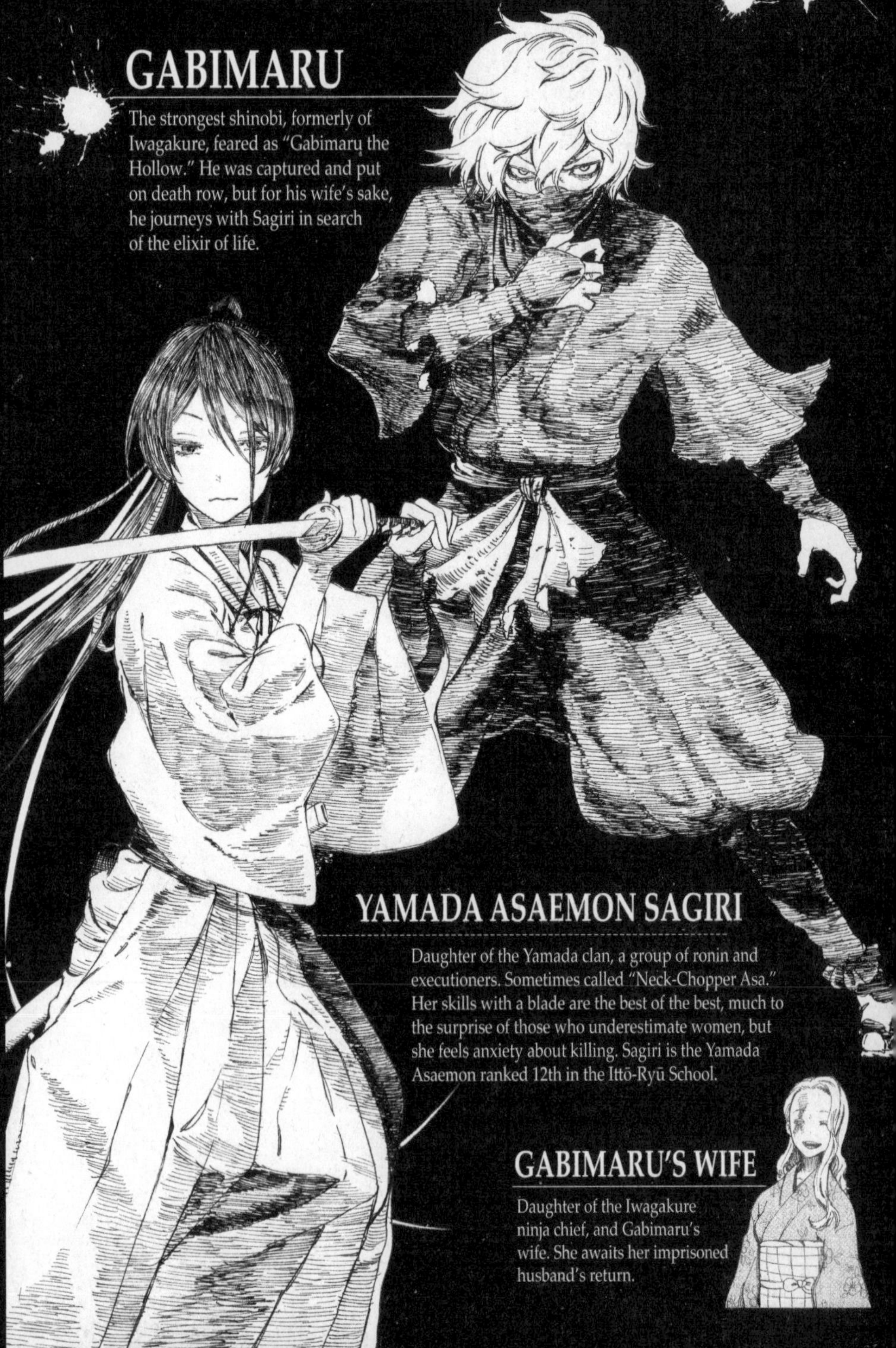

GABIMARU

The strongest shinobi, formerly of Iwagakure, feared as "Gabimaru the Hollow." He was captured and put on death row, but for his wife's sake, he journeys with Sagiri in search of the elixir of life.

YAMADA ASAEMON SAGIRI

Daughter of the Yamada clan, a group of ronin and executioners. Sometimes called "Neck-Chopper Asa." Her skills with a blade are the best of the best, much to the surprise of those who underestimate women, but she feels anxiety about killing. Sagiri is the Yamada Asaemon ranked 12th in the Ittō-Ryū School.

GABIMARU'S WIFE

Daughter of the Iwagakure ninja chief, and Gabimaru's wife. She awaits her imprisoned husband's return.

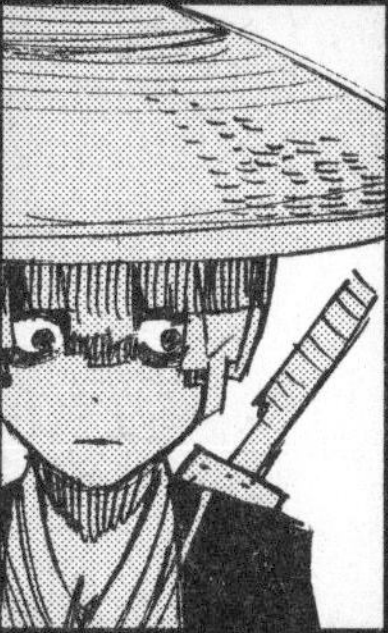

FUCHI

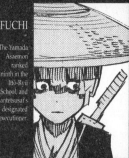

The Yamada Asaemon ranked ninth in the Ittō-Ryū School, and Gantetsusai's designated executioner.

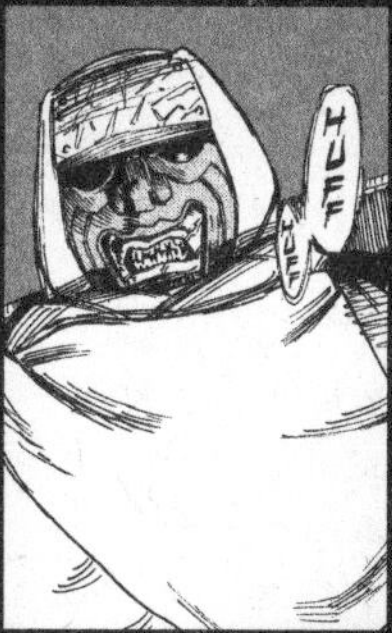
HUFF
HUFF

KEIUN

A monk nicknamed "Hunter of the Hundred." Notable for his "living armor" plates stitched directly onto his body.

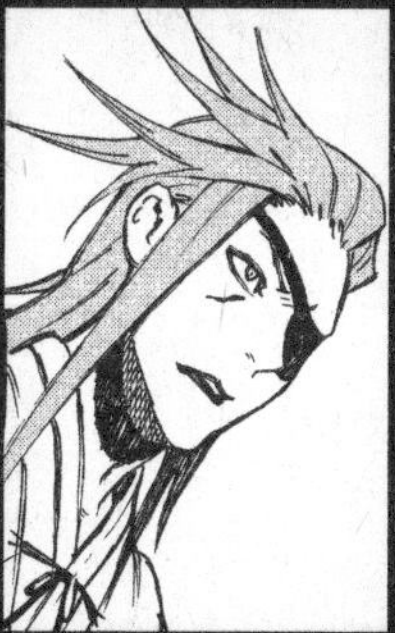

EIZEN

The Yamada Asaemon ranked number one in the Ittō-Ryū School, and Rokurota's designated executioner.

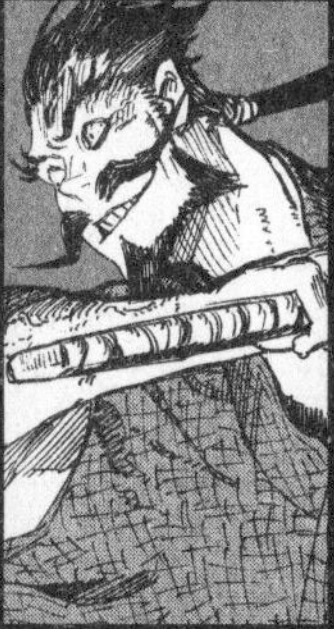

TAMIYA GANTETSUSAI

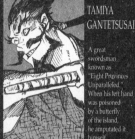

A great swordsman known as "Eight Provinces Unparalleled." When his left hand was poisoned by a butterfly of the island, he amputated it himself.

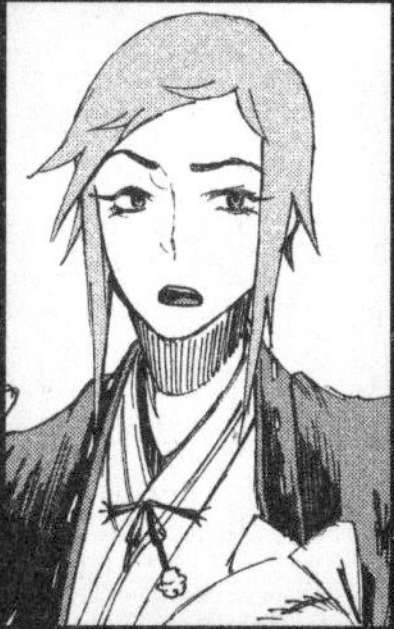

KISHO

The Yamada Asaemon ranked 11th in the Ittō-Ryū School, and Keiun's designated executioner.

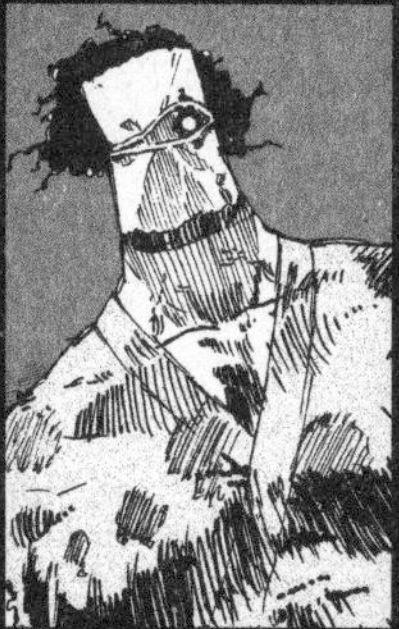

ROKUROTA

Known as "the Giant of Bizen." Swords cannot pierce his hide, and he's rumored to have once eaten a bear headfirst.

OTHER CONVICTS

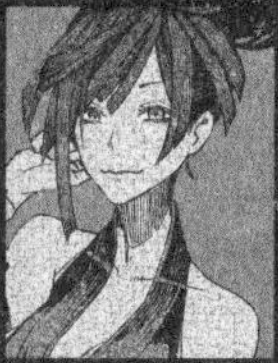

KUNOICHI: YUZURIHA OF KEISHU

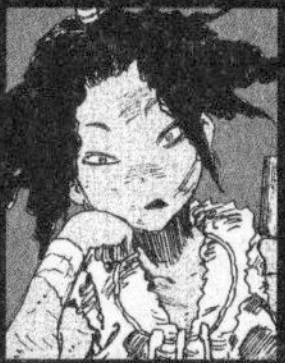

NURUGAI OF THE SANKA

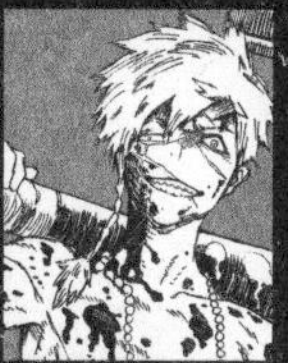

BANDIT KING: AZA CHOBE

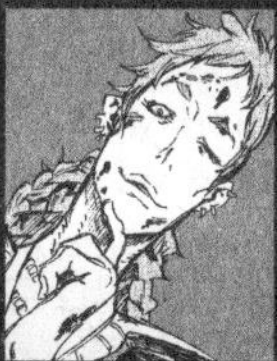

MORO MAKIYA THE APOSTATE

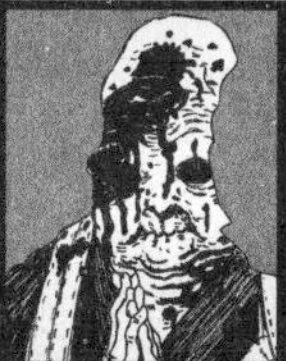

KILLING BUDDHIST PRAYER: HORUBO

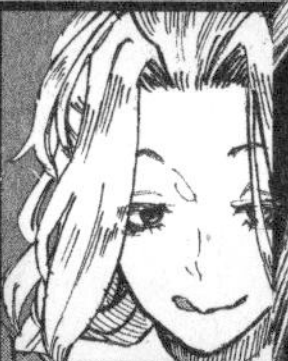

CANNIBAL COURTESAN: AKAGINU

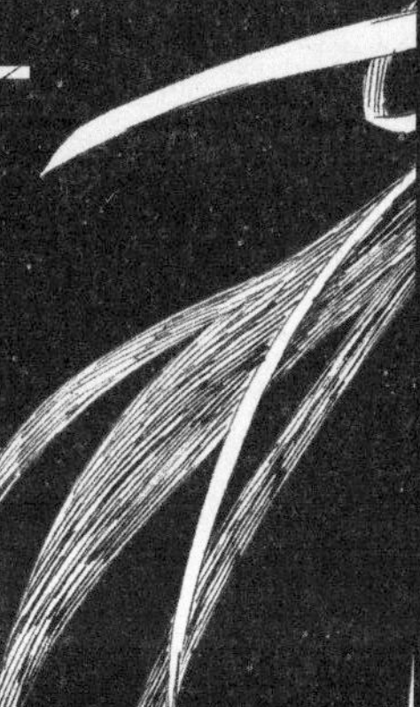

STORY

In the waning years of the Edo Period…

Once hailed as the strongest shinobi, the much-feared Gabimaru goes astray and is soon captured. In prison, executioner Yamada Asaemon Sagiri tells him of an island rumored to be paradise itself. Should he find the legendary elixir of life there, he will be granted the highest pardon from the shogunate. Gabimaru accepts the mission in the hope of one day reuniting with his beloved wife, and he travels to the island with Sagiri. However, his fellow death row convicts and the mysterious beings inhabiting this so-called paradise stand in their way!

Will Gabimaru and Sagiri find the elixir of life and escape the hellish island with their lives?

HELL'S

PARADISE

JIGOKURAKU

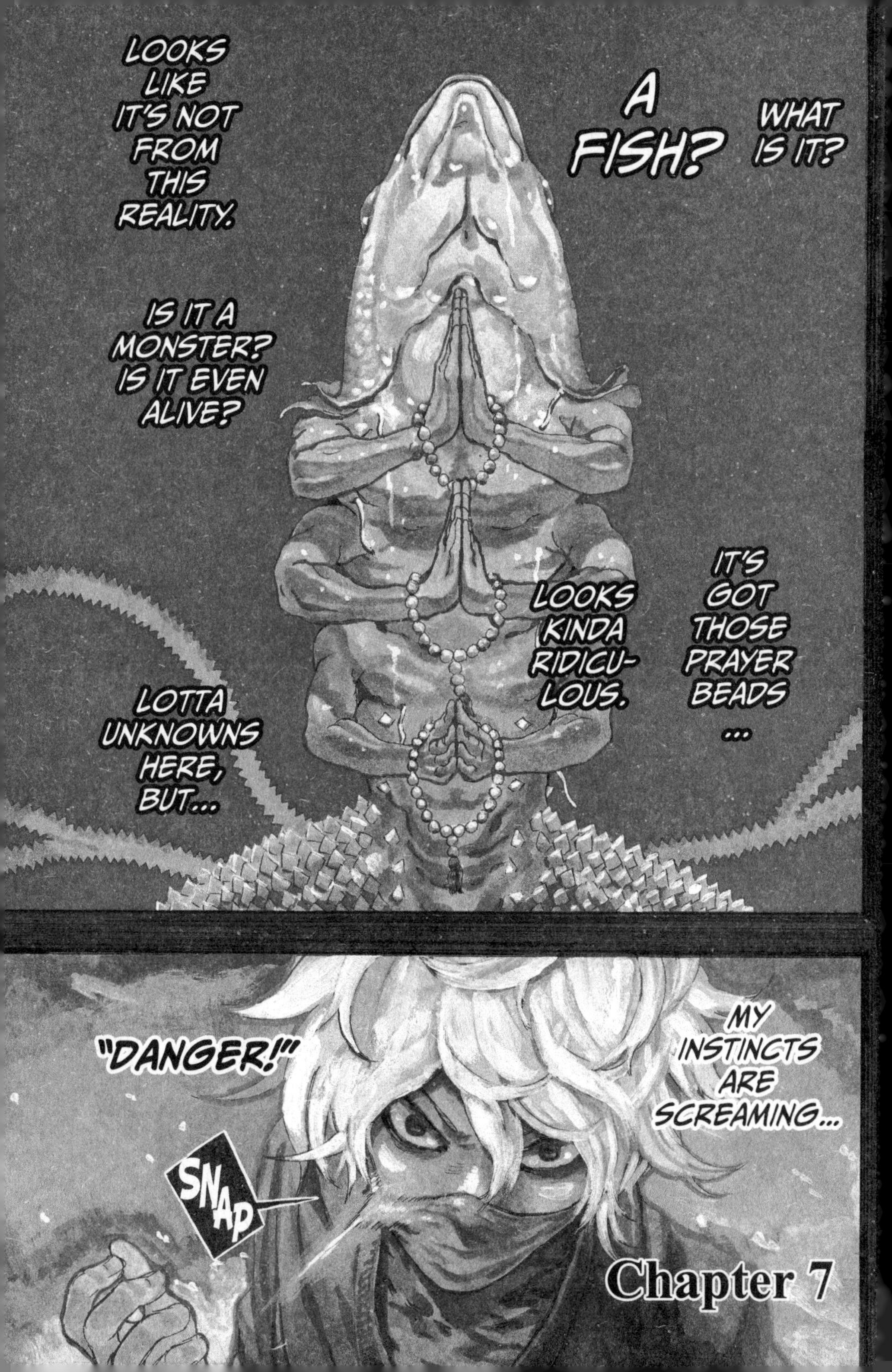
WHAT IS IT?
A FISH?
LOOKS LIKE IT'S NOT FROM THIS REALITY.
IS IT A MONSTER? IS IT EVEN ALIVE?
IT'S GOT THOSE PRAYER BEADS...
LOOKS KINDA RIDICU-LOUS.
LOTTA UNKNOWNS HERE, BUT...
MY INSTINCTS ARE SCREAMING...
"DANGER!"
SNAP

Chapter 7

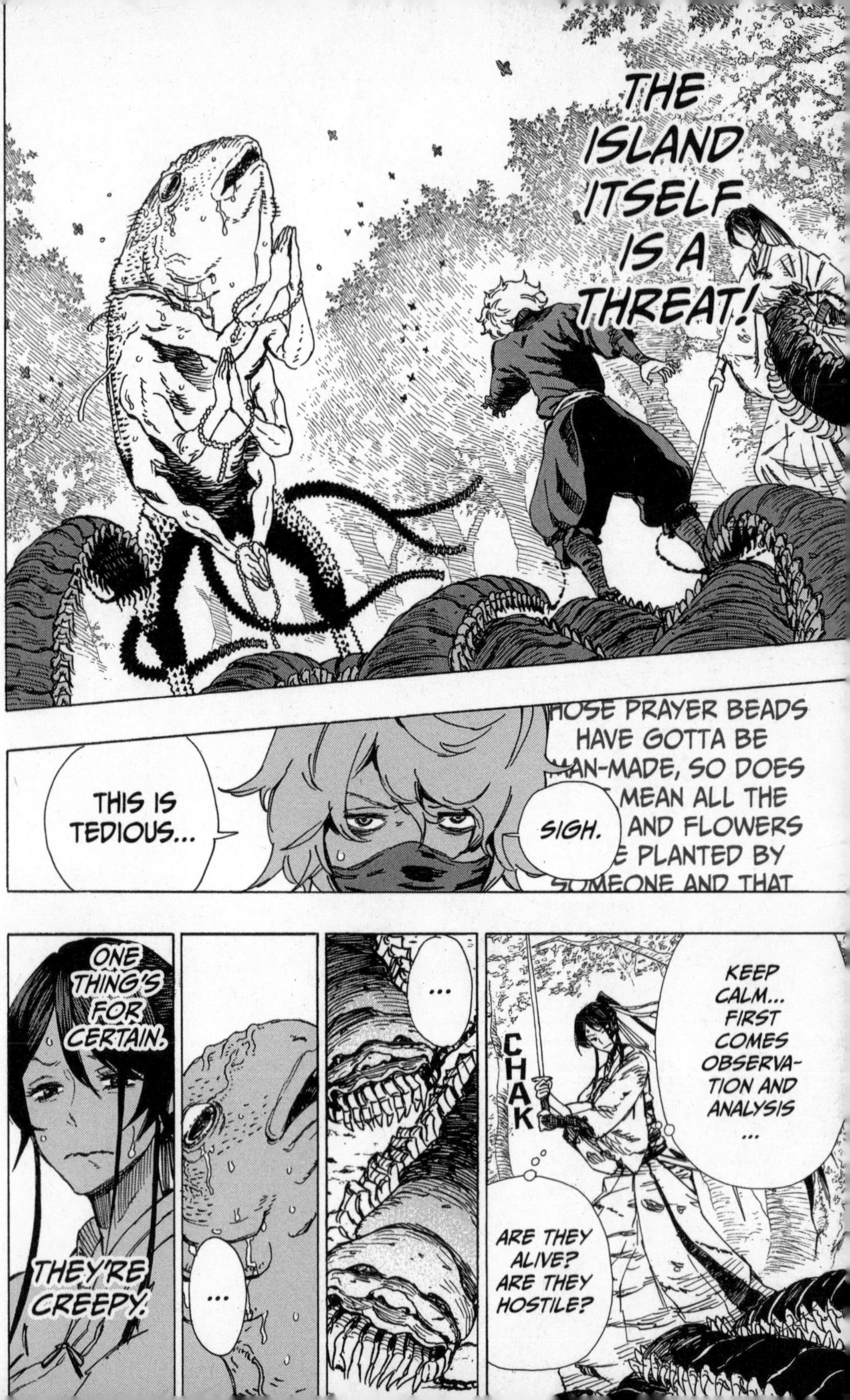
THE ISLAND ITSELF IS A THREAT!
HOSE PRAYER BEADS HAVE GOTTA BE MAN-MADE, SO DOES
MEAN ALL THE
AND FLOWERS
E PLANTED BY
SOMEONE AND THAT
SIGH.
THIS IS TEDIOUS...
KEEP CALM... FIRST COMES OBSERVATION AND ANALYSIS ...
CHAK
ARE THEY ALIVE? ARE THEY HOSTILE?
...
...
ONE THING'S FOR CERTAIN.
THEY'RE CREEPY.

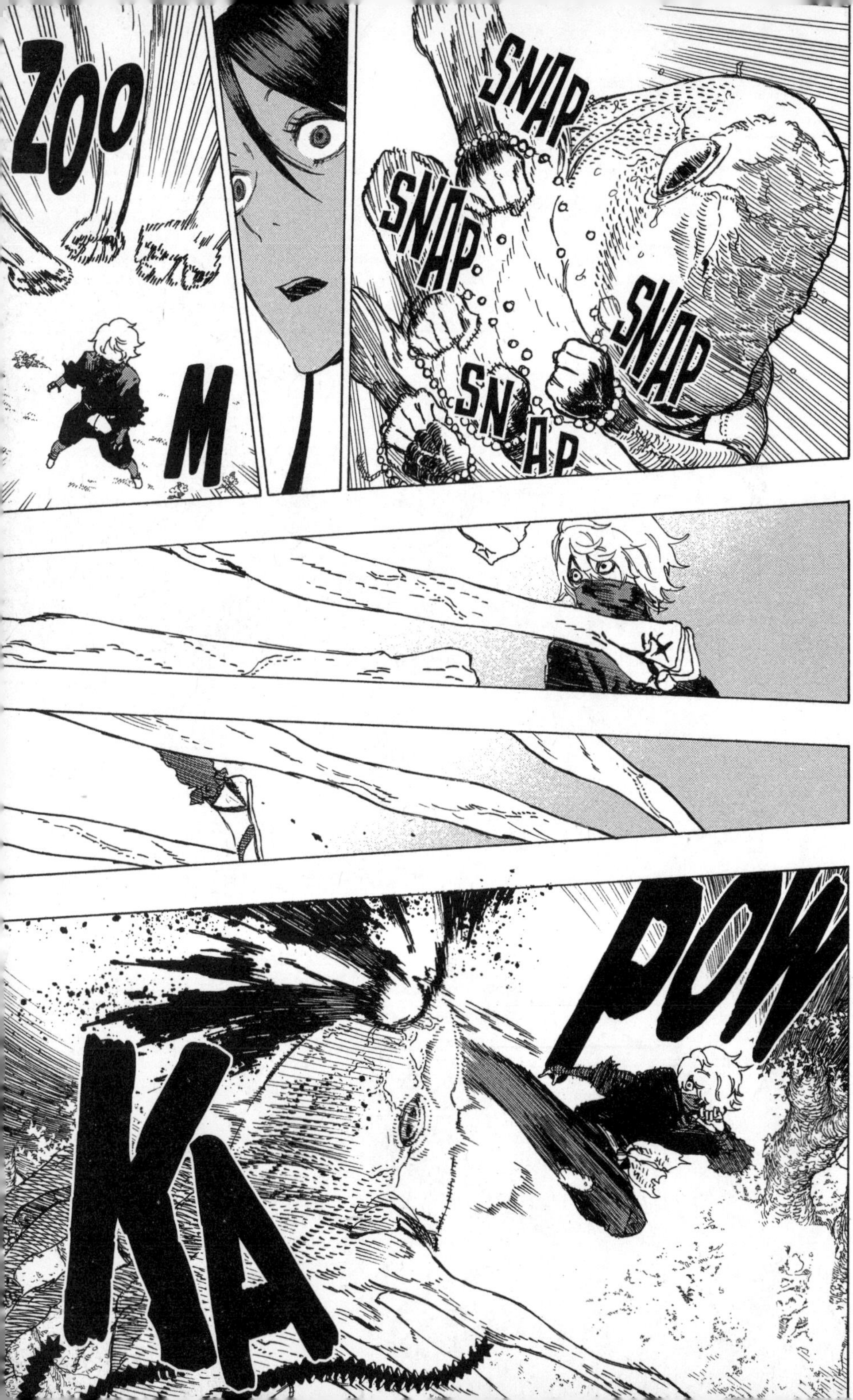
SNAP
SNAP
SNAP
SNAP
SNAP
ZOOM
POW
KA

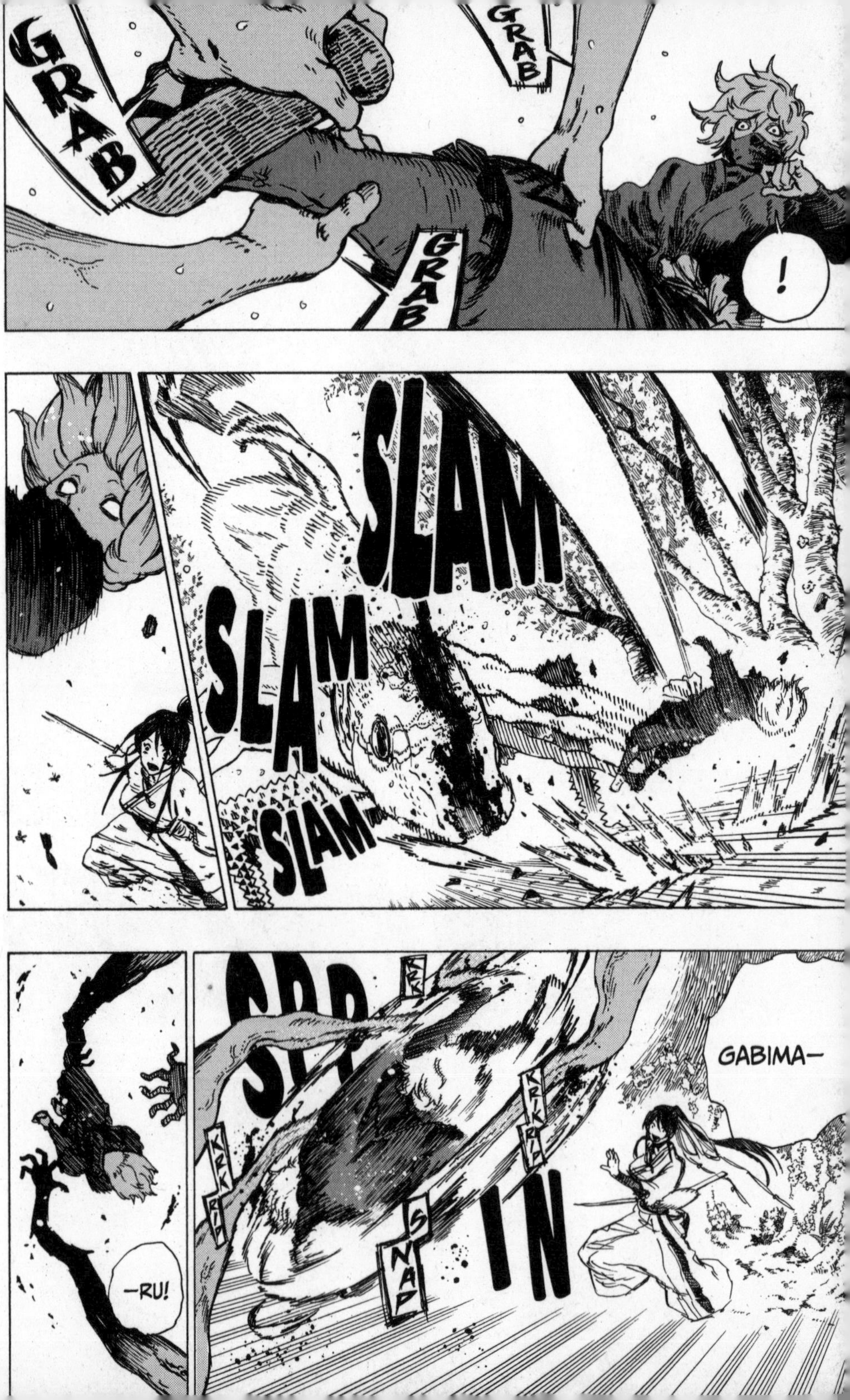
GRAB
!
GRAB
GRAB
SLAM
SLAM
SLAM
GABIMA—
KRK
KRK RIP
SPR
IN
KRK RIP
SNAP
—RU!

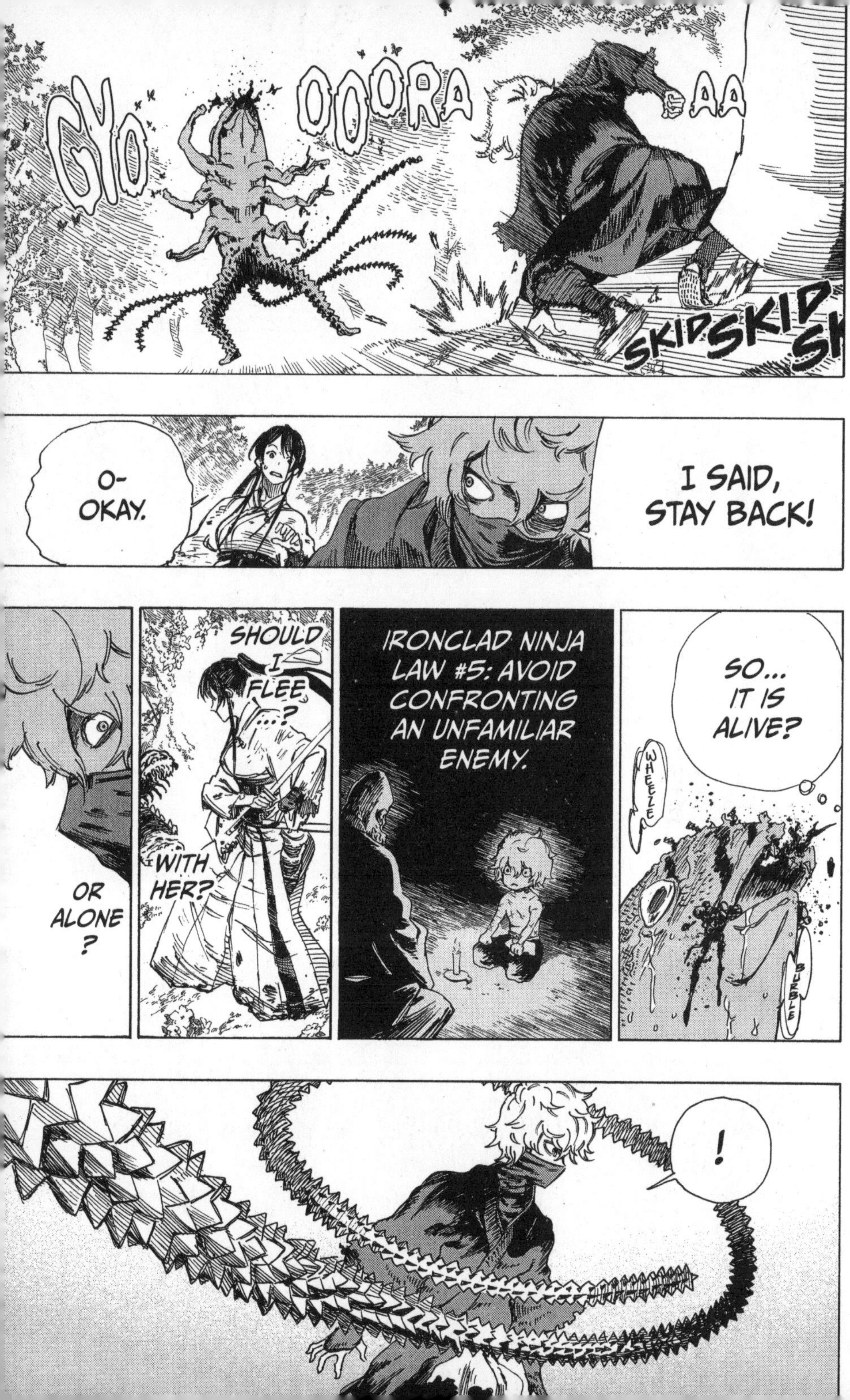
GYOOOORAAA
SKID SKID SK
I SAID, STAY BACK!
O-OKAY.
SO... IT IS ALIVE?
WHEEZE
BUBBLE
IRONCLAD NINJA LAW #5: AVOID CONFRONTING AN UNFAMILIAR ENEMY.
SHOULD I FLEE...?
WITH HER?
OR ALONE?
!

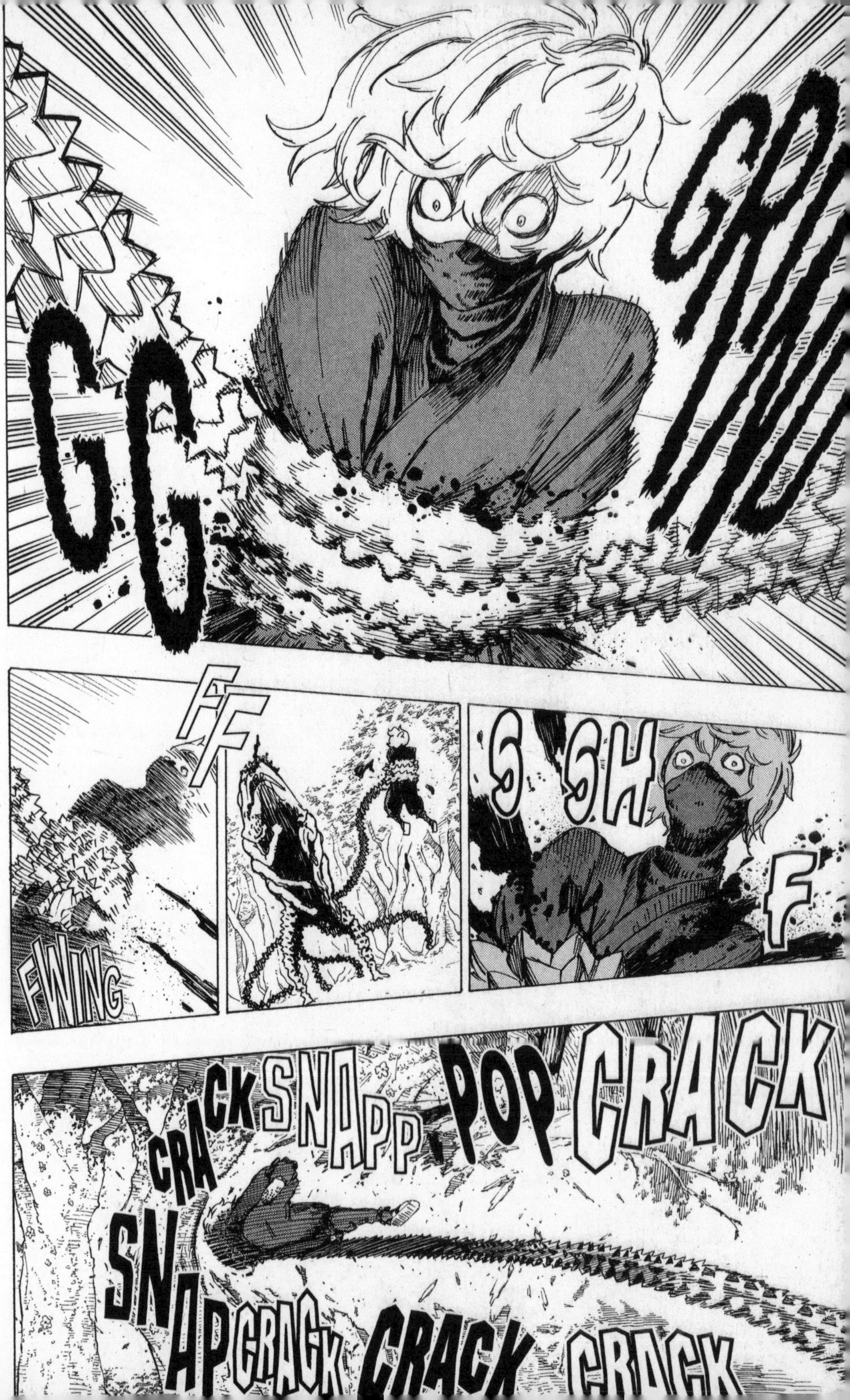
GRA
GG
S SH
F
FF
FWING
CRACK
POP
SNAPP
CRACK
SNAP
CRACK
CRACK
CRACK

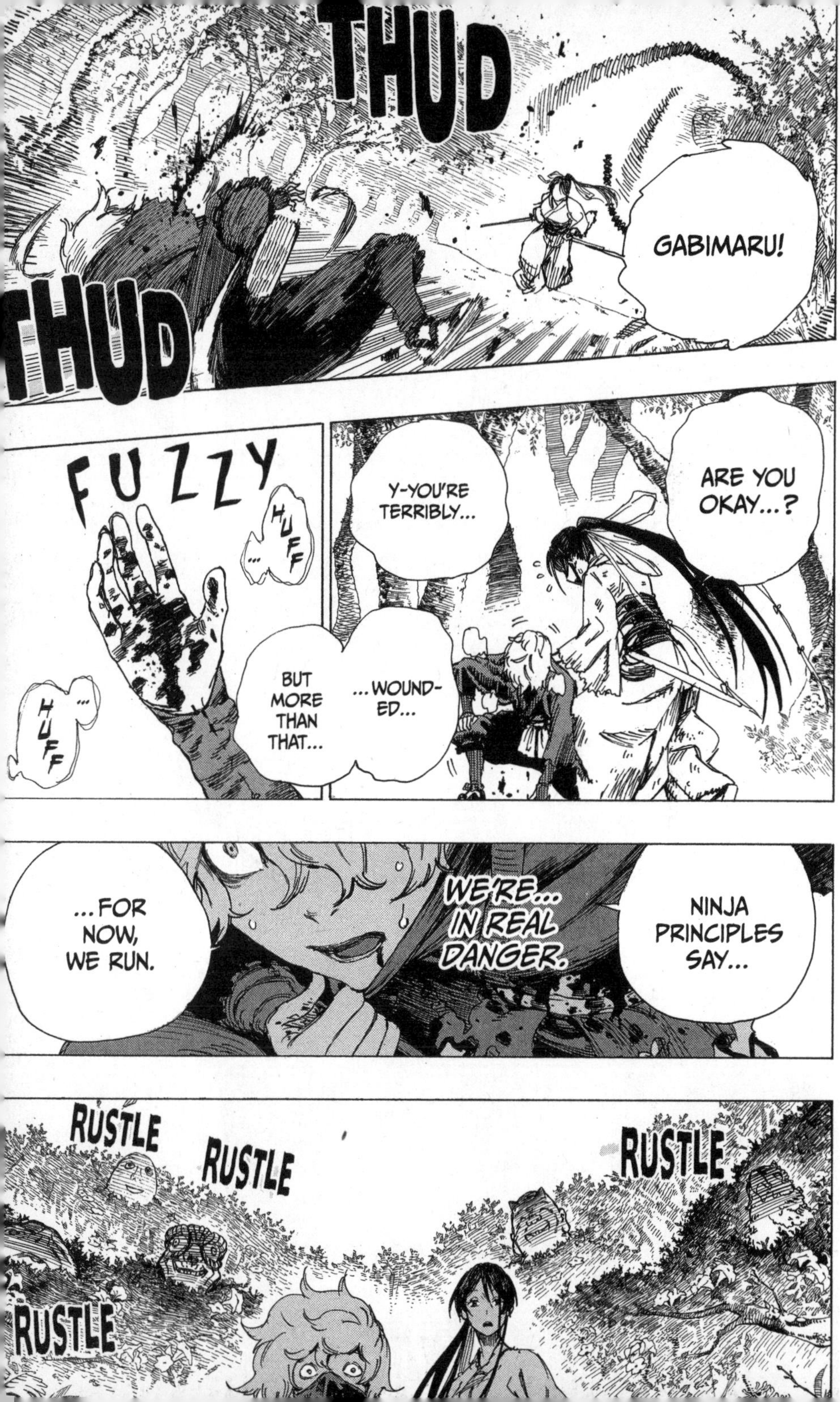
THUD
GABIMARU!
THUD
ARE YOU OKAY...?
Y-YOU'RE TERRIBLY...
...WOUND-ED...
BUT MORE THAN THAT...
FUZZY
...HUFF
...HUFF
NINJA PRINCIPLES SAY...
WE'RE... IN REAL DANGER.
...FOR NOW, WE RUN.
RUSTLE
RUSTLE
RUSTLE
RUSTLE

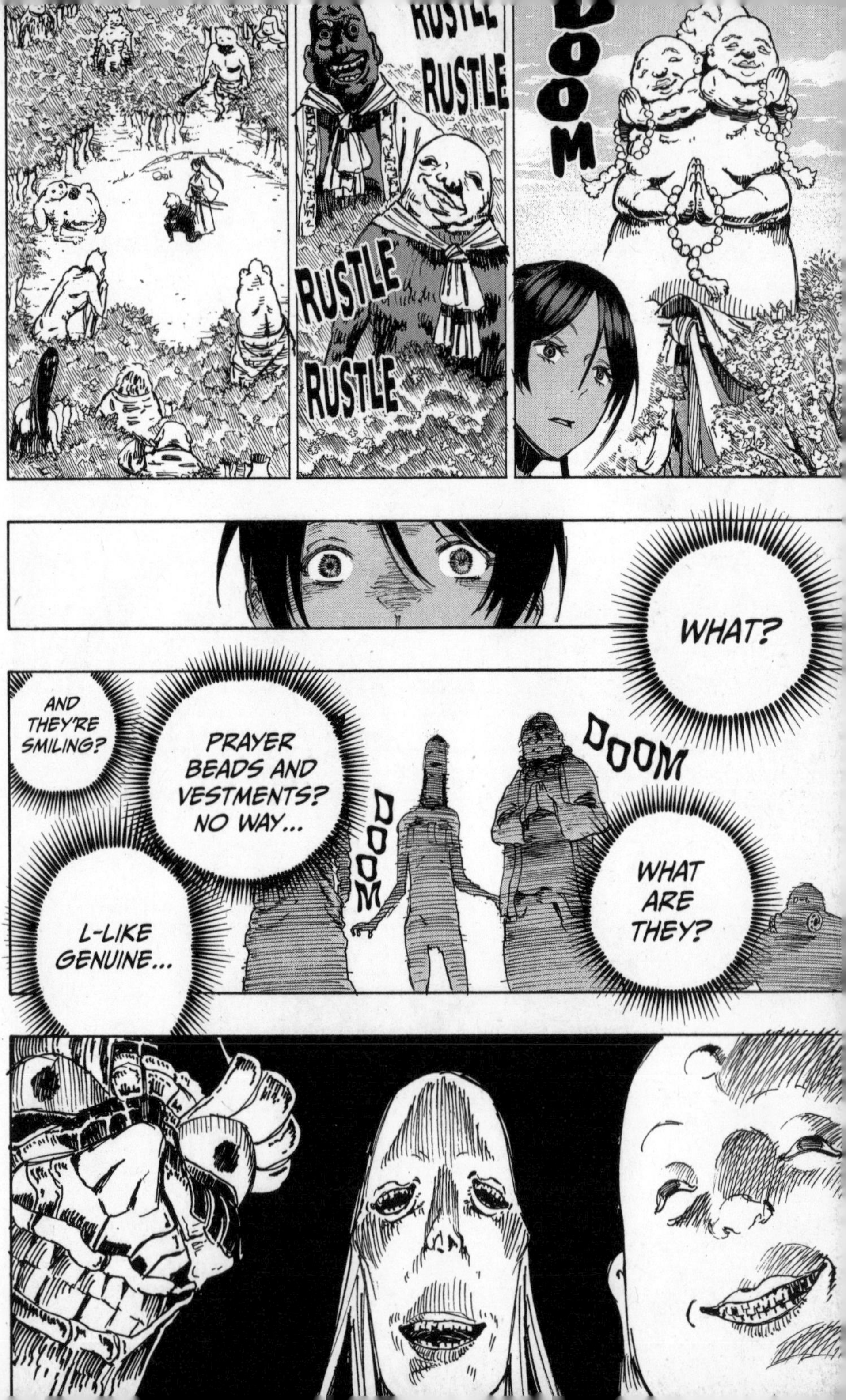
DOOM
RUSTLE
RUSTLE
RUSTLE
RUSTLE
WHAT?
DOOM
WHAT ARE THEY?
DOOM
PRAYER BEADS AND VESTMENTS? NO WAY...
AND THEY'RE SMILING?
L-LIKE GENUINE...

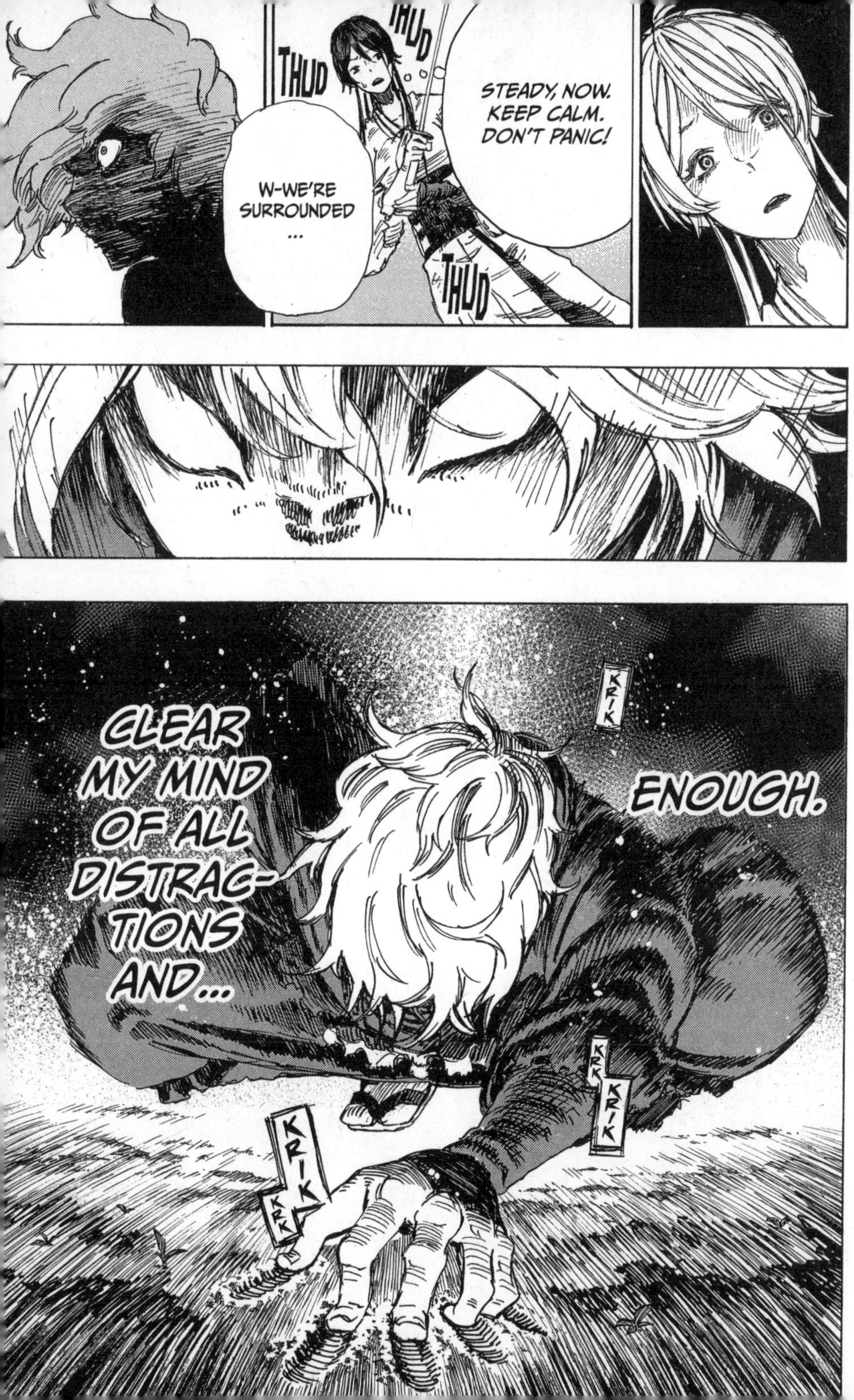
THUD
THUD
STEADY, NOW. KEEP CALM. DON'T PANIC!
W-WE'RE SURROUNDED ...
THUD
ENOUGH.
KRIK
CLEAR MY MIND OF ALL DISTRAC-TIONS AND...
KRK KRIK
KRIK KRK

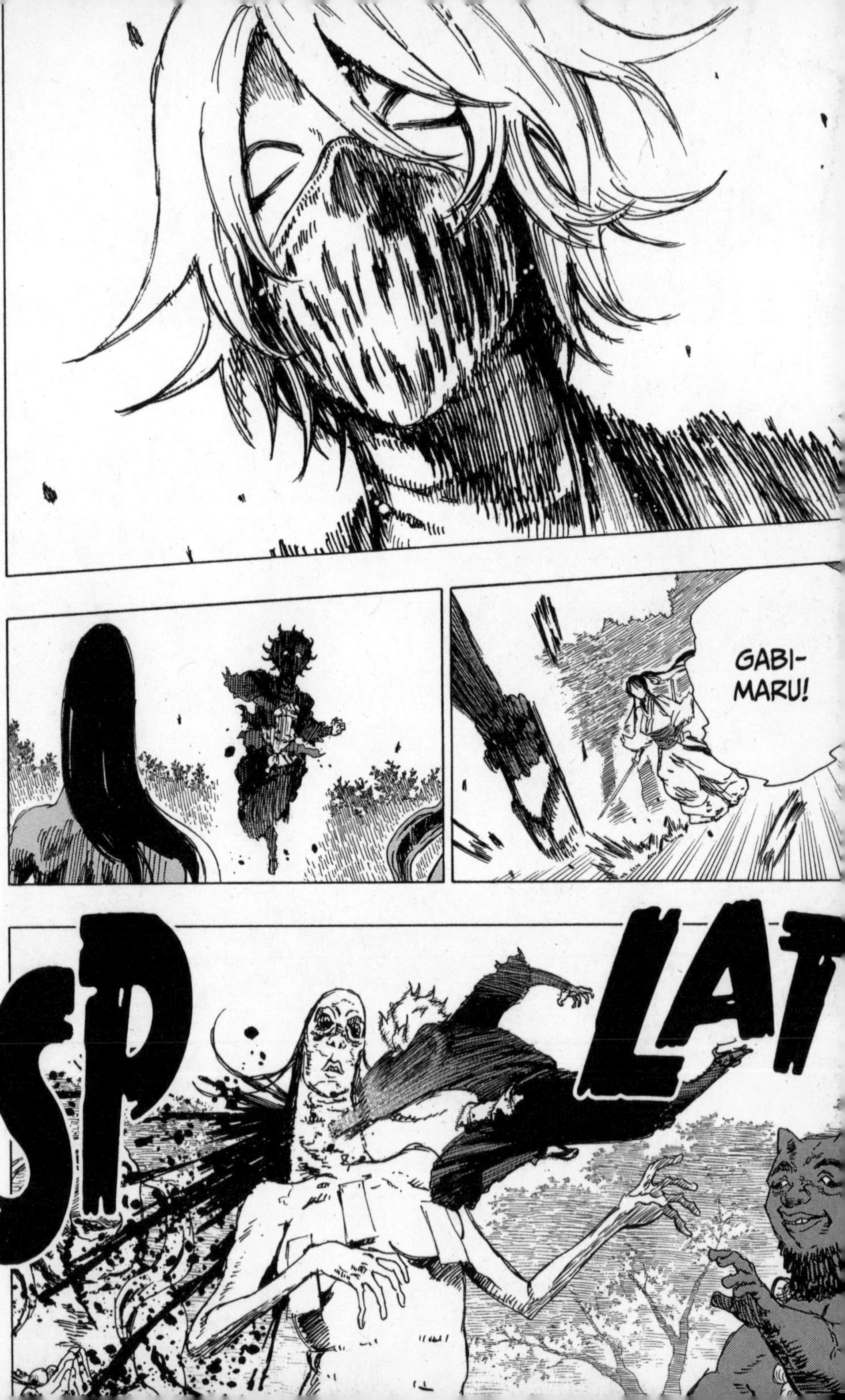
GABI-
MARU!
SPLAT

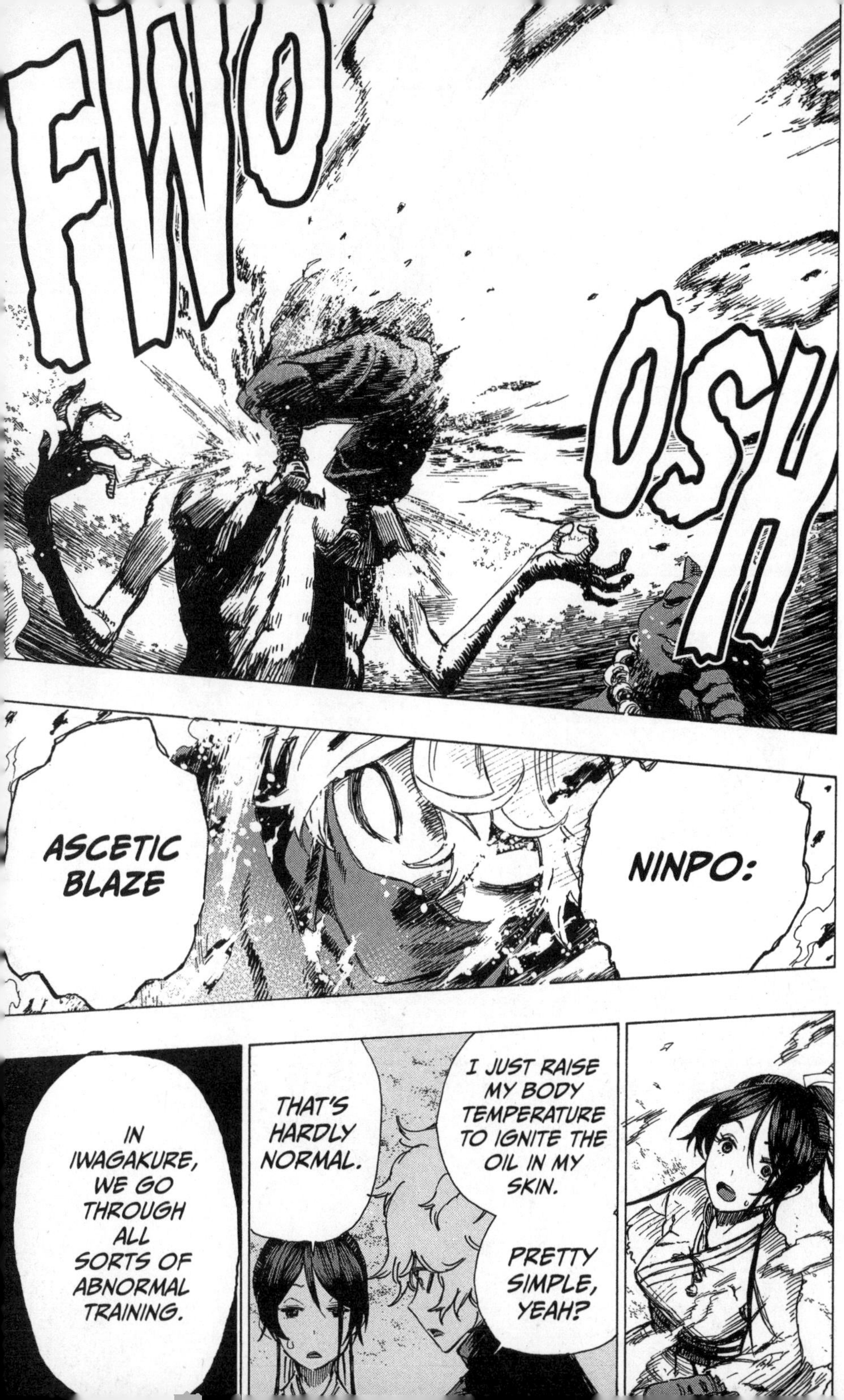
FWO
OSH
NINPO:
ASCETIC BLAZE
I JUST RAISE MY BODY TEMPERATURE TO IGNITE THE OIL IN MY SKIN.
PRETTY SIMPLE, YEAH?
THAT'S HARDLY NORMAL.
IN IWAGAKURE, WE GO THROUGH ALL SORTS OF ABNORMAL TRAINING.

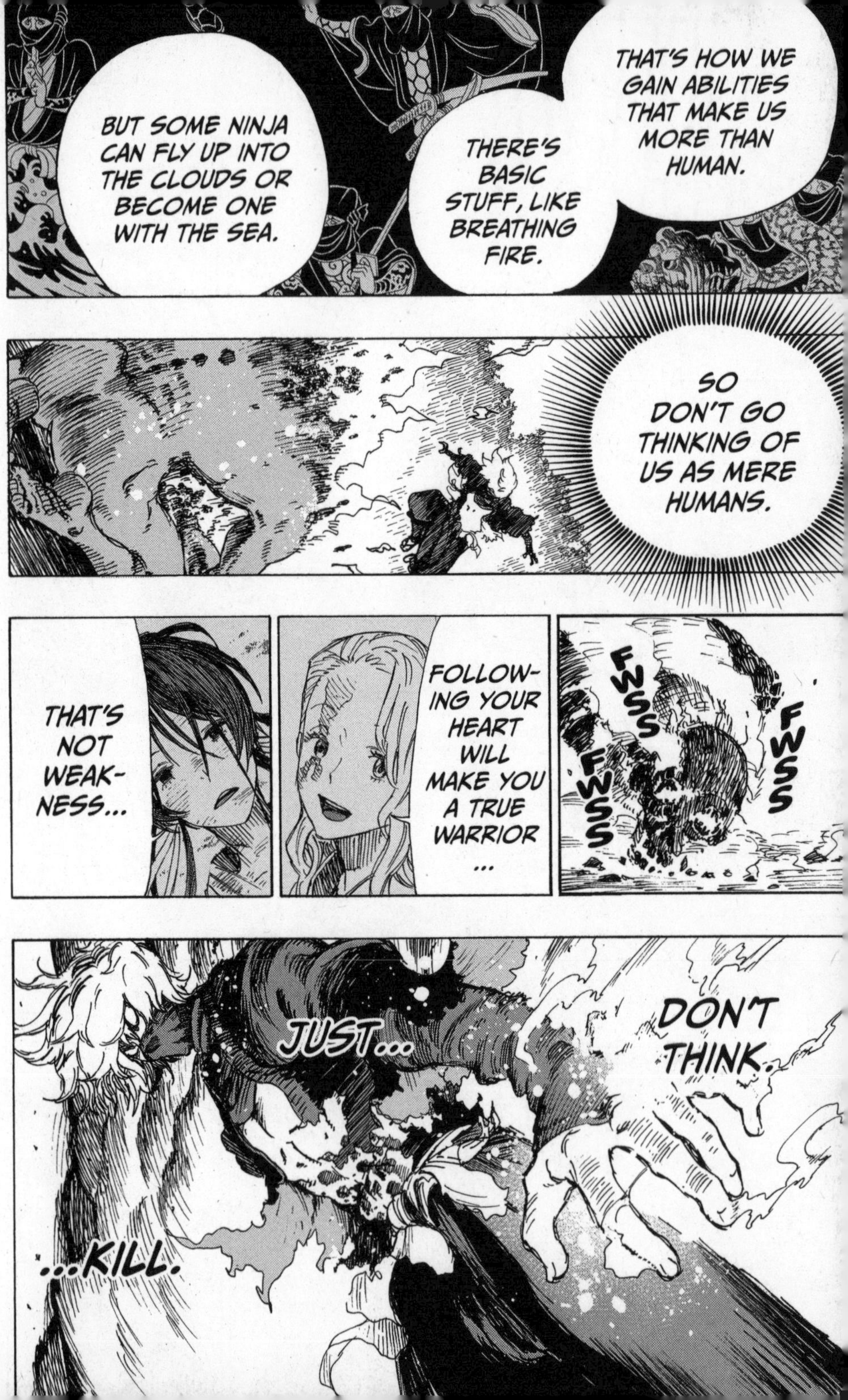
THAT'S HOW WE GAIN ABILITIES THAT MAKE US MORE THAN HUMAN.
THERE'S BASIC STUFF, LIKE BREATHING FIRE.
BUT SOME NINJA CAN FLY UP INTO THE CLOUDS OR BECOME ONE WITH THE SEA.
SO DON'T GO THINKING OF US AS MERE HUMANS.
FWSS
FWSS
FWSS
FOLLOWING YOUR HEART WILL MAKE YOU A TRUE WARRIOR...
THAT'S NOT WEAKNESS...
DON'T THINK.
JUST...
...KILL.

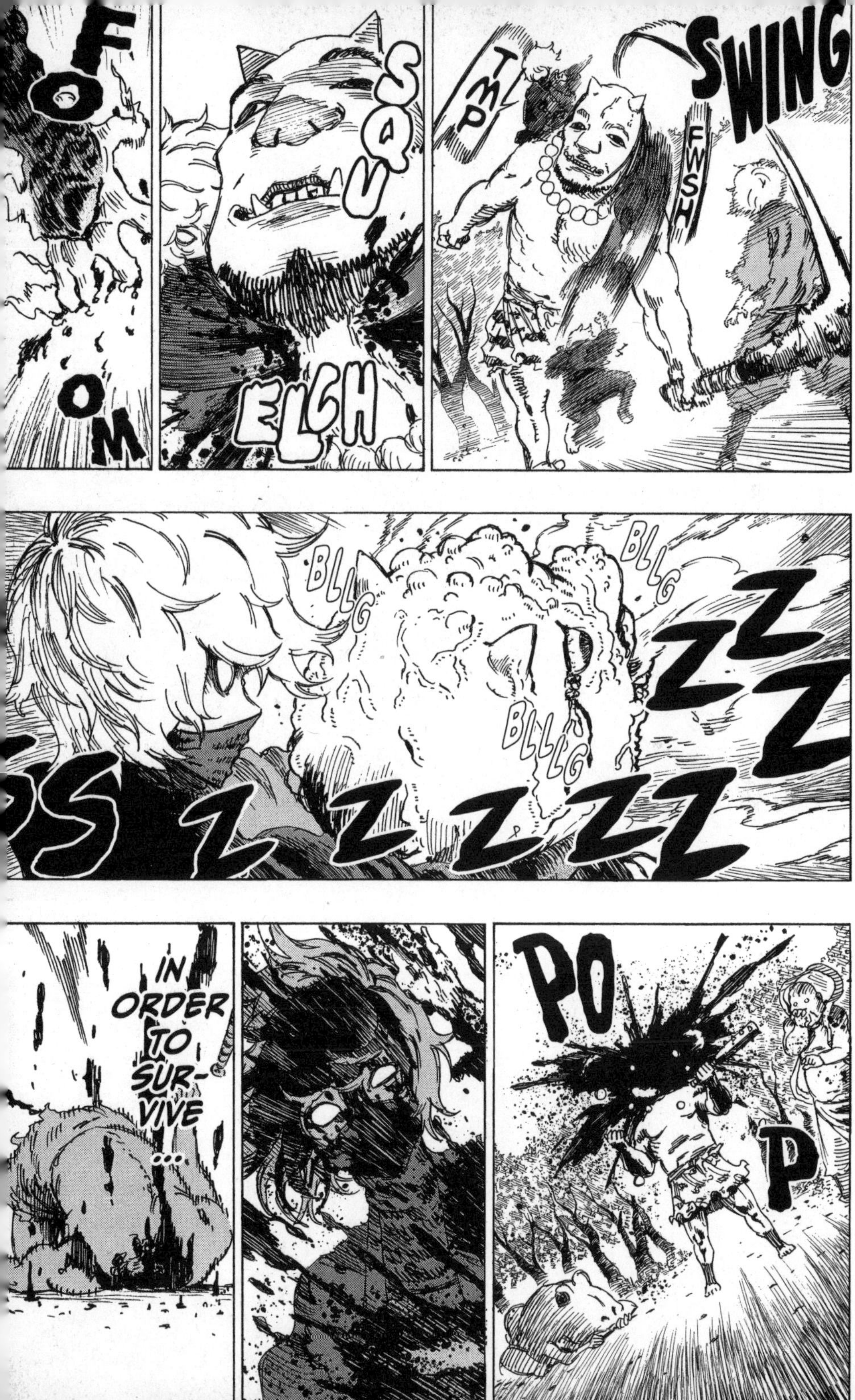
SWING
FWSH
TMP
SQU
ELCH
F
O
OM
BLLG
BLLG
BLLLG
ZZZ
ZZZZ
Z
PS
PO
P
IN ORDER TO SUR-VIVE ...

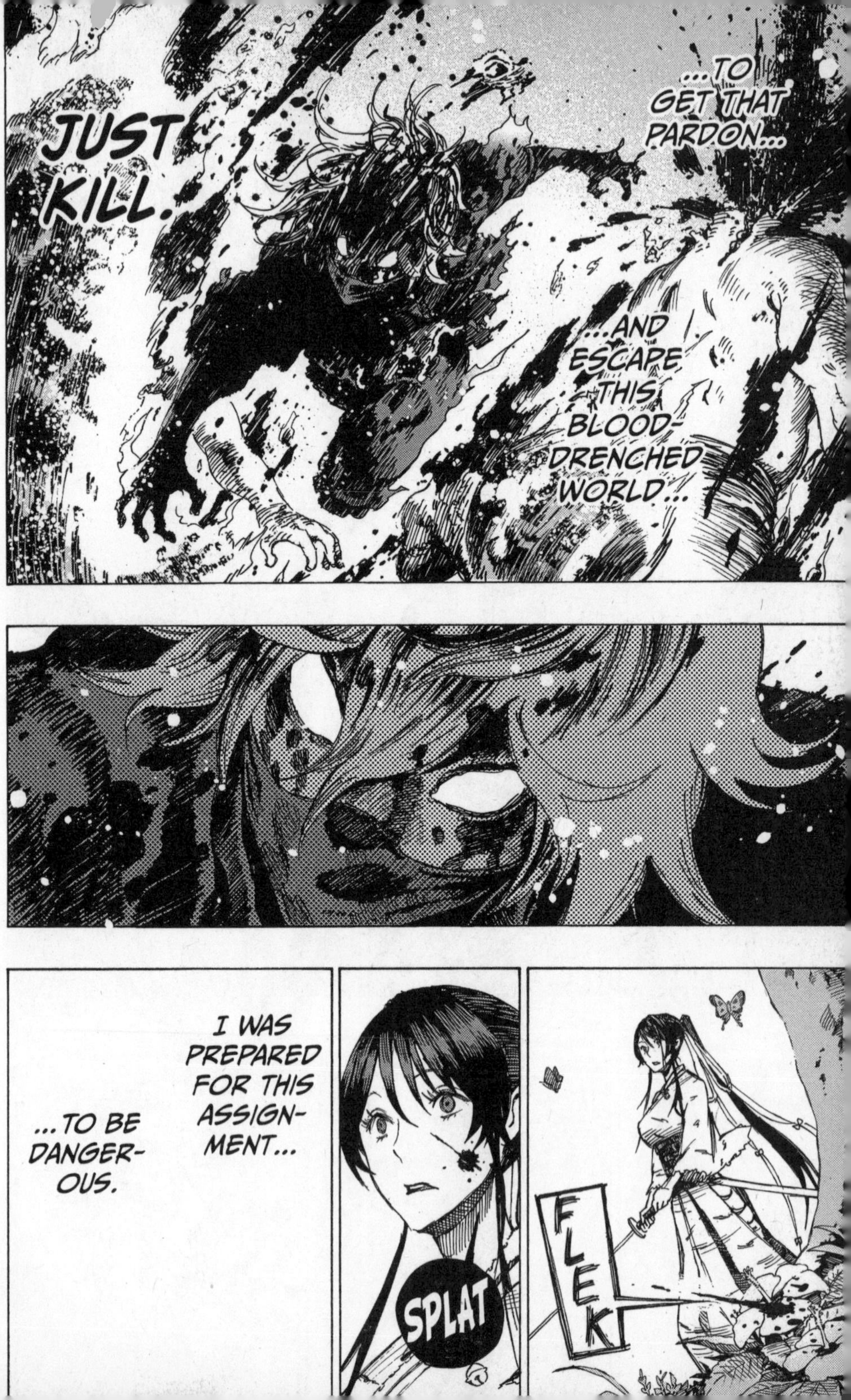
...TO GET THAT PARDON...
...AND ESCAPE THIS BLOOD-DRENCHED WORLD...
JUST KILL.
FLEK
SPLAT
I WAS PREPARED FOR THIS ASSIGNMENT...
...TO BE DANGEROUS.

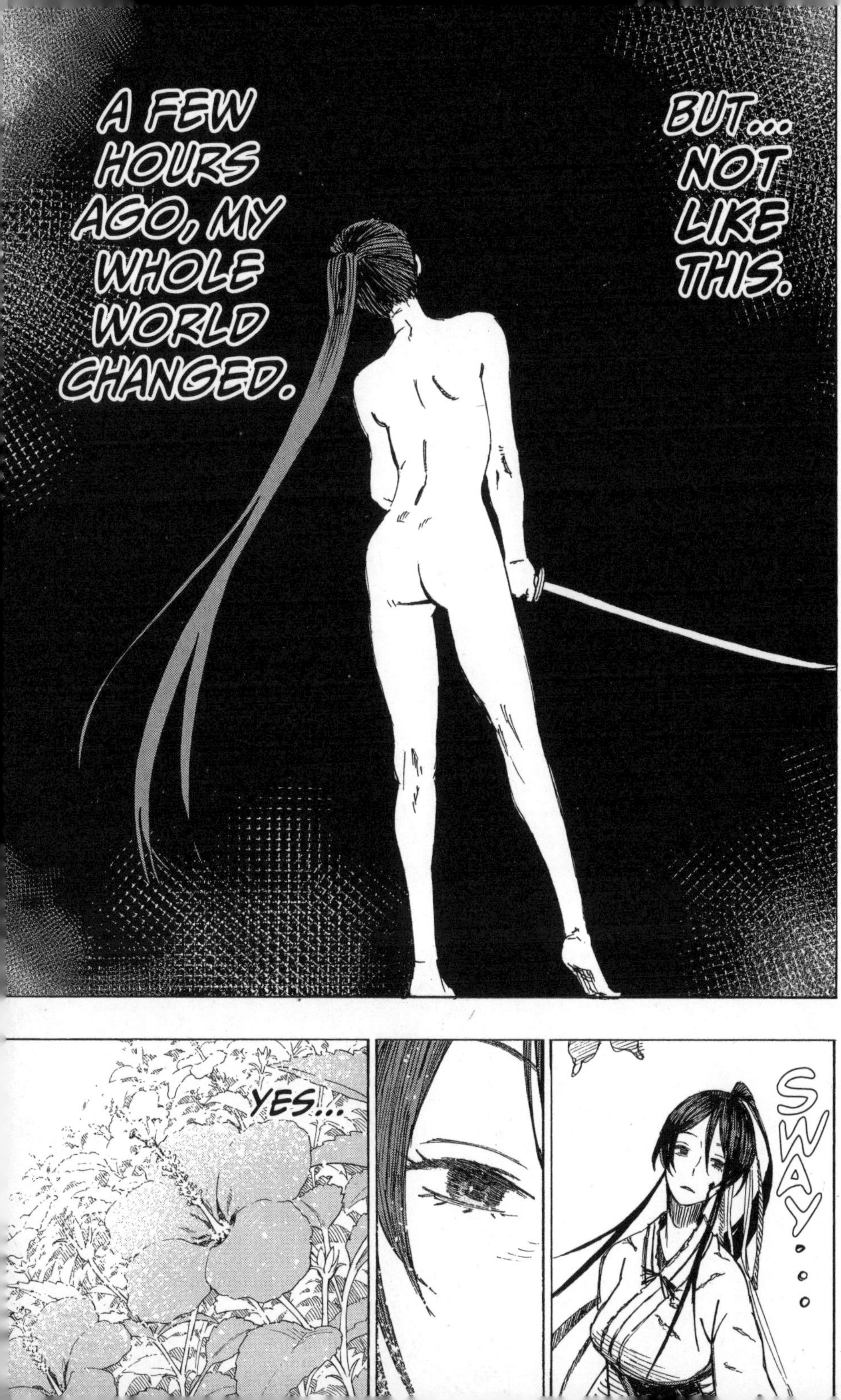
A FEW HOURS AGO, MY WHOLE WORLD CHANGED.
BUT... NOT LIKE THIS.
SWAY...
YES...

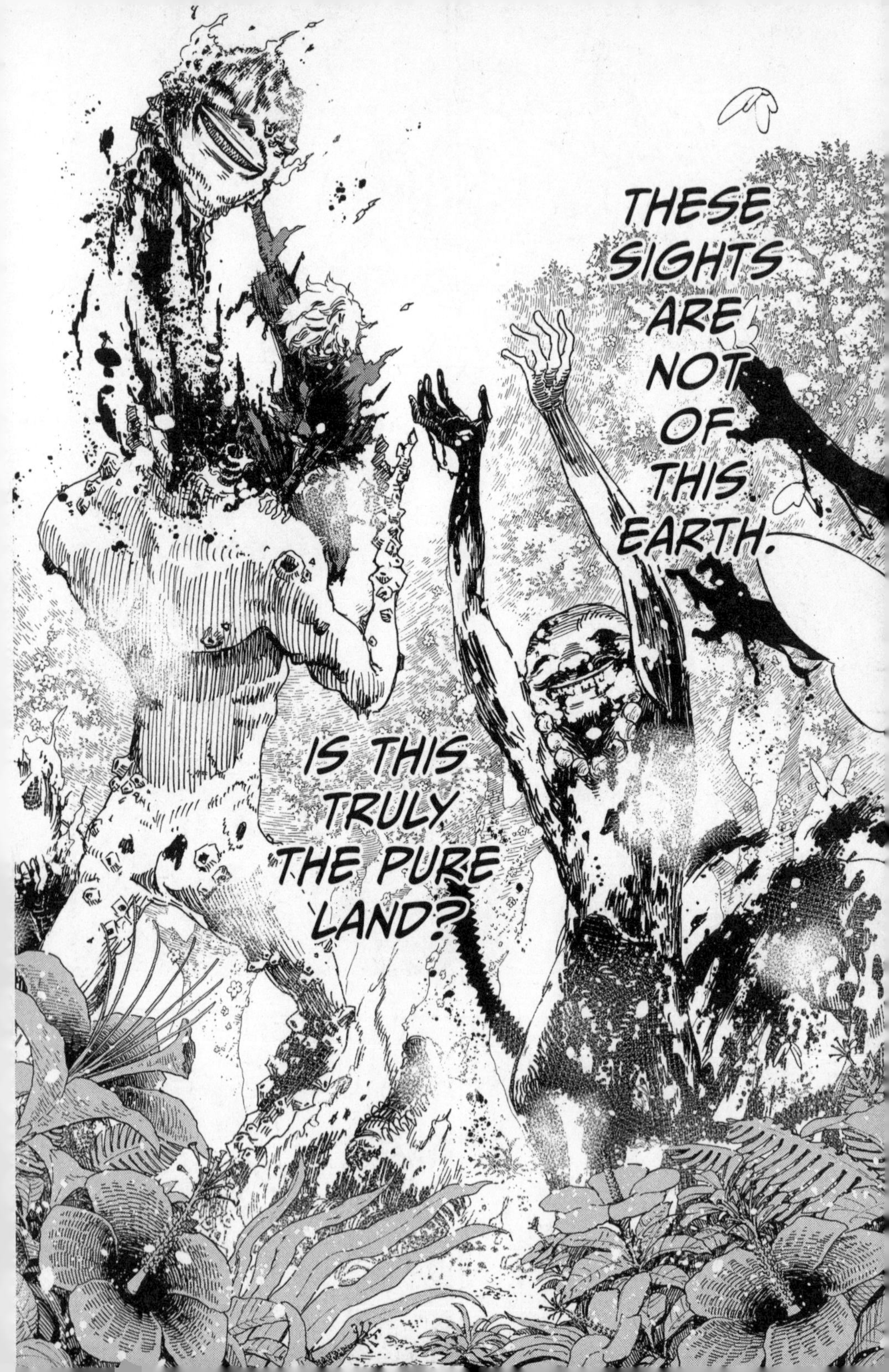
THESE SIGHTS ARE NOT OF THIS EARTH.
IS THIS TRULY THE PURE LAND?

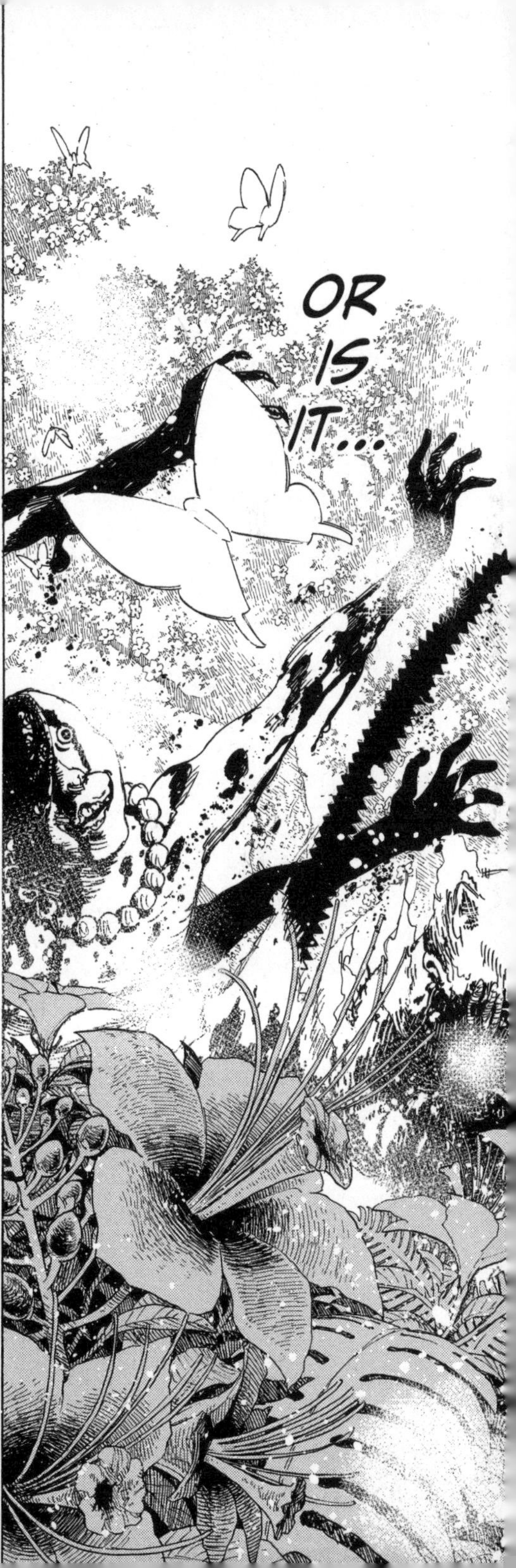
OR IS IT...
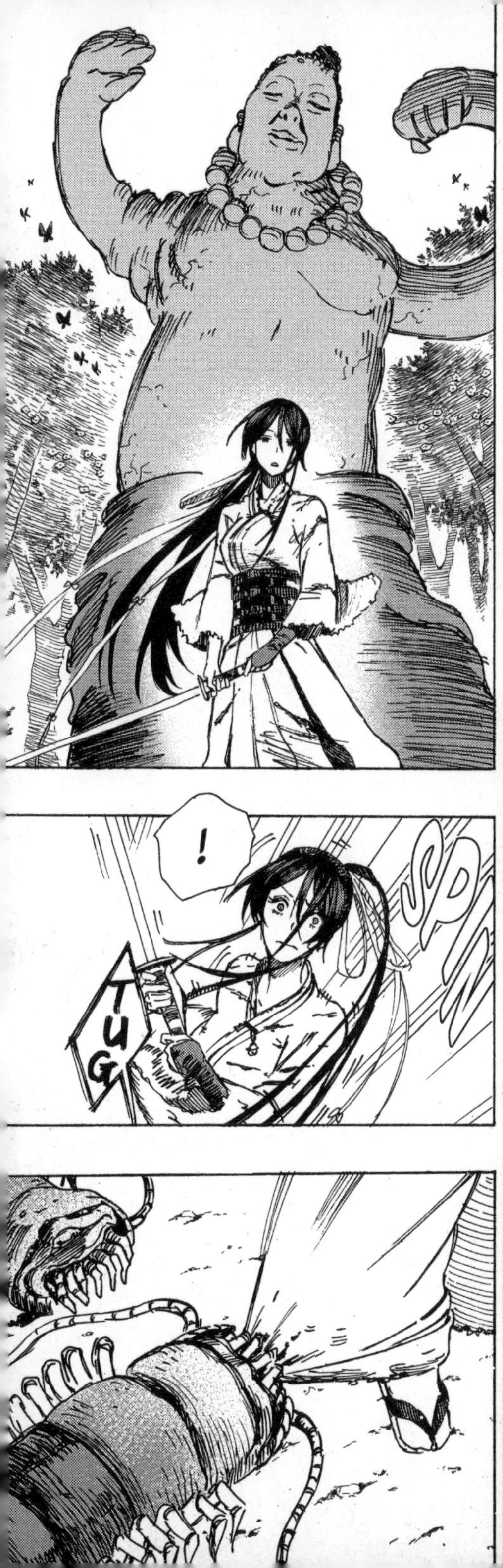
!
SPIN
TUG

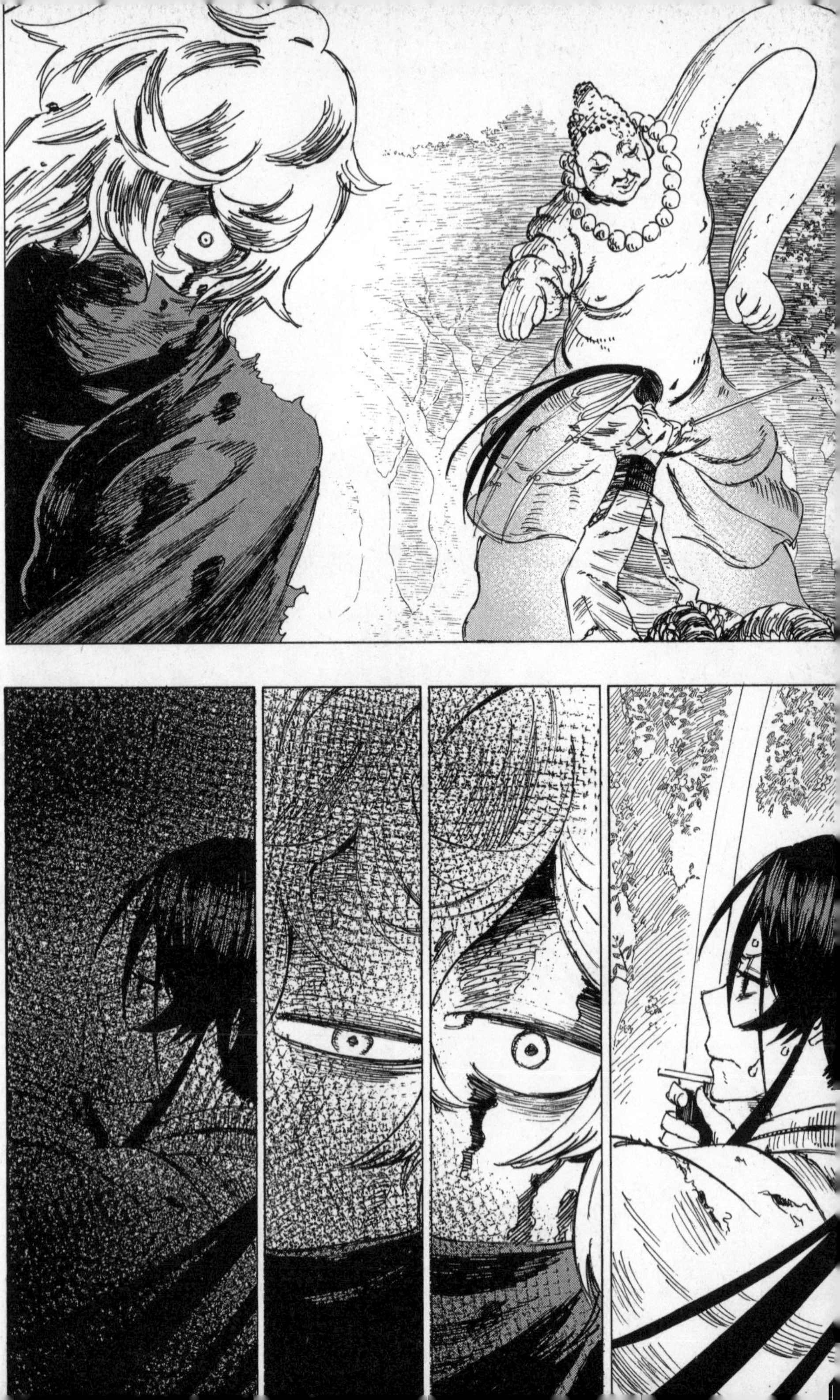

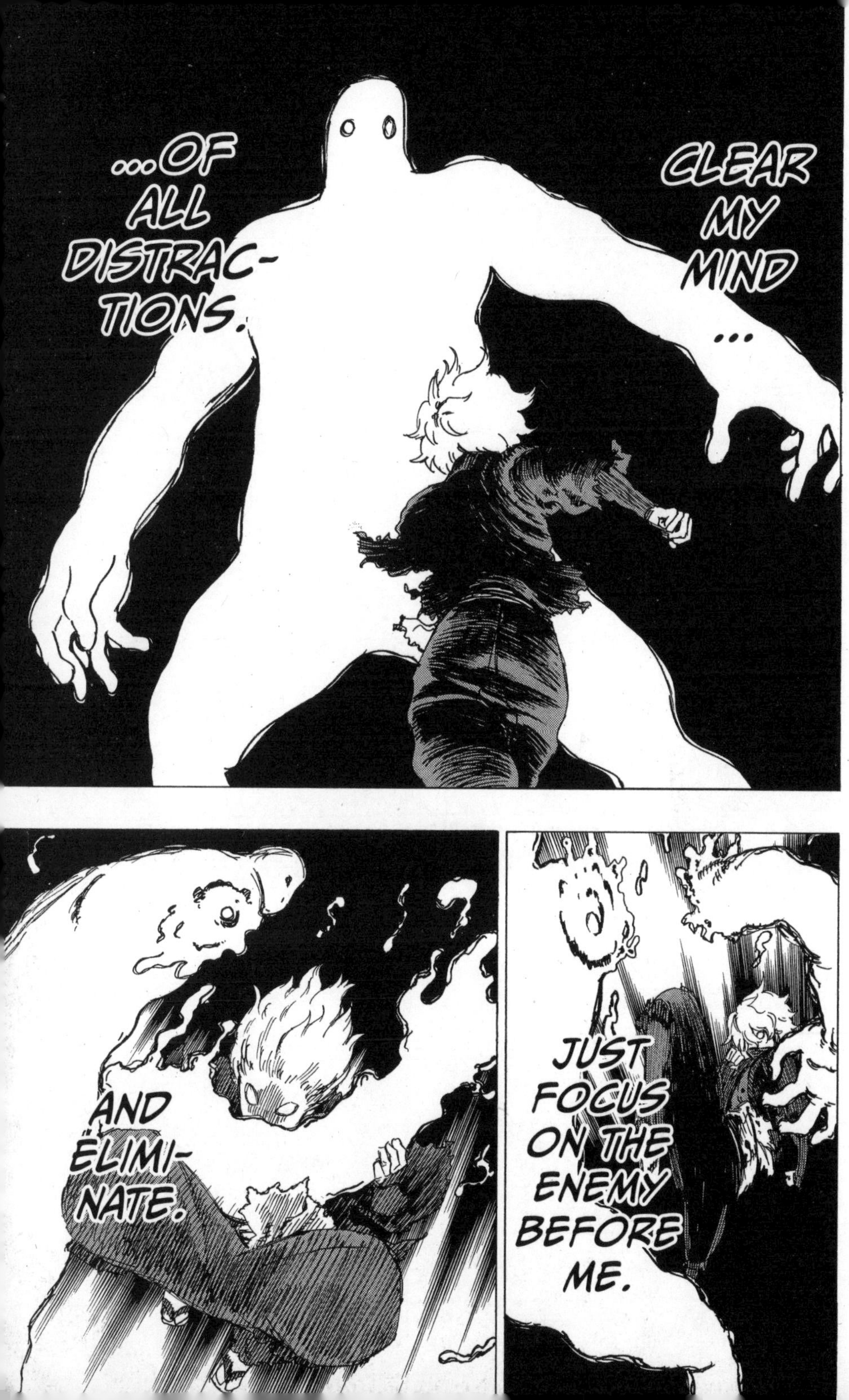
CLEAR MY MIND...
...OF ALL DISTRACTIONS.
JUST FOCUS ON THE ENEMY BEFORE ME.
AND ELIMINATE.

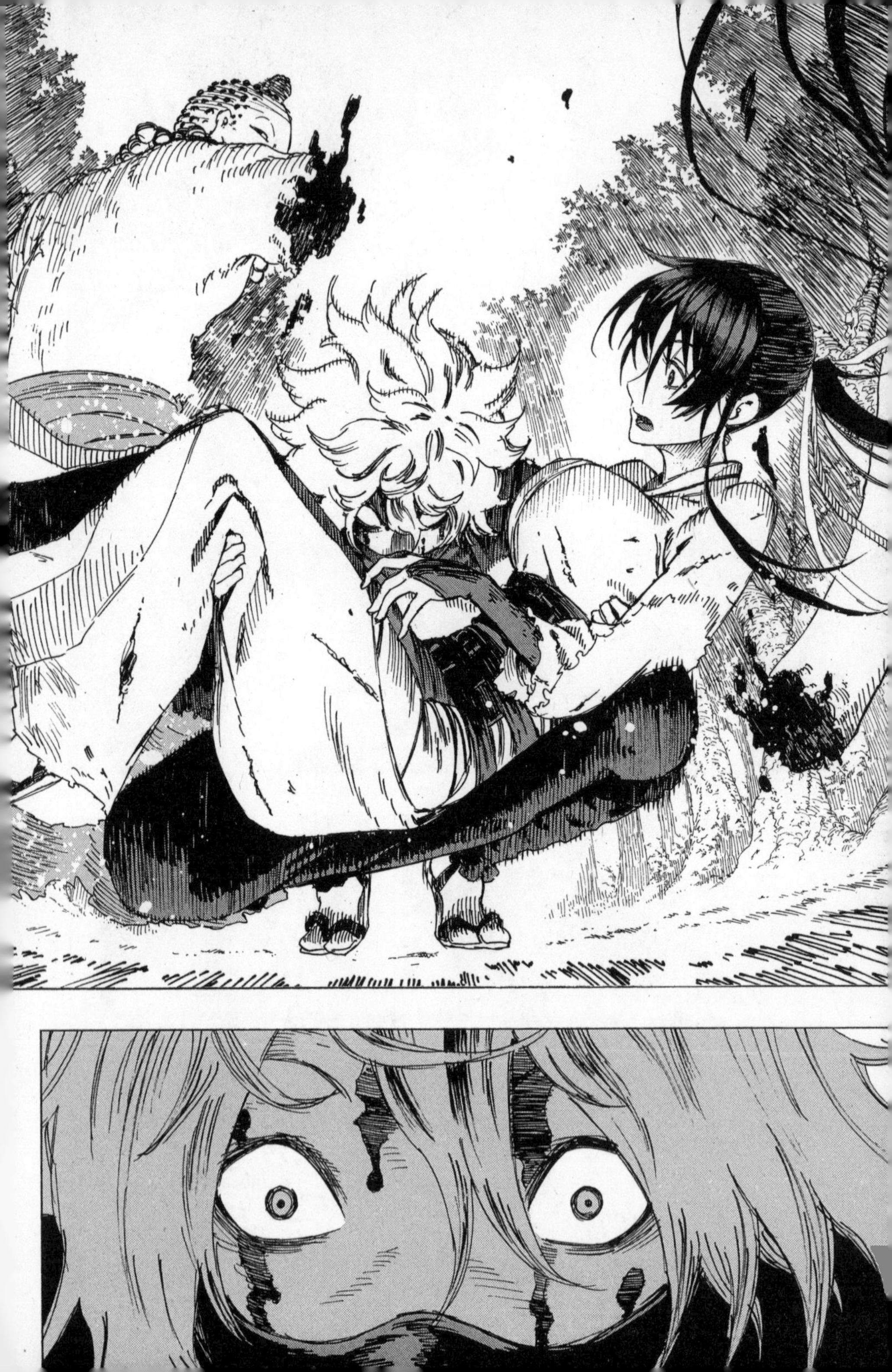

AH...

GABI...

GABIMARU?

UMM.

FWIPPP

...

I-I'M IN YOUR DEBT...

WHAP

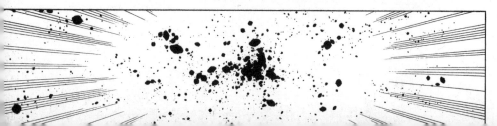

Chapter 8

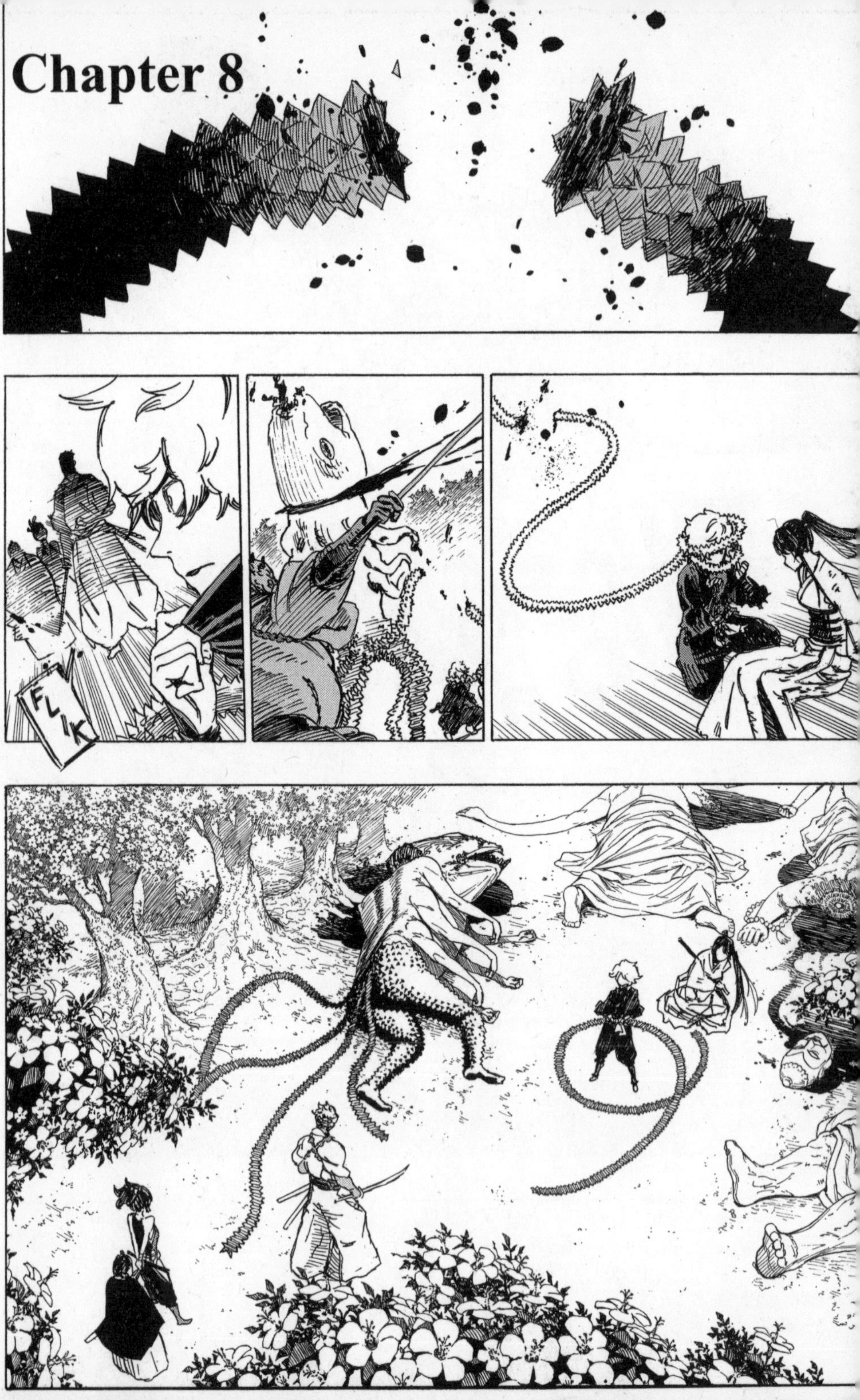
FLIK

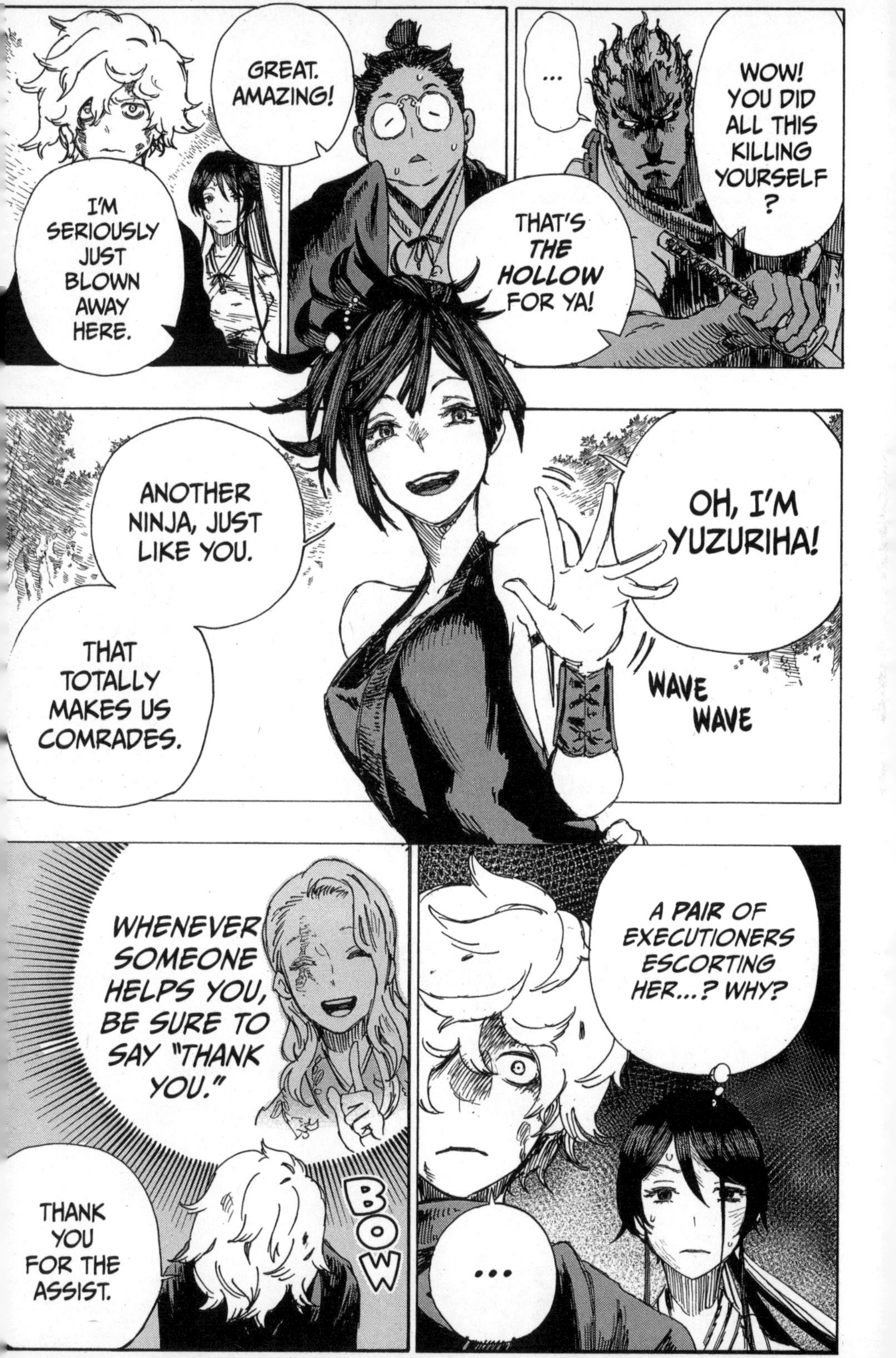
WOW! YOU DID ALL THIS KILLING YOURSELF?
...
THAT'S *THE HOLLOW* FOR YA!
GREAT. AMAZING!
I'M SERIOUSLY JUST BLOWN AWAY HERE.
OH, I'M YUZURIHA!
WAVE WAVE
ANOTHER NINJA, JUST LIKE YOU.
THAT TOTALLY MAKES US COMRADES.
A *PAIR* OF EXECUTIONERS ESCORTING HER...? WHY?
...
WHENEVER SOMEONE HELPS YOU, BE SURE TO SAY "THANK YOU."
BOW
THANK YOU FOR THE ASSIST.

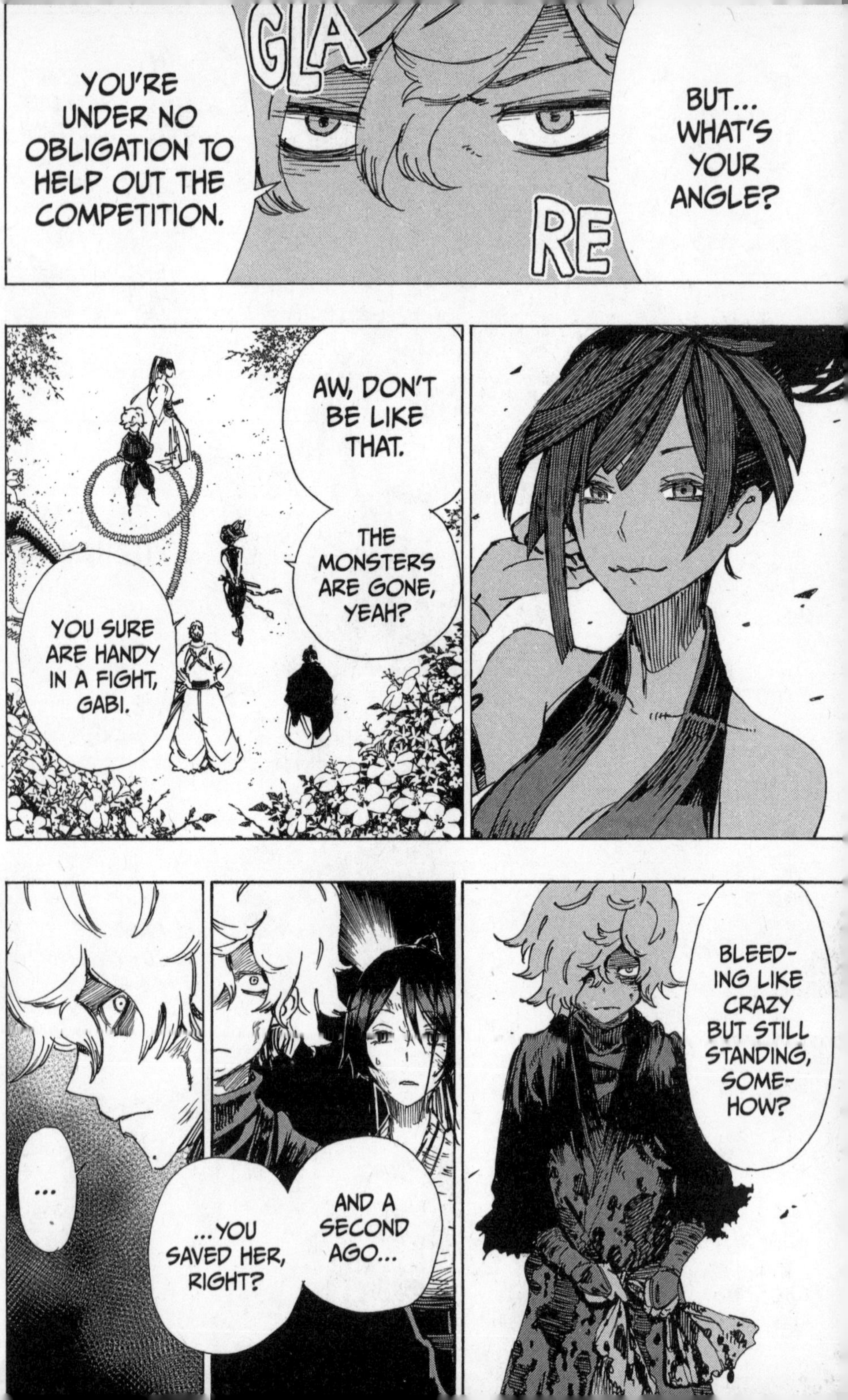
GLA
RE
YOU'RE UNDER NO OBLIGATION TO HELP OUT THE COMPETITION.
BUT... WHAT'S YOUR ANGLE?
AW, DON'T BE LIKE THAT.
THE MONSTERS ARE GONE, YEAH?
YOU SURE ARE HANDY IN A FIGHT, GABI.
BLEED-ING LIKE CRAZY BUT STILL STANDING, SOME-HOW?
AND A SECOND AGO...
...YOU SAVED HER, RIGHT?
...

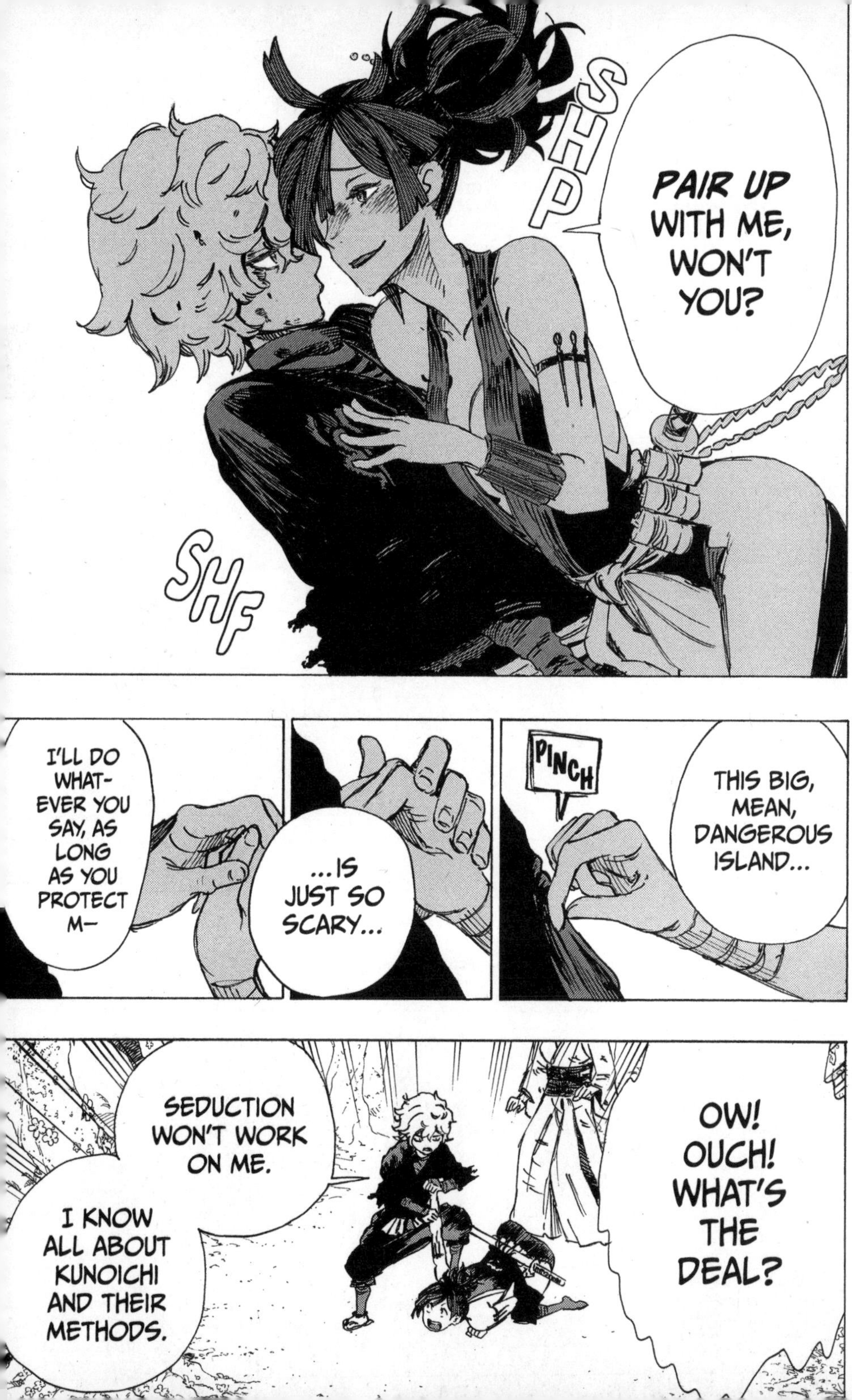
SHP
PAIR UP WITH ME, WON'T YOU?
SHF
PINCH
THIS BIG, MEAN, DANGEROUS ISLAND...
...IS JUST SO SCARY...
I'LL DO WHAT-EVER YOU SAY, AS LONG AS YOU PROTECT M—
OW! OUCH! WHAT'S THE DEAL?
SEDUCTION WON'T WORK ON ME.
I KNOW ALL ABOUT KUNOICHI AND THEIR METHODS.

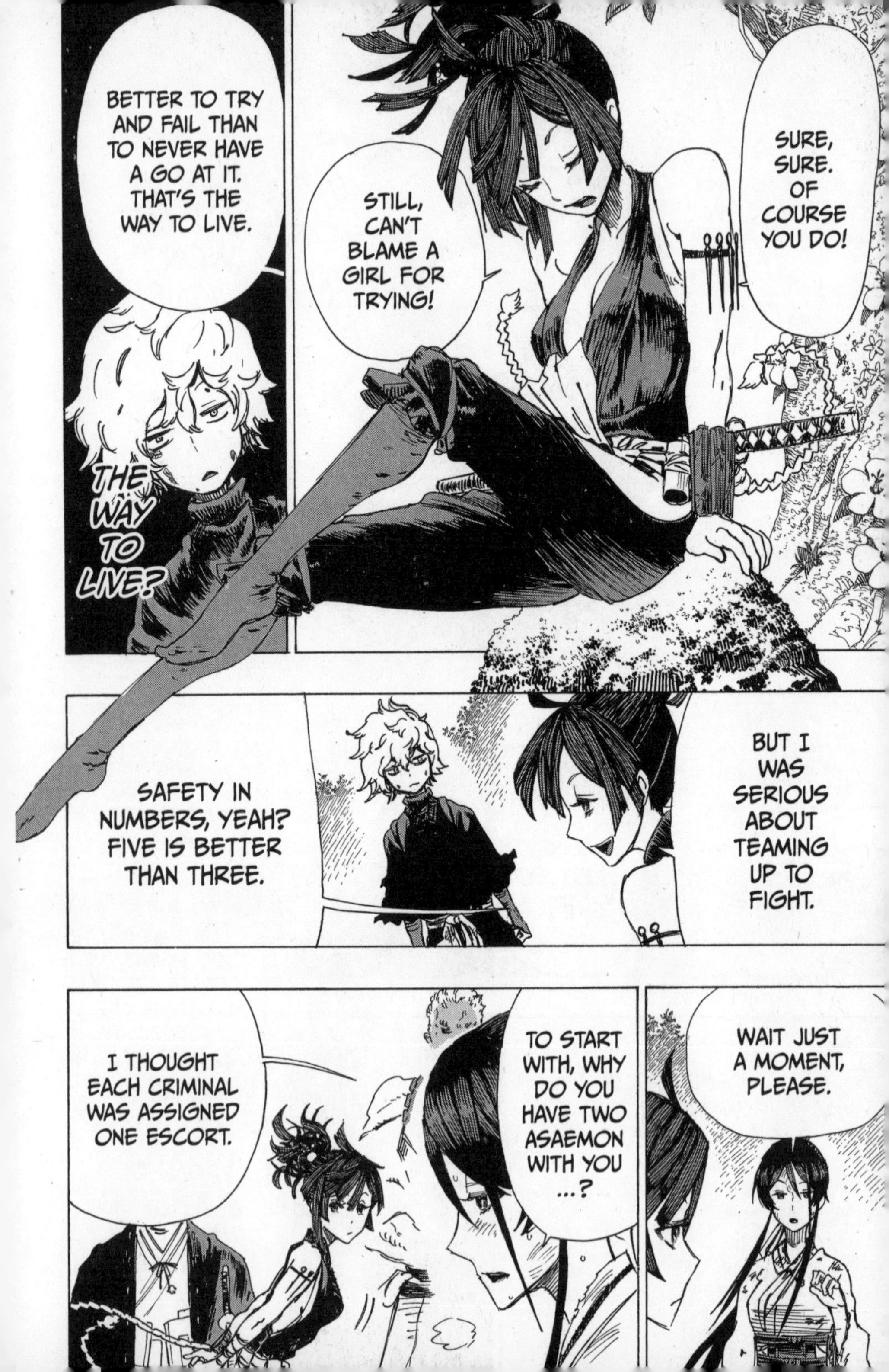
SURE, SURE. OF COURSE YOU DO!
STILL, CAN'T BLAME A GIRL FOR TRYING!
BETTER TO TRY AND FAIL THAN TO NEVER HAVE A GO AT IT. THAT'S THE WAY TO LIVE.
THE WAY TO LIVE?
BUT I WAS SERIOUS ABOUT TEAMING UP TO FIGHT.
SAFETY IN NUMBERS, YEAH? FIVE IS BETTER THAN THREE.
WAIT JUST A MOMENT, PLEASE.
TO START WITH, WHY DO YOU HAVE TWO ASAEMON WITH YOU ...?
I THOUGHT EACH CRIMINAL WAS ASSIGNED ONE ESCORT.

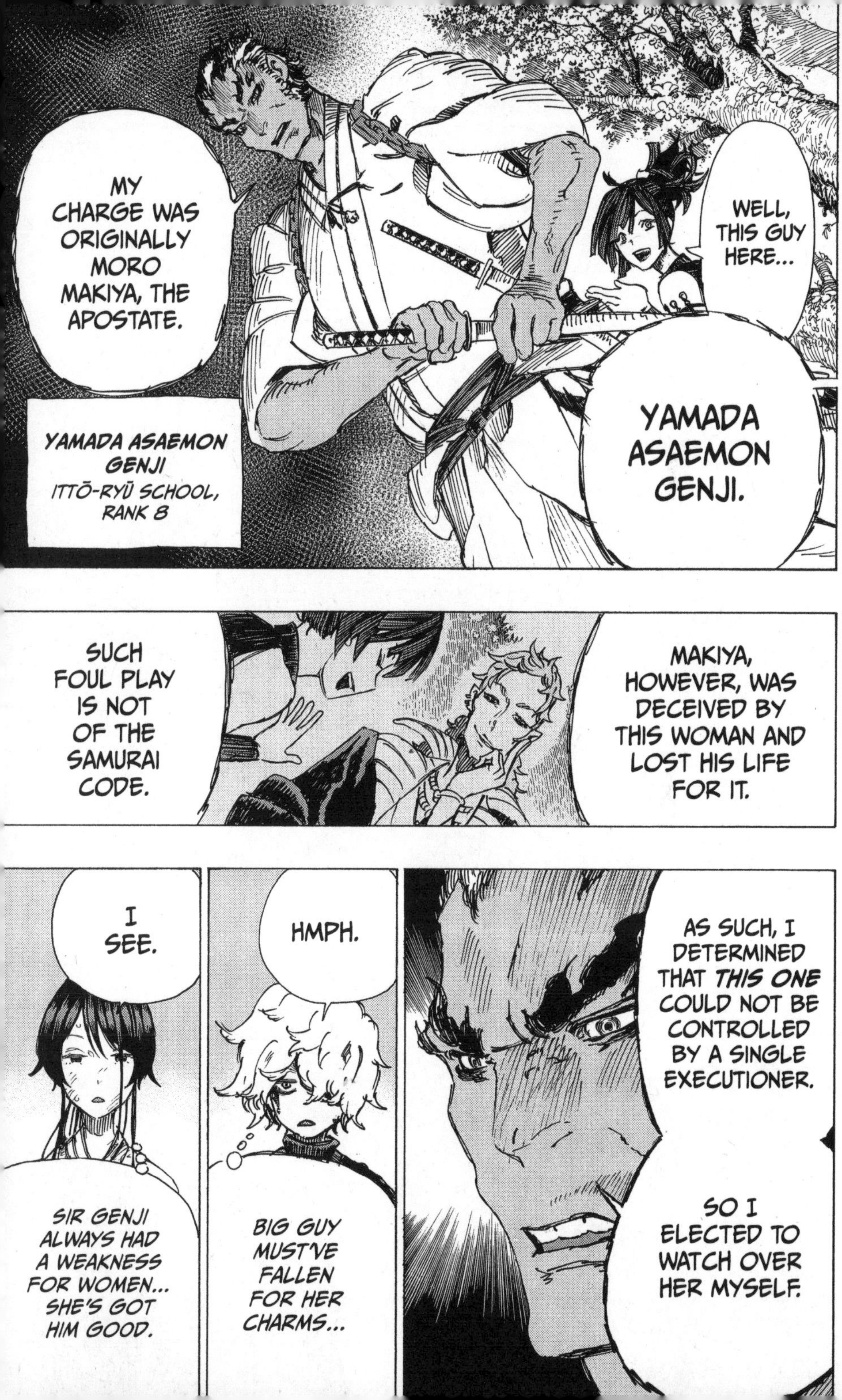
WELL, THIS GUY HERE...
YAMADA ASAEMON GENJI.
MY CHARGE WAS ORIGINALLY MORO MAKIYA, THE APOSTATE.
YAMADA ASAEMON GENJI
ITTŌ-RYŪ SCHOOL, RANK 8
MAKIYA, HOWEVER, WAS DECEIVED BY THIS WOMAN AND LOST HIS LIFE FOR IT.
SUCH FOUL PLAY IS NOT OF THE SAMURAI CODE.
AS SUCH, I DETERMINED THAT THIS ONE COULD NOT BE CONTROLLED BY A SINGLE EXECUTIONER.
SO I ELECTED TO WATCH OVER HER MYSELF.
HMPH.
BIG GUY MUST'VE FALLEN FOR HER CHARMS...
I SEE.
SIR GENJI ALWAYS HAD A WEAKNESS FOR WOMEN... SHE'S GOT HIM GOOD.

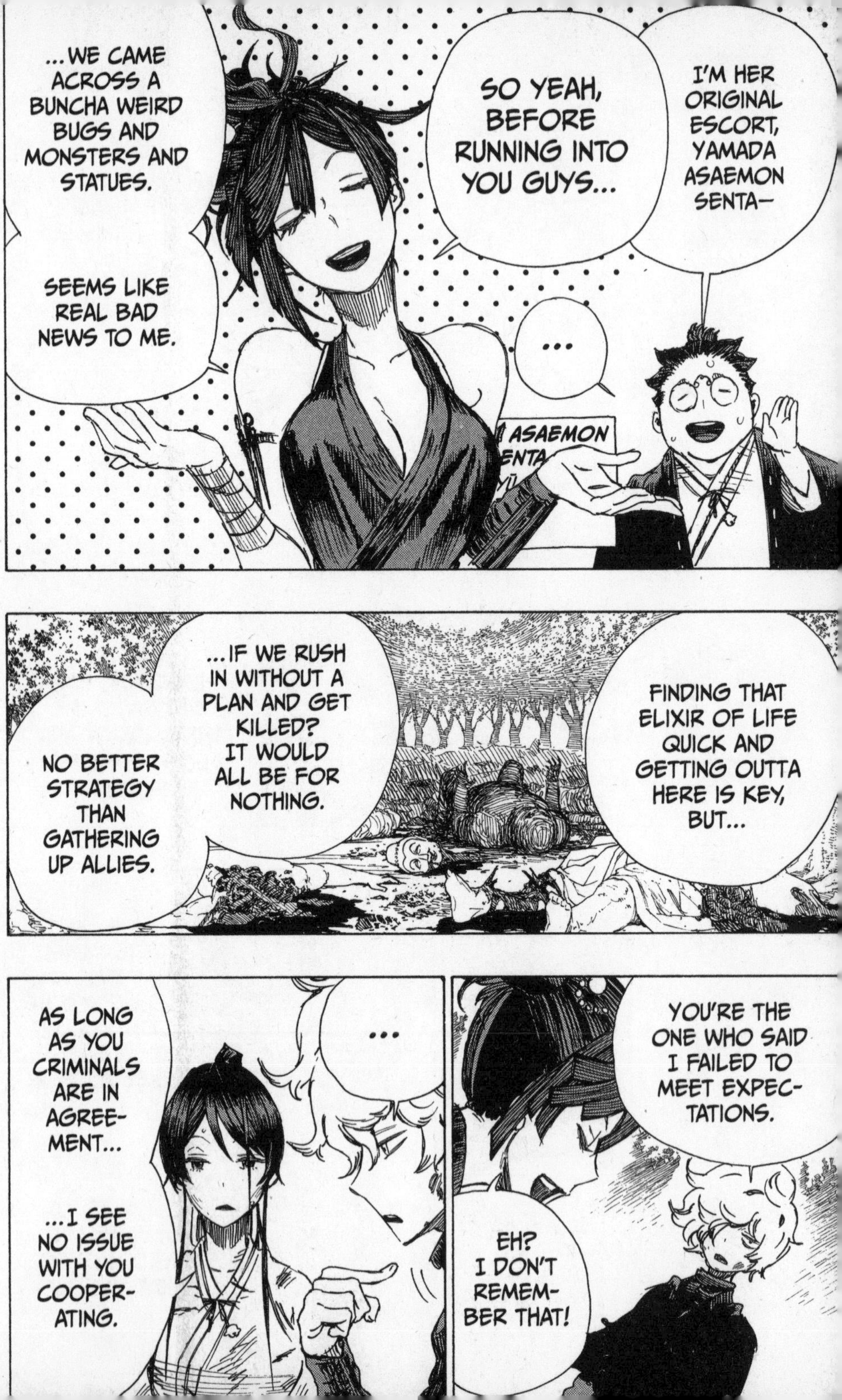
I'M HER ORIGINAL ESCORT, YAMADA ASAEMON SENTA—
SO YEAH, BEFORE RUNNING INTO YOU GUYS...
...
...WE CAME ACROSS A BUNCHA WEIRD BUGS AND MONSTERS AND STATUES.
SEEMS LIKE REAL BAD NEWS TO ME.
FINDING THAT ELIXIR OF LIFE QUICK AND GETTING OUTTA HERE IS KEY, BUT...
...IF WE RUSH IN WITHOUT A PLAN AND GET KILLED? IT WOULD ALL BE FOR NOTHING.
NO BETTER STRATEGY THAN GATHERING UP ALLIES.
YOU'RE THE ONE WHO SAID I FAILED TO MEET EXPECTATIONS.
EH? I DON'T REMEMBER THAT!
...
AS LONG AS YOU CRIMINALS ARE IN AGREEMENT...
...I SEE NO ISSUE WITH YOU COOPERATING.

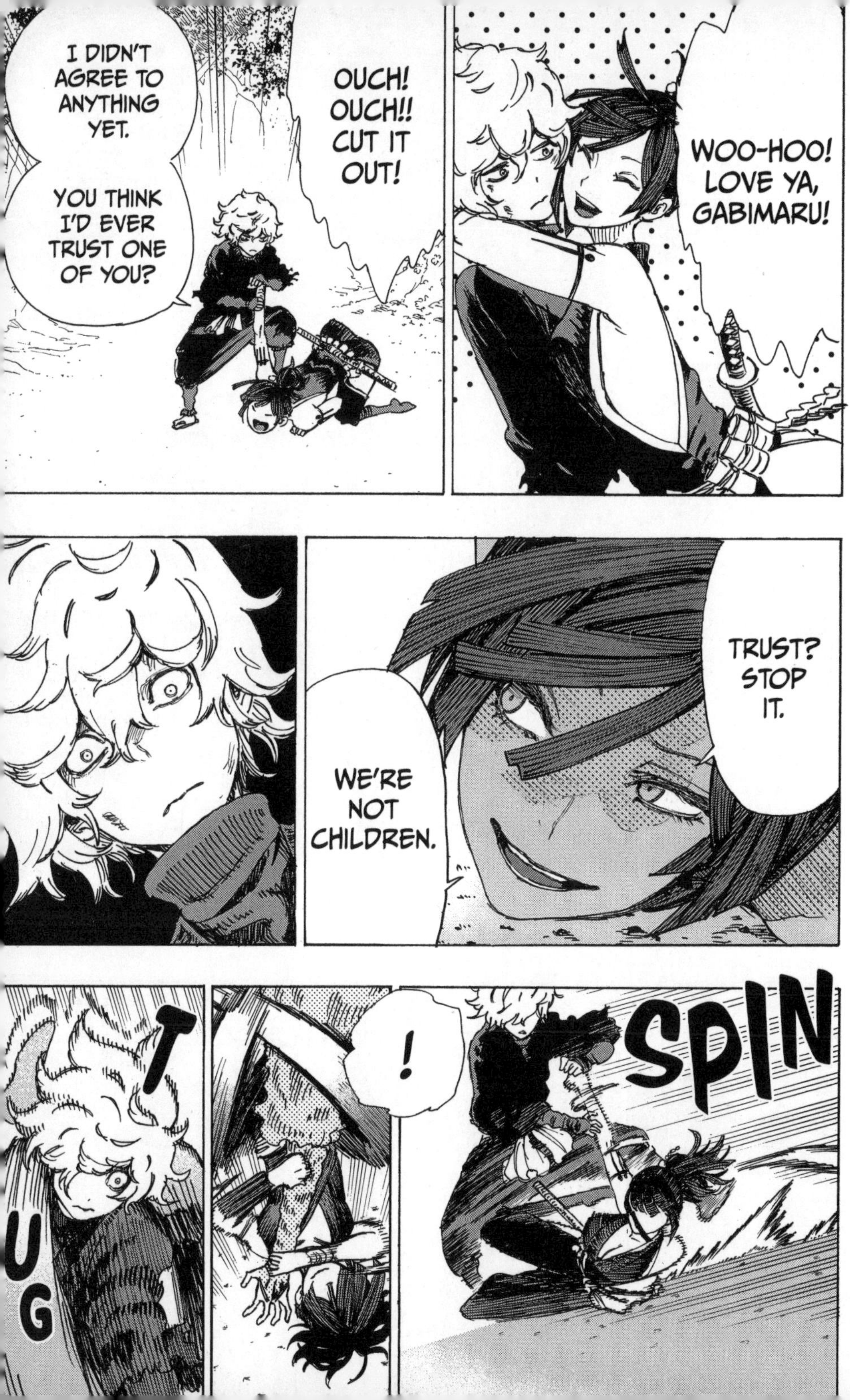
WOO-HOO! LOVE YA, GABIMARU!
OUCH! OUCH!! CUT IT OUT!
I DIDN'T AGREE TO ANYTHING YET.
YOU THINK I'D EVER TRUST ONE OF YOU?
TRUST? STOP IT.
WE'RE NOT CHILDREN.
SPIN
!
TUG

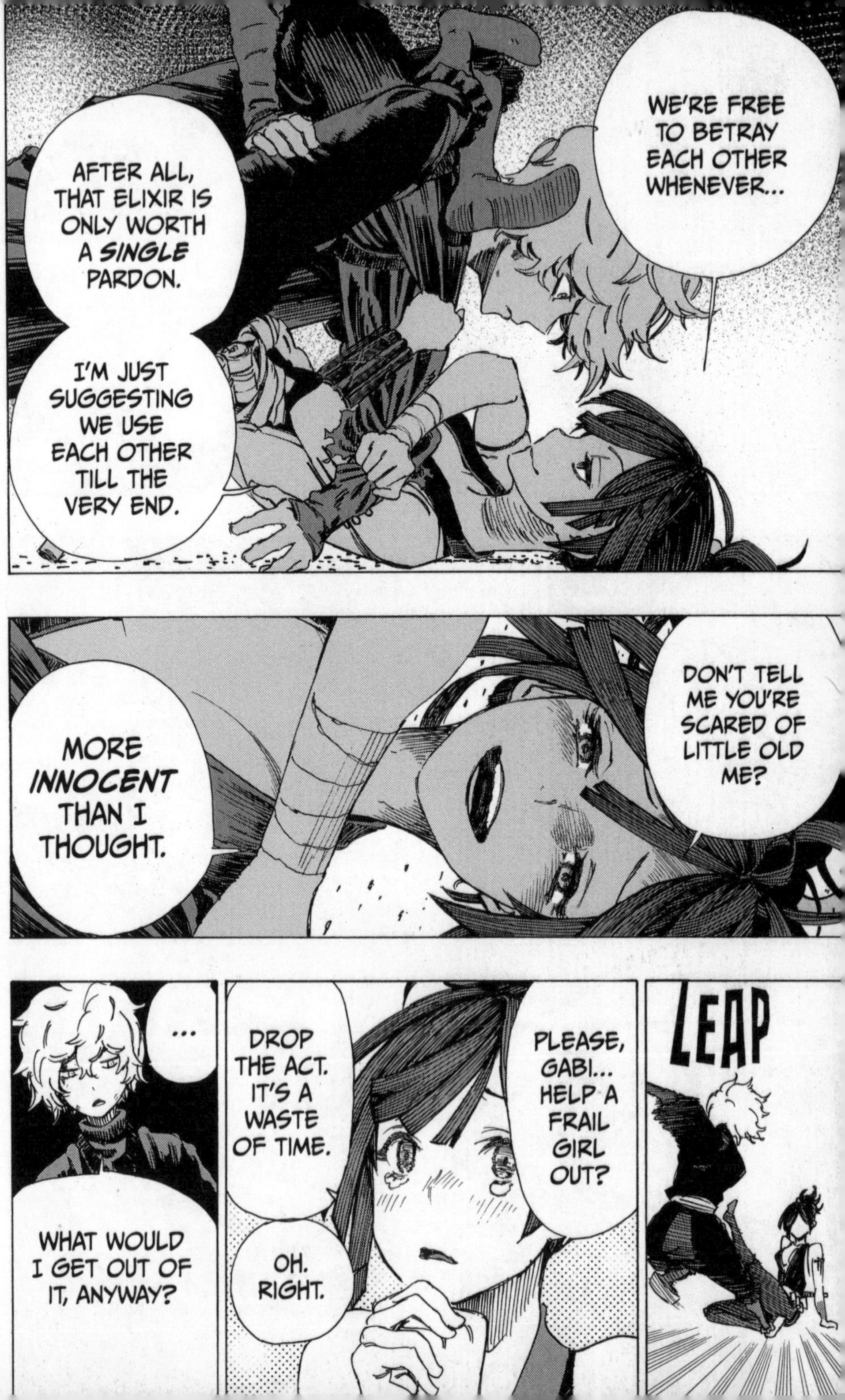
WE'RE FREE TO BETRAY EACH OTHER WHENEVER...
AFTER ALL, THAT ELIXIR IS ONLY WORTH A *SINGLE* PARDON.
I'M JUST SUGGESTING WE USE EACH OTHER TILL THE VERY END.
DON'T TELL ME YOU'RE SCARED OF LITTLE OLD ME?
MORE *INNOCENT* THAN I THOUGHT.
LEAP
PLEASE, GABI... HELP A FRAIL GIRL OUT?
DROP THE ACT. IT'S A WASTE OF TIME.
OH. RIGHT.
...
WHAT WOULD I GET OUT OF IT, ANYWAY?

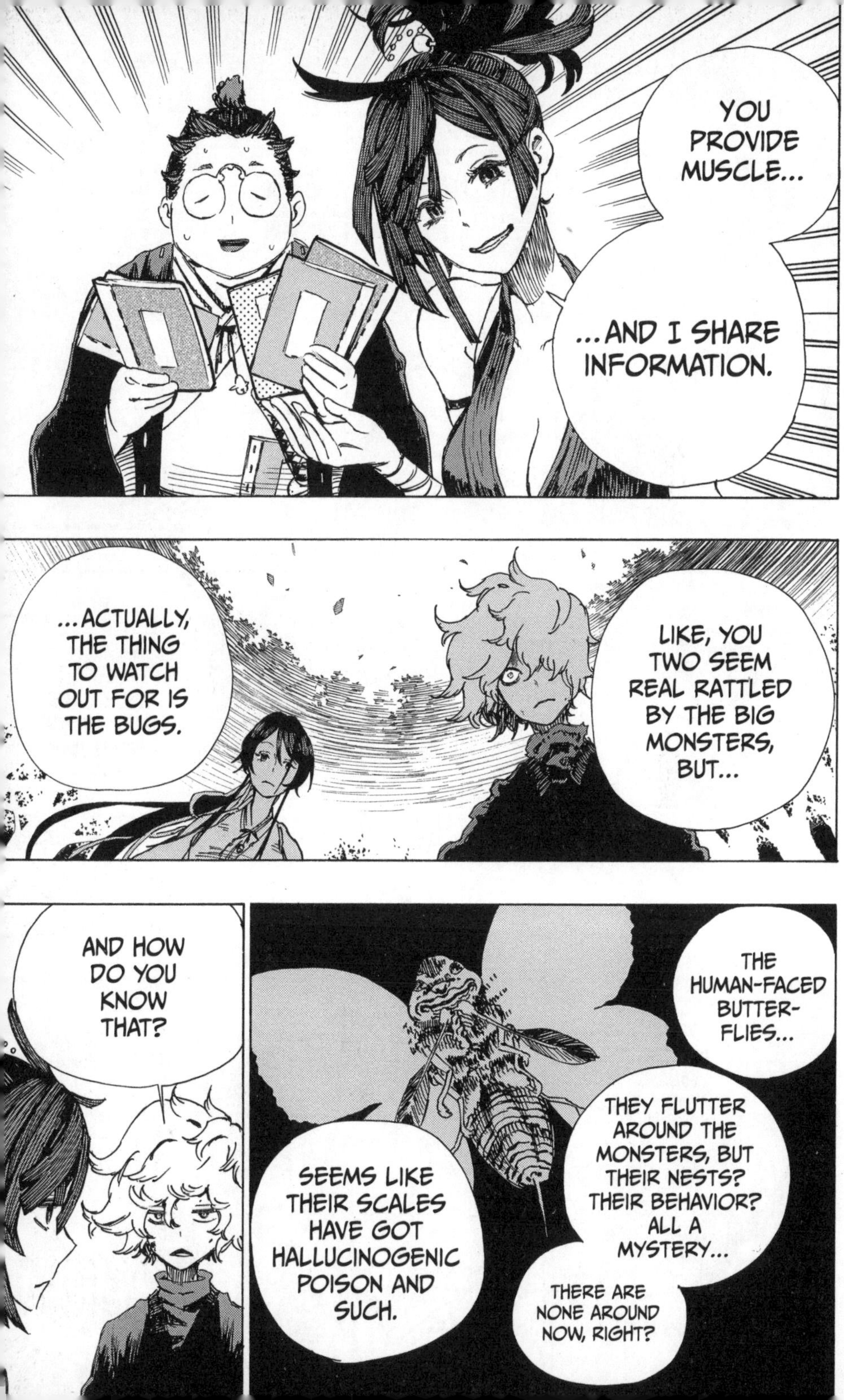
YOU PROVIDE MUSCLE...
...AND I SHARE INFORMATION.
LIKE, YOU TWO SEEM REAL RATTLED BY THE BIG MONSTERS, BUT...
...ACTUALLY, THE THING TO WATCH OUT FOR IS THE BUGS.
THE HUMAN-FACED BUTTER-FLIES...
THEY FLUTTER AROUND THE MONSTERS, BUT THEIR NESTS? THEIR BEHAVIOR? ALL A MYSTERY...
SEEMS LIKE THEIR SCALES HAVE GOT HALLUCINOGENIC POISON AND SUCH.
THERE ARE NONE AROUND NOW, RIGHT?
AND HOW DO YOU KNOW THAT?

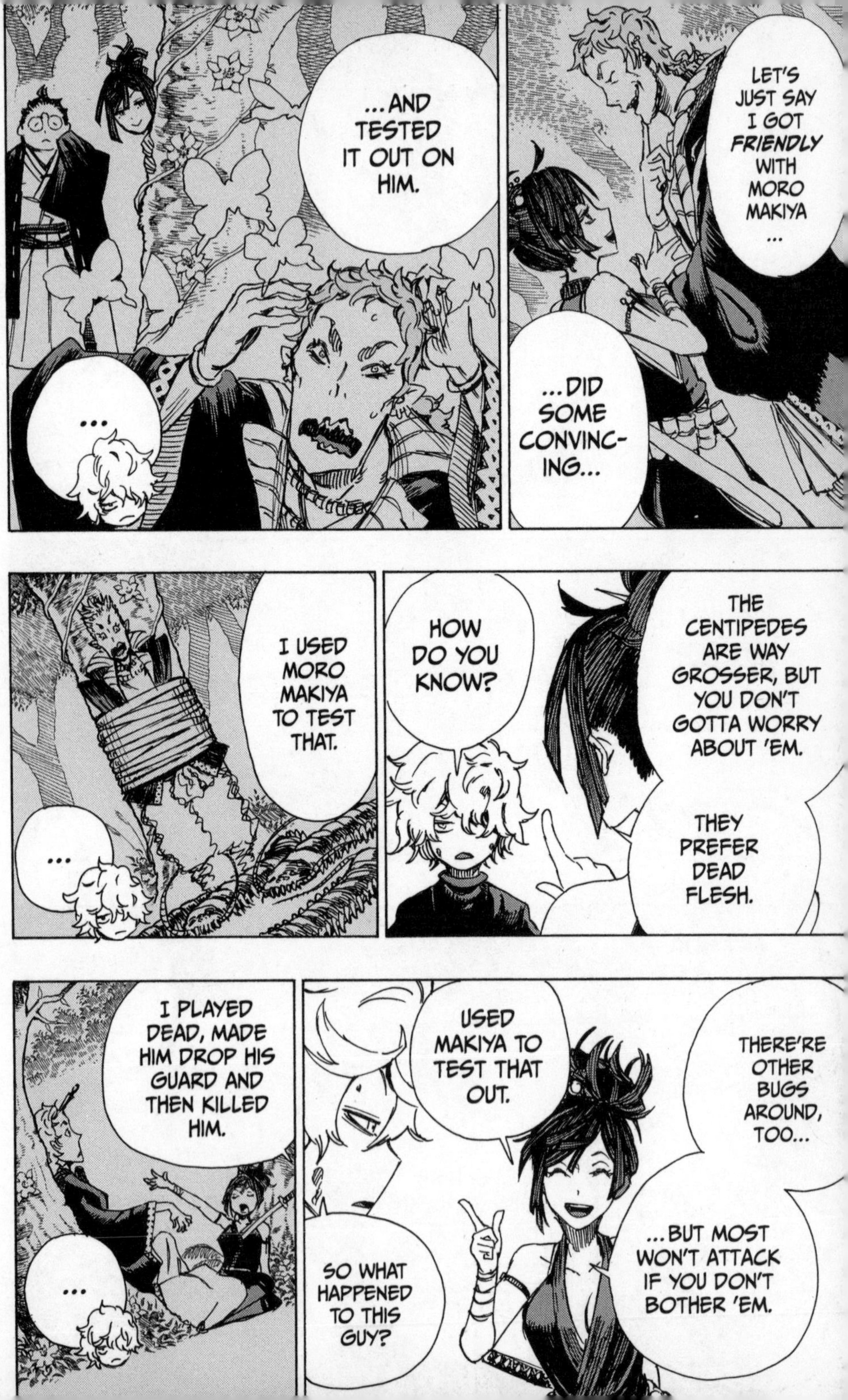
LET'S JUST SAY I GOT FRIENDLY WITH MORO MAKIYA ...
...DID SOME CONVINCING...
...AND TESTED IT OUT ON HIM.
...
THE CENTIPEDES ARE WAY GROSSER, BUT YOU DON'T GOTTA WORRY ABOUT 'EM.
THEY PREFER DEAD FLESH.
HOW DO YOU KNOW?
I USED MORO MAKIYA TO TEST THAT.
...
THERE'RE OTHER BUGS AROUND, TOO...
...BUT MOST WON'T ATTACK IF YOU DON'T BOTHER 'EM.
USED MAKIYA TO TEST THAT OUT.
SO WHAT HAPPENED TO THIS GUY?
I PLAYED DEAD, MADE HIM DROP HIS GUARD AND THEN KILLED HIM.
...

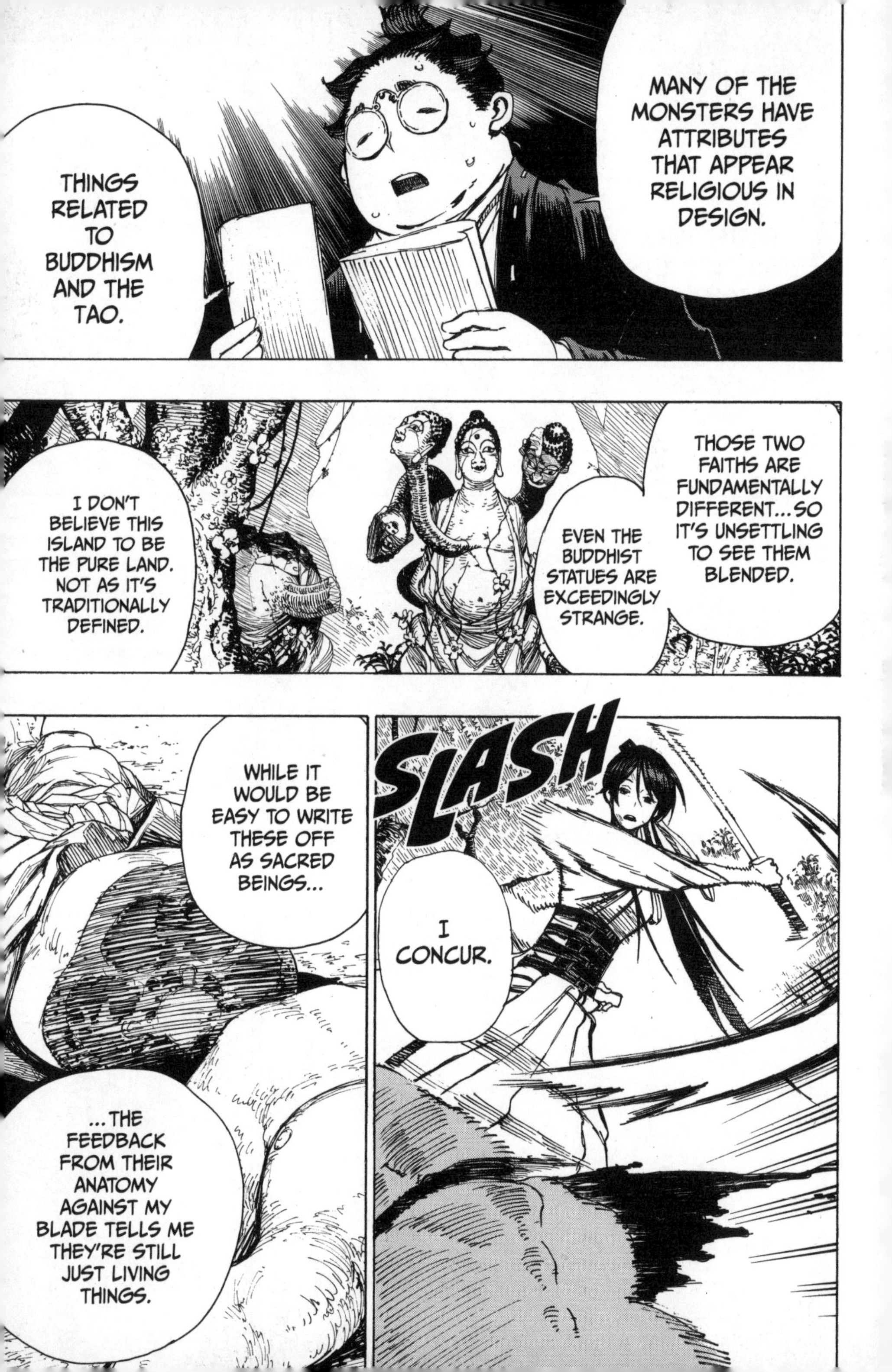
MANY OF THE MONSTERS HAVE ATTRIBUTES THAT APPEAR RELIGIOUS IN DESIGN.
THINGS RELATED TO BUDDHISM AND THE TAO.
THOSE TWO FAITHS ARE FUNDAMENTALLY DIFFERENT...SO IT'S UNSETTLING TO SEE THEM BLENDED.
EVEN THE BUDDHIST STATUES ARE EXCEEDINGLY STRANGE.
I DON'T BELIEVE THIS ISLAND TO BE THE PURE LAND. NOT AS IT'S TRADITIONALLY DEFINED.
SLASH
I CONCUR.
WHILE IT WOULD BE EASY TO WRITE THESE OFF AS SACRED BEINGS...
...THE FEEDBACK FROM THEIR ANATOMY AGAINST MY BLADE TELLS ME THEY'RE STILL JUST LIVING THINGS.

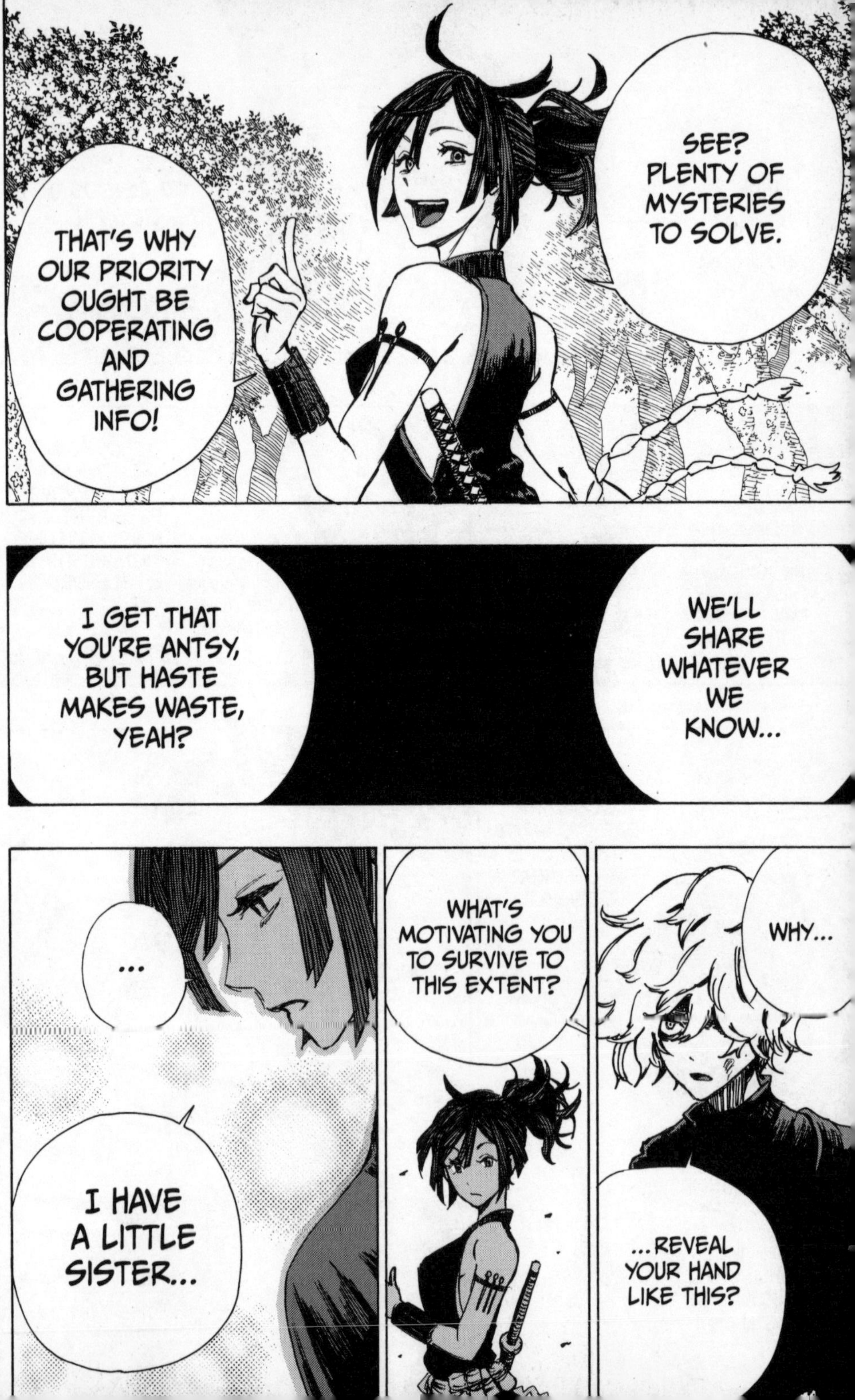
SEE? PLENTY OF MYSTERIES TO SOLVE.
THAT'S WHY OUR PRIORITY OUGHT BE COOPERATING AND GATHERING INFO!
WE'LL SHARE WHATEVER WE KNOW...
I GET THAT YOU'RE ANTSY, BUT HASTE MAKES WASTE, YEAH?
WHY...
...REVEAL YOUR HAND LIKE THIS?
WHAT'S MOTIVATING YOU TO SURVIVE TO THIS EXTENT?
...
I HAVE A LITTLE SISTER...

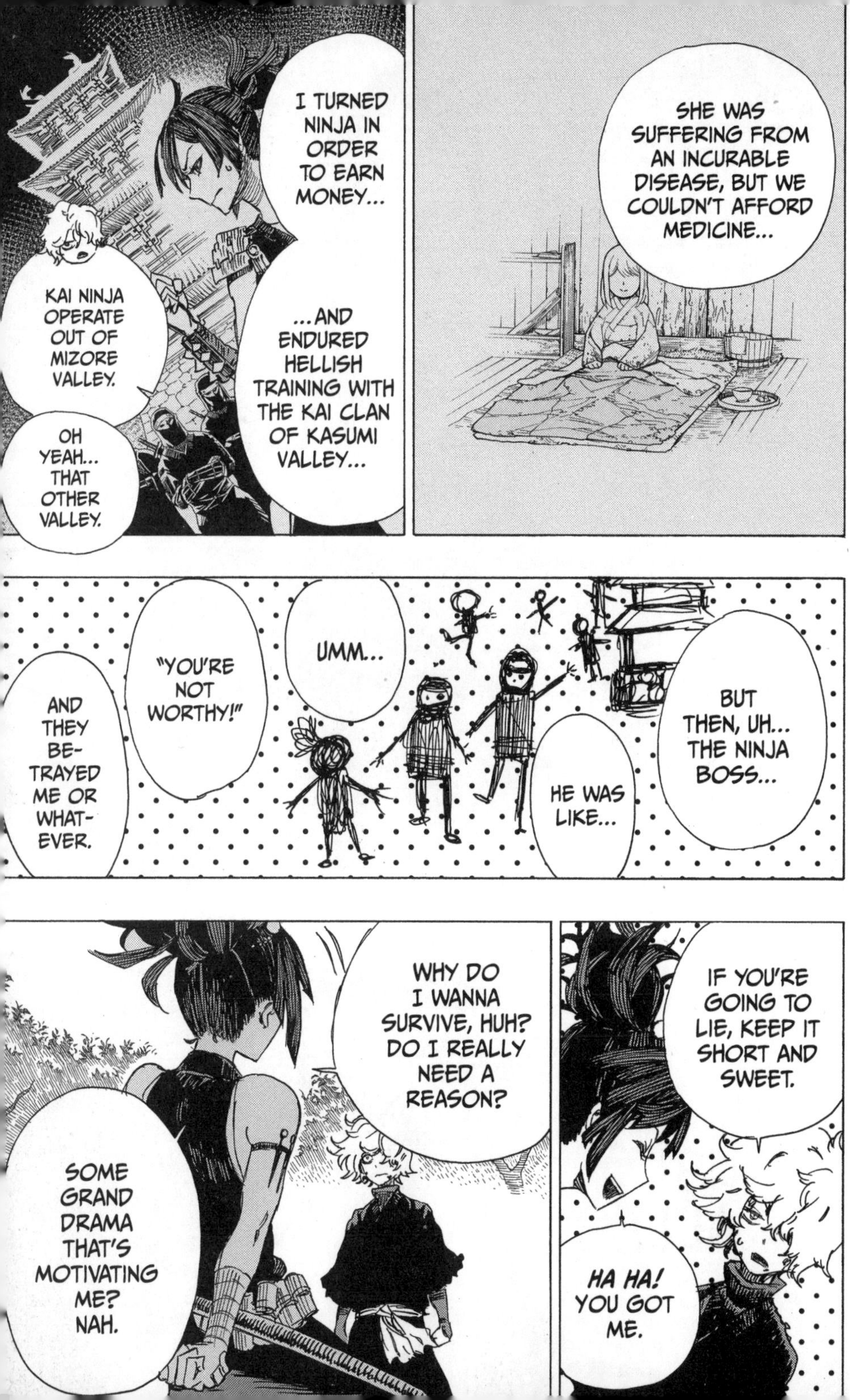
SHE WAS SUFFERING FROM AN INCURABLE DISEASE, BUT WE COULDN'T AFFORD MEDICINE...
I TURNED NINJA IN ORDER TO EARN MONEY...
...AND ENDURED HELLISH TRAINING WITH THE KAI CLAN OF KASUMI VALLEY...
KAI NINJA OPERATE OUT OF MIZORE VALLEY.
OH YEAH... THAT OTHER VALLEY.
BUT THEN, UH... THE NINJA BOSS...
HE WAS LIKE...
UMM...
"YOU'RE NOT WORTHY!"
AND THEY BE-TRAYED ME OR WHAT-EVER.
IF YOU'RE GOING TO LIE, KEEP IT SHORT AND SWEET.
HA HA! YOU GOT ME.
WHY DO I WANNA SURVIVE, HUH? DO I REALLY NEED A REASON?
SOME GRAND DRAMA THAT'S MOTIVATING ME? NAH.

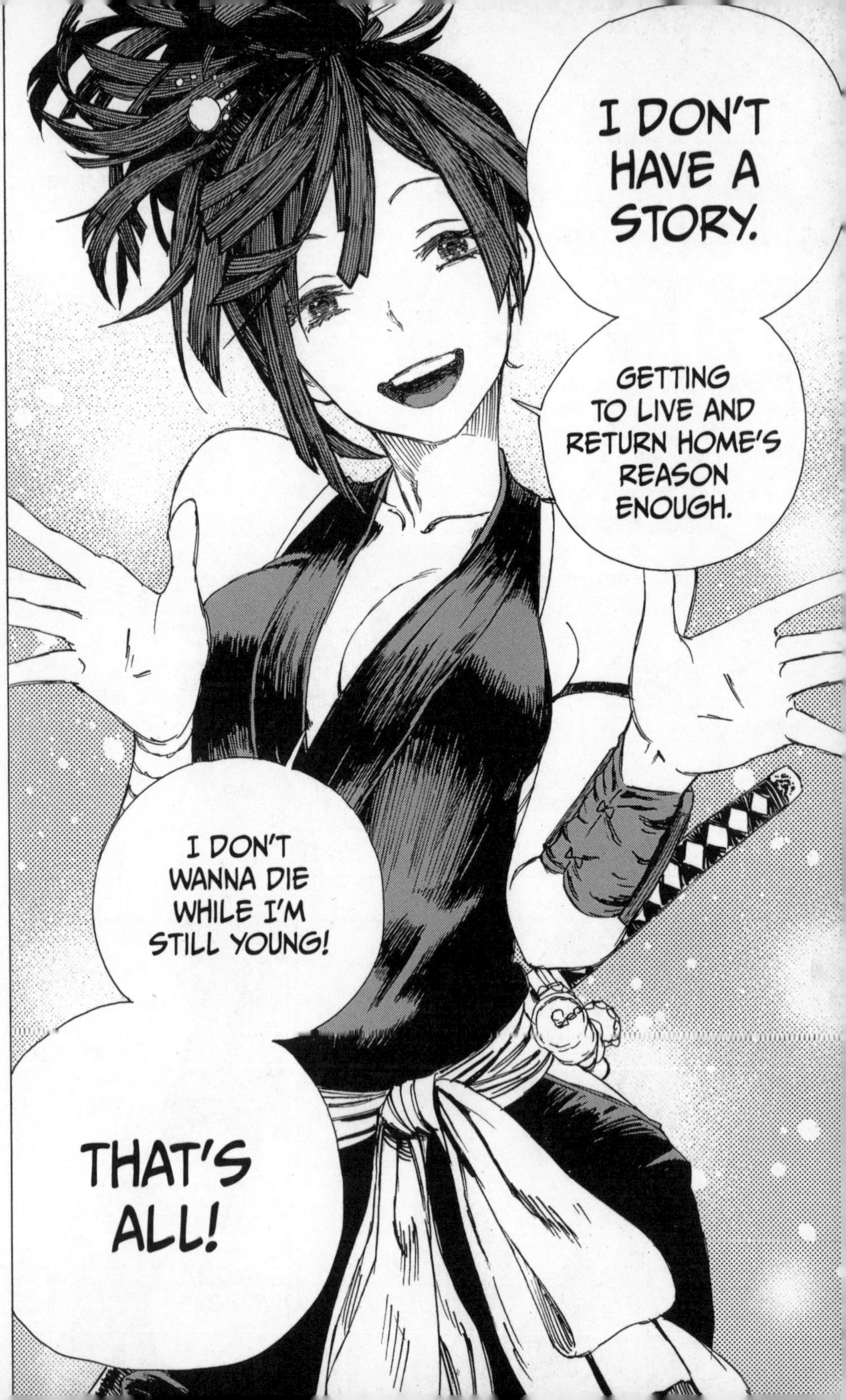
I DON'T HAVE A STORY.
GETTING TO LIVE AND RETURN HOME'S REASON ENOUGH.
I DON'T WANNA DIE WHILE I'M STILL YOUNG!
THAT'S ALL!

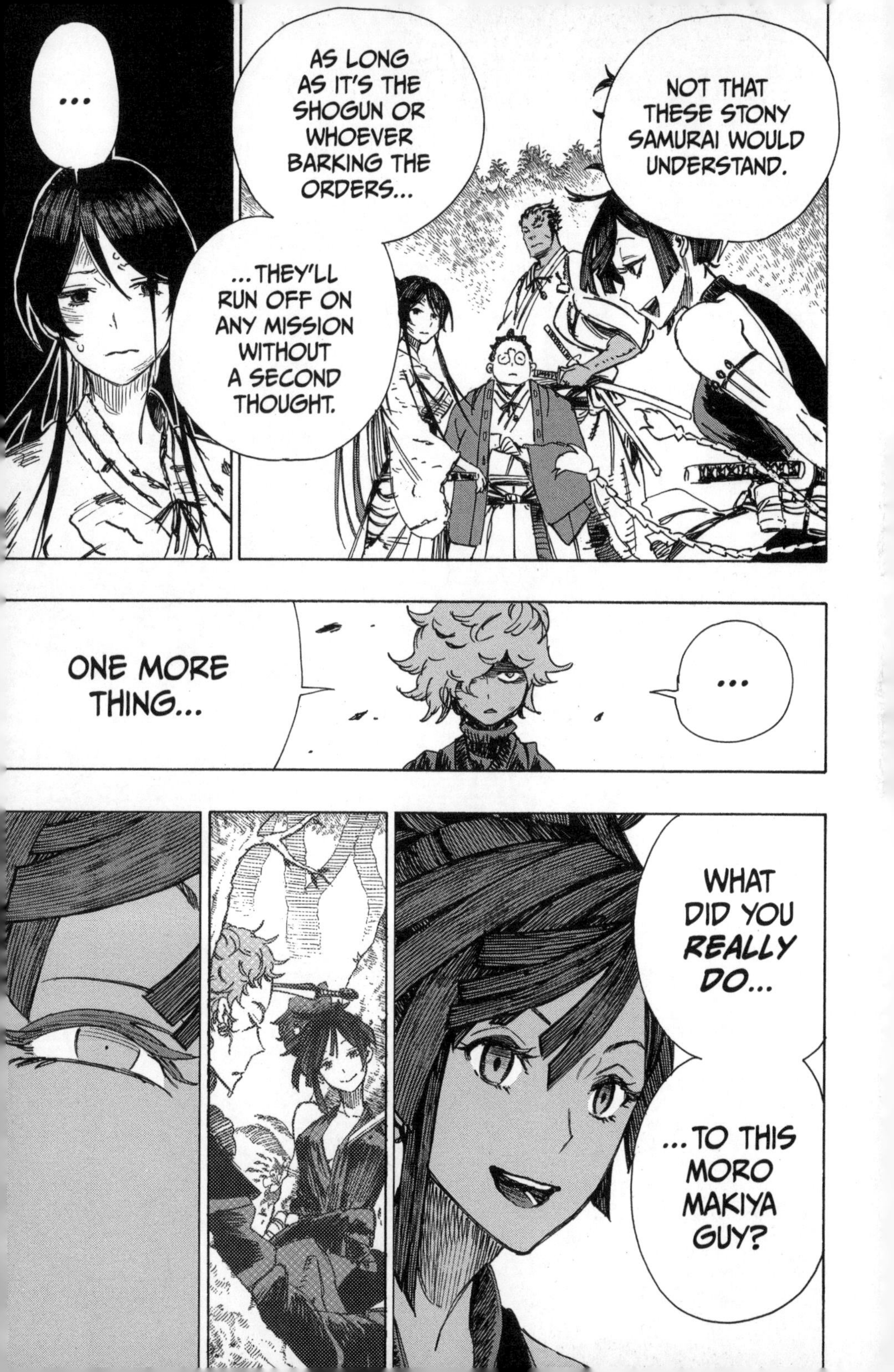
NOT THAT THESE STONY SAMURAI WOULD UNDERSTAND.
AS LONG AS IT'S THE SHOGUN OR WHOEVER BARKING THE ORDERS...
...THEY'LL RUN OFF ON ANY MISSION WITHOUT A SECOND THOUGHT.
...
...
ONE MORE THING...
WHAT DID YOU *REALLY DO*...
...TO THIS MORO MAKIYA GUY?

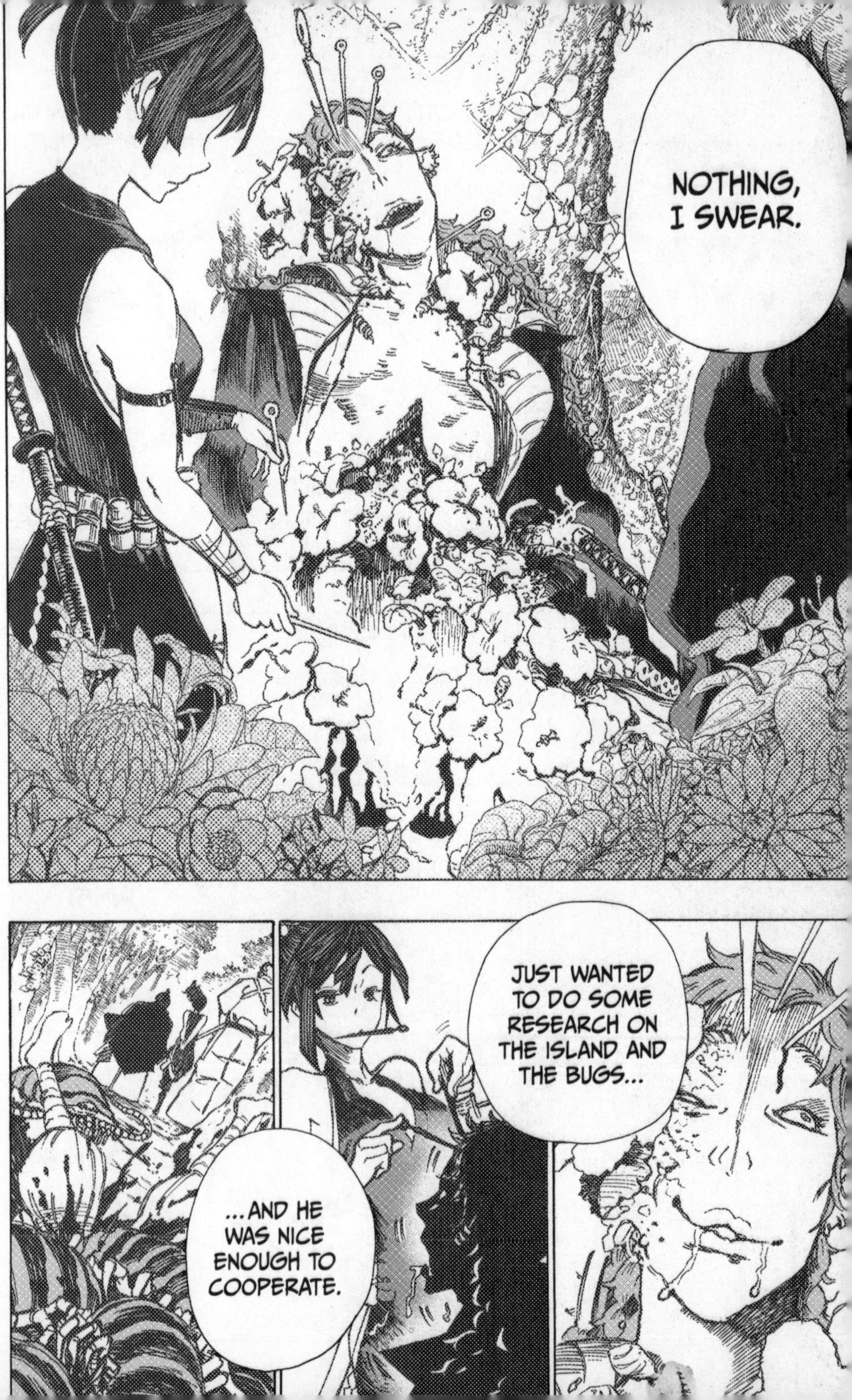
NOTHING, I SWEAR.
JUST WANTED TO DO SOME RESEARCH ON THE ISLAND AND THE BUGS...
...AND HE WAS NICE ENOUGH TO COOPERATE.

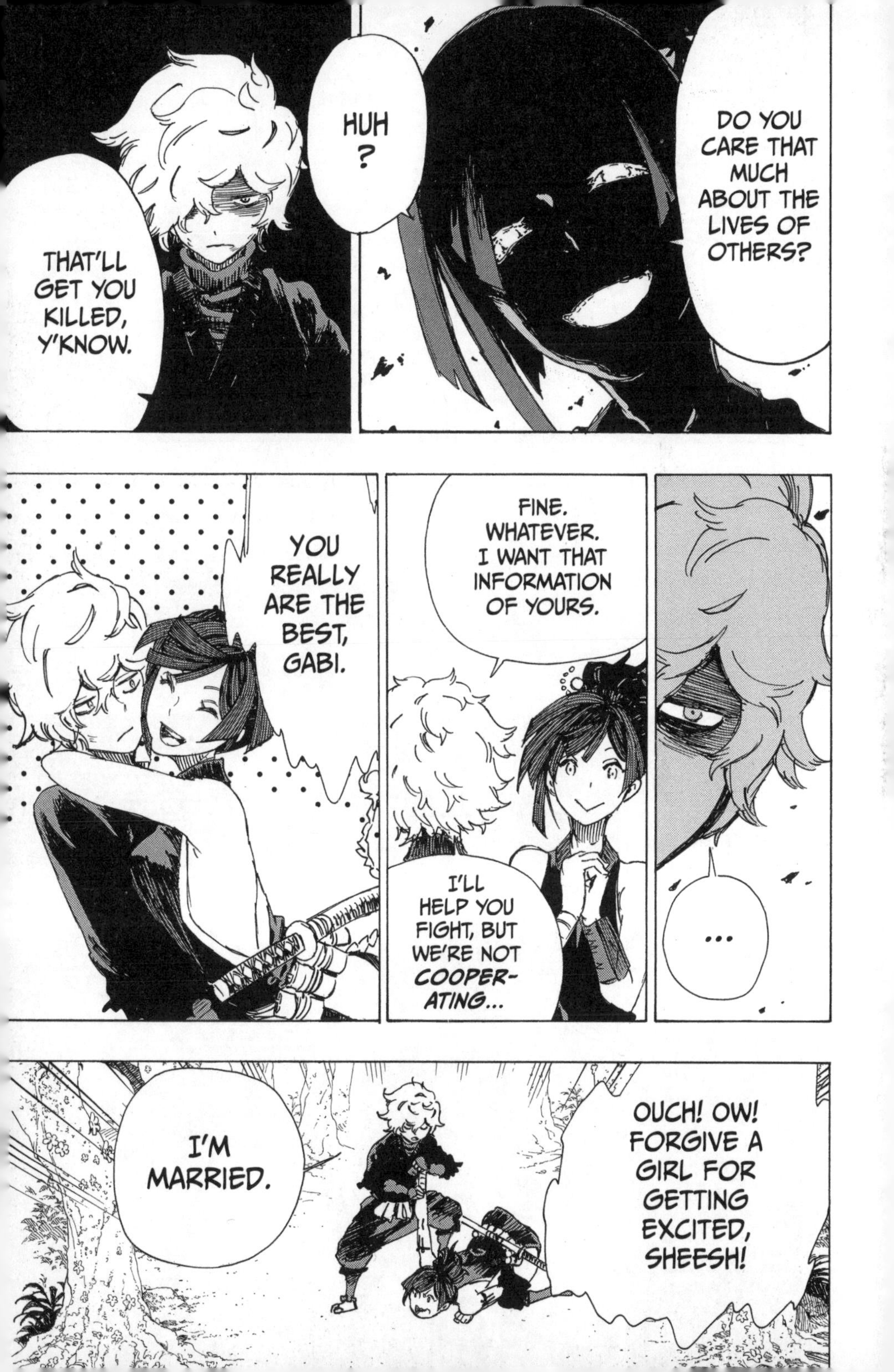
DO YOU CARE THAT MUCH ABOUT THE LIVES OF OTHERS?
HUH?
THAT'LL GET YOU KILLED, Y'KNOW.
...
FINE. WHATEVER. I WANT THAT INFORMATION OF YOURS.
I'LL HELP YOU FIGHT, BUT WE'RE NOT *COOPERATING*...
YOU REALLY ARE THE BEST, GABI.
I'M MARRIED.
OUCH! OW! FORGIVE A GIRL FOR GETTING EXCITED, SHEESH!

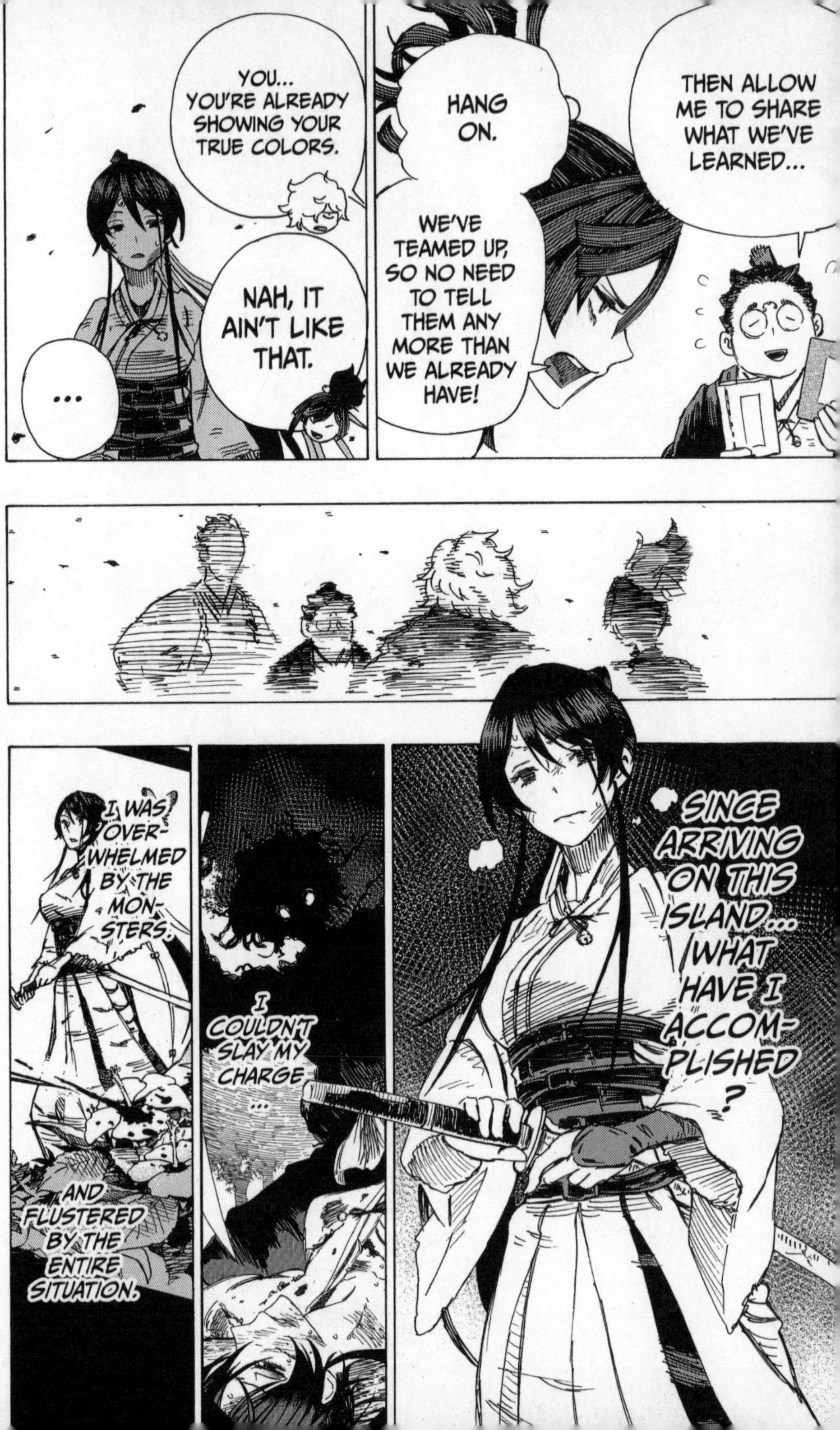
THEN ALLOW ME TO SHARE WHAT WE'VE LEARNED...
HANG ON.
WE'VE TEAMED UP, SO NO NEED TO TELL THEM ANY MORE THAN WE ALREADY HAVE!
YOU... YOU'RE ALREADY SHOWING YOUR TRUE COLORS.
NAH, IT AIN'T LIKE THAT.
...
SINCE ARRIVING ON THIS ISLAND... WHAT HAVE I ACCOMPLISHED?
I COULDN'T SLAY MY CHARGE...
I WAS OVERWHELMED BY THE MONSTERS.
AND FLUSTERED BY THE ENTIRE SITUATION.

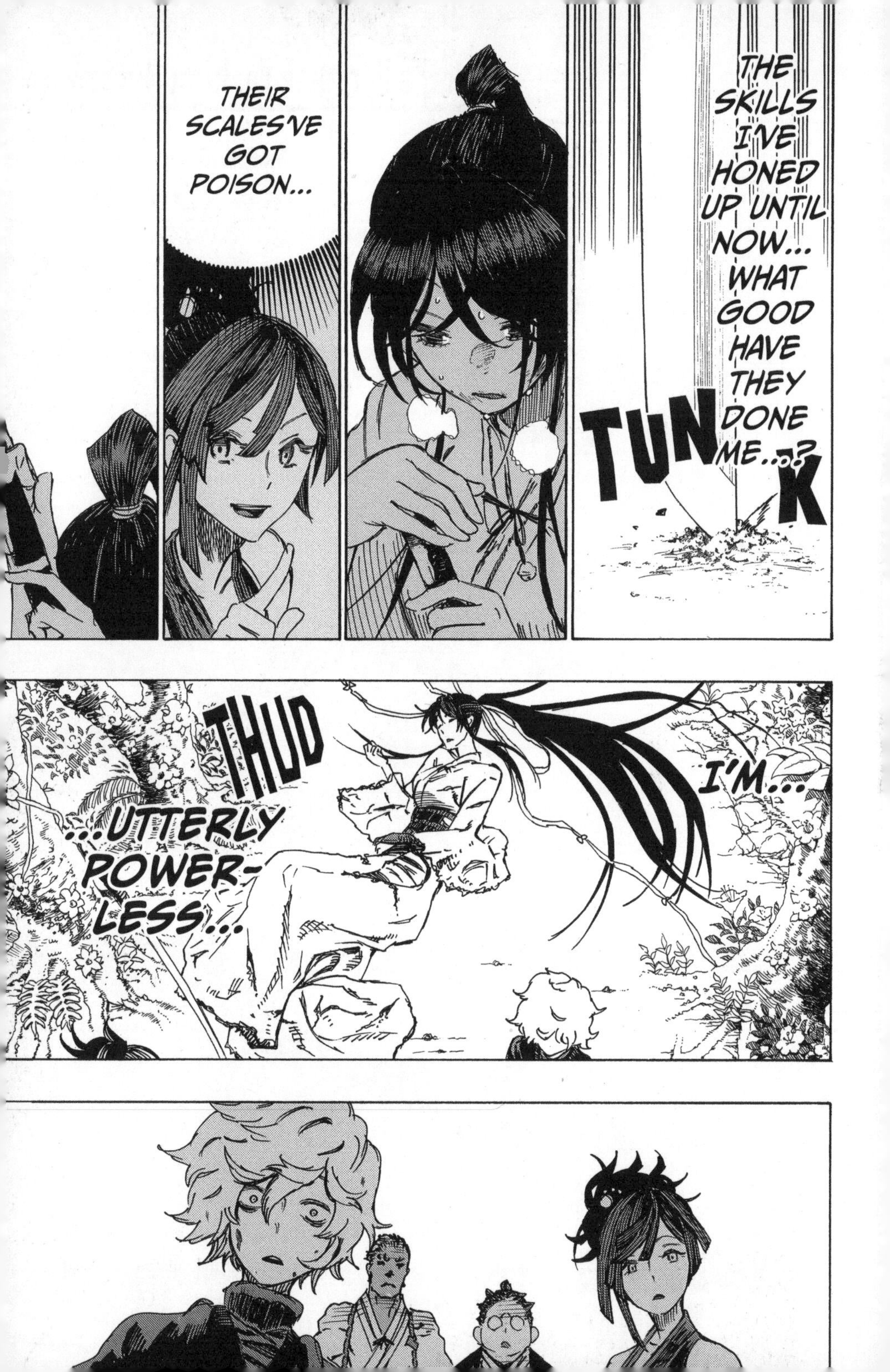
THE SKILLS I'VE HONED UP UNTIL NOW... WHAT GOOD HAVE THEY DONE ME...?
TUNK
THEIR SCALES'VE GOT POISON...
I'M...
THUD
...UTTERLY POWER-LESS...

Hell's Paradise Fashion Review

Yuzuriha of Keishu
KUNOICHI

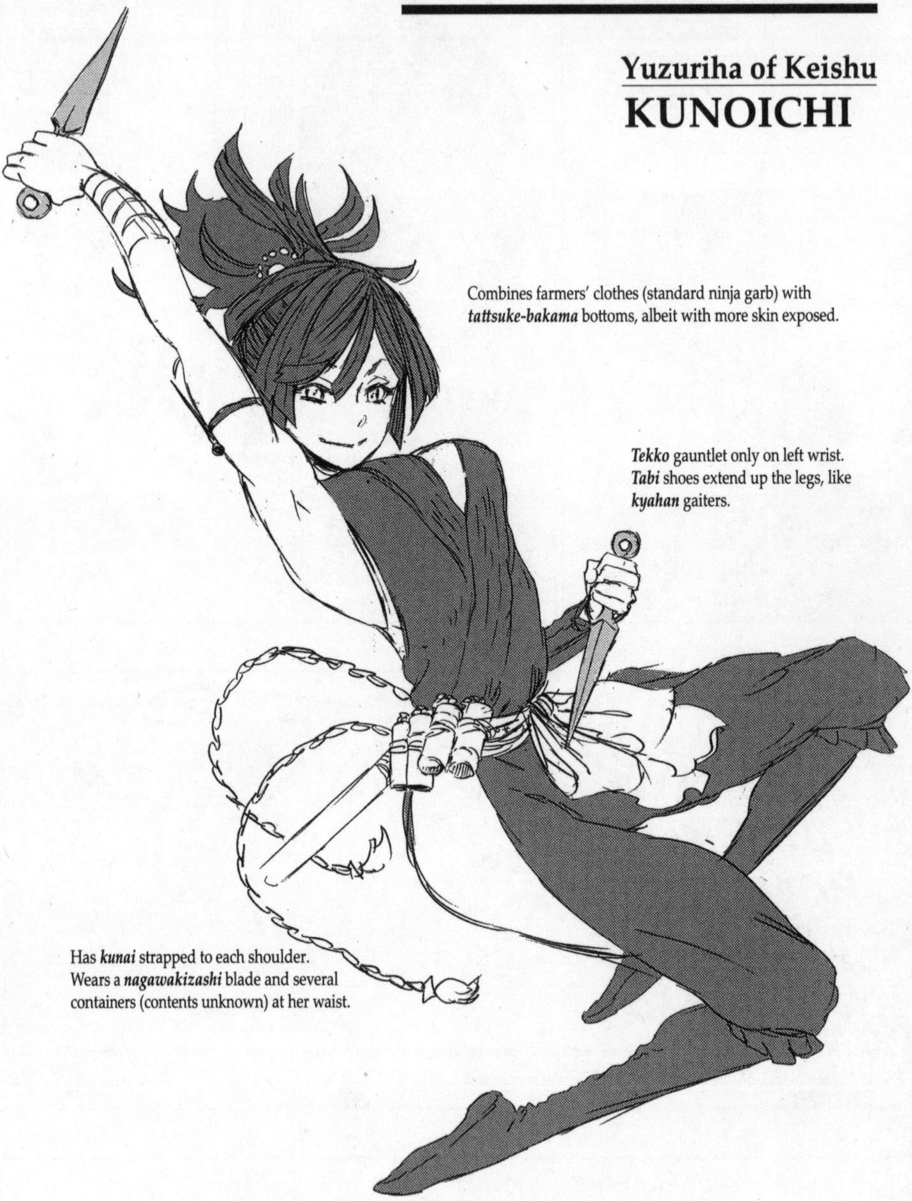

Combines farmers' clothes (standard ninja garb) with ***tattsuke-bakama*** bottoms, albeit with more skin exposed.

Tekko gauntlet only on left wrist.
Tabi shoes extend up the legs, like ***kyahan*** gaiters.

Has ***kunai*** strapped to each shoulder.
Wears a ***nagawakizashi*** blade and several containers (contents unknown) at her waist.

EVALUATION ► STYLISH ELITE ★★★ ALL THAT EXPOSED SKIN CONTRASTS BEAUTIFULLY WITH HER MASSIVE ARSENAL. VERY NICE.

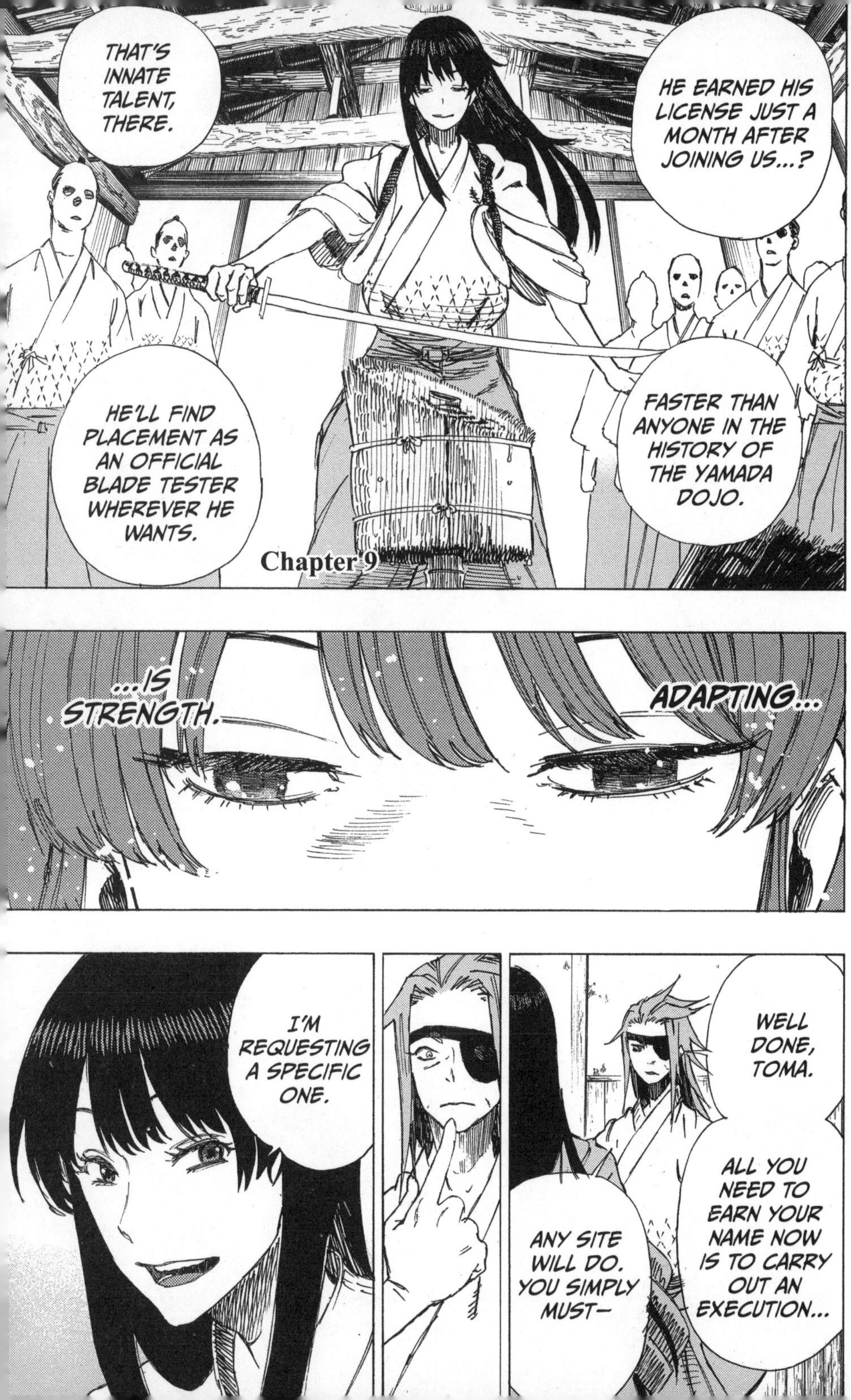
HE EARNED HIS LICENSE JUST A MONTH AFTER JOINING US...?
FASTER THAN ANYONE IN THE HISTORY OF THE YAMADA DOJO.
THAT'S INNATE TALENT, THERE.
HE'LL FIND PLACEMENT AS AN OFFICIAL BLADE TESTER WHEREVER HE WANTS.
Chapter 9
ADAPTING...
...IS STRENGTH.
WELL DONE, TOMA.
ALL YOU NEED TO EARN YOUR NAME NOW IS TO CARRY OUT AN EXECUTION...
ANY SITE WILL DO. YOU SIMPLY MUST—
I'M REQUESTING A SPECIFIC ONE.

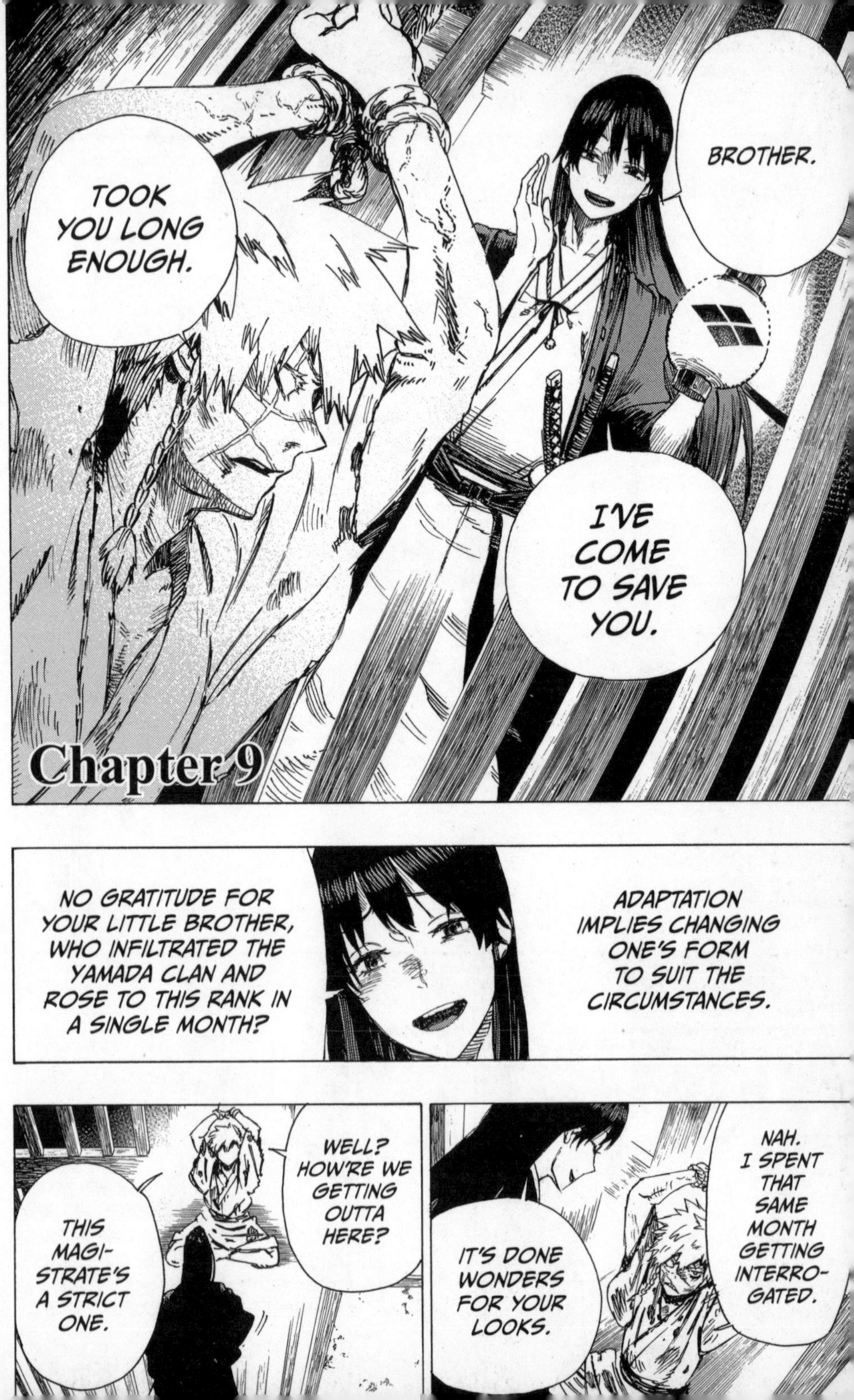
BROTHER.
I'VE COME TO SAVE YOU.
TOOK YOU LONG ENOUGH.
Chapter 9
ADAPTATION IMPLIES CHANGING ONE'S FORM TO SUIT THE CIRCUMSTANCES.
NO GRATITUDE FOR YOUR LITTLE BROTHER, WHO INFILTRATED THE YAMADA CLAN AND ROSE TO THIS RANK IN A SINGLE MONTH?
NAH. I SPENT THAT SAME MONTH GETTING INTERRO-GATED.
IT'S DONE WONDERS FOR YOUR LOOKS.
WELL? HOW'RE WE GETTING OUTTA HERE?
THIS MAGI-STRATE'S A STRICT ONE.

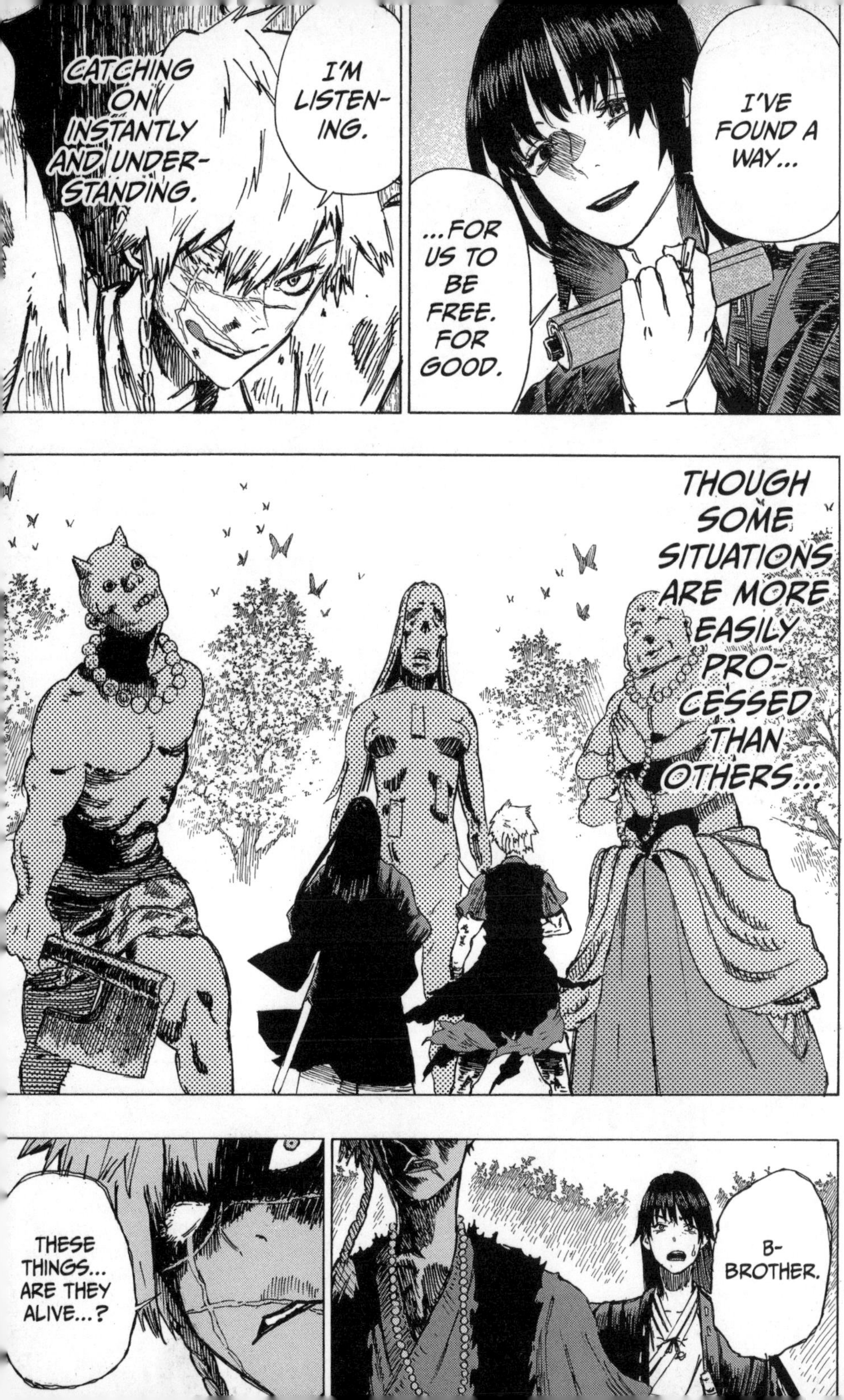
I'VE FOUND A WAY...
...FOR US TO BE FREE. FOR GOOD.
I'M LISTEN-ING.
CATCHING ON INSTANTLY AND UNDER-STANDING.
THOUGH SOME SITUATIONS ARE MORE EASILY PRO-CESSED THAN OTHERS...
B-BROTHER.
THESE THINGS... ARE THEY ALIVE...?

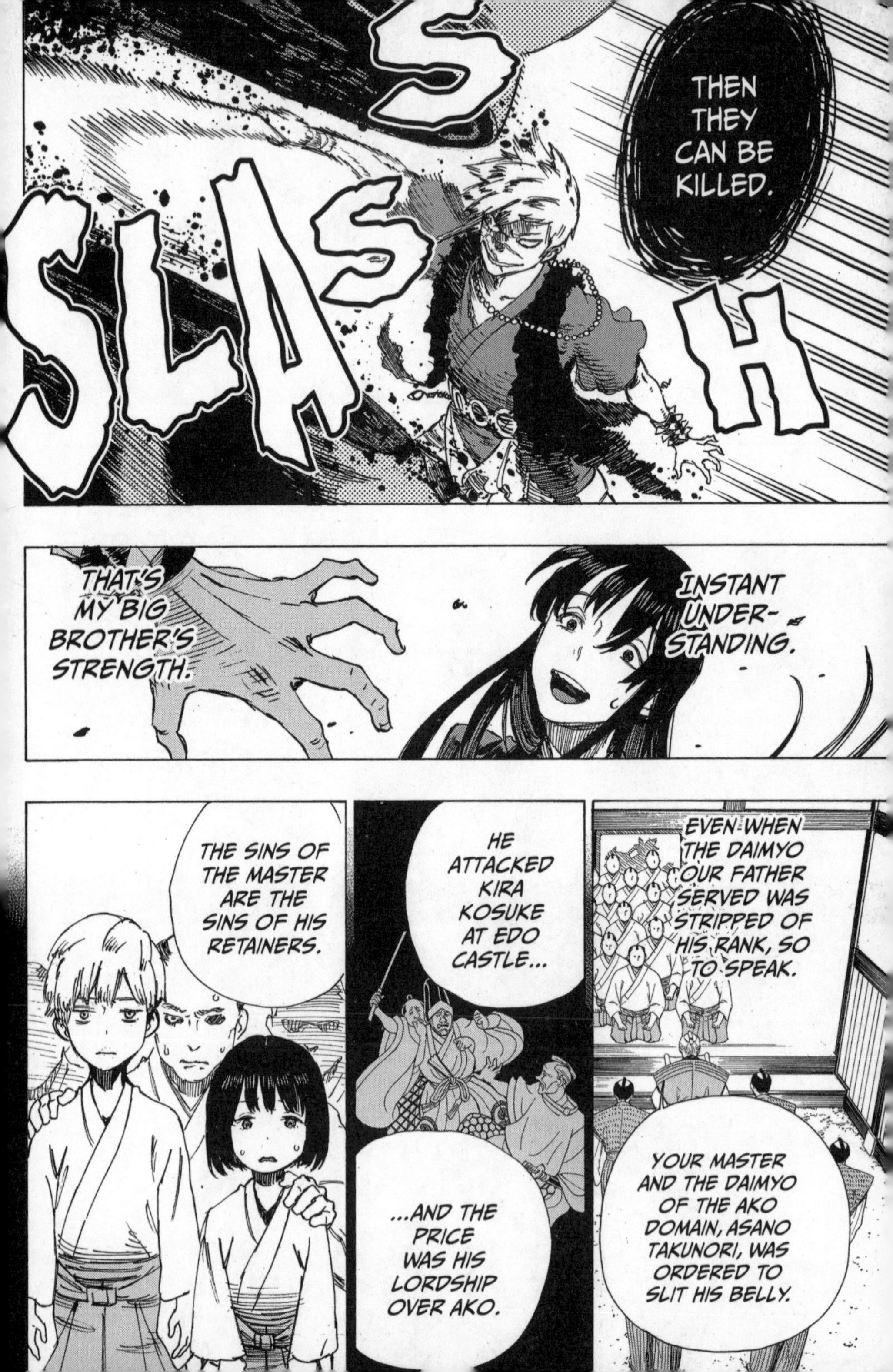
THEN THEY CAN BE KILLED.
SLASH
INSTANT UNDER-STANDING.
THAT'S MY BIG BROTHER'S STRENGTH.
EVEN WHEN THE DAIMYO OUR FATHER SERVED WAS STRIPPED OF HIS RANK, SO TO SPEAK.
YOUR MASTER AND THE DAIMYO OF THE AKO DOMAIN, ASANO TAKUNORI, WAS ORDERED TO SLIT HIS BELLY.
HE ATTACKED KIRA KOSUKE AT EDO CASTLE...
...AND THE PRICE WAS HIS LORDSHIP OVER AKO.
THE SINS OF THE MASTER ARE THE SINS OF HIS RETAINERS.

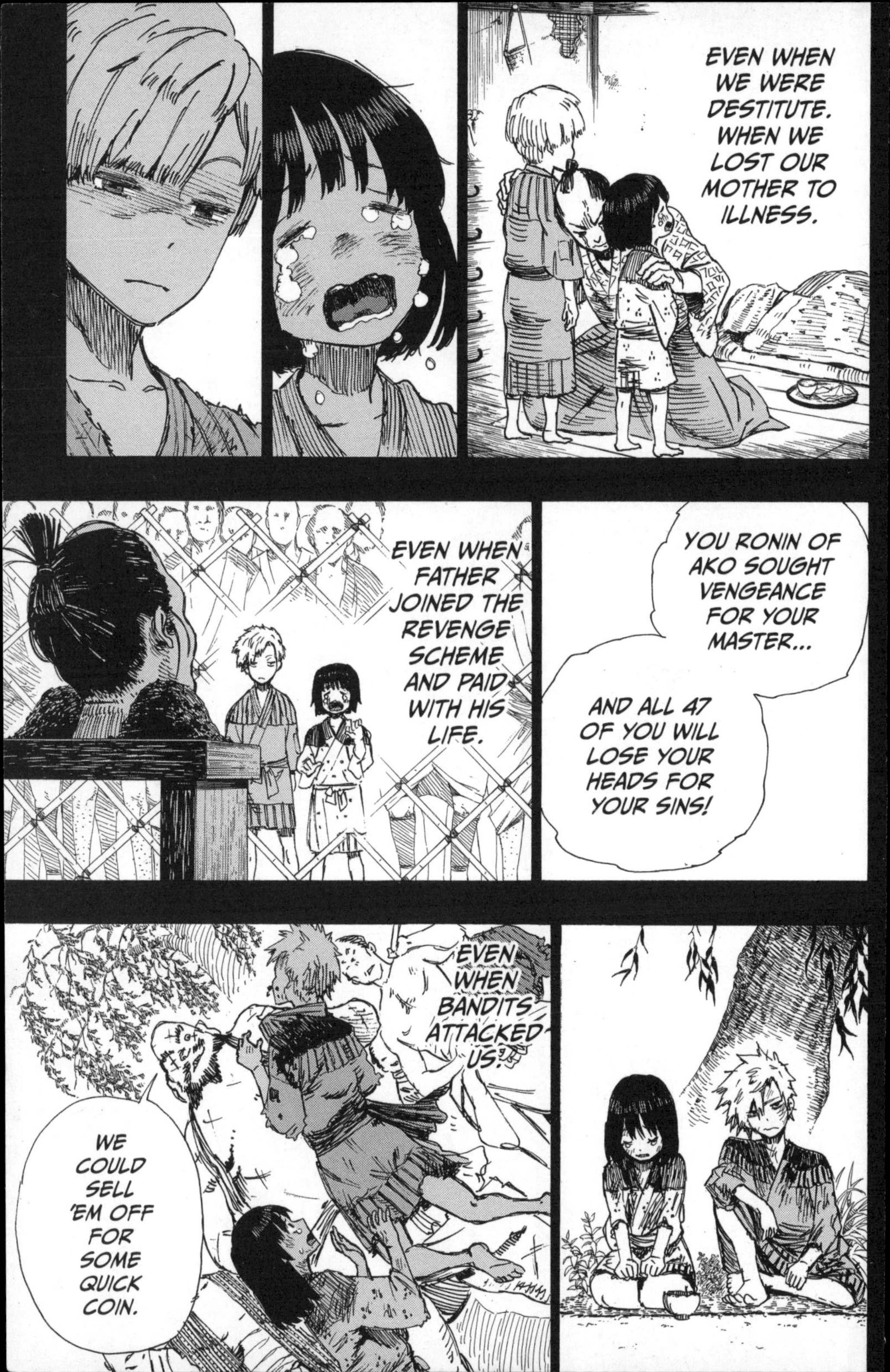
EVEN WHEN WE WERE DESTITUTE. WHEN WE LOST OUR MOTHER TO ILLNESS.
YOU RONIN OF AKO SOUGHT VENGEANCE FOR YOUR MASTER...
AND ALL 47 OF YOU WILL LOSE YOUR HEADS FOR YOUR SINS!
EVEN WHEN FATHER JOINED THE REVENGE SCHEME AND PAID WITH HIS LIFE.
EVEN WHEN BANDITS ATTACKED US.
WE COULD SELL 'EM OFF FOR SOME QUICK COIN.

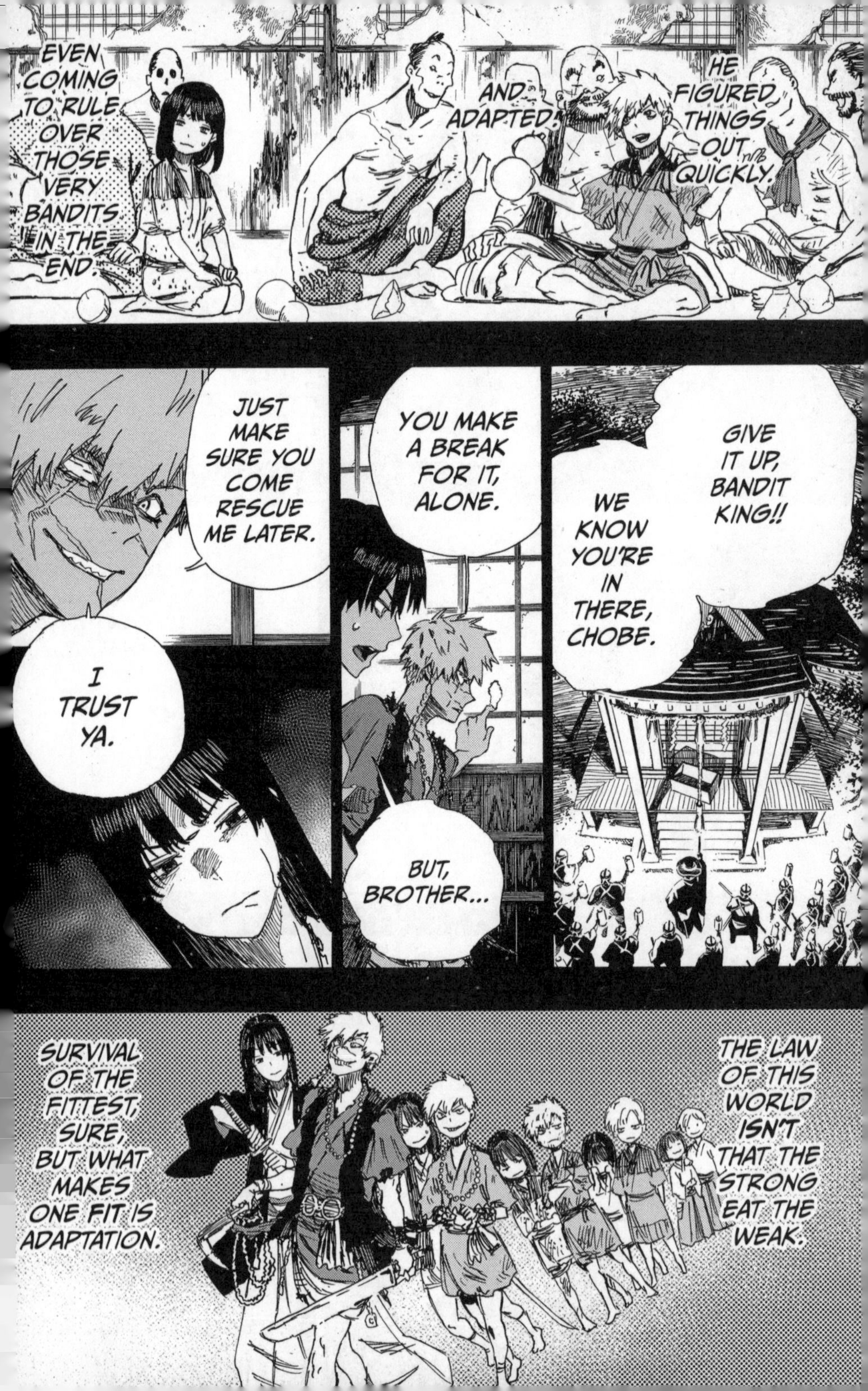
HE FIGURED THINGS OUT QUICKLY.
AND ADAPTED.
EVEN COMING TO RULE OVER THOSE VERY BANDITS IN THE END.
GIVE IT UP, BANDIT KING!!
WE KNOW YOU'RE IN THERE, CHOBE.
YOU MAKE A BREAK FOR IT, ALONE.
BUT, BROTHER...
JUST MAKE SURE YOU COME RESCUE ME LATER.
I TRUST YA.
THE LAW OF THIS WORLD ISN'T THAT THE STRONG EAT THE WEAK.
SURVIVAL OF THE FITTEST, SURE, BUT WHAT MAKES ONE FIT IS ADAPTATION.

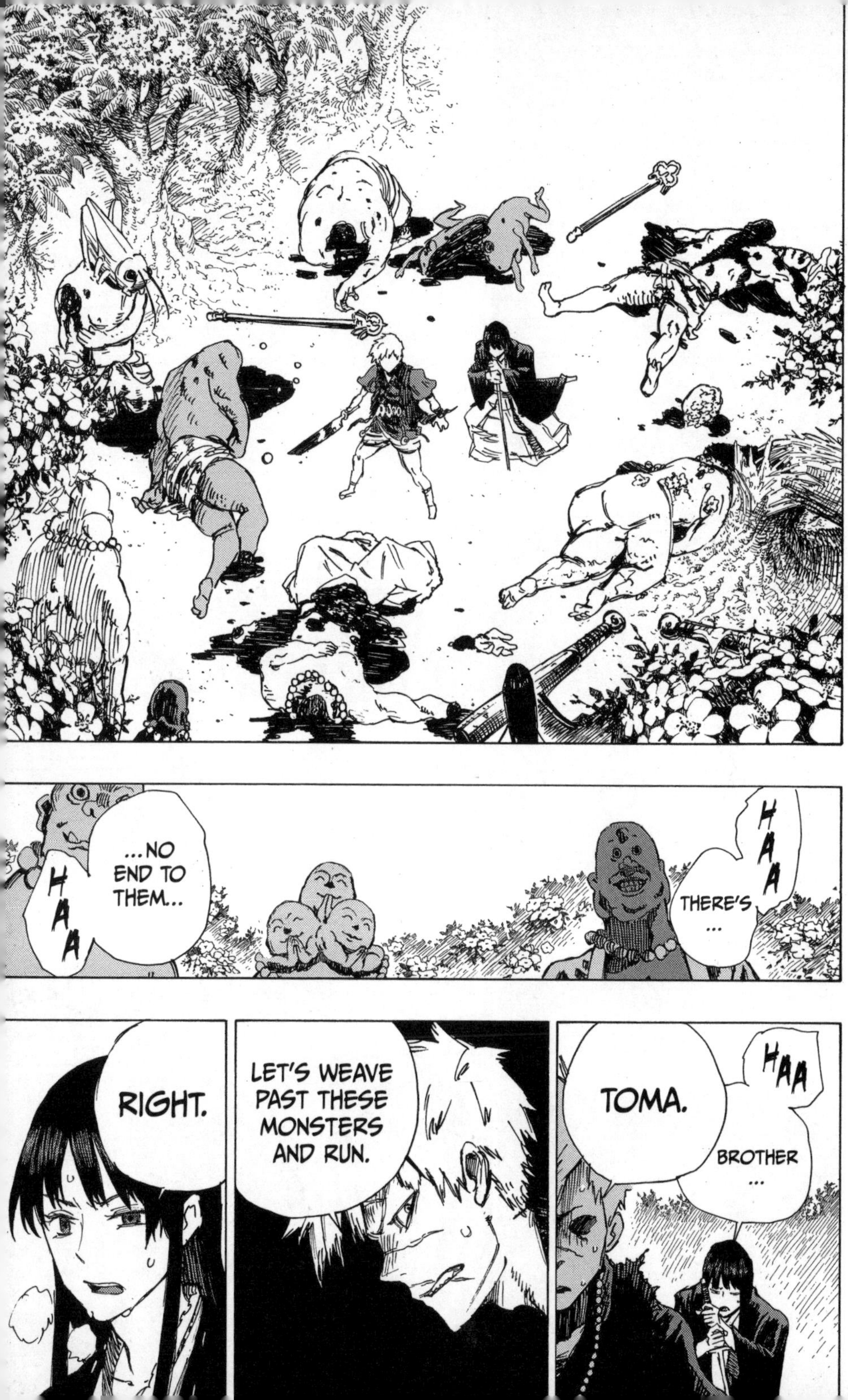
HAAA
THERE'S ...
...NO END TO THEM...
HAAA
HAAA
TOMA.
BROTHER ...
LET'S WEAVE PAST THESE MONSTERS AND RUN.
RIGHT.

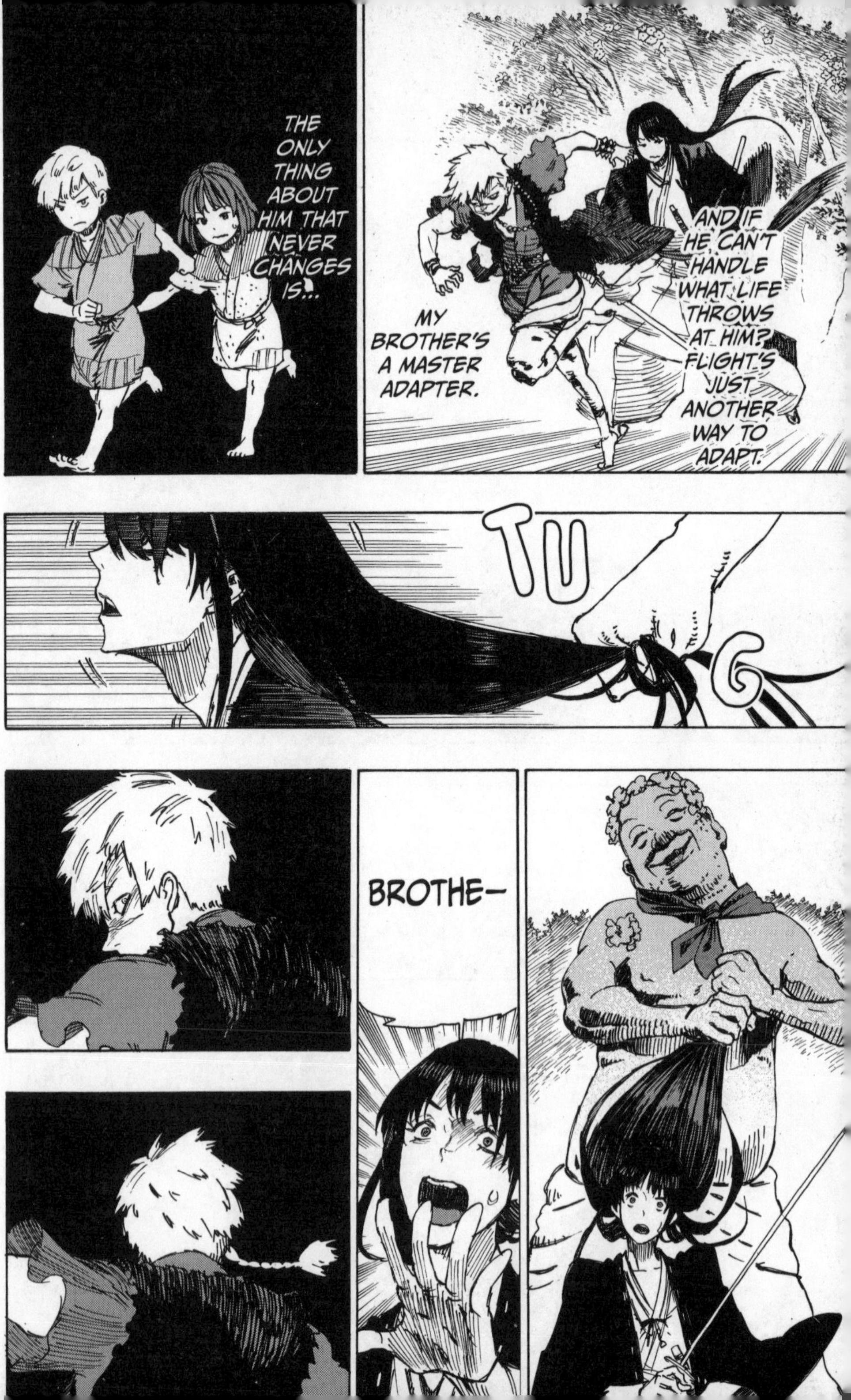
MY BROTHER'S A MASTER ADAPTER.
AND IF HE CAN'T HANDLE WHAT LIFE THROWS AT HIM? FLIGHT'S JUST ANOTHER WAY TO ADAPT.
THE ONLY THING ABOUT HIM THAT NEVER CHANGES IS...
TUG
BROTHE-

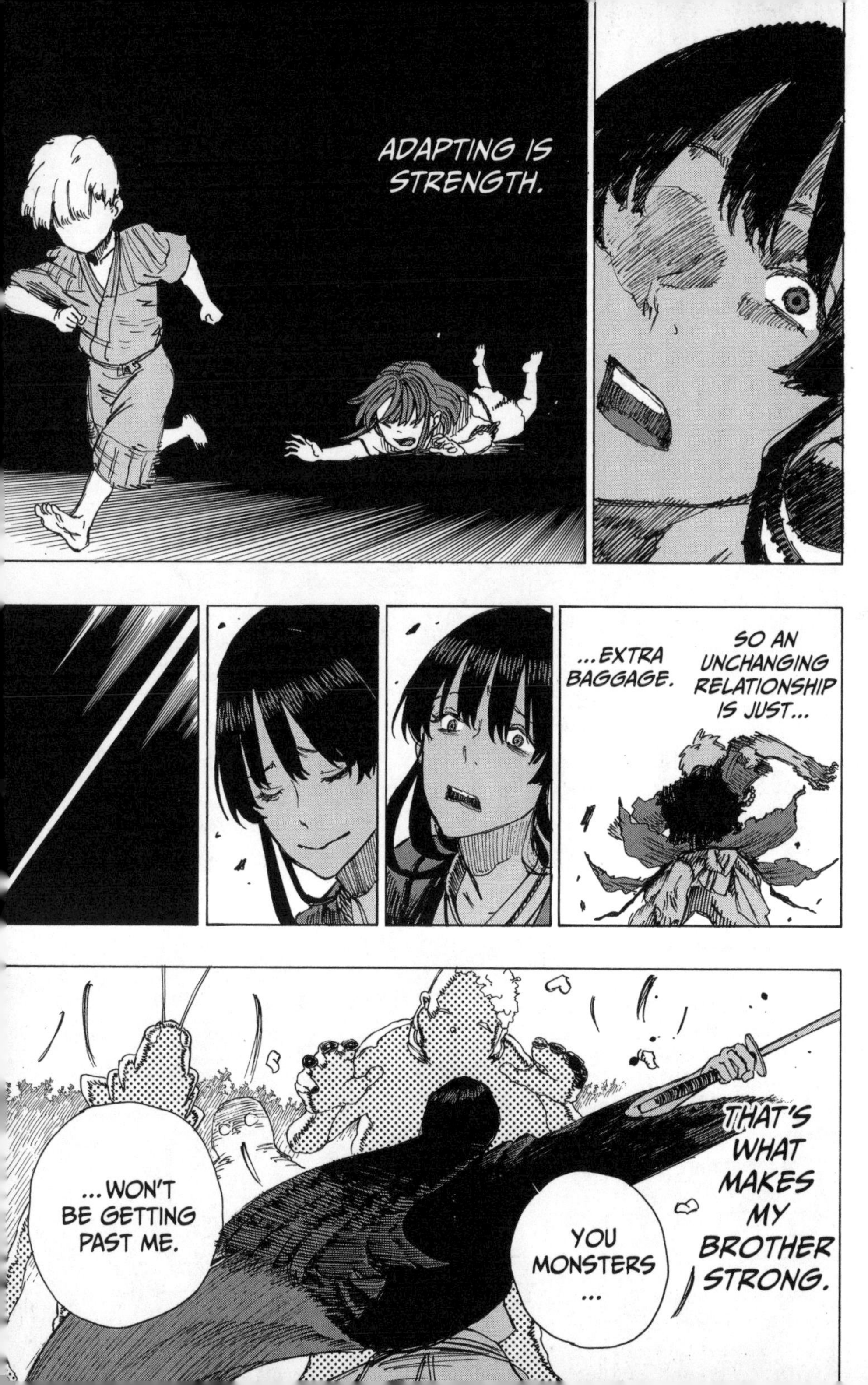
ADAPTING IS STRENGTH.
SO AN UNCHANGING RELATIONSHIP IS JUST...
...EXTRA BAGGAGE.
THAT'S WHAT MAKES MY BROTHER STRONG.
YOU MONSTERS ...
...WON'T BE GETTING PAST ME.

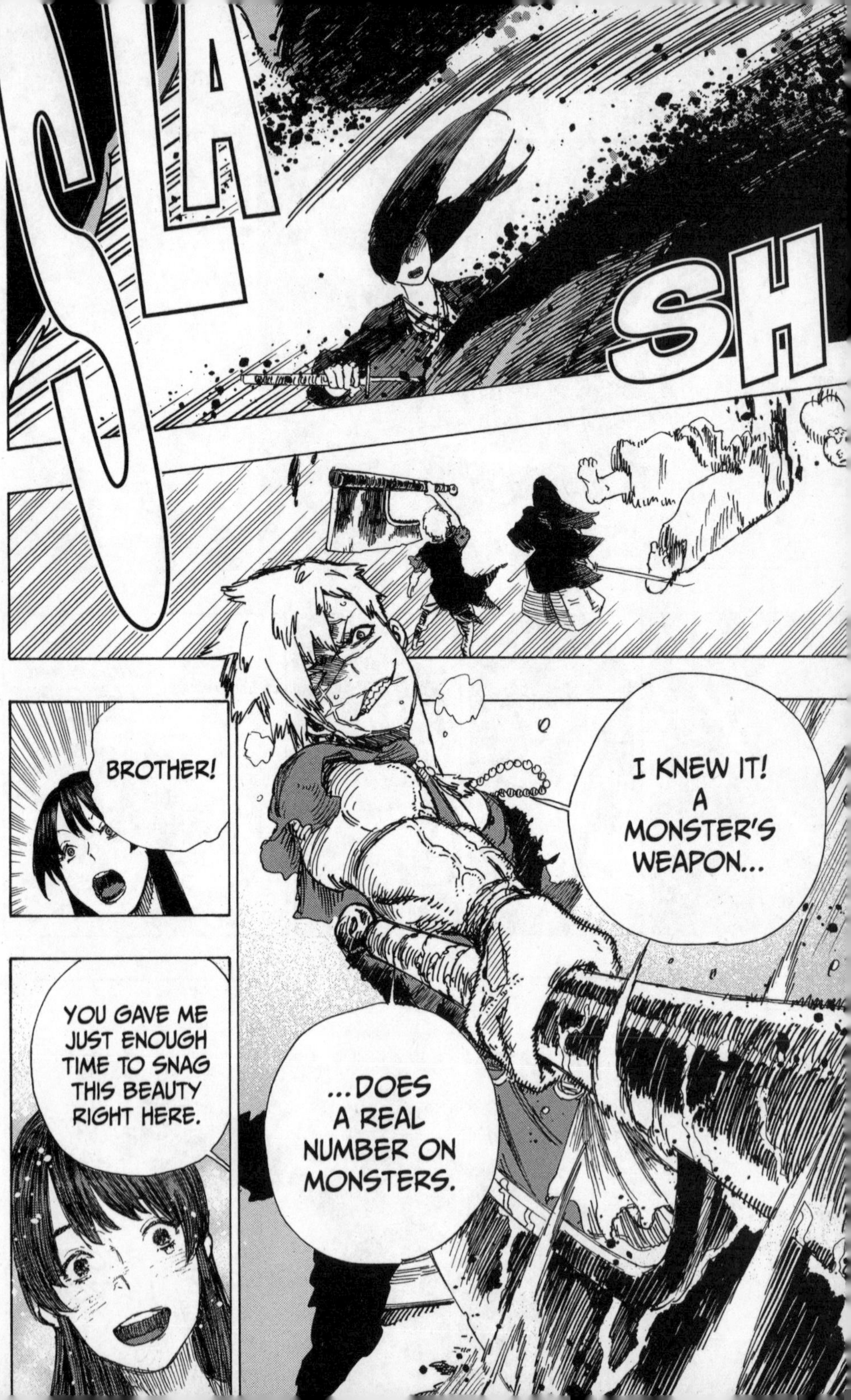
SLA
SH
I KNEW IT! A MONSTER'S WEAPON...
...DOES A REAL NUMBER ON MONSTERS.
BROTHER!
YOU GAVE ME JUST ENOUGH TIME TO SNAG THIS BEAUTY RIGHT HERE.

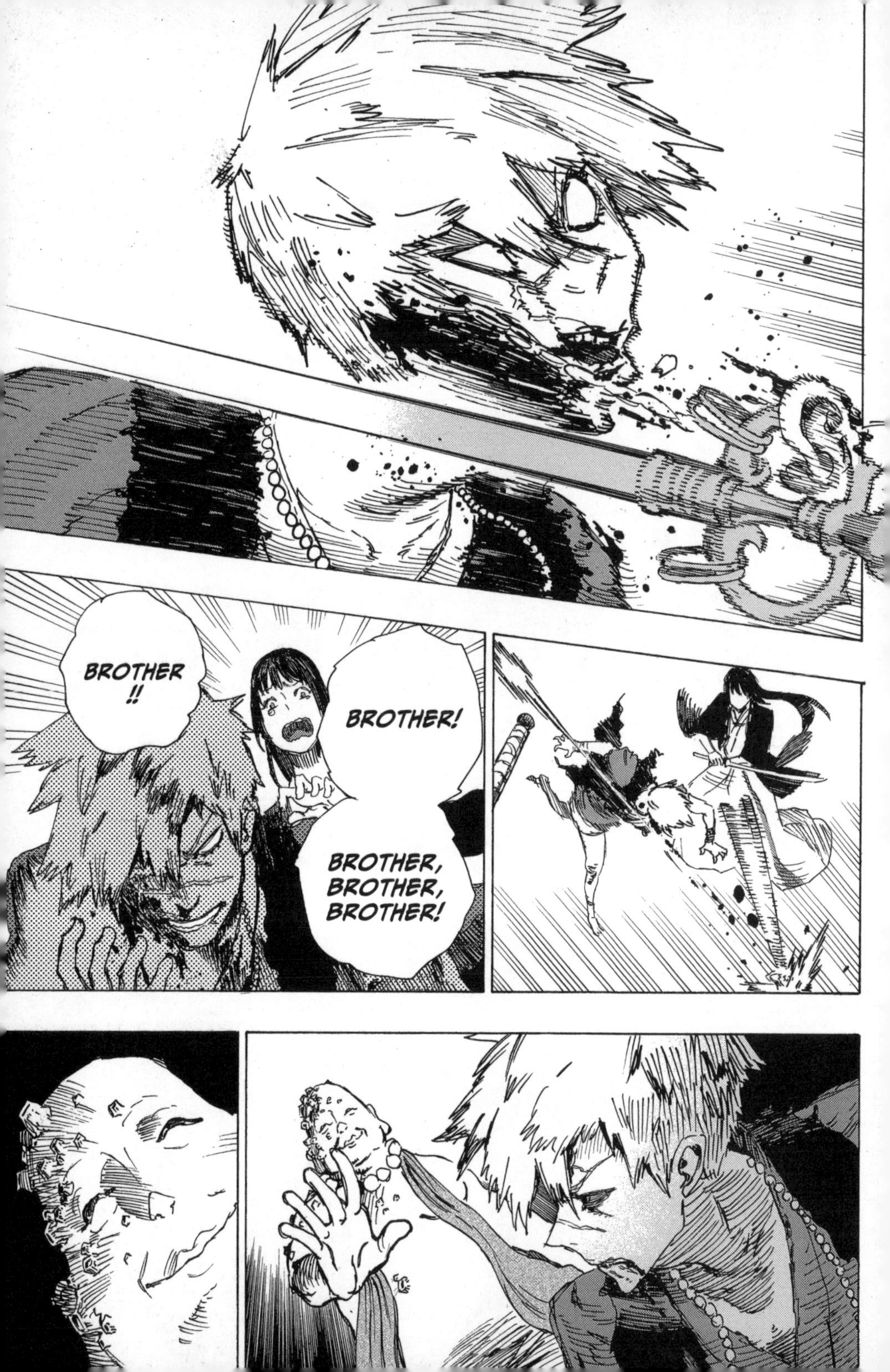
BROTHER!
BROTHER !!
BROTHER, BROTHER, BROTHER!

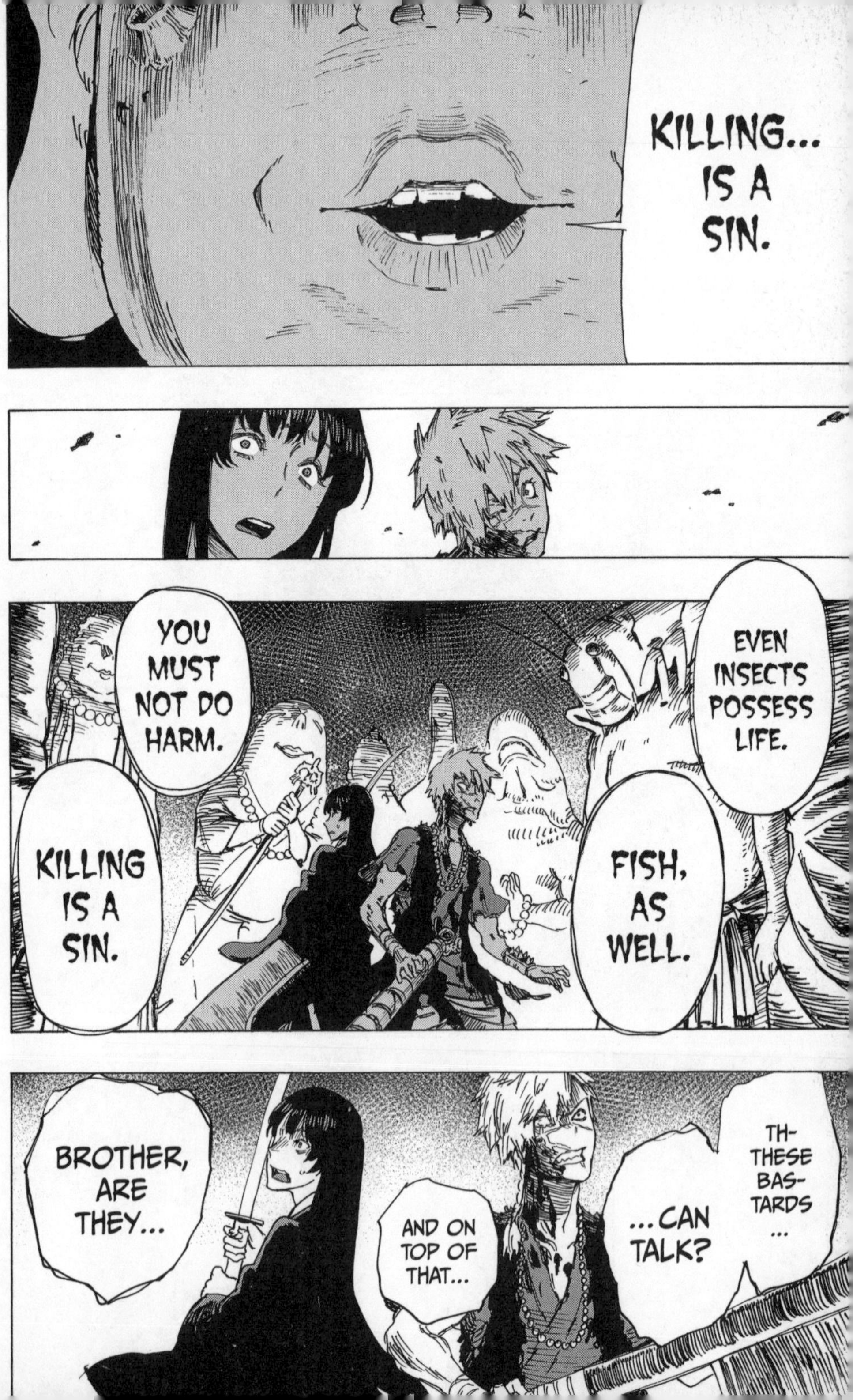
KILLING... IS A SIN.
EVEN INSECTS POSSESS LIFE.
YOU MUST NOT DO HARM.
FISH, AS WELL.
KILLING IS A SIN.
TH-THESE BAS-TARDS...
...CAN TALK?
AND ON TOP OF THAT...
BROTHER, ARE THEY...

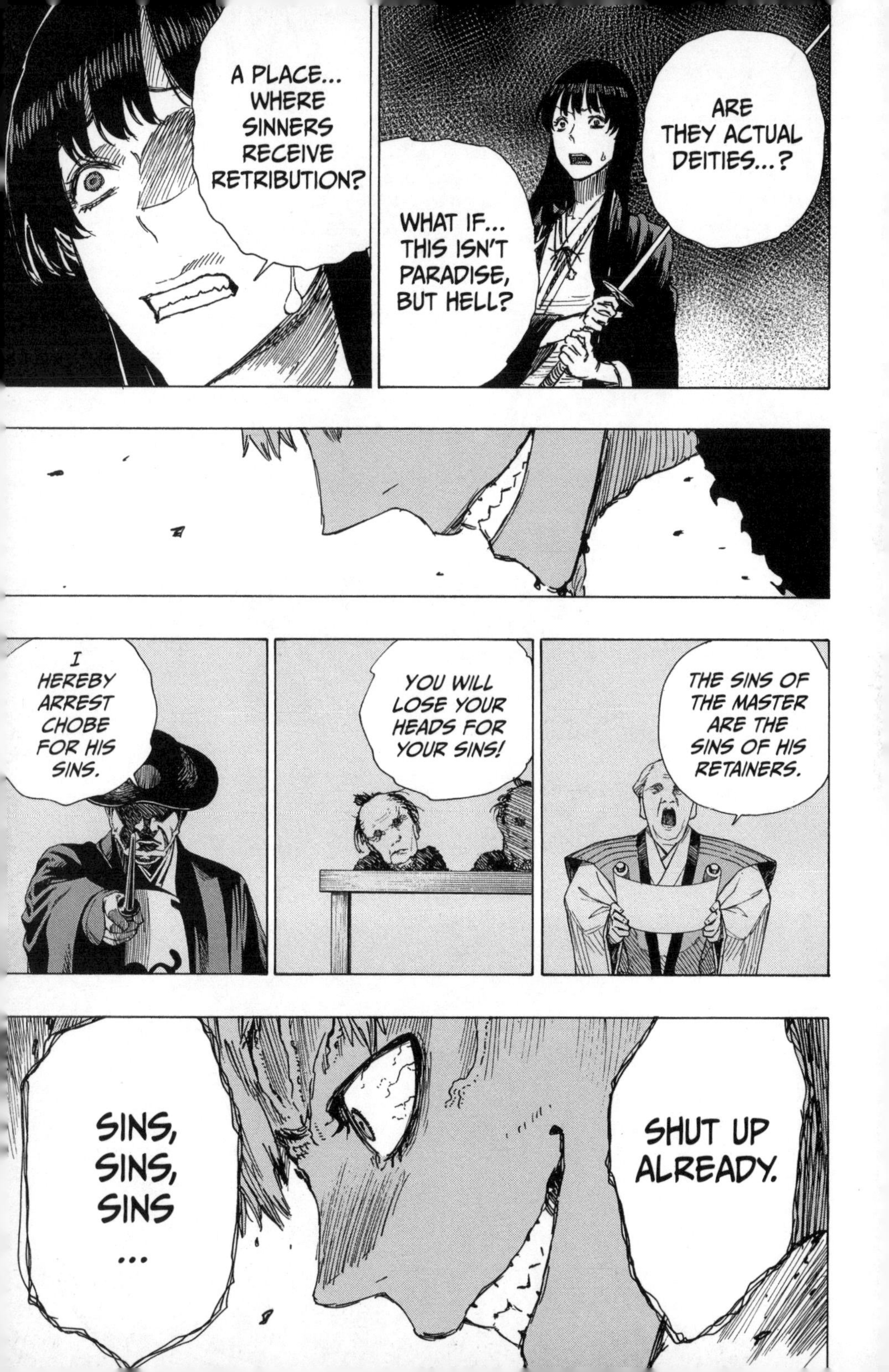
ARE THEY ACTUAL DEITIES...?
WHAT IF... THIS ISN'T PARADISE, BUT HELL?
A PLACE... WHERE SINNERS RECEIVE RETRIBUTION?
THE SINS OF THE MASTER ARE THE SINS OF HIS RETAINERS.
YOU WILL LOSE YOUR HEADS FOR YOUR SINS!
I HEREBY ARREST CHOBE FOR HIS SINS.
SHUT UP ALREADY.
SINS, SINS, SINS ...

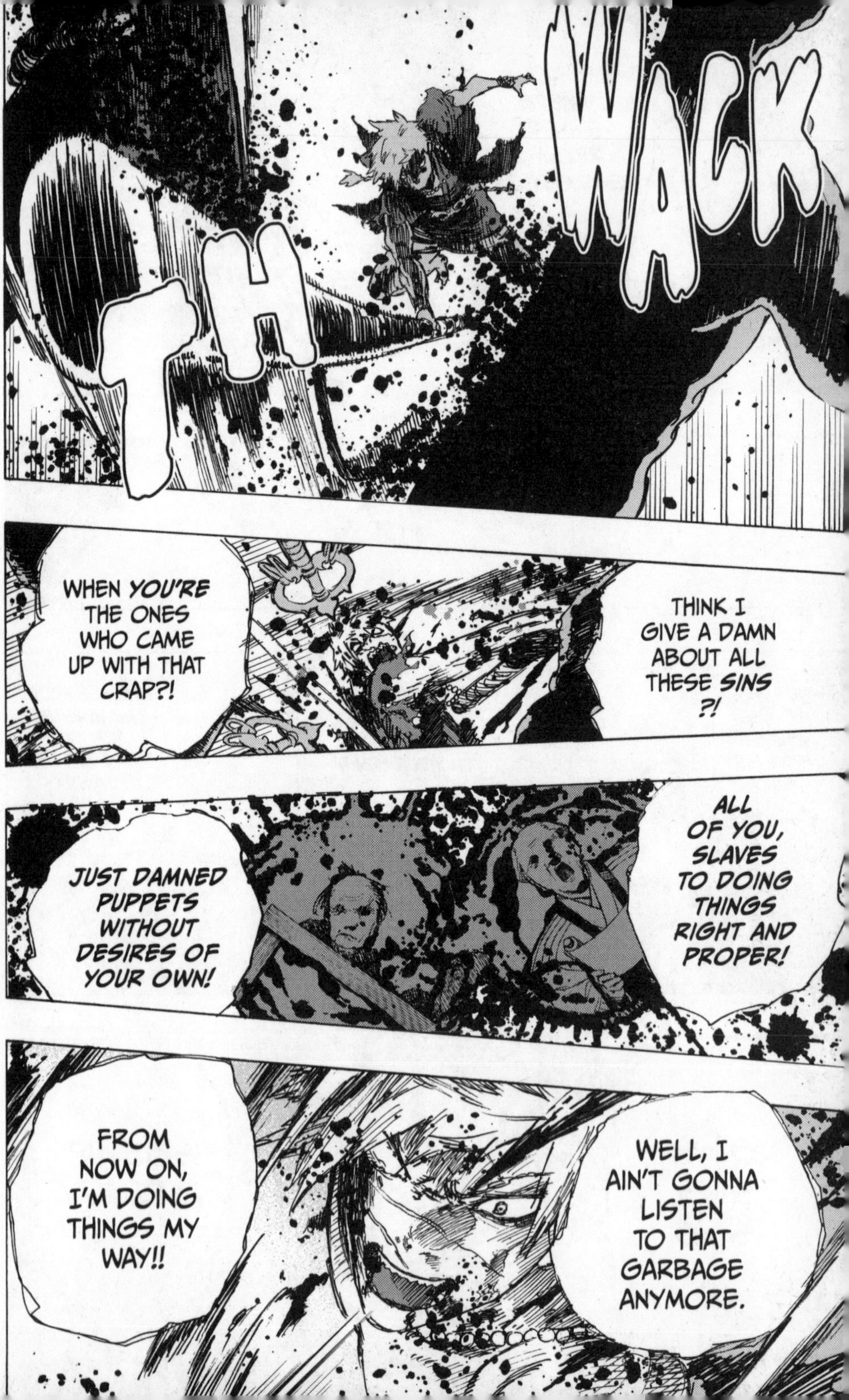
WACK
TH
THINK I GIVE A DAMN ABOUT ALL THESE *SINS* ?!
WHEN *YOU'RE* THE ONES WHO CAME UP WITH THAT CRAP?!
ALL OF YOU, SLAVES TO DOING THINGS RIGHT AND PROPER!
JUST DAMNED PUPPETS WITHOUT DESIRES OF YOUR OWN!
WELL, I AIN'T GONNA LISTEN TO THAT GARBAGE ANYMORE.
FROM NOW ON, I'M DOING THINGS MY WAY!!

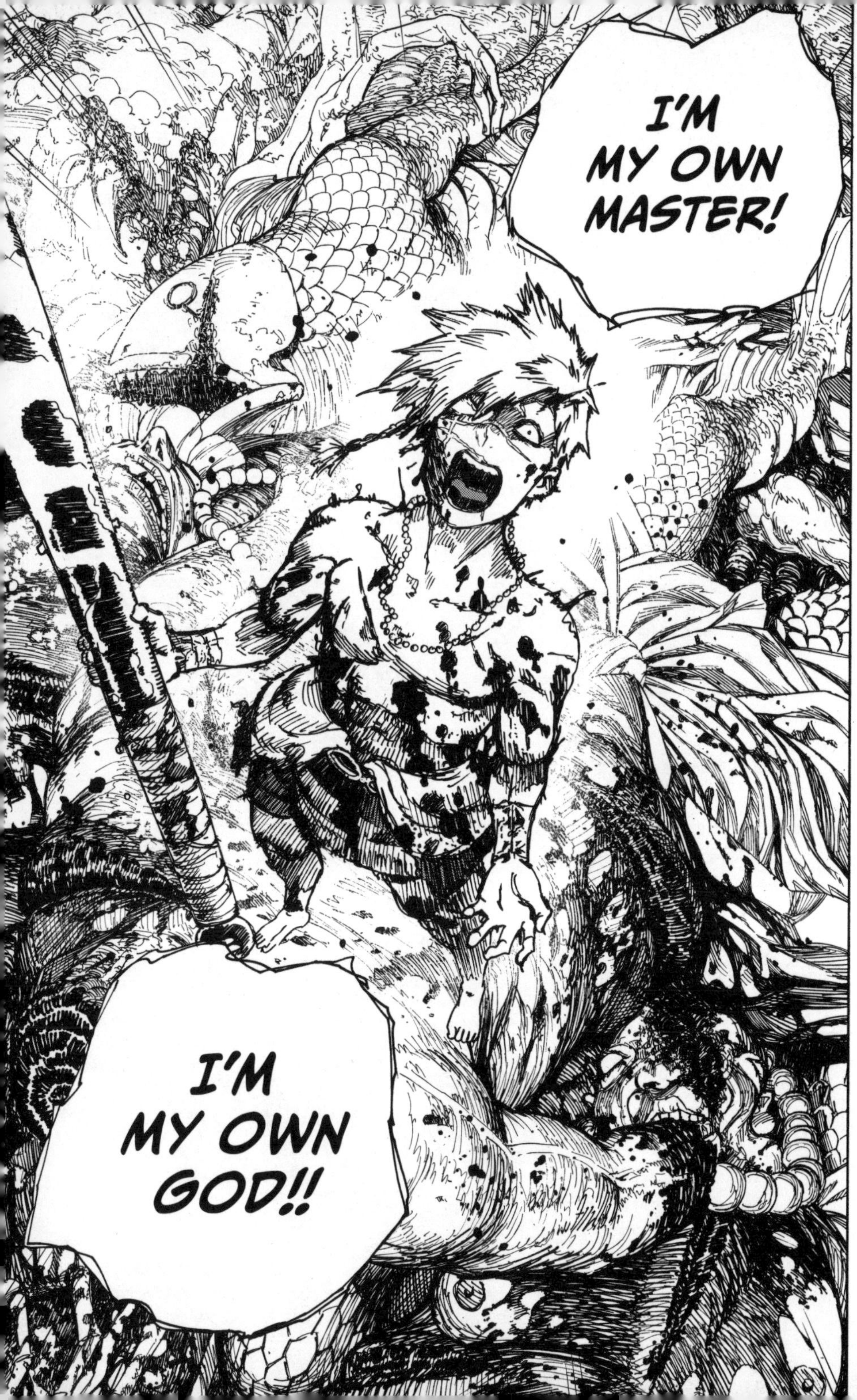
I'M MY OWN MASTER!
I'M MY OWN GOD!!

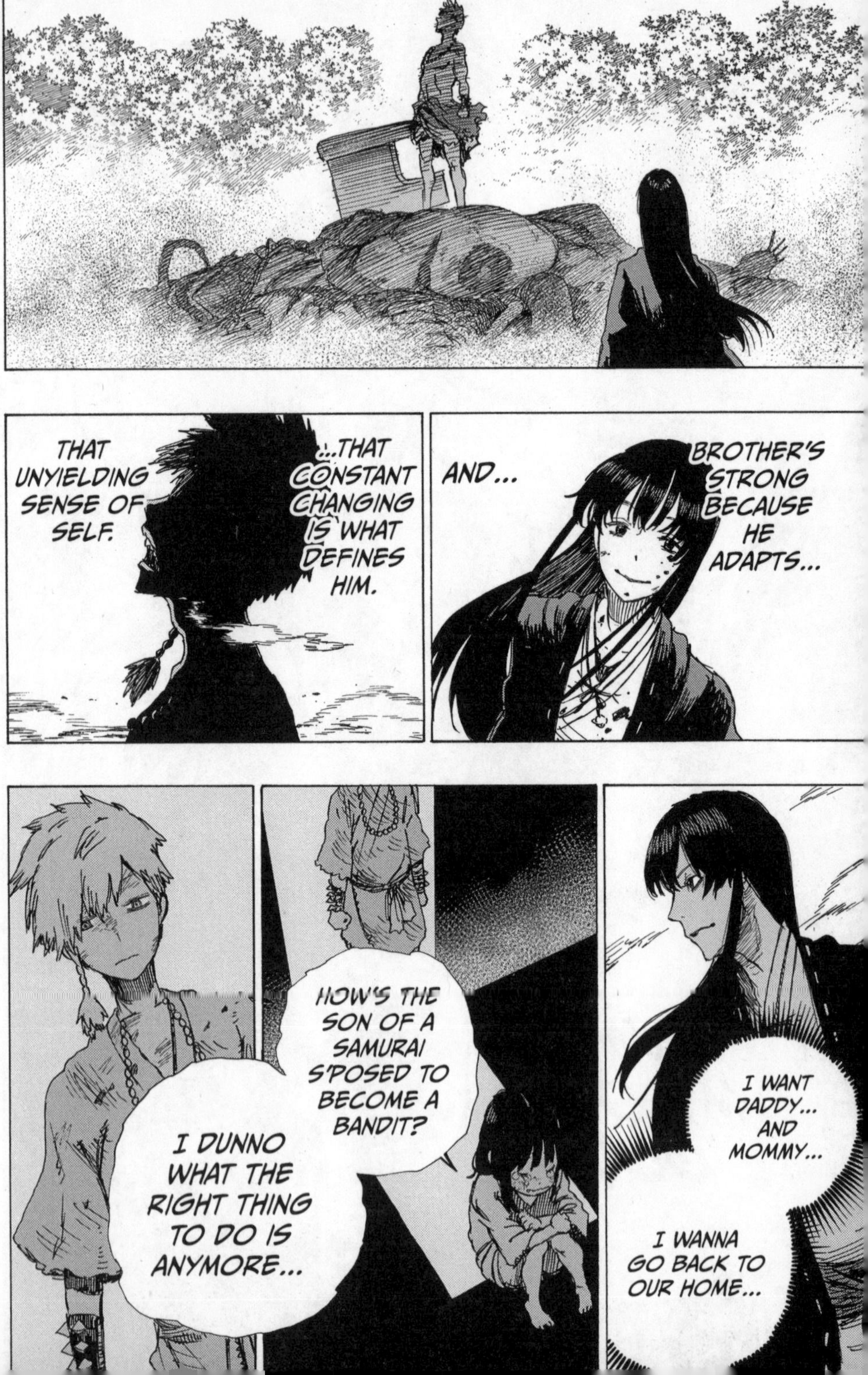
BROTHER'S STRONG BECAUSE HE ADAPTS...
AND...
...THAT CONSTANT CHANGING IS WHAT DEFINES HIM.
THAT UNYIELDING SENSE OF SELF.
I WANT DADDY... AND MOMMY...
I WANNA GO BACK TO OUR HOME...
HOW'S THE SON OF A SAMURAI S'POSED TO BECOME A BANDIT?
I DUNNO WHAT THE RIGHT THING TO DO IS ANYMORE...

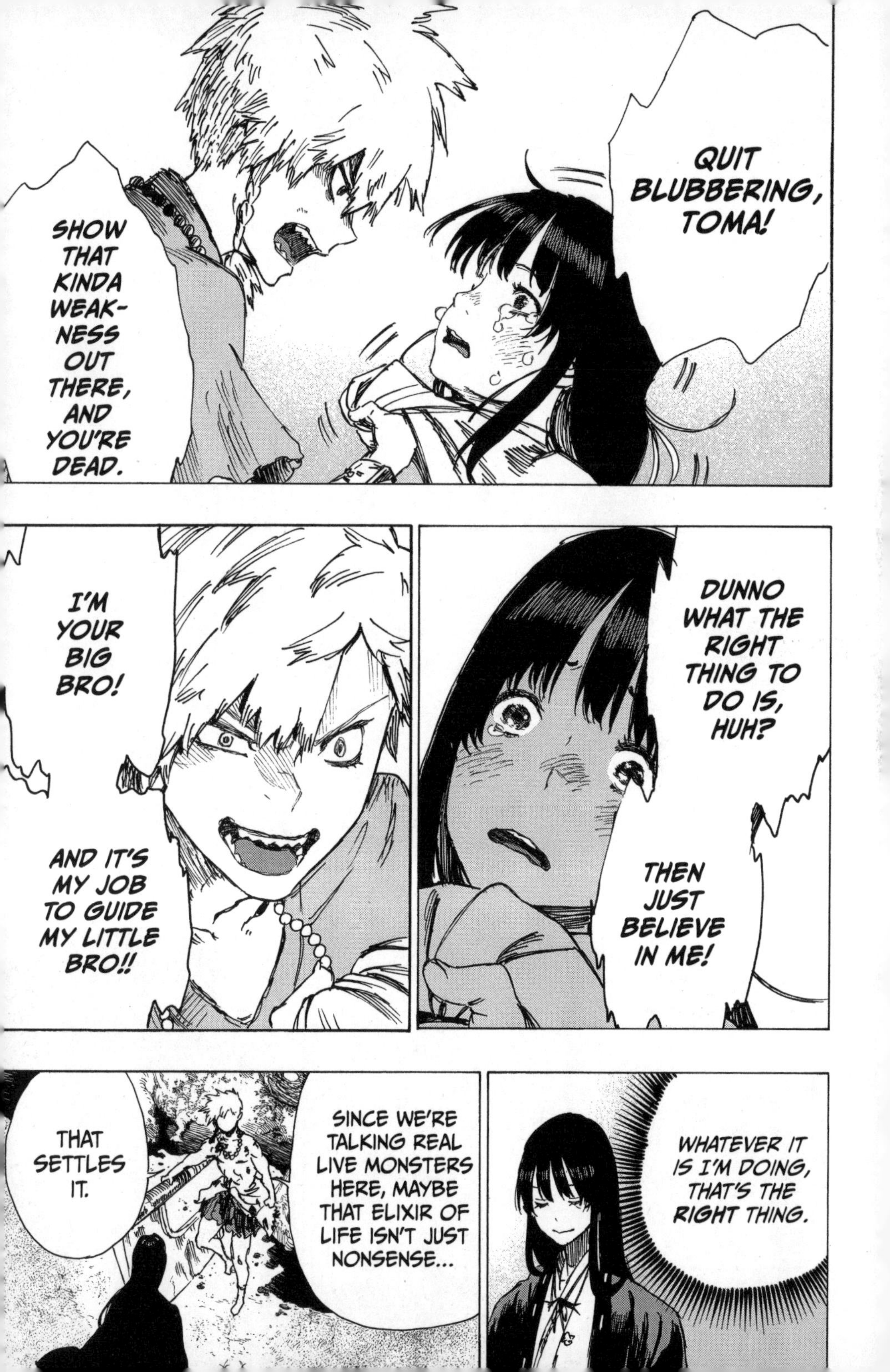
QUIT BLUBBERING, TOMA!
SHOW THAT KINDA WEAKNESS OUT THERE, AND YOU'RE DEAD.
DUNNO WHAT THE RIGHT THING TO DO IS, HUH?
THEN JUST BELIEVE IN ME!
I'M YOUR BIG BRO!
AND IT'S MY JOB TO GUIDE MY LITTLE BRO!!
WHATEVER IT IS I'M DOING, THAT'S THE RIGHT THING.
SINCE WE'RE TALKING REAL LIVE MONSTERS HERE, MAYBE THAT ELIXIR OF LIFE ISN'T JUST NONSENSE...
THAT SETTLES IT.

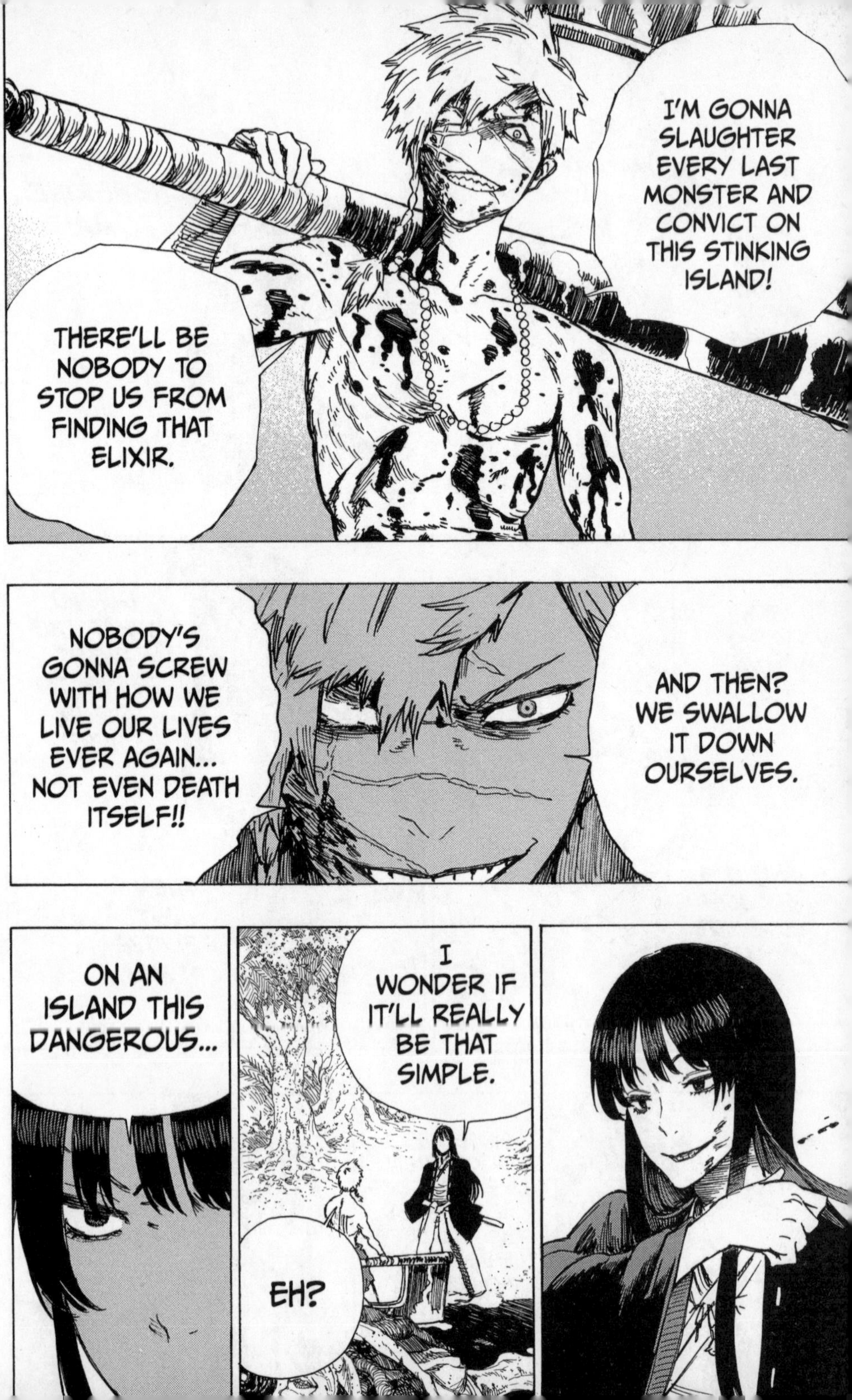
I'M GONNA SLAUGHTER EVERY LAST MONSTER AND CONVICT ON THIS STINKING ISLAND!
THERE'LL BE NOBODY TO STOP US FROM FINDING THAT ELIXIR.
AND THEN? WE SWALLOW IT DOWN OURSELVES.
NOBODY'S GONNA SCREW WITH HOW WE LIVE OUR LIVES EVER AGAIN... NOT EVEN DEATH ITSELF!!
I WONDER IF IT'LL REALLY BE THAT SIMPLE.
EH?
ON AN ISLAND THIS DANGEROUS...

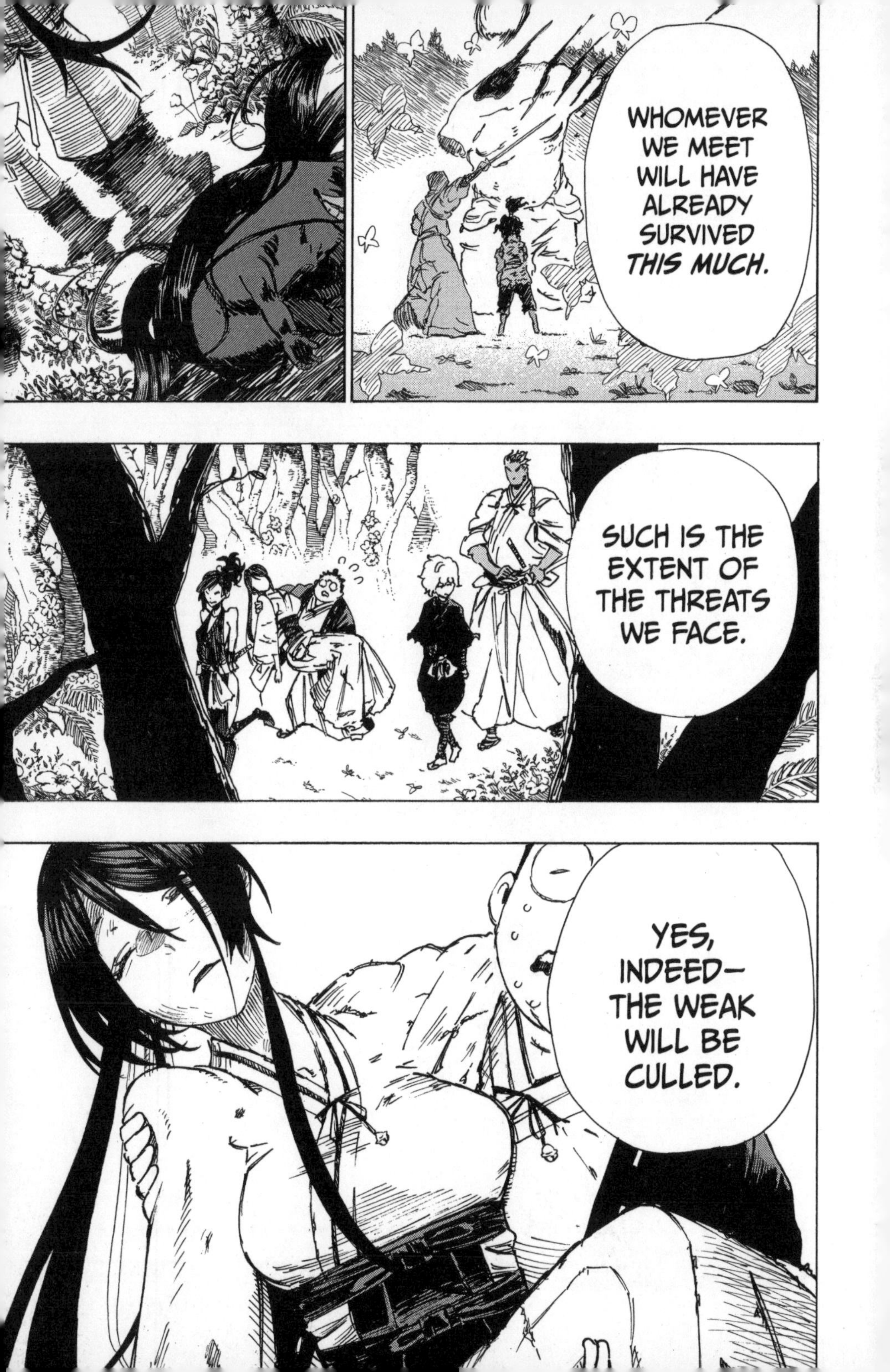
WHOMEVER WE MEET WILL HAVE ALREADY SURVIVED *THIS MUCH.*
SUCH IS THE EXTENT OF THE THREATS WE FACE.
YES, INDEED— THE WEAK WILL BE CULLED.

Hell's Paradise Fashion Review

Aza Brother Bandits
CHOBE & TOMA

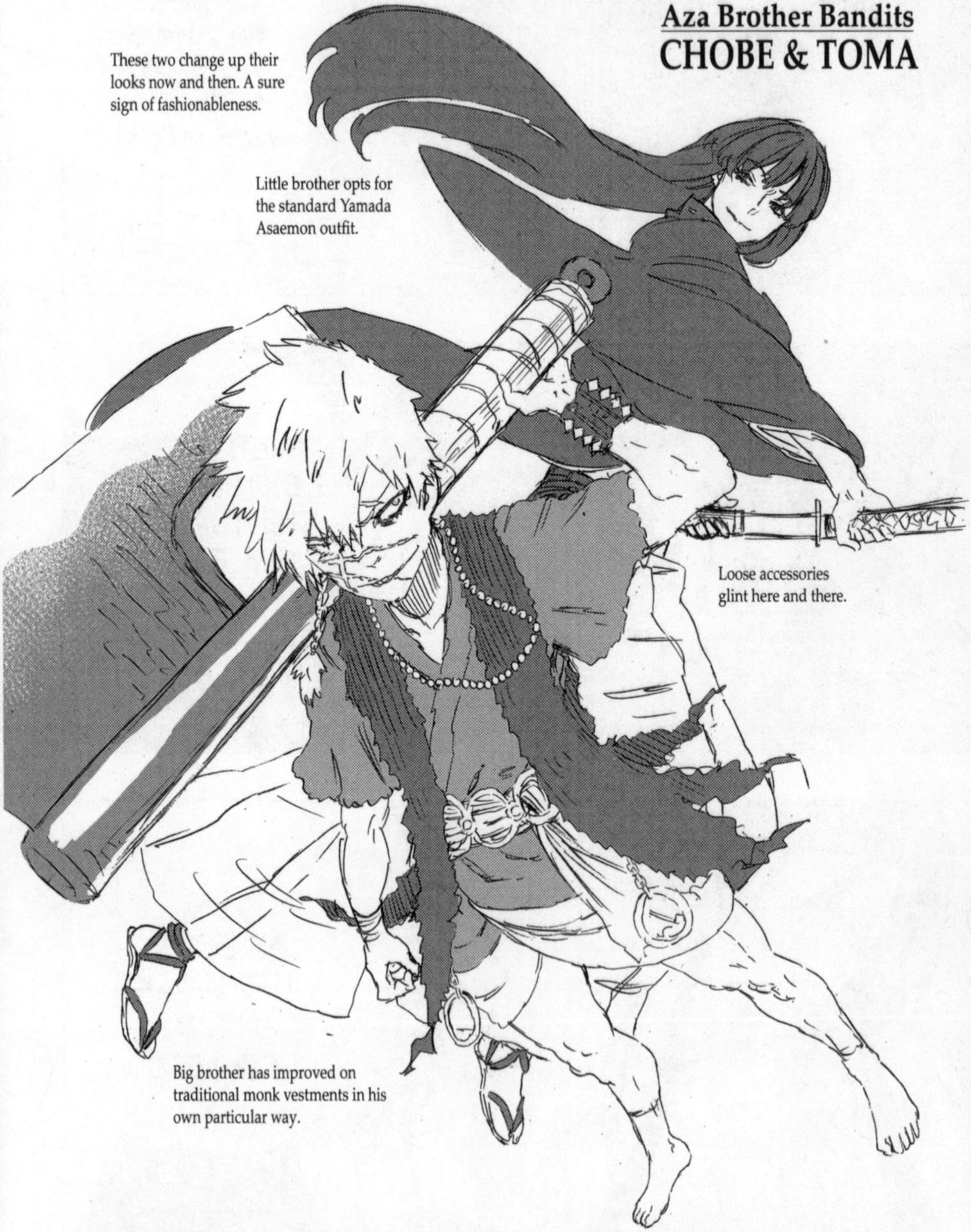
These two change up their looks now and then. A sure sign of fashionableness.
Little brother opts for the standard Yamada Asaemon outfit.
Loose accessories glint here and there.
Big brother has improved on traditional monk vestments in his own particular way.

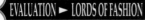

EVALUATION ► LORDS OF FASHION ★★★ FASHION IS NOT ONLY LIMITED TO EXTERNAL GARB, BUT ALSO INCLUDES THE WAY ONE LIVES ONE'S LIFE.

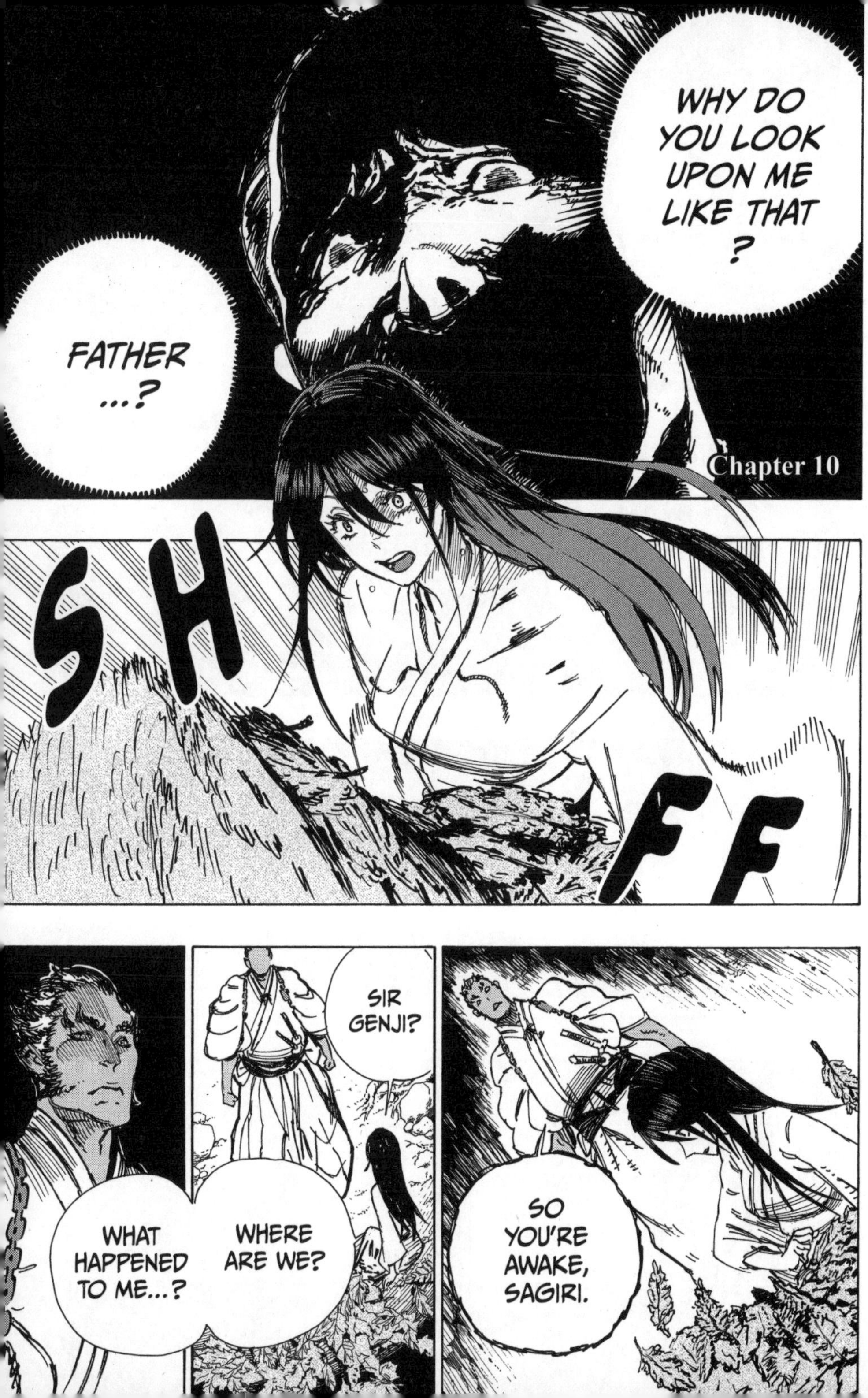
WHY DO YOU LOOK UPON ME LIKE THAT?
FATHER...?
Chapter 10
SHFF
SO YOU'RE AWAKE, SAGIRI.
SIR GENJI?
WHERE ARE WE?
WHAT HAPPENED TO ME...?

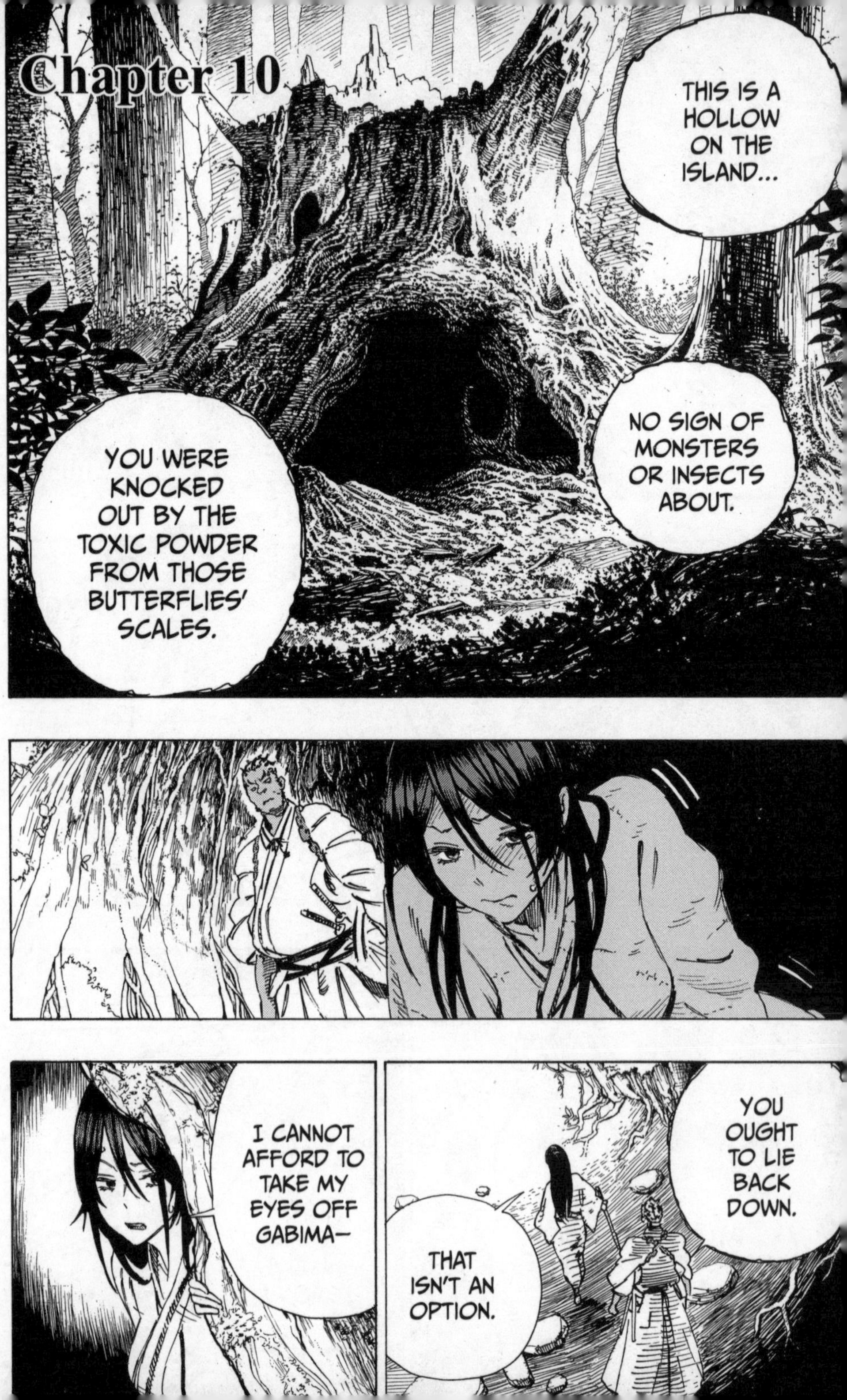
Chapter 10
THIS IS A HOLLOW ON THE ISLAND...
NO SIGN OF MONSTERS OR INSECTS ABOUT.
YOU WERE KNOCKED OUT BY THE TOXIC POWDER FROM THOSE BUTTERFLIES' SCALES.
YOU OUGHT TO LIE BACK DOWN.
THAT ISN'T AN OPTION.
I CANNOT AFFORD TO TAKE MY EYES OFF GABIMA—

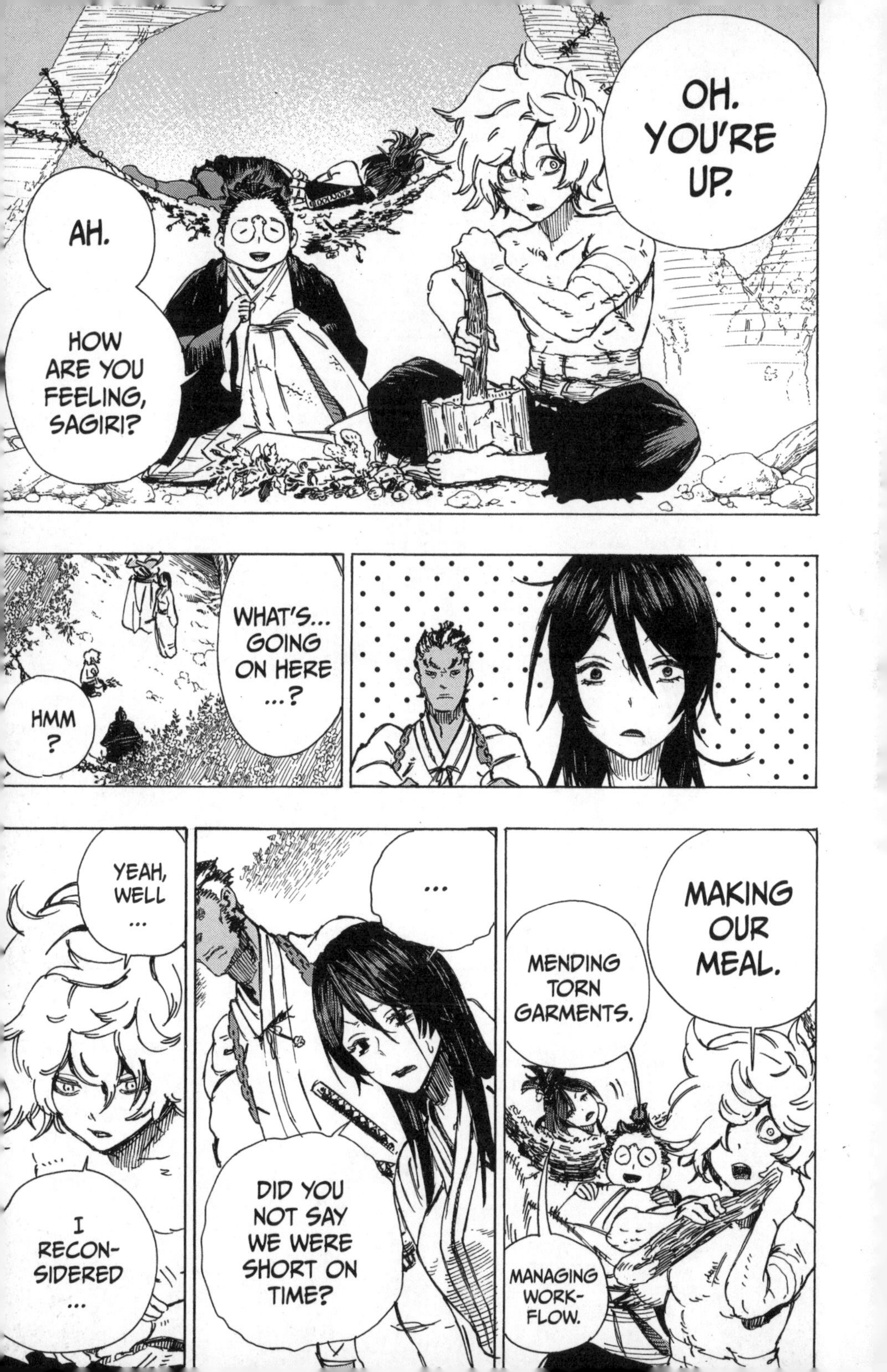
OH. YOU'RE UP.
AH.
HOW ARE YOU FEELING, SAGIRI?
WHAT'S... GOING ON HERE ...?
HMM ?
MAKING OUR MEAL.
MENDING TORN GARMENTS.
MANAGING WORK-FLOW.
...
DID YOU NOT SAY WE WERE SHORT ON TIME?
YEAH, WELL ...
I RECON-SIDERED ...

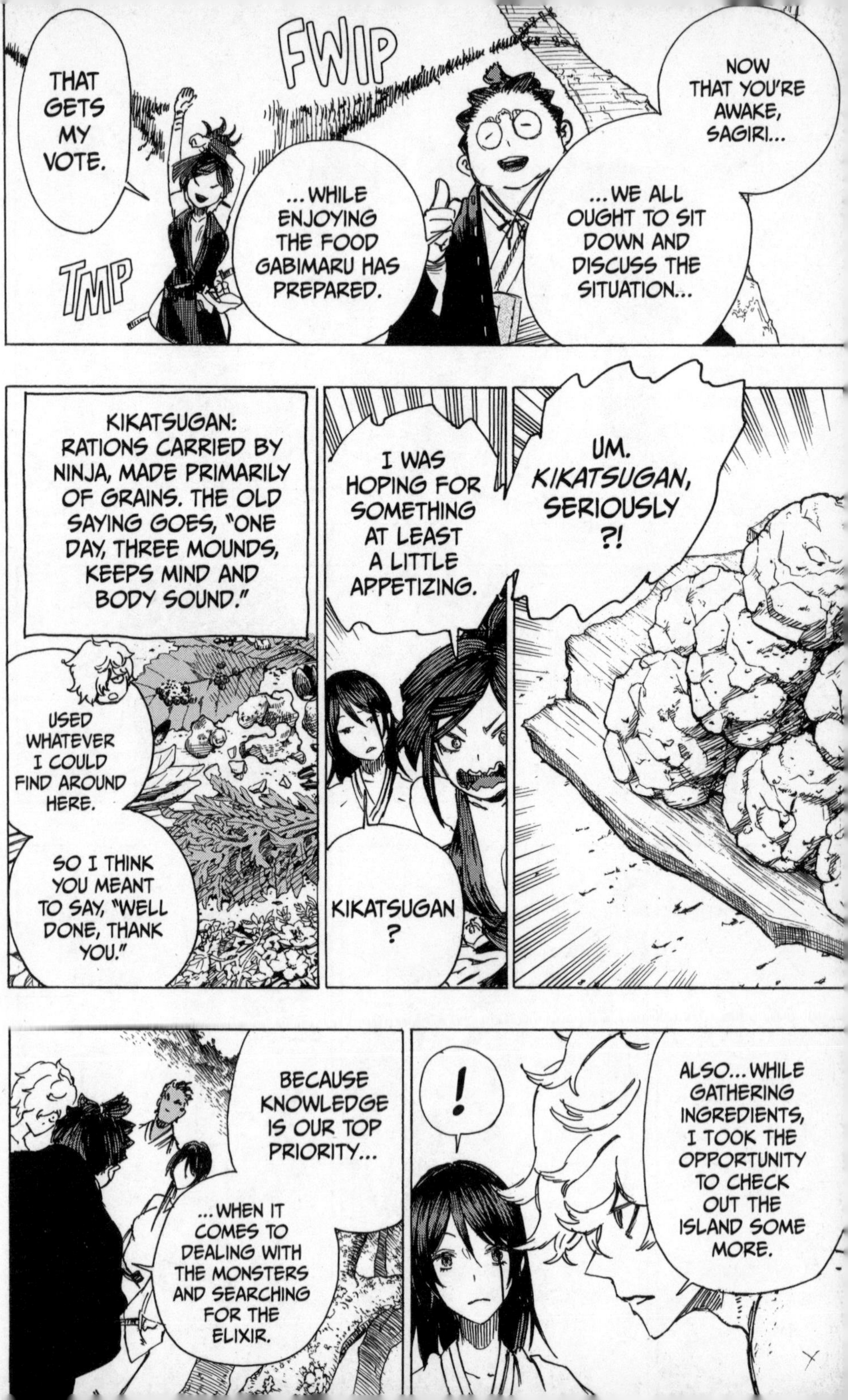
FWIP
NOW THAT YOU'RE AWAKE, SAGIRI...
...WE ALL OUGHT TO SIT DOWN AND DISCUSS THE SITUATION...
...WHILE ENJOYING THE FOOD GABIMARU HAS PREPARED.
THAT GETS MY VOTE.
TMP
UM. KIKATSUGAN, SERIOUSLY?!
I WAS HOPING FOR SOMETHING AT LEAST A LITTLE APPETIZING.
KIKATSUGAN?
KIKATSUGAN: RATIONS CARRIED BY NINJA, MADE PRIMARILY OF GRAINS. THE OLD SAYING GOES, "ONE DAY, THREE MOUNDS, KEEPS MIND AND BODY SOUND."
USED WHATEVER I COULD FIND AROUND HERE.
SO I THINK YOU MEANT TO SAY, "WELL DONE, THANK YOU."
ALSO...WHILE GATHERING INGREDIENTS, I TOOK THE OPPORTUNITY TO CHECK OUT THE ISLAND SOME MORE.
!
BECAUSE KNOWLEDGE IS OUR TOP PRIORITY...
...WHEN IT COMES TO DEALING WITH THE MONSTERS AND SEARCHING FOR THE ELIXIR.

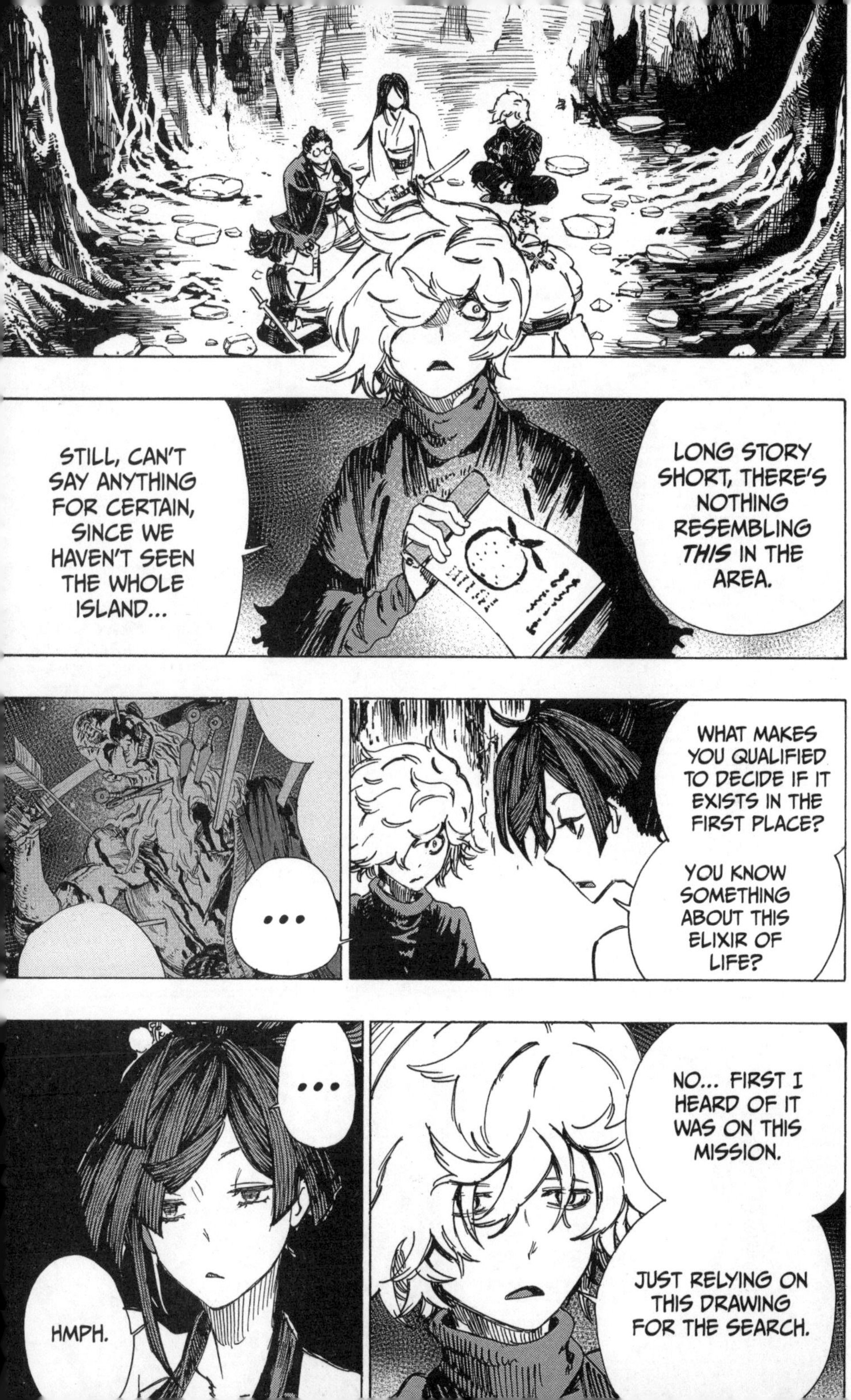
LONG STORY SHORT, THERE'S NOTHING RESEMBLING *THIS* IN THE AREA.
STILL, CAN'T SAY ANYTHING FOR CERTAIN, SINCE WE HAVEN'T SEEN THE WHOLE ISLAND...
WHAT MAKES YOU QUALIFIED TO DECIDE IF IT EXISTS IN THE FIRST PLACE?
YOU KNOW SOMETHING ABOUT THIS ELIXIR OF LIFE?
...
NO... FIRST I HEARD OF IT WAS ON THIS MISSION.
JUST RELYING ON THIS DRAWING FOR THE SEARCH.
...
HMPH.

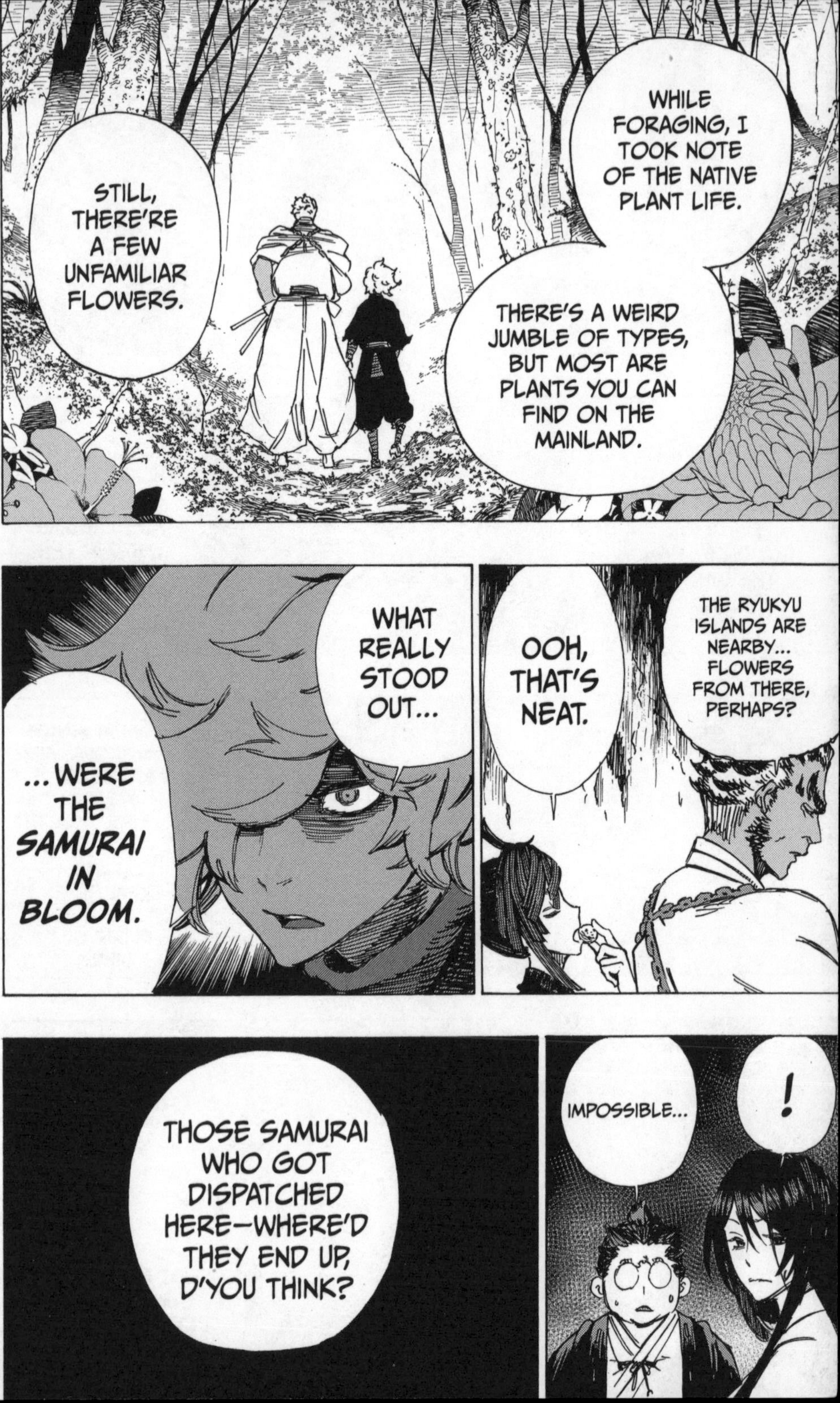
WHILE FORAGING, I TOOK NOTE OF THE NATIVE PLANT LIFE.
THERE'S A WEIRD JUMBLE OF TYPES, BUT MOST ARE PLANTS YOU CAN FIND ON THE MAINLAND.
STILL, THERE'RE A FEW UNFAMILIAR FLOWERS.
THE RYUKYU ISLANDS ARE NEARBY... FLOWERS FROM THERE, PERHAPS?
OOH, THAT'S NEAT.
WHAT REALLY STOOD OUT...
...WERE THE SAMURAI IN BLOOM.
!
IMPOSSIBLE...
THOSE SAMURAI WHO GOT DISPATCHED HERE—WHERE'D THEY END UP, D'YOU THINK?

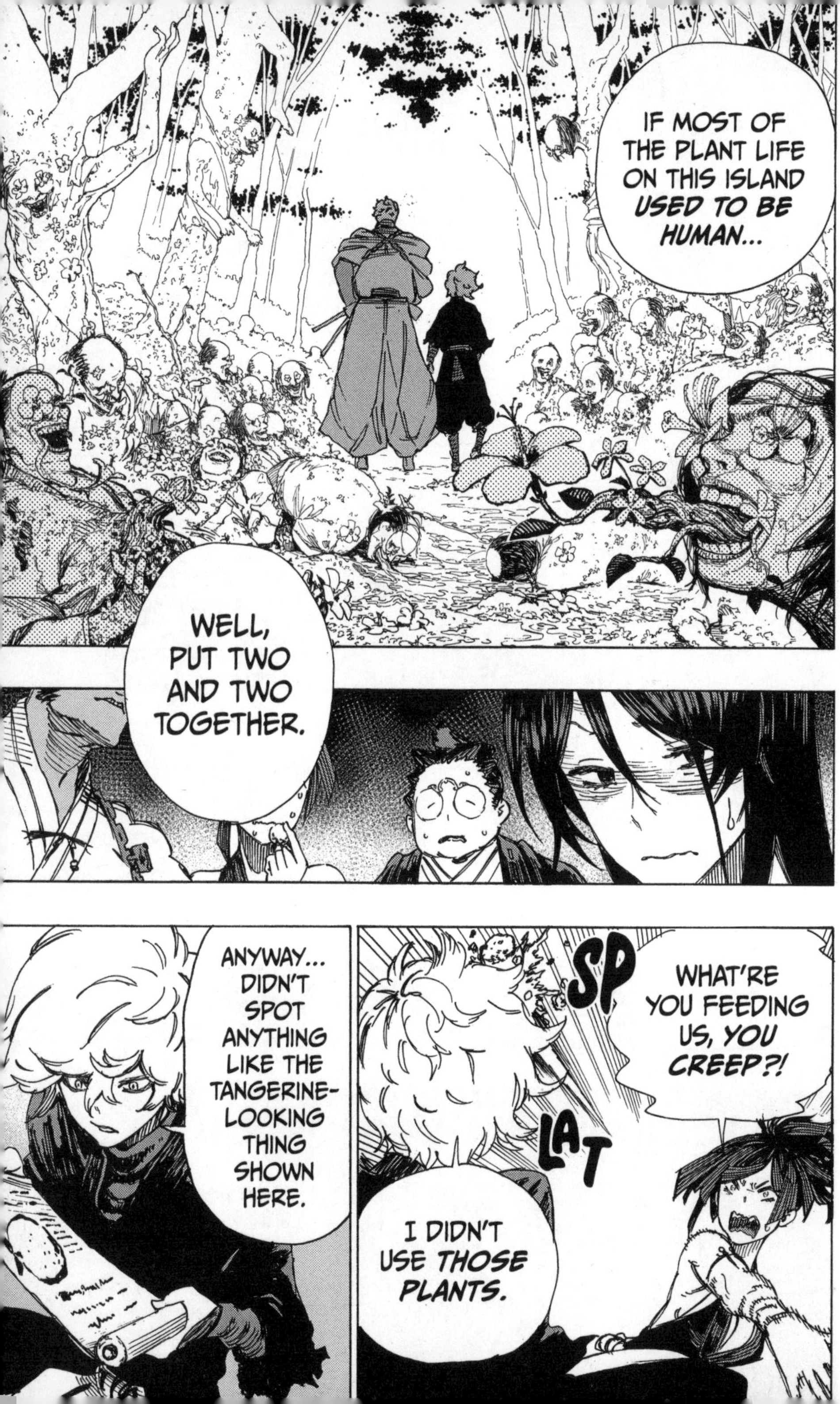
IF MOST OF THE PLANT LIFE ON THIS ISLAND *USED TO BE HUMAN...*
WELL, PUT TWO AND TWO TOGETHER.
WHAT'RE YOU FEEDING US, *YOU CREEP?!*
SPLAT
I DIDN'T USE *THOSE PLANTS.*
ANYWAY... DIDN'T SPOT ANYTHING LIKE THE TANGERINE-LOOKING THING SHOWN HERE.

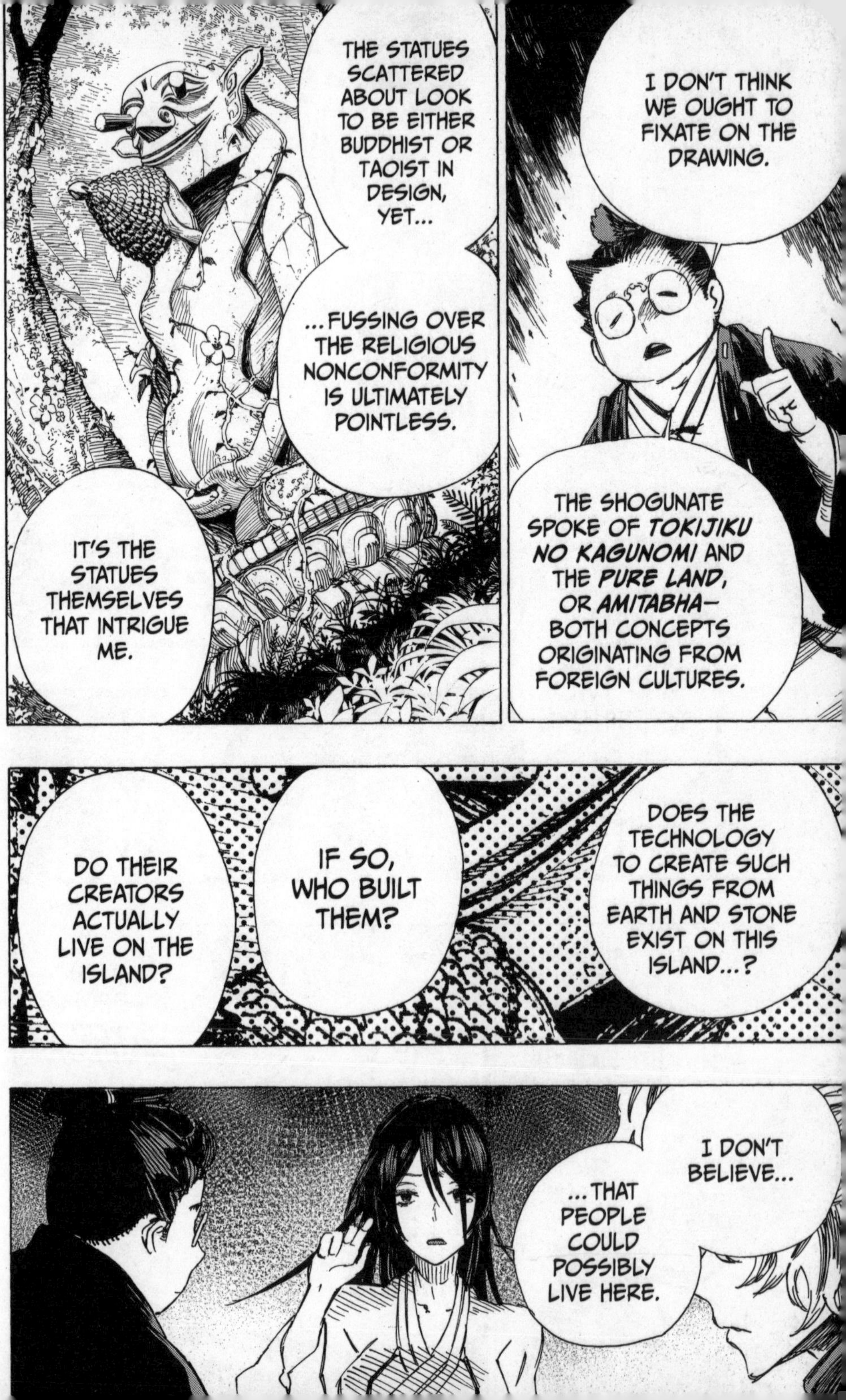
I DON'T THINK WE OUGHT TO FIXATE ON THE DRAWING.
THE SHOGUNATE SPOKE OF *TOKIJIKU NO KAGUNOMI* AND THE *PURE LAND*, OR *AMITABHA*— BOTH CONCEPTS ORIGINATING FROM FOREIGN CULTURES.
THE STATUES SCATTERED ABOUT LOOK TO BE EITHER BUDDHIST OR TAOIST IN DESIGN, YET...
...FUSSING OVER THE RELIGIOUS NONCONFORMITY IS ULTIMATELY POINTLESS.
IT'S THE STATUES THEMSELVES THAT INTRIGUE ME.
DOES THE TECHNOLOGY TO CREATE SUCH THINGS FROM EARTH AND STONE EXIST ON THIS ISLAND...?
IF SO, WHO BUILT THEM?
DO THEIR CREATORS ACTUALLY LIVE ON THE ISLAND?
I DON'T BELIEVE...
...THAT PEOPLE COULD POSSIBLY LIVE HERE.

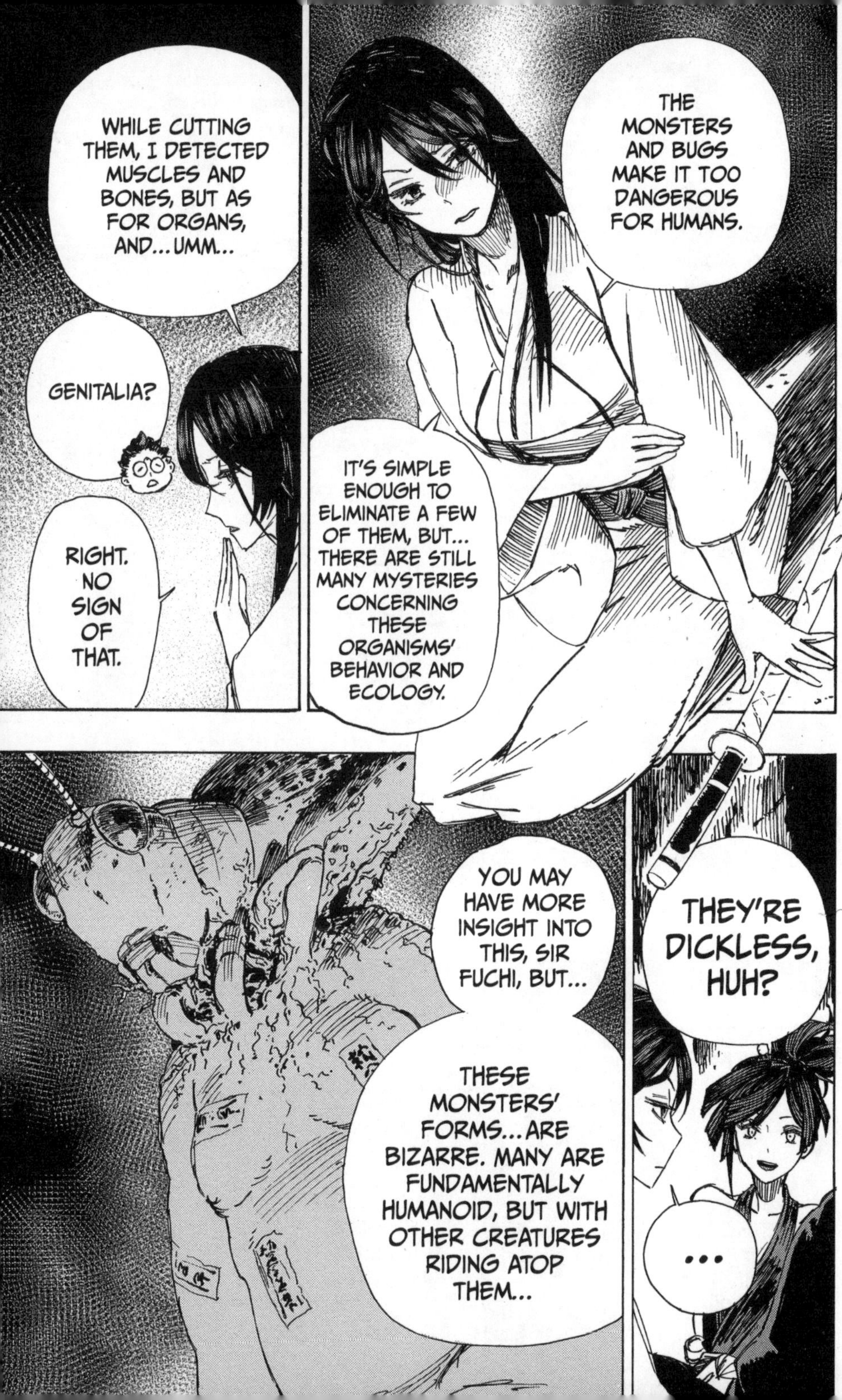
THE MONSTERS AND BUGS MAKE IT TOO DANGEROUS FOR HUMANS.
IT'S SIMPLE ENOUGH TO ELIMINATE A FEW OF THEM, BUT... THERE ARE STILL MANY MYSTERIES CONCERNING THESE ORGANISMS' BEHAVIOR AND ECOLOGY.
WHILE CUTTING THEM, I DETECTED MUSCLES AND BONES, BUT AS FOR ORGANS, AND... UMM...
GENITALIA?
RIGHT. NO SIGN OF THAT.
THEY'RE DICKLESS, HUH?
...
YOU MAY HAVE MORE INSIGHT INTO THIS, SIR FUCHI, BUT...
THESE MONSTERS' FORMS... ARE BIZARRE. MANY ARE FUNDAMENTALLY HUMANOID, BUT WITH OTHER CREATURES RIDING ATOP THEM...

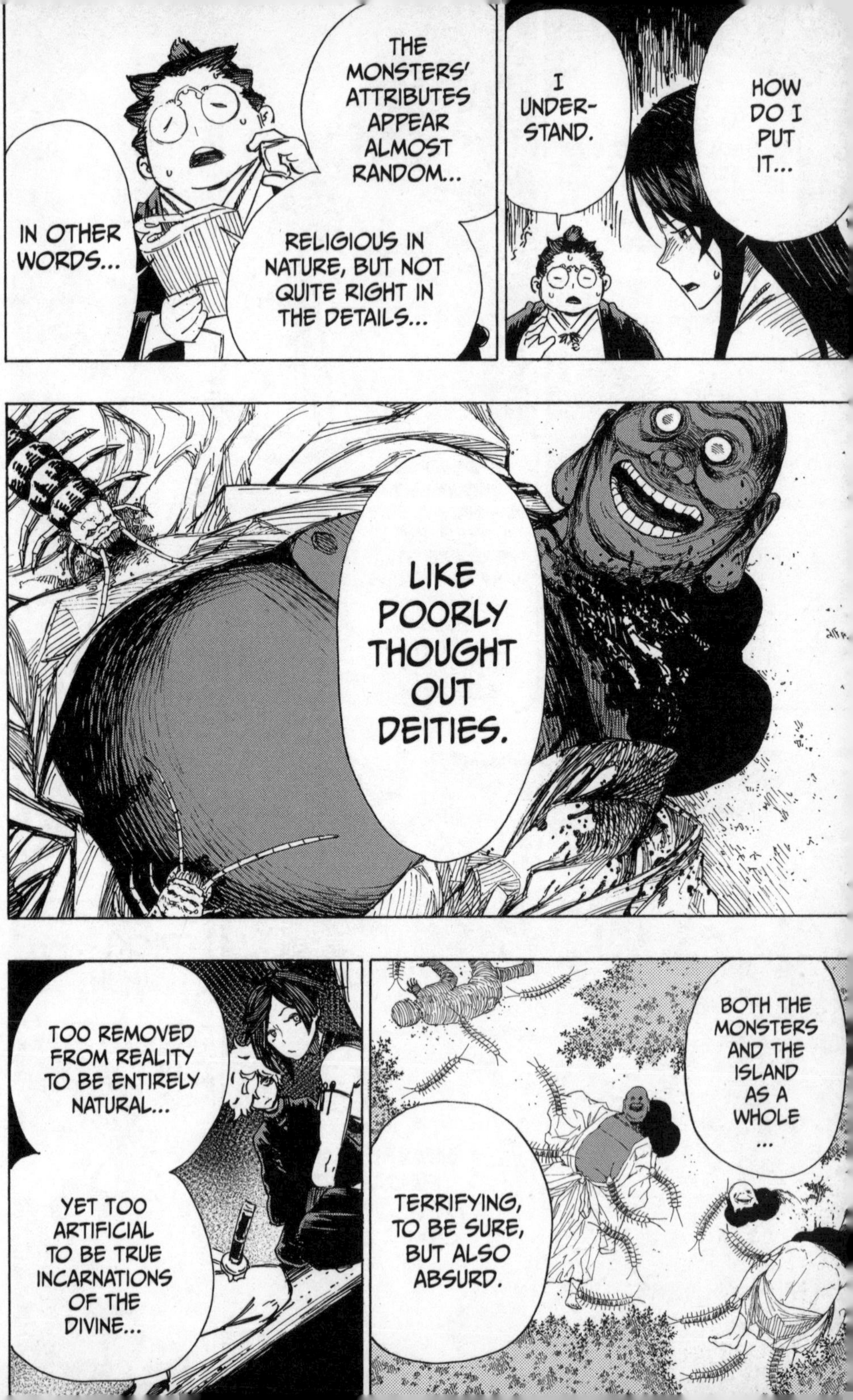
HOW DO I PUT IT...
I UNDER-STAND.
THE MONSTERS' ATTRIBUTES APPEAR ALMOST RANDOM...
RELIGIOUS IN NATURE, BUT NOT QUITE RIGHT IN THE DETAILS...
IN OTHER WORDS...
LIKE POORLY THOUGHT OUT DEITIES.
BOTH THE MONSTERS AND THE ISLAND AS A WHOLE...
TERRIFYING, TO BE SURE, BUT ALSO ABSURD.
TOO REMOVED FROM REALITY TO BE ENTIRELY NATURAL...
YET TOO ARTIFICIAL TO BE TRUE INCARNATIONS OF THE DIVINE...

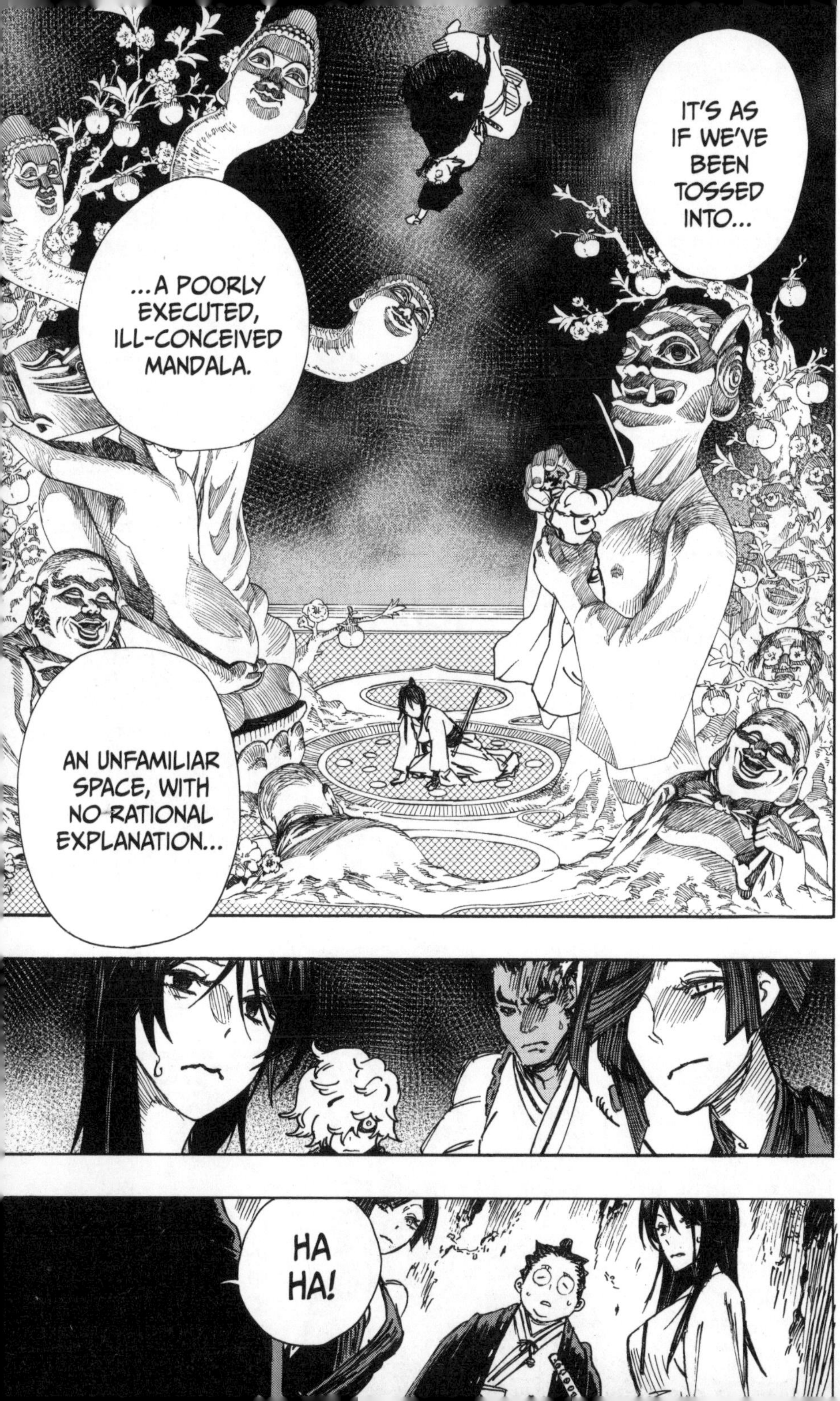
IT'S AS IF WE'VE BEEN TOSSED INTO...
...A POORLY EXECUTED, ILL-CONCEIVED MANDALA.
AN UNFAMILIAR SPACE, WITH NO RATIONAL EXPLANATION...
HA HA!

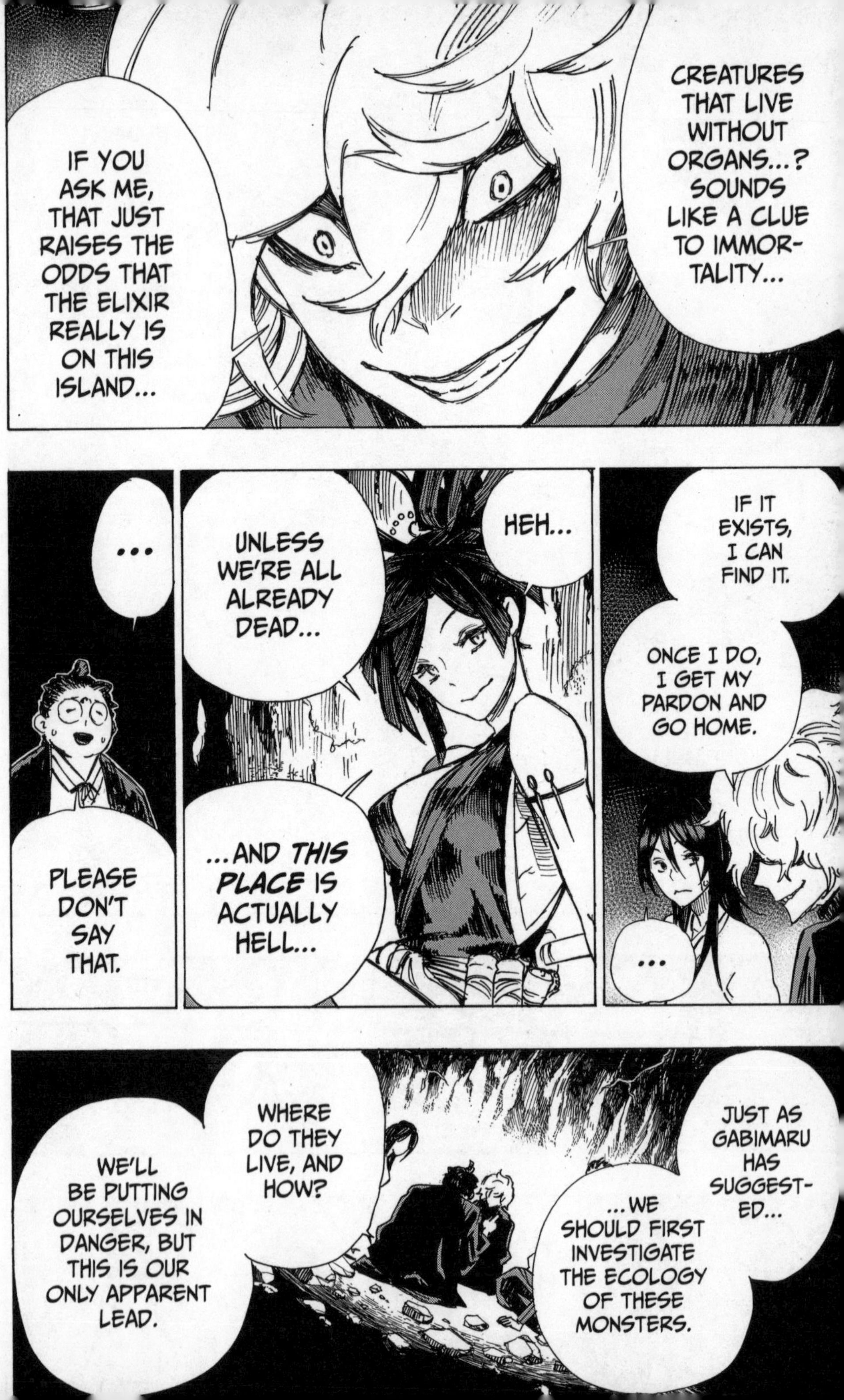
CREATURES THAT LIVE WITHOUT ORGANS...? SOUNDS LIKE A CLUE TO IMMORTALITY...
IF YOU ASK ME, THAT JUST RAISES THE ODDS THAT THE ELIXIR REALLY IS ON THIS ISLAND...
IF IT EXISTS, I CAN FIND IT.
ONCE I DO, I GET MY PARDON AND GO HOME.
...
HEH...
UNLESS WE'RE ALL ALREADY DEAD...
...AND *THIS PLACE* IS ACTUALLY HELL...
...
PLEASE DON'T SAY THAT.
JUST AS GABIMARU HAS SUGGESTED...
...WE SHOULD FIRST INVESTIGATE THE ECOLOGY OF THESE MONSTERS.
WHERE DO THEY LIVE, AND HOW?
WE'LL BE PUTTING OURSELVES IN DANGER, BUT THIS IS OUR ONLY APPARENT LEAD.

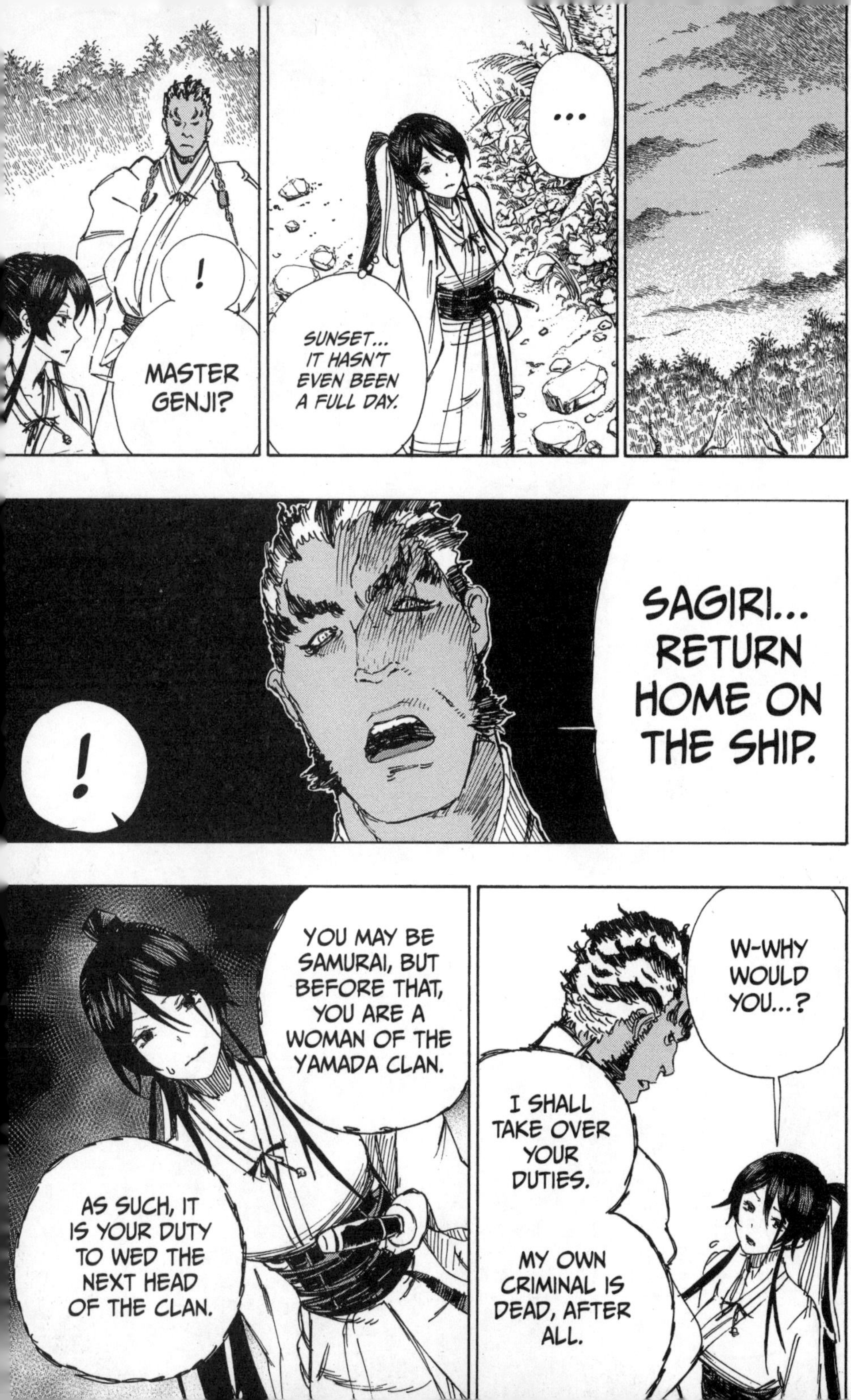
...
SUNSET... IT HASN'T EVEN BEEN A FULL DAY.
!
MASTER GENJI?
SAGIRI... RETURN HOME ON THE SHIP.
!
W-WHY WOULD YOU...?
I SHALL TAKE OVER YOUR DUTIES.
MY OWN CRIMINAL IS DEAD, AFTER ALL.
YOU MAY BE SAMURAI, BUT BEFORE THAT, YOU ARE A WOMAN OF THE YAMADA CLAN.
AS SUCH, IT IS YOUR DUTY TO WED THE NEXT HEAD OF THE CLAN.

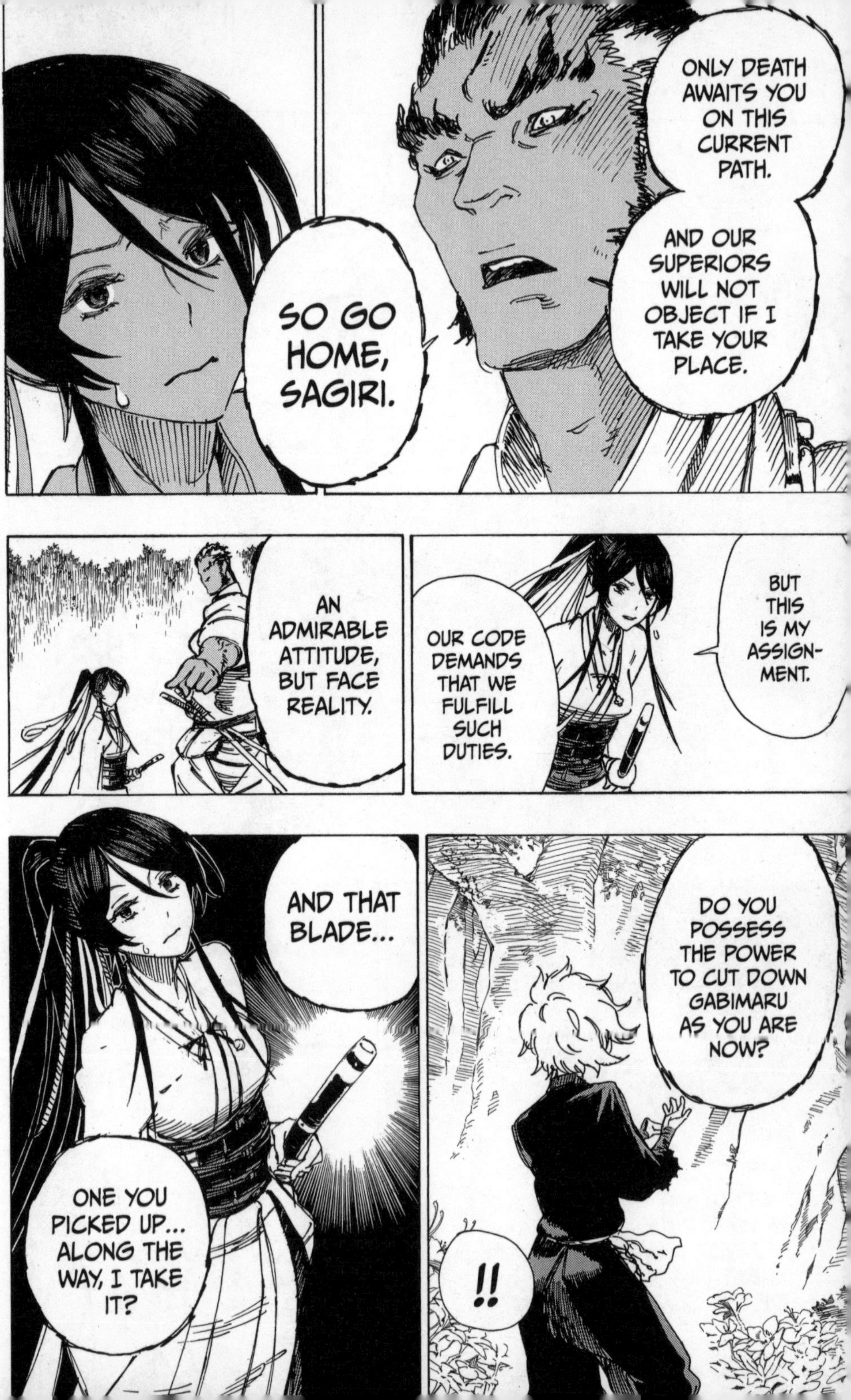
ONLY DEATH AWAITS YOU ON THIS CURRENT PATH.
AND OUR SUPERIORS WILL NOT OBJECT IF I TAKE YOUR PLACE.
SO GO HOME, SAGIRI.
BUT THIS IS MY ASSIGN-MENT.
OUR CODE DEMANDS THAT WE FULFILL SUCH DUTIES.
AN ADMIRABLE ATTITUDE, BUT FACE REALITY.
DO YOU POSSESS THE POWER TO CUT DOWN GABIMARU AS YOU ARE NOW?
!!
AND THAT BLADE...
ONE YOU PICKED UP... ALONG THE WAY, I TAKE IT?

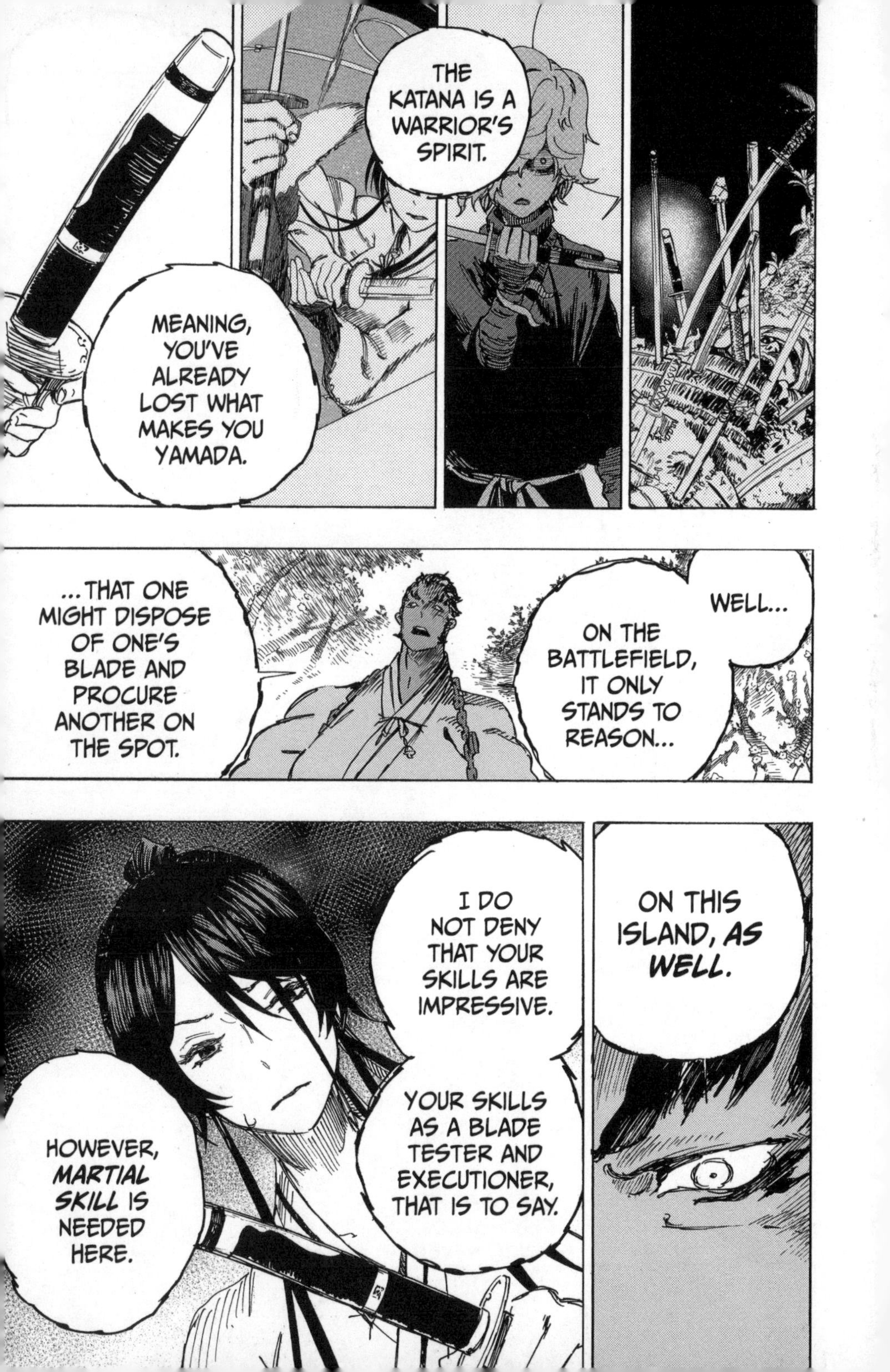
THE KATANA IS A WARRIOR'S SPIRIT.
MEANING, YOU'VE ALREADY LOST WHAT MAKES YOU YAMADA.
WELL...
ON THE BATTLEFIELD, IT ONLY STANDS TO REASON...
...THAT ONE MIGHT DISPOSE OF ONE'S BLADE AND PROCURE ANOTHER ON THE SPOT.
ON THIS ISLAND, AS WELL.
I DO NOT DENY THAT YOUR SKILLS ARE IMPRESSIVE.
YOUR SKILLS AS A BLADE TESTER AND EXECUTIONER, THAT IS TO SAY.
HOWEVER, MARTIAL SKILL IS NEEDED HERE.

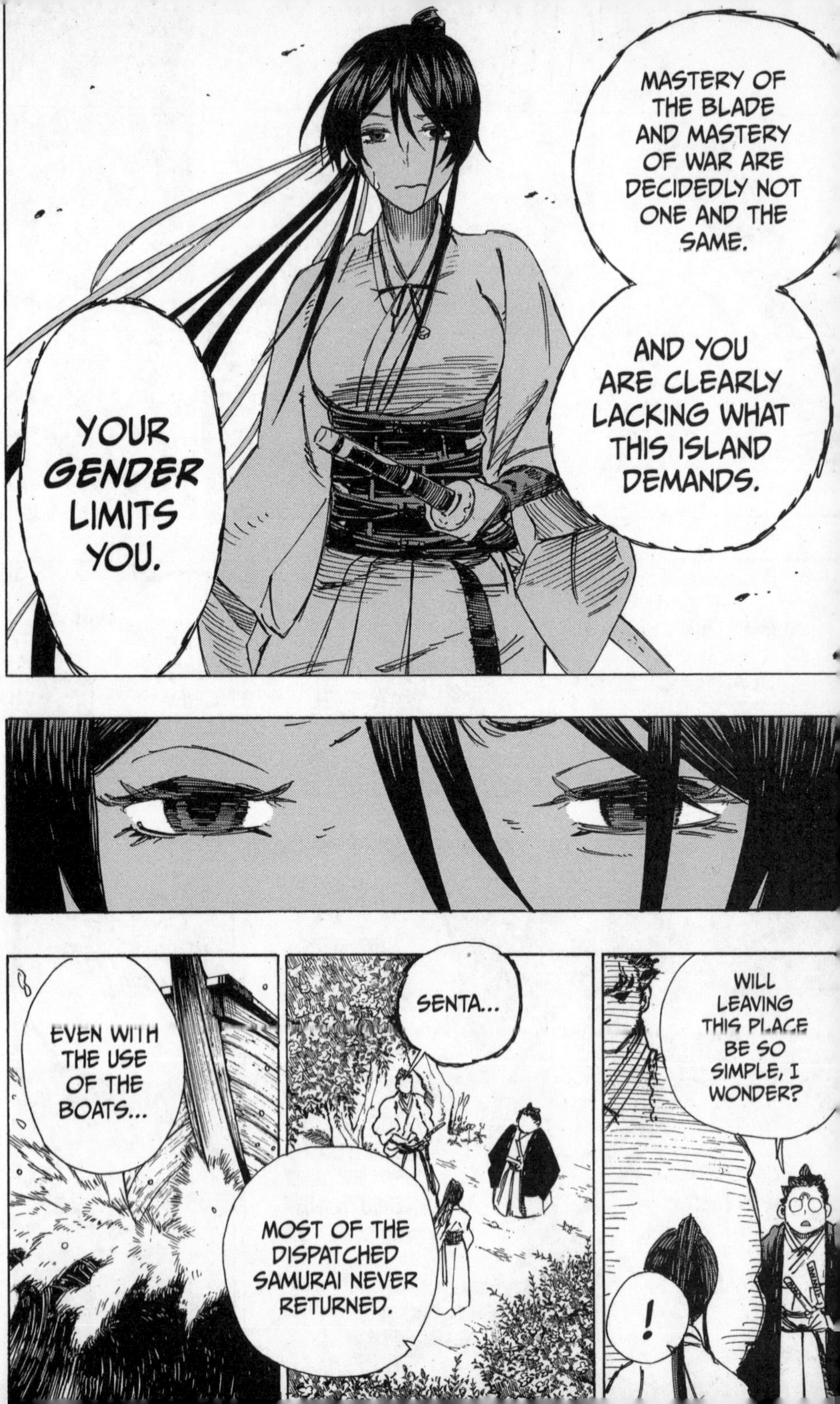
MASTERY OF THE BLADE AND MASTERY OF WAR ARE DECIDEDLY NOT ONE AND THE SAME.
AND YOU ARE CLEARLY LACKING WHAT THIS ISLAND DEMANDS.
YOUR GENDER LIMITS YOU.
WILL LEAVING THIS PLACE BE SO SIMPLE, I WONDER?
!
SENTA...
EVEN WITH THE USE OF THE BOATS...
MOST OF THE DISPATCHED SAMURAI NEVER RETURNED.

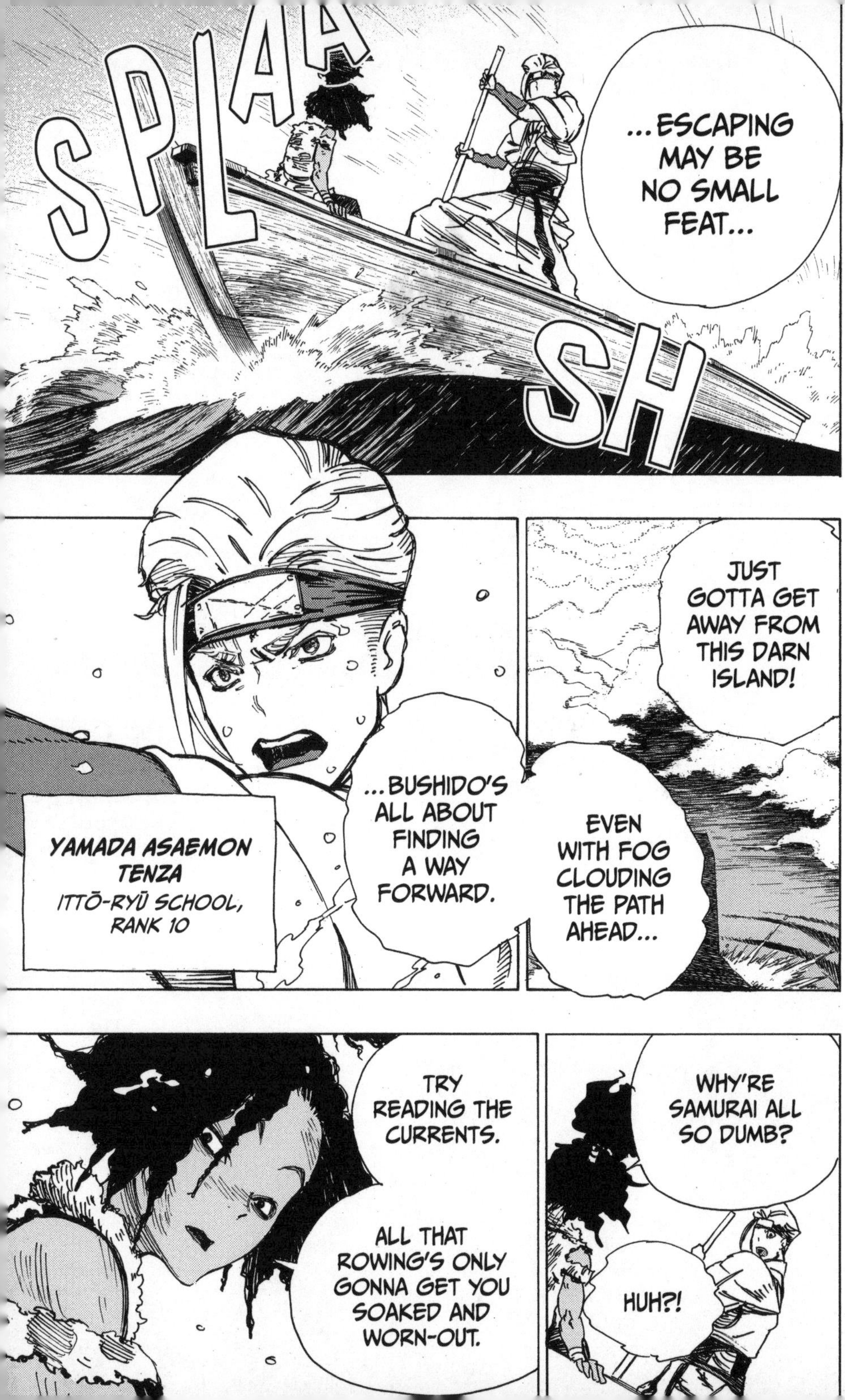
SPLAASH
...ESCAPING MAY BE NO SMALL FEAT...
JUST GOTTA GET AWAY FROM THIS DARN ISLAND!
EVEN WITH FOG CLOUDING THE PATH AHEAD...
...BUSHIDO'S ALL ABOUT FINDING A WAY FORWARD.
YAMADA ASAEMON TENZA
ITTŌ-RYŪ SCHOOL, RANK 10
WHY'RE SAMURAI ALL SO DUMB?
HUH?!
TRY READING THE CURRENTS.
ALL THAT ROWING'S ONLY GONNA GET YOU SOAKED AND WORN-OUT.

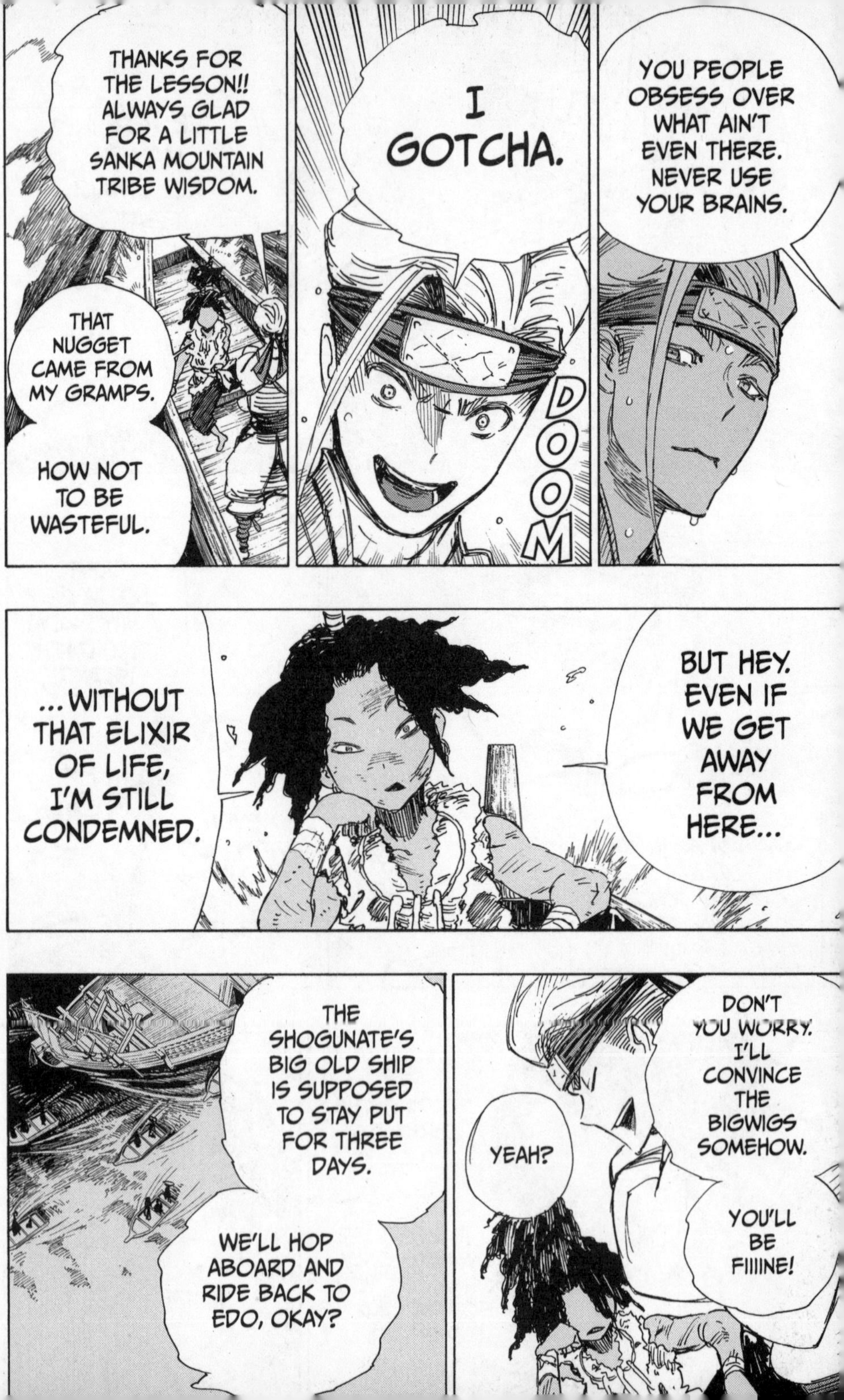
YOU PEOPLE OBSESS OVER WHAT AIN'T EVEN THERE. NEVER USE YOUR BRAINS.
I GOTCHA.
DOOM
THANKS FOR THE LESSON!! ALWAYS GLAD FOR A LITTLE SANKA MOUNTAIN TRIBE WISDOM.
THAT NUGGET CAME FROM MY GRAMPS.
HOW NOT TO BE WASTEFUL.
BUT HEY. EVEN IF WE GET AWAY FROM HERE...
...WITHOUT THAT ELIXIR OF LIFE, I'M STILL CONDEMNED.
DON'T YOU WORRY. I'LL CONVINCE THE BIGWIGS SOMEHOW.
YEAH?
YOU'LL BE FIIIINE!
THE SHOGUNATE'S BIG OLD SHIP IS SUPPOSED TO STAY PUT FOR THREE DAYS.
WE'LL HOP ABOARD AND RIDE BACK TO EDO, OKAY?

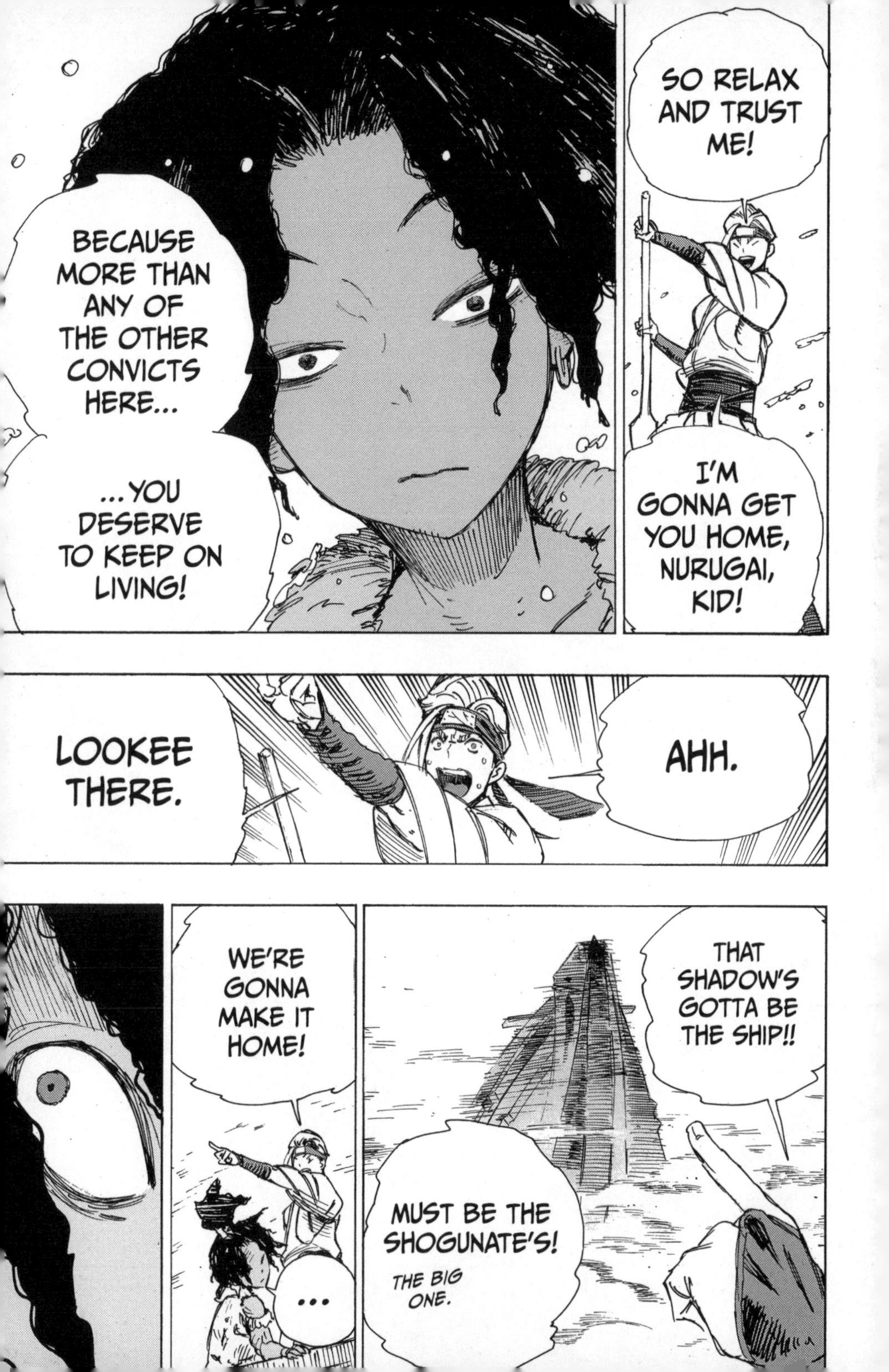
SO RELAX AND TRUST ME!
I'M GONNA GET YOU HOME, NURUGAI, KID!
BECAUSE MORE THAN ANY OF THE OTHER CONVICTS HERE...
...YOU DESERVE TO KEEP ON LIVING!
AHH.
LOOKEE THERE.
THAT SHADOW'S GOTTA BE THE SHIP!!
MUST BE THE SHOGUNATE'S!
THE BIG ONE.
WE'RE GONNA MAKE IT HOME!
...

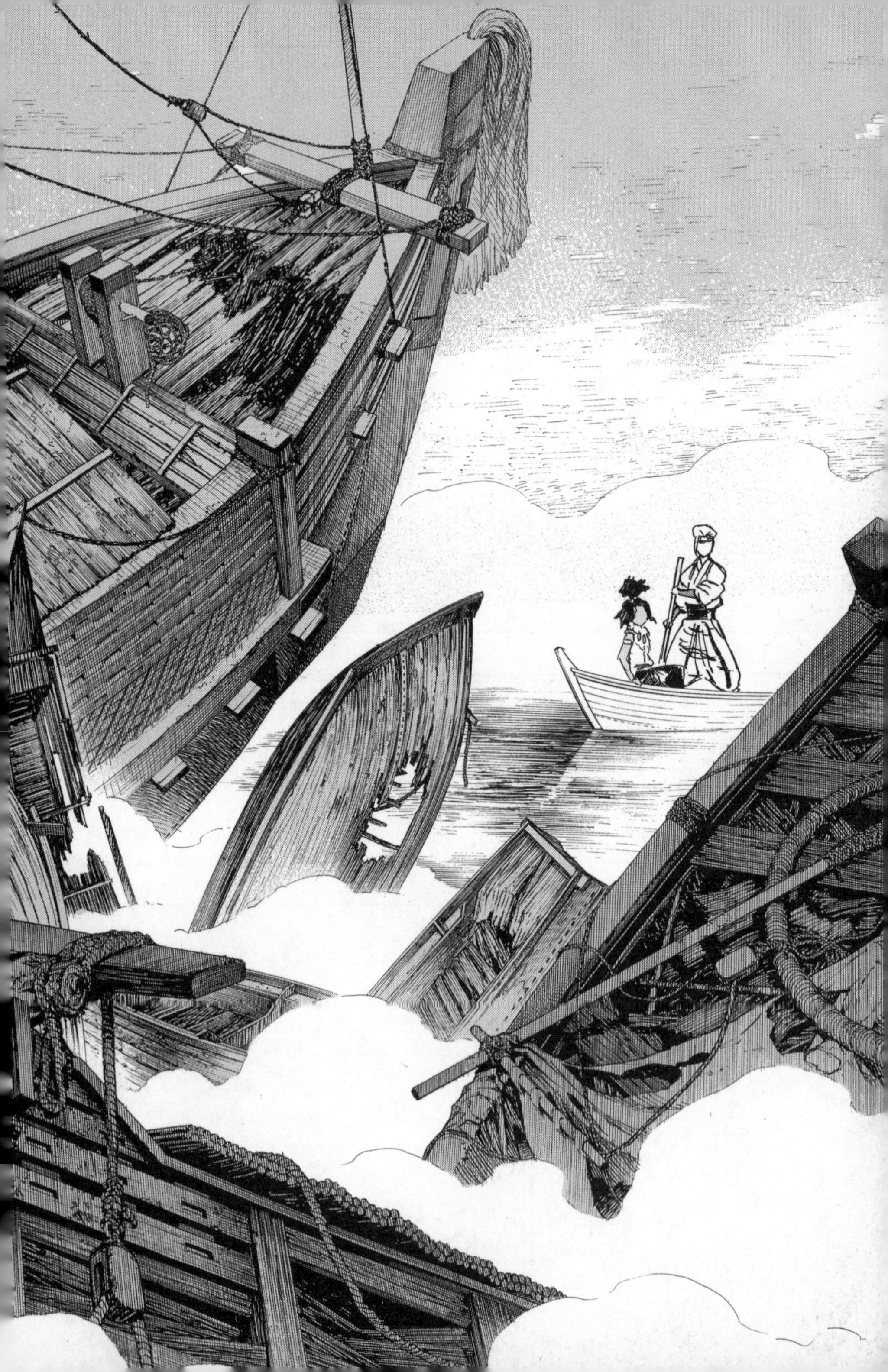

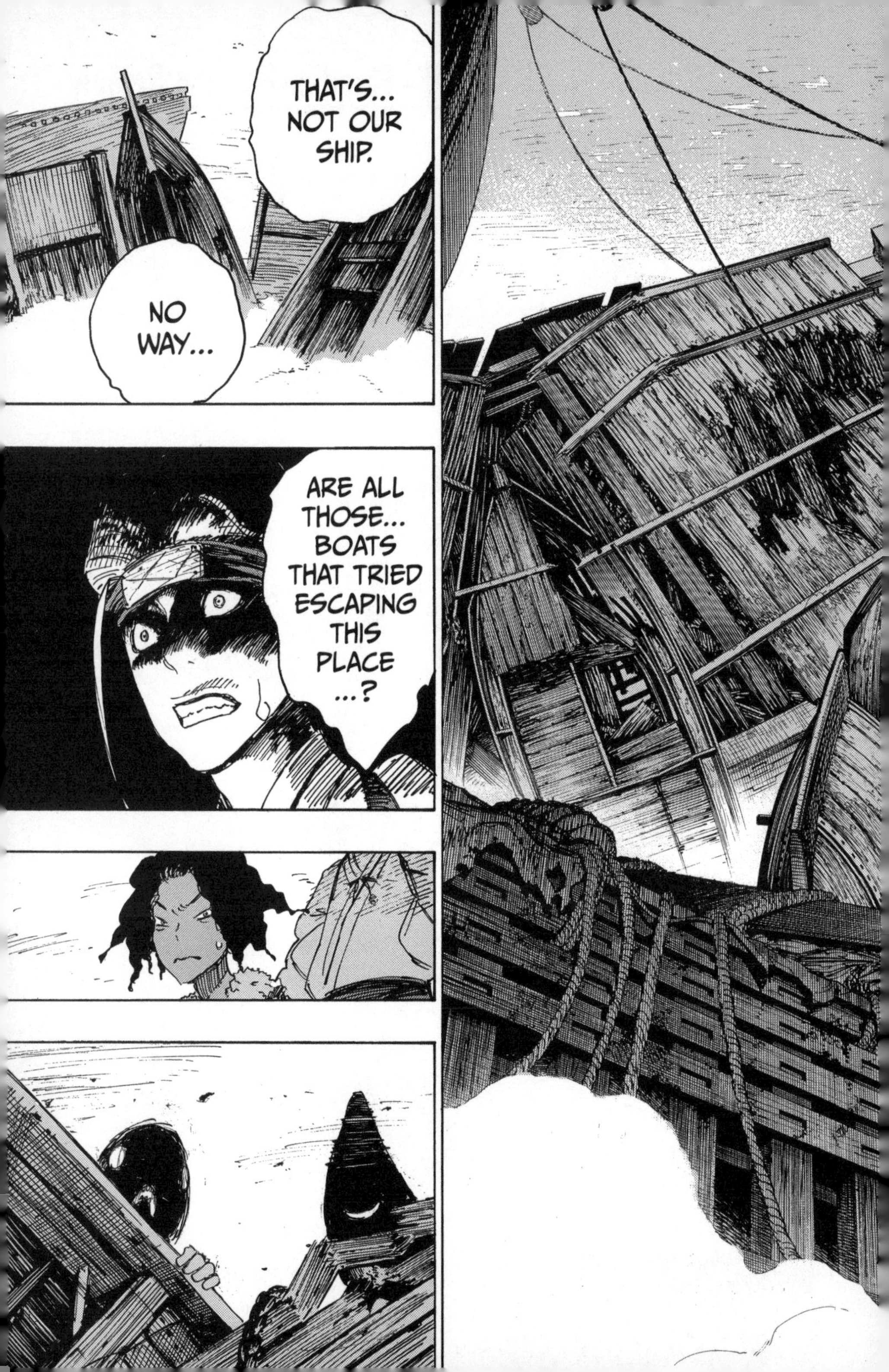
THAT'S... NOT OUR SHIP.
NO WAY...
ARE ALL THOSE... BOATS THAT TRIED ESCAPING THIS PLACE ...?

Hell's Paradise Fashion Review

Yamada Asaemon
TENZA

Standard Yamada Asaemon garb with a few personal touches.

Tucks up kimono sleeves with *tasuki* cords and wears *tekko* gauntlets on both arms. The *hitai-ate* forehead protector looks well-worn.

Incorporates a *do'ate* belt into the *hakama* bottoms and wears *kyahan* gaiters on lower legs for increased mobility.

 EVALUATION ► DECKED-OUT TROOPER ★☆☆ HIS ATTEMPT AT MIXING UP HIS LOOK IS ADMIRABLE, BUT HE'S PRIORITIZED BATTLE READINESS A BIT TOO MUCH. NOT VERY FASHIONABLE.

Chapter 11

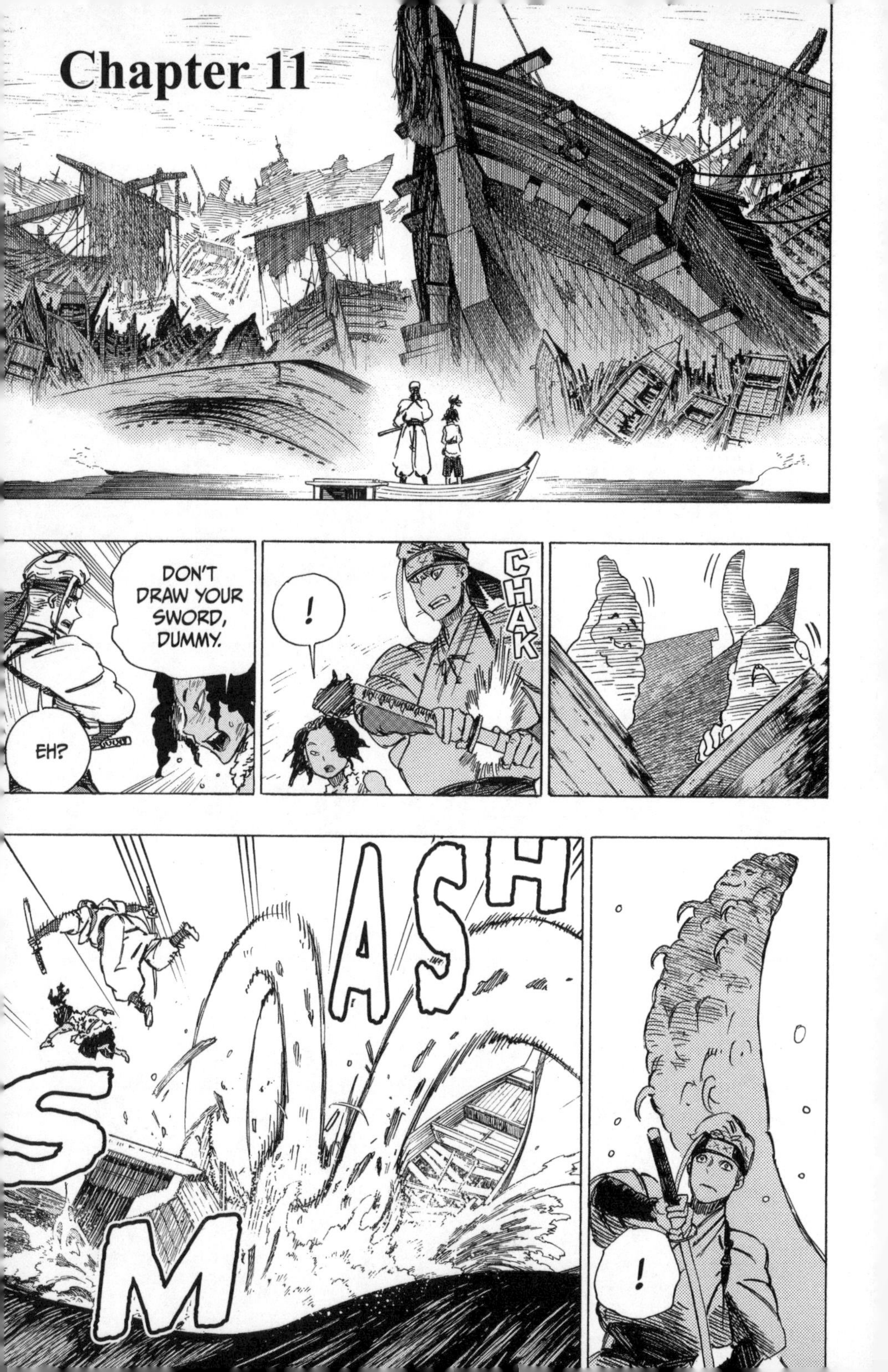

CHAK
!
DON'T DRAW YOUR SWORD, DUMMY.
EH?
!
SMASH

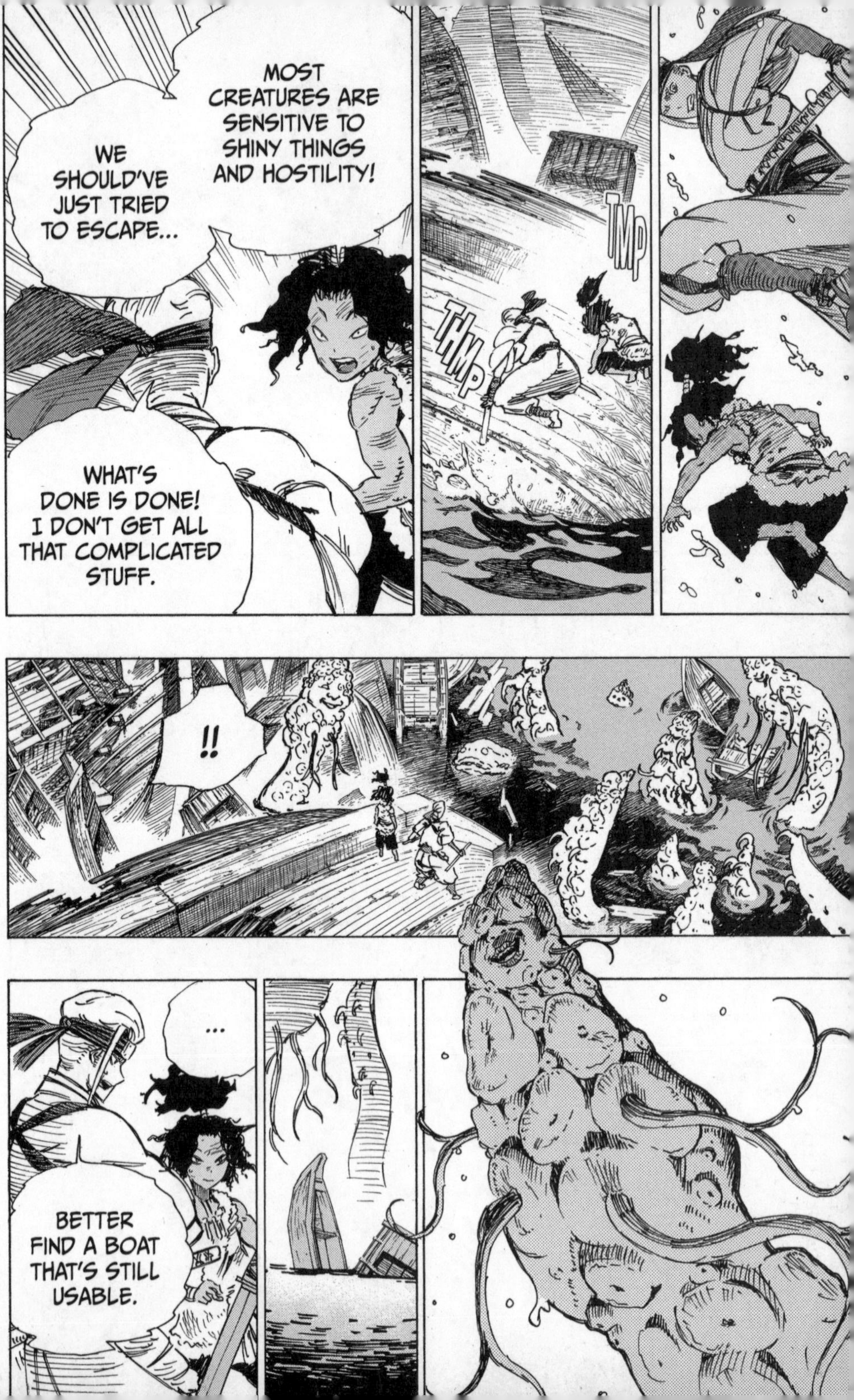
TMP
THMP
MOST CREATURES ARE SENSITIVE TO SHINY THINGS AND HOSTILITY!
WE SHOULD'VE JUST TRIED TO ESCAPE...
WHAT'S DONE IS DONE! I DON'T GET ALL THAT COMPLICATED STUFF.
!!
...
BETTER FIND A BOAT THAT'S STILL USABLE.

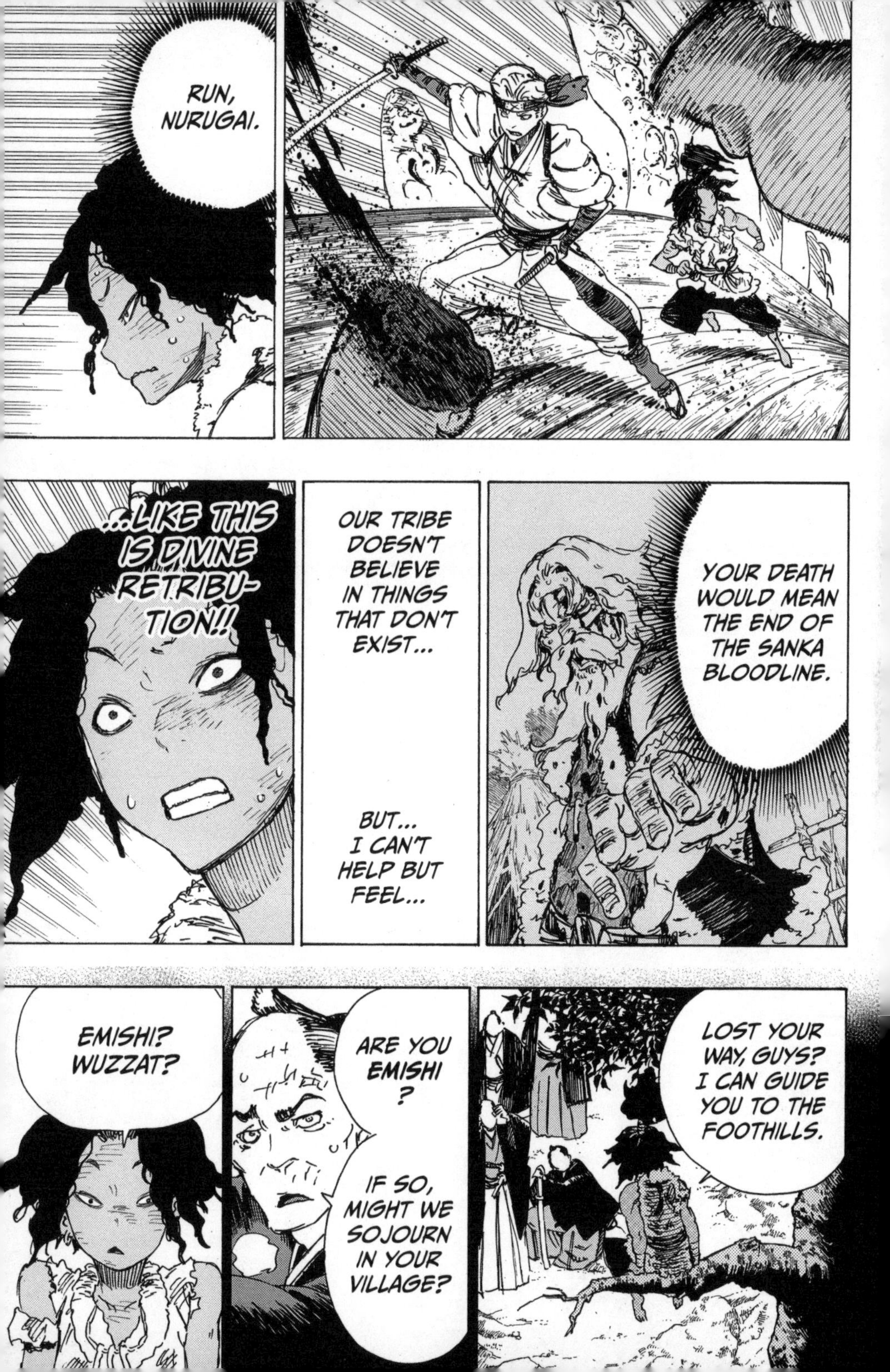
RUN, NURUGAI.
YOUR DEATH WOULD MEAN THE END OF THE SANKA BLOODLINE.
OUR TRIBE DOESN'T BELIEVE IN THINGS THAT DON'T EXIST...
BUT... I CAN'T HELP BUT FEEL...
...LIKE THIS IS DIVINE RETRIBU-TION!!
LOST YOUR WAY, GUYS? I CAN GUIDE YOU TO THE FOOTHILLS.
ARE YOU EMISHI?
IF SO, MIGHT WE SOJOURN IN YOUR VILLAGE?
EMISHI? WUZZAT?

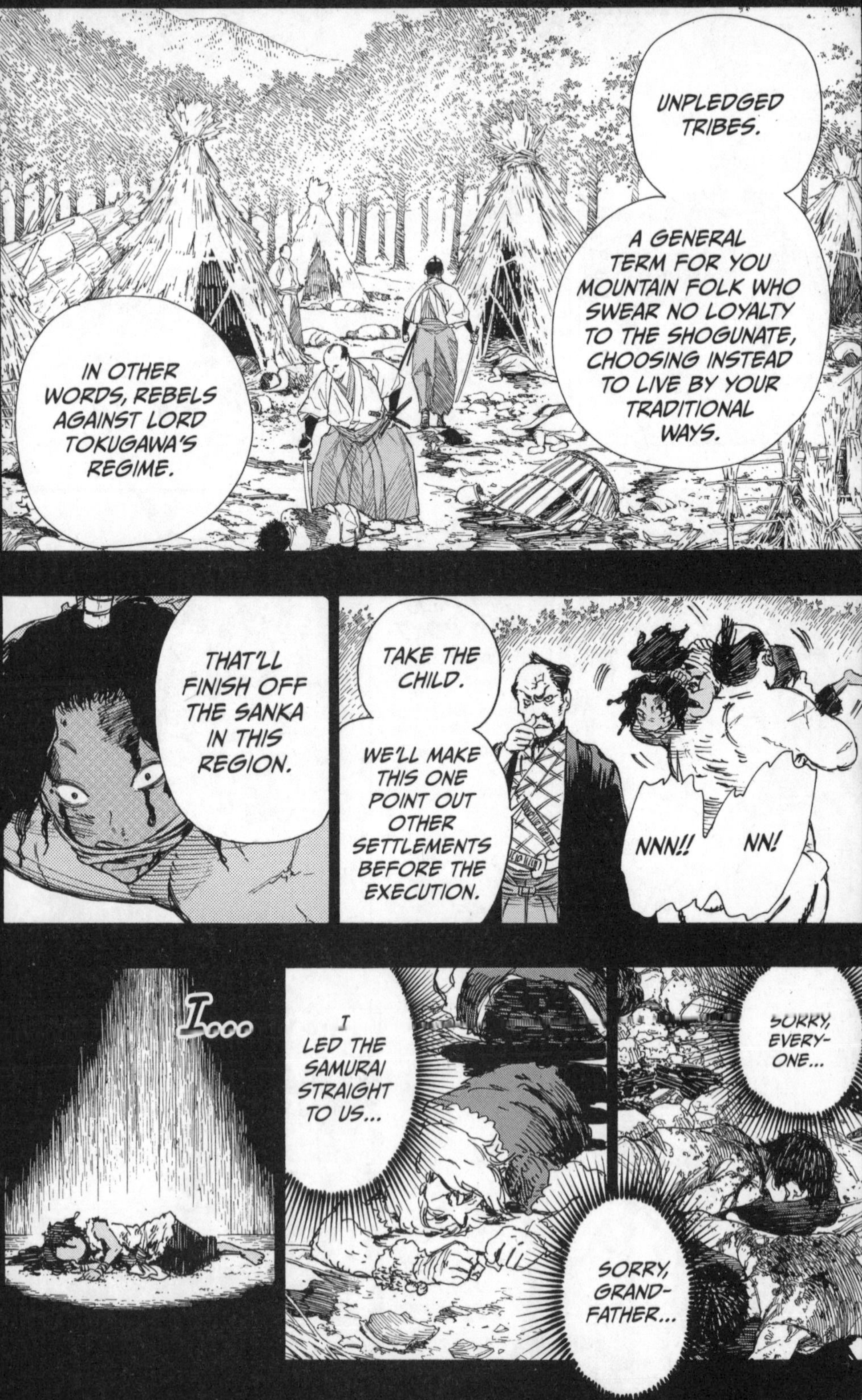
UNPLEDGED TRIBES.
A GENERAL TERM FOR YOU MOUNTAIN FOLK WHO SWEAR NO LOYALTY TO THE SHOGUNATE, CHOOSING INSTEAD TO LIVE BY YOUR TRADITIONAL WAYS.
IN OTHER WORDS, REBELS AGAINST LORD TOKUGAWA'S REGIME.
TAKE THE CHILD.
WE'LL MAKE THIS ONE POINT OUT OTHER SETTLEMENTS BEFORE THE EXECUTION.
NN!
NNN!!
THAT'LL FINISH OFF THE SANKA IN THIS REGION.
SORRY, EVERY-ONE...
SORRY, GRAND-FATHER...
I LED THE SAMURAI STRAIGHT TO US...
I...

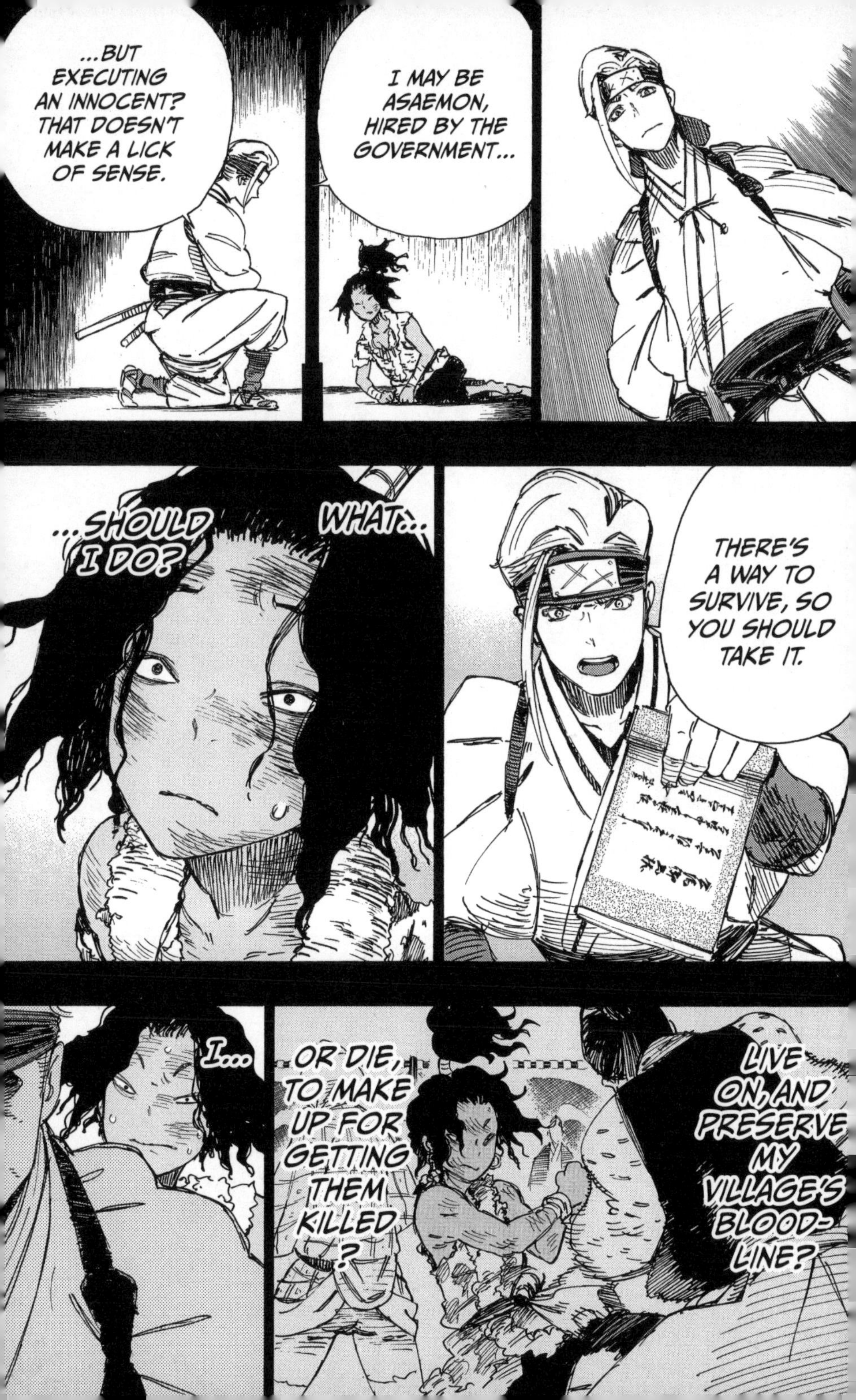
I MAY BE ASAEMON, HIRED BY THE GOVERNMENT...
...BUT EXECUTING AN INNOCENT? THAT DOESN'T MAKE A LICK OF SENSE.
THERE'S A WAY TO SURVIVE, SO YOU SHOULD TAKE IT.
WHAT...
...SHOULD I DO?
LIVE ON, AND PRESERVE MY VILLAGE'S BLOOD-LINE?
OR DIE, TO MAKE UP FOR GETTING THEM KILLED?
I...

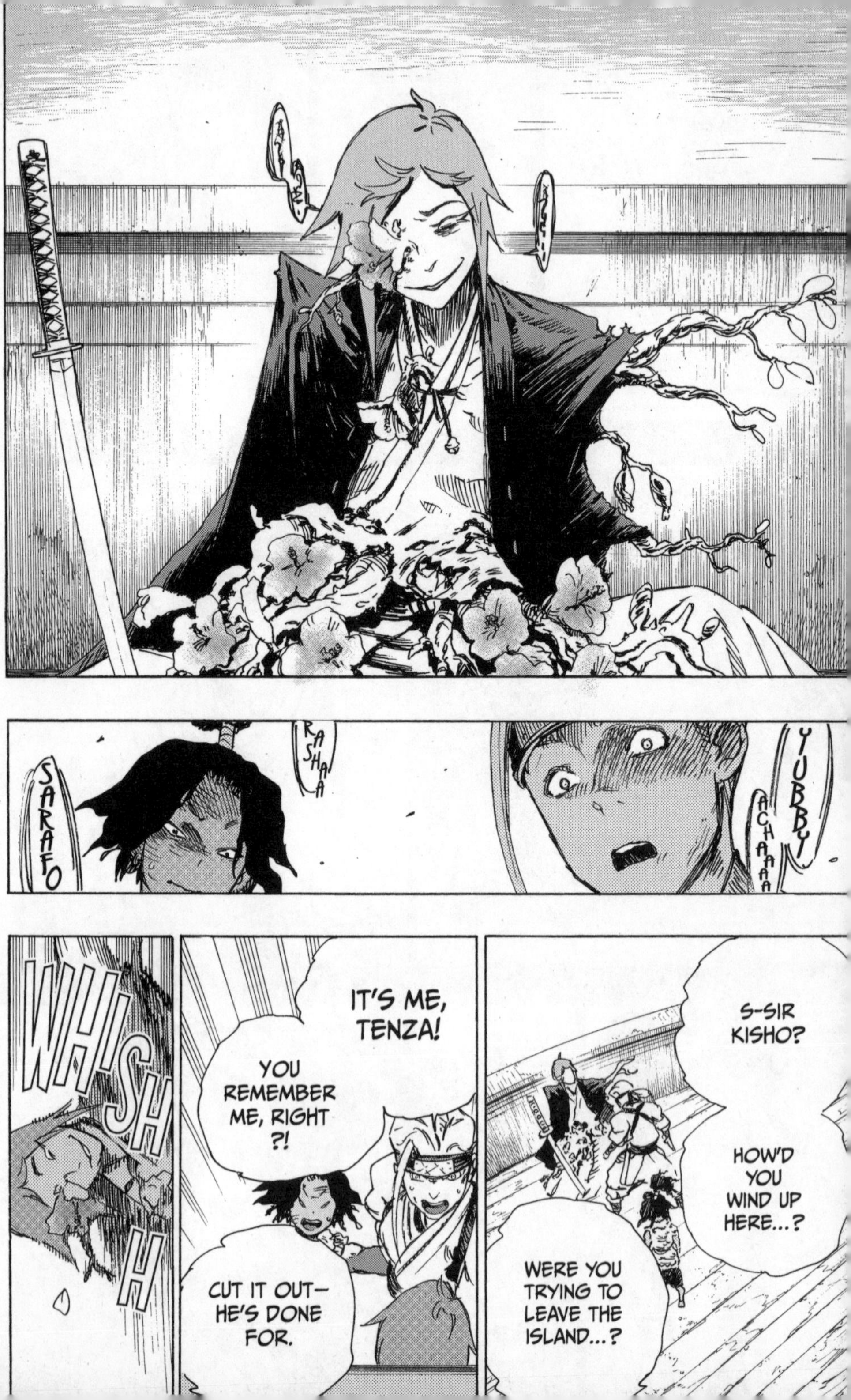
YUBBY!
ACHAAAAA
RASHAA
SARAFO
S-SIR KISHO?
HOW'D YOU WIND UP HERE...?
WERE YOU TRYING TO LEAVE THE ISLAND...?
IT'S ME, TENZA!
YOU REMEMBER ME, RIGHT?!
CUT IT OUT—HE'S DONE FOR.
WHISHH

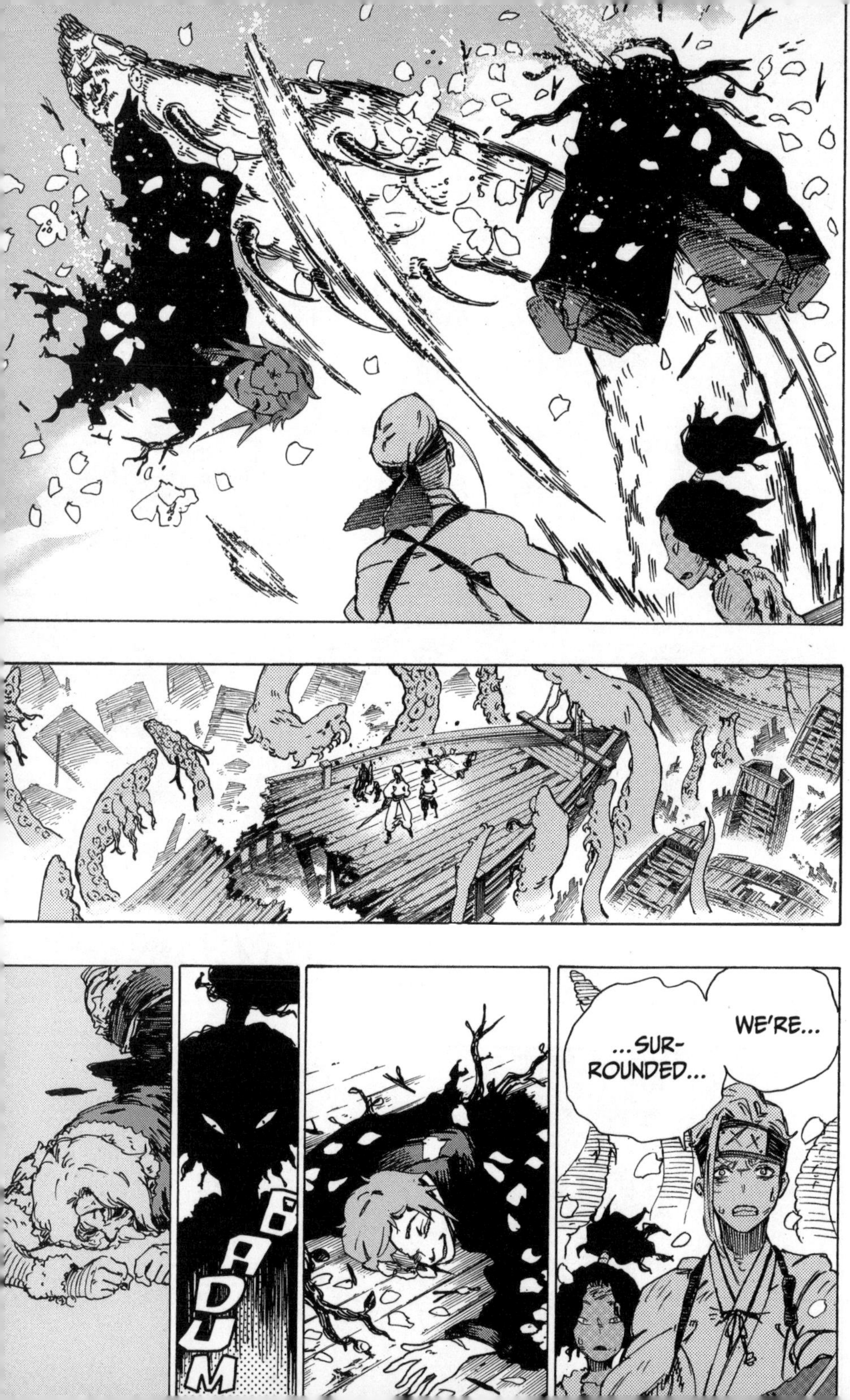
WE'RE...
...SUR-
ROUNDED...
BADUM

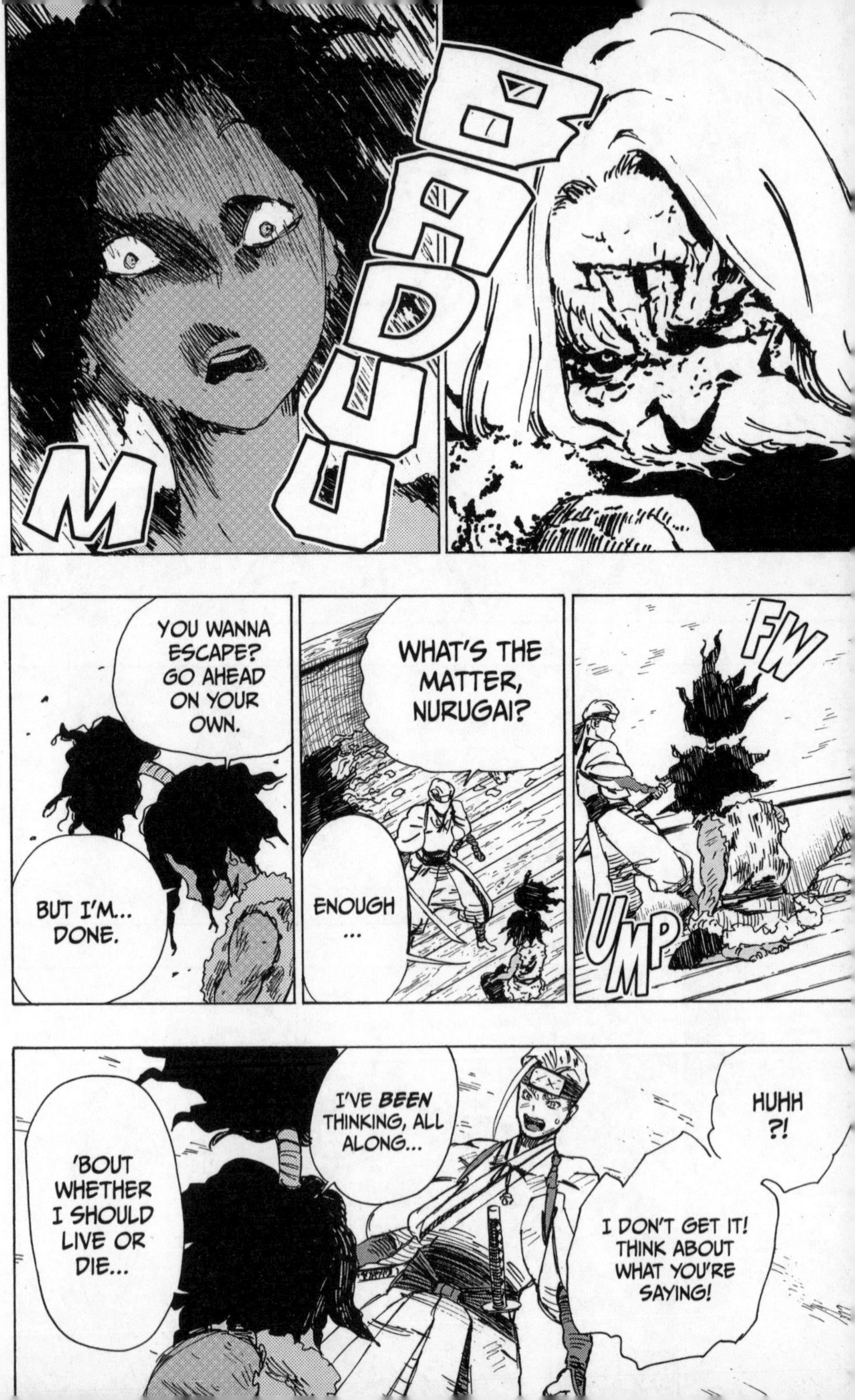
BADUU
M
FW
UMP
WHAT'S THE MATTER, NURUGAI?
ENOUGH ...
YOU WANNA ESCAPE? GO AHEAD ON YOUR OWN.
BUT I'M... DONE.
HUHH ?!
I DON'T GET IT! THINK ABOUT WHAT YOU'RE SAYING!
I'VE *BEEN* THINKING, ALL ALONG...
'BOUT WHETHER I SHOULD LIVE OR DIE...

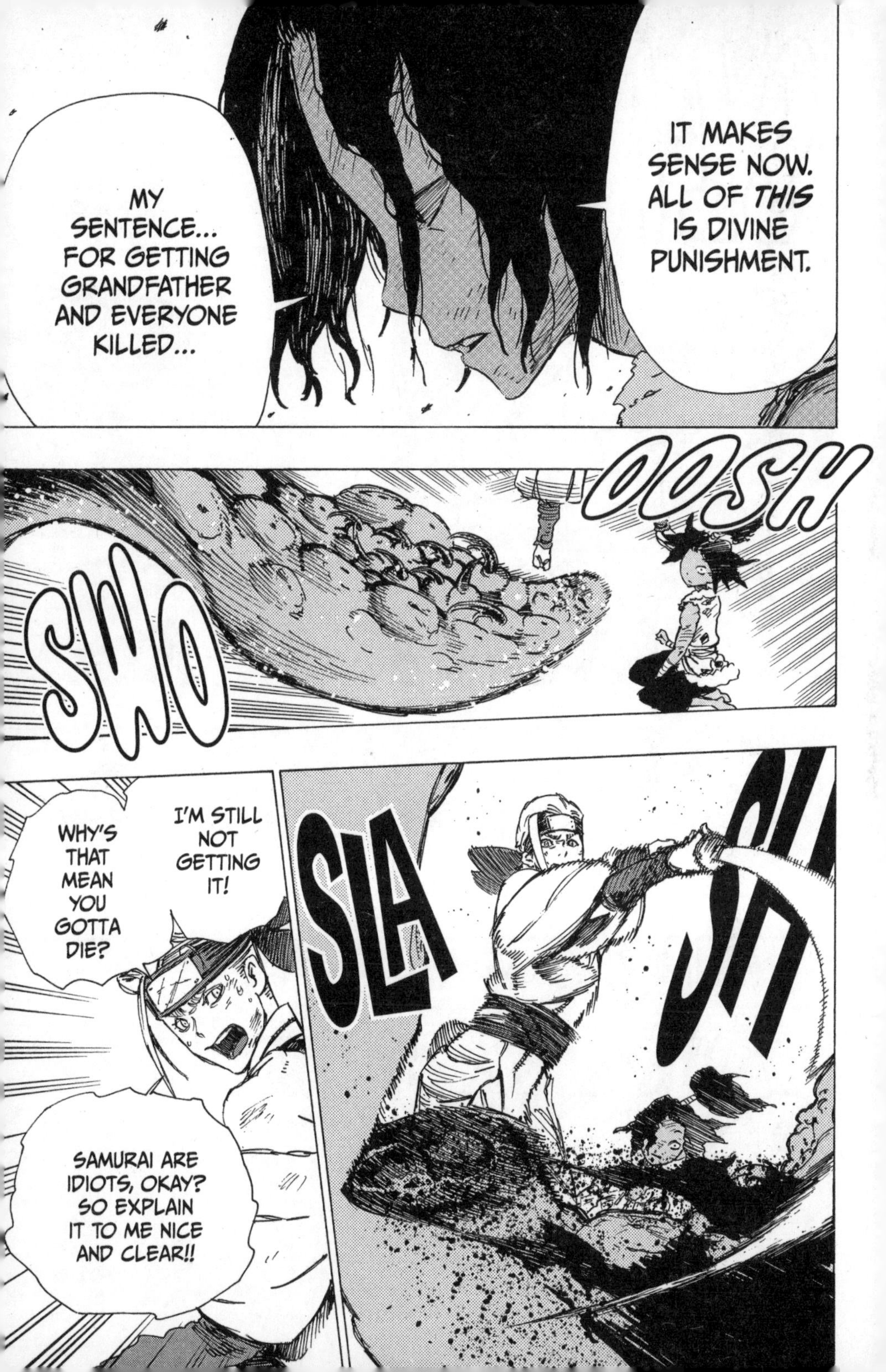
IT MAKES SENSE NOW. ALL OF *THIS* IS DIVINE PUNISHMENT.
MY SENTENCE... FOR GETTING GRANDFATHER AND EVERYONE KILLED...
OOSH
SWO
SLA
SH
I'M STILL NOT GETTING IT!
WHY'S THAT MEAN YOU GOTTA DIE?
SAMURAI ARE IDIOTS, OKAY? SO EXPLAIN IT TO ME NICE AND CLEAR!!

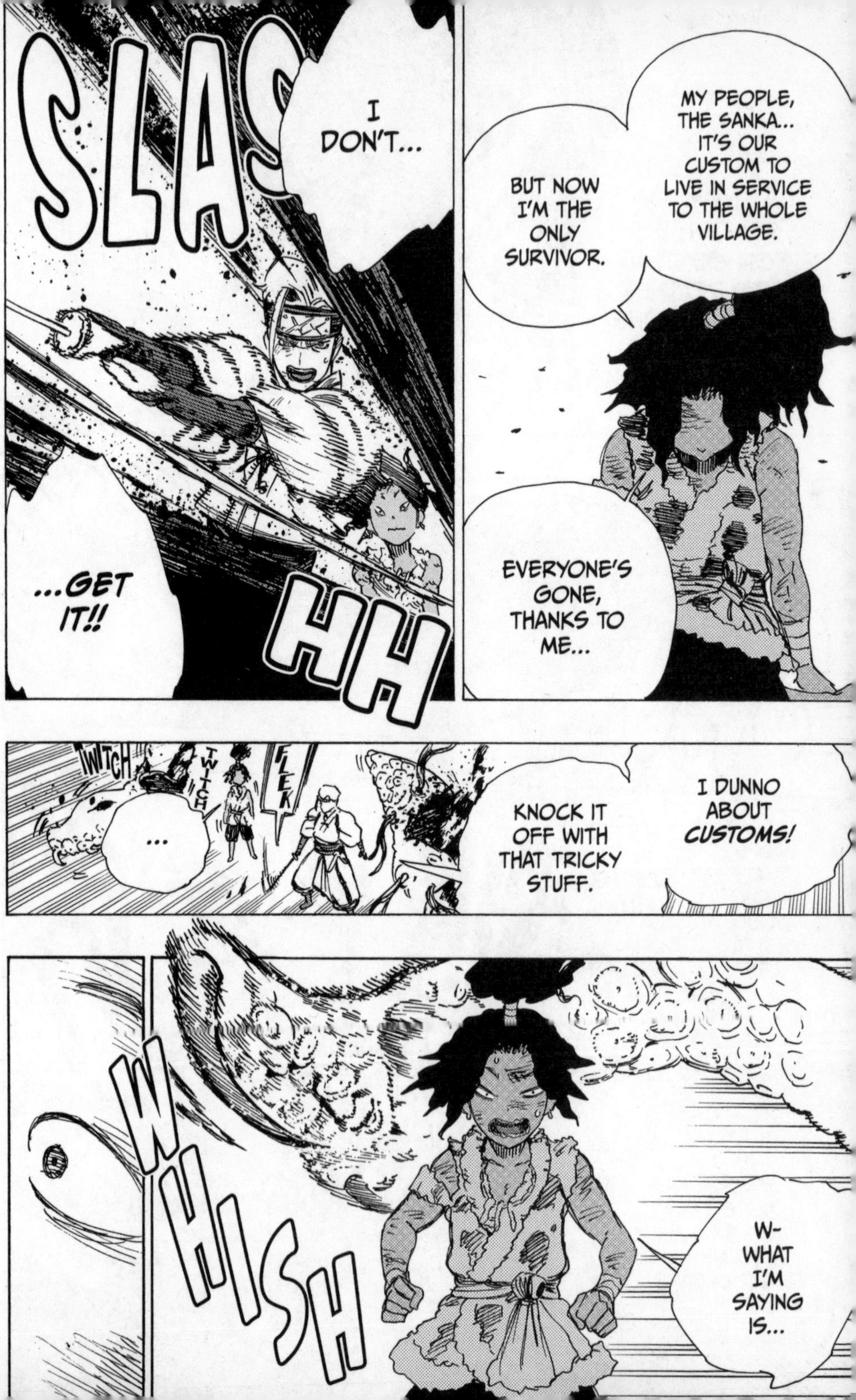
MY PEOPLE, THE SANKA... IT'S OUR CUSTOM TO LIVE IN SERVICE TO THE WHOLE VILLAGE.
BUT NOW I'M THE ONLY SURVIVOR.
EVERYONE'S GONE, THANKS TO ME...
I DON'T...
SLASHHH
...GET IT!!
I DUNNO ABOUT *CUSTOMS!*
KNOCK IT OFF WITH THAT TRICKY STUFF.
FLEK
TWITCH
TWITCH
...
W-WHAT I'M SAYING IS...
WHISH

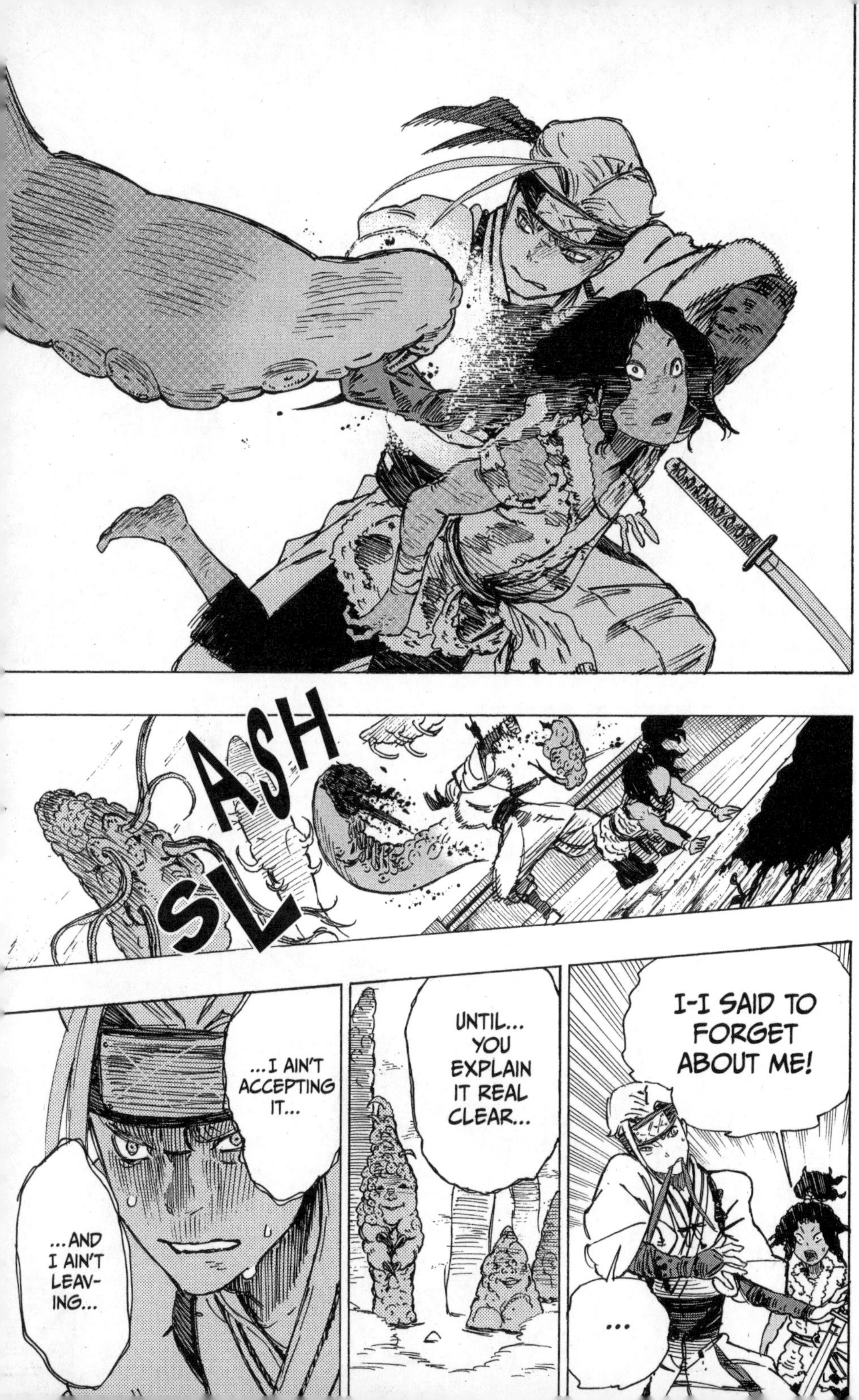
SLASH
I-I SAID TO FORGET ABOUT ME!
...
UNTIL... YOU EXPLAIN IT REAL CLEAR...
...I AIN'T ACCEPTING IT...
...AND I AIN'T LEAVING...

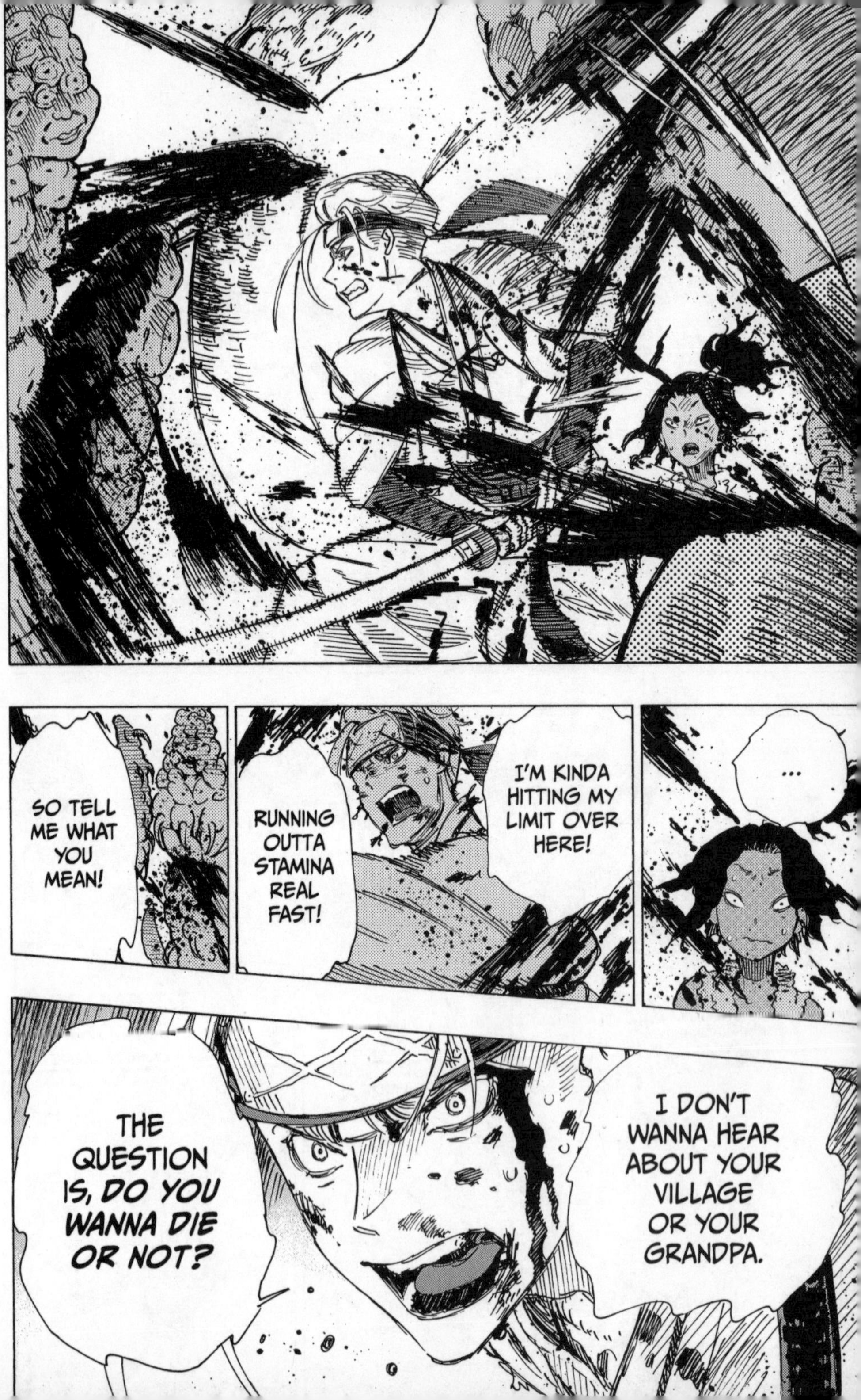
...
I'M KINDA HITTING MY LIMIT OVER HERE!
RUNNING OUTTA STAMINA REAL FAST!
SO TELL ME WHAT YOU MEAN!
I DON'T WANNA HEAR ABOUT YOUR VILLAGE OR YOUR GRANDPA.
THE QUESTION IS, DO YOU WANNA DIE OR NOT?

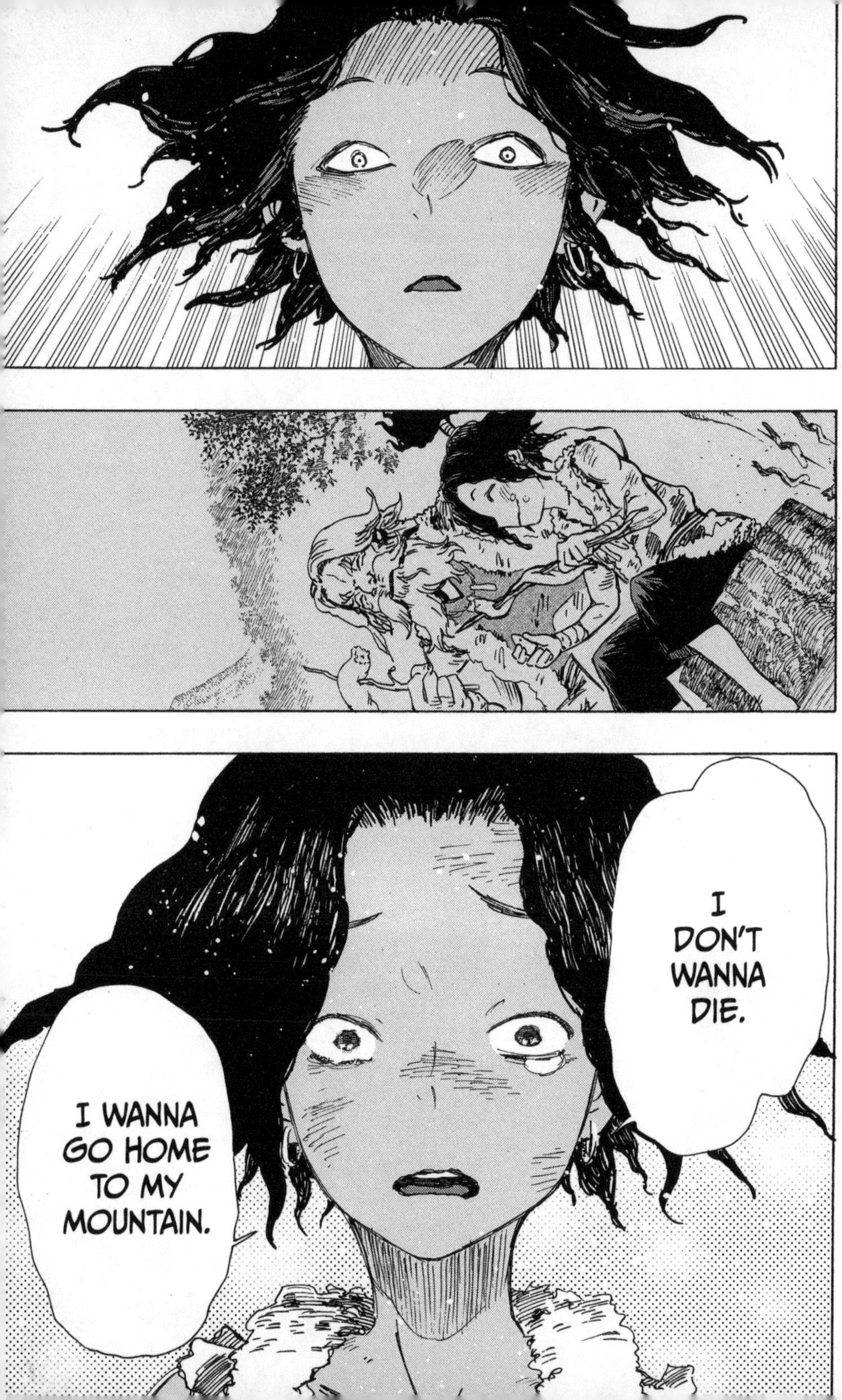
I DON'T WANNA DIE.
I WANNA GO HOME TO MY MOUNTAIN.

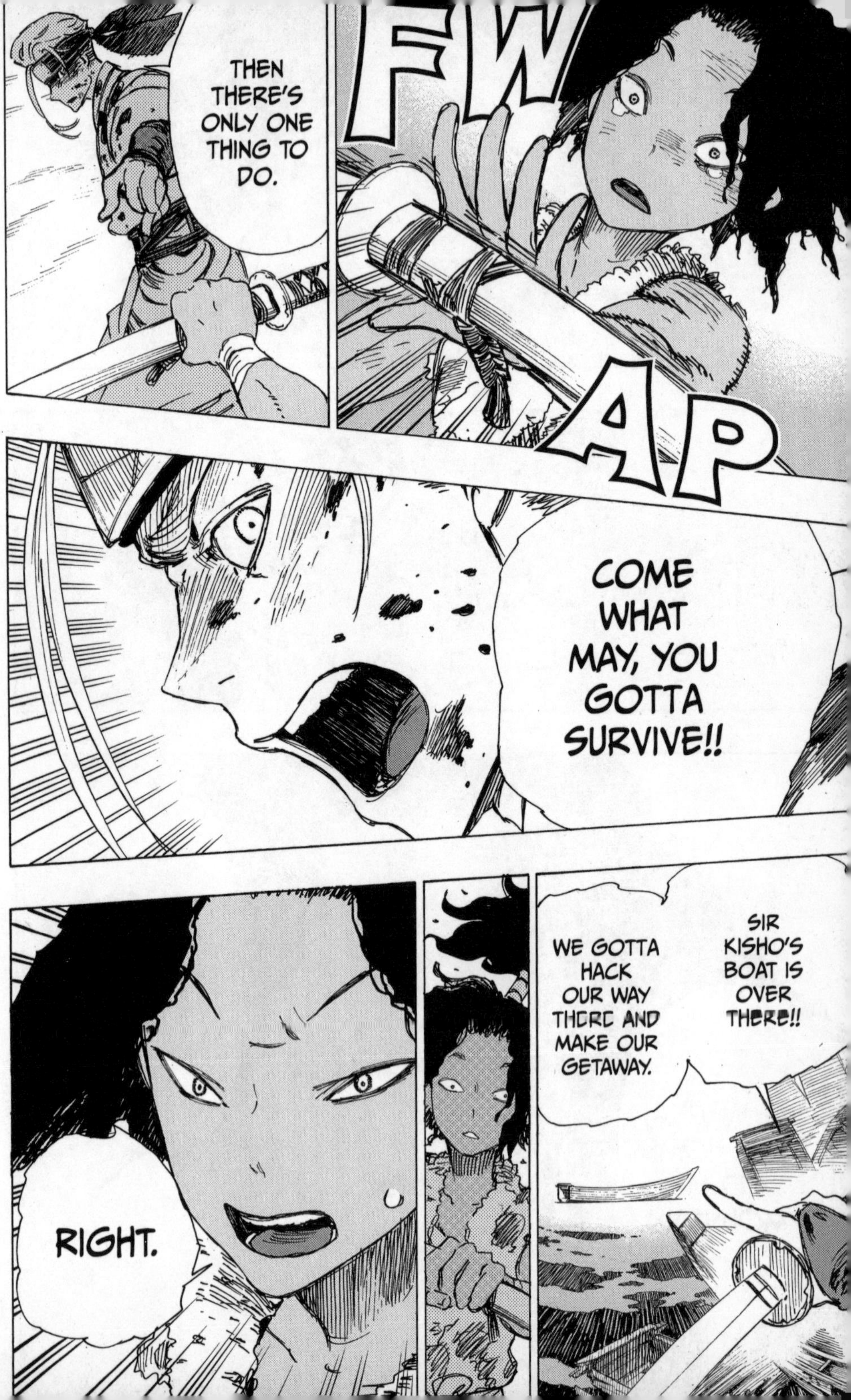
FW
AP
THEN THERE'S ONLY ONE THING TO DO.
COME WHAT MAY, YOU GOTTA SURVIVE!!
SIR KISHO'S BOAT IS OVER THERE!!
WE GOTTA HACK OUR WAY THERE AND MAKE OUR GETAWAY.
RIGHT.

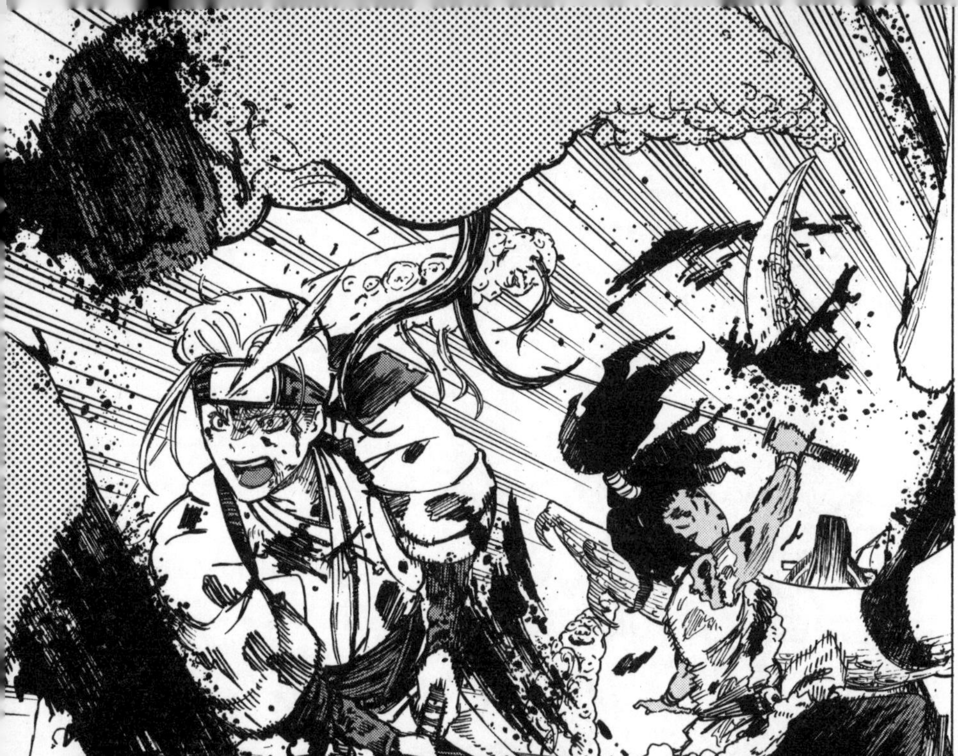
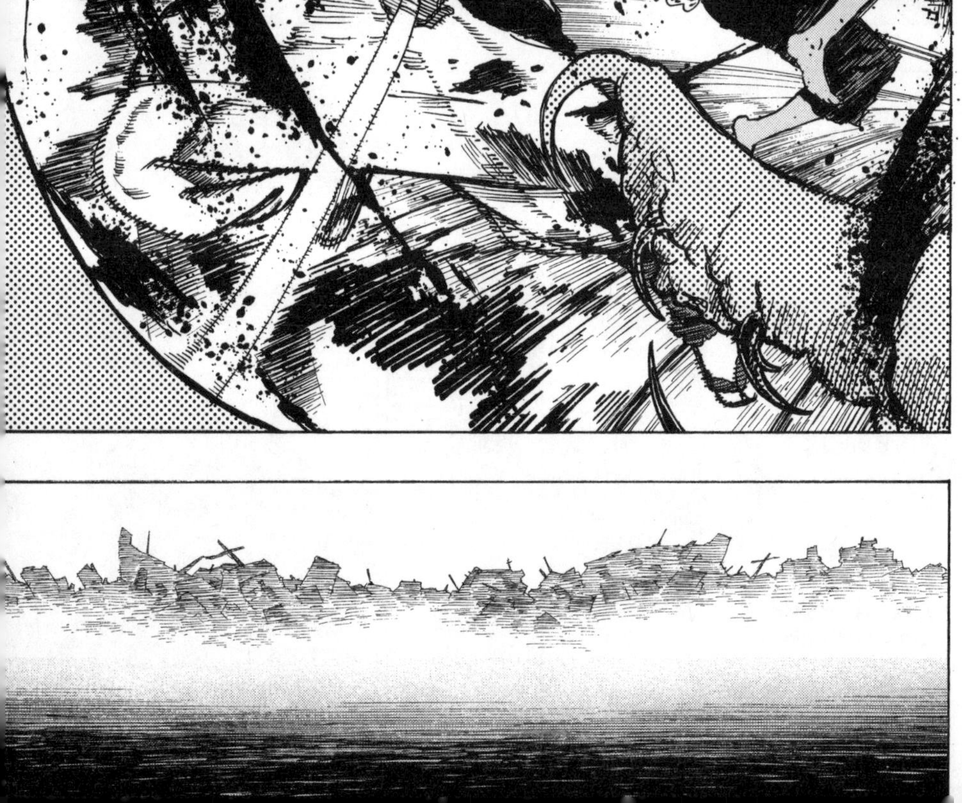

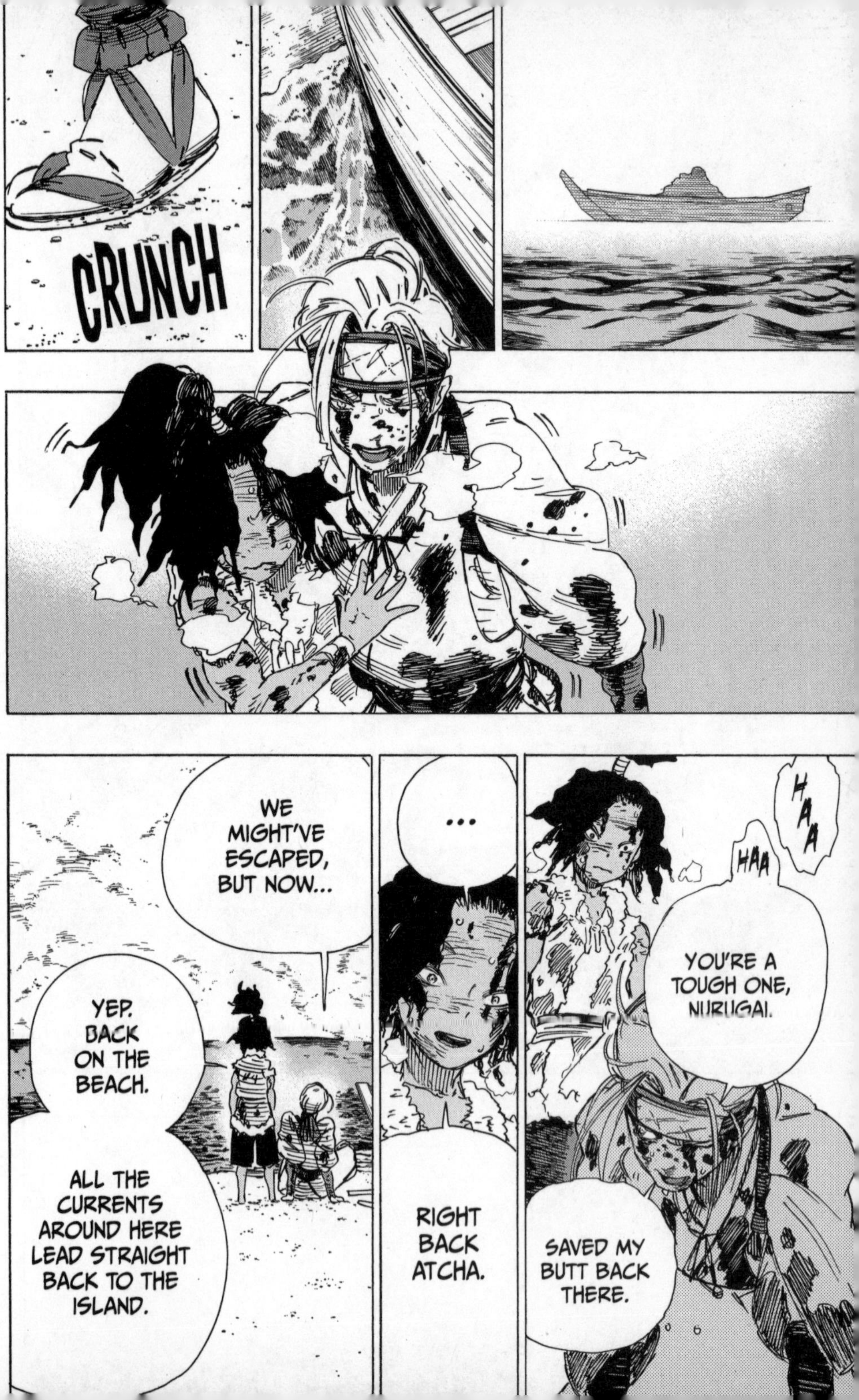
CRUNCH
HAA
HAA
YOU'RE A TOUGH ONE, NURUGAI.
SAVED MY BUTT BACK THERE.
...
RIGHT BACK ATCHA.
WE MIGHT'VE ESCAPED, BUT NOW...
YEP. BACK ON THE BEACH.
ALL THE CURRENTS AROUND HERE LEAD STRAIGHT BACK TO THE ISLAND.

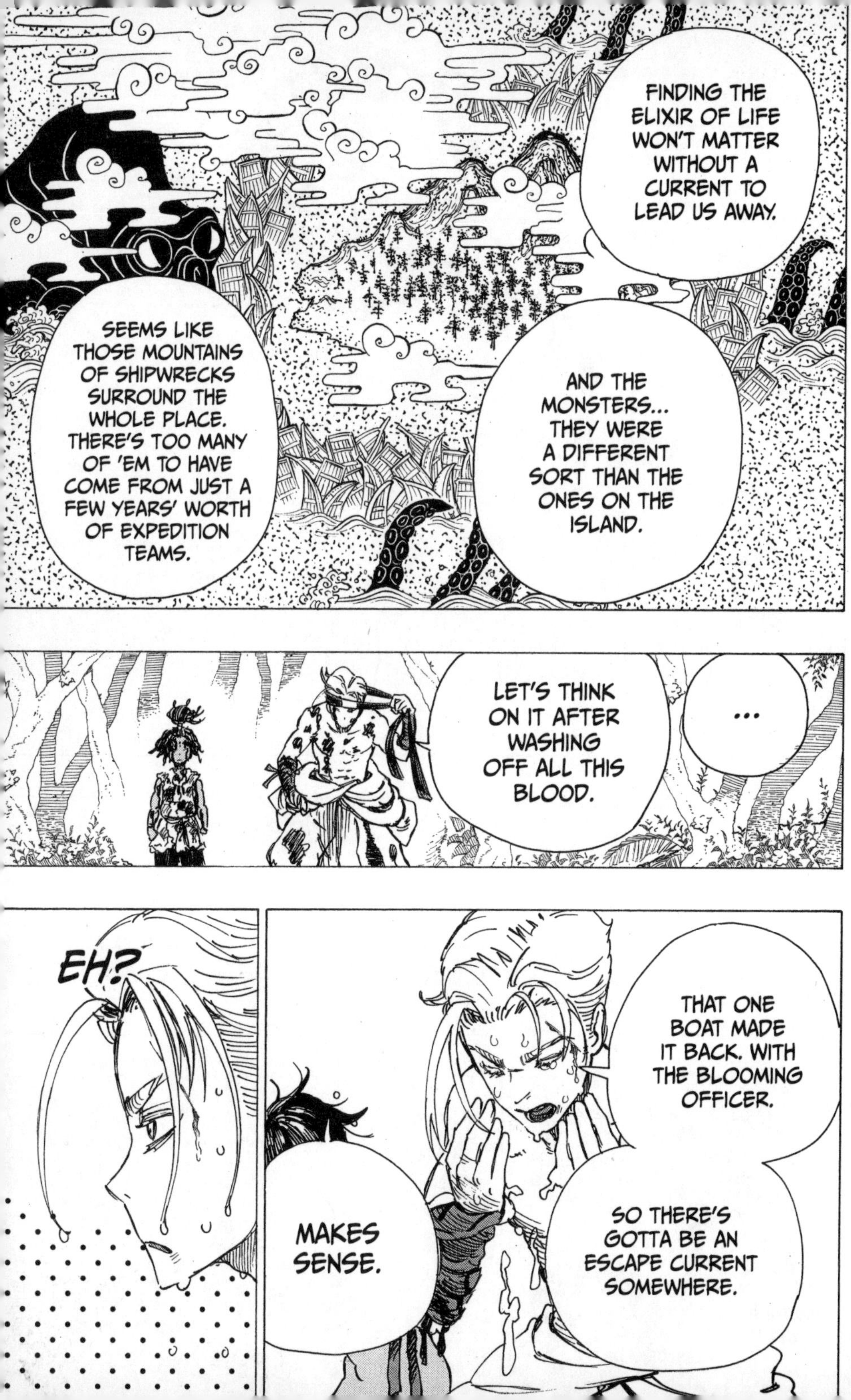
FINDING THE ELIXIR OF LIFE WON'T MATTER WITHOUT A CURRENT TO LEAD US AWAY.
SEEMS LIKE THOSE MOUNTAINS OF SHIPWRECKS SURROUND THE WHOLE PLACE. THERE'S TOO MANY OF 'EM TO HAVE COME FROM JUST A FEW YEARS' WORTH OF EXPEDITION TEAMS.
AND THE MONSTERS... THEY WERE A DIFFERENT SORT THAN THE ONES ON THE ISLAND.
...
LET'S THINK ON IT AFTER WASHING OFF ALL THIS BLOOD.
THAT ONE BOAT MADE IT BACK. WITH THE BLOOMING OFFICER.
SO THERE'S GOTTA BE AN ESCAPE CURRENT SOMEWHERE.
MAKES SENSE.
EH?

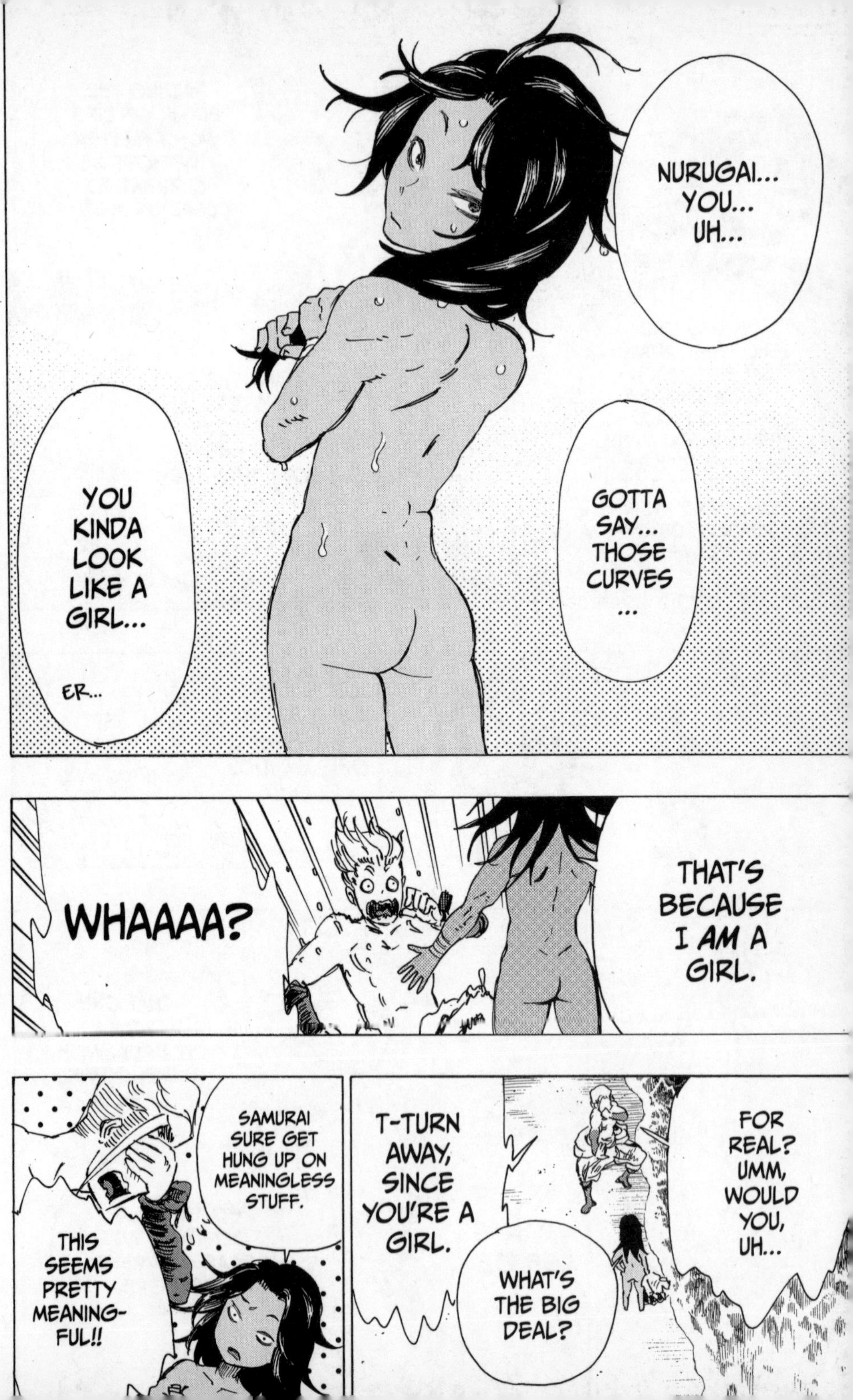
NURUGAI... YOU... UH...
GOTTA SAY... THOSE CURVES ...
YOU KINDA LOOK LIKE A GIRL...
ER...
THAT'S BECAUSE I *AM* A GIRL.
WHAAAA?
FOR REAL? UMM, WOULD YOU, UH...
T-TURN AWAY, SINCE YOU'RE A GIRL.
WHAT'S THE BIG DEAL?
SAMURAI SURE GET HUNG UP ON MEANINGLESS STUFF.
THIS SEEMS PRETTY MEANING-FUL!!

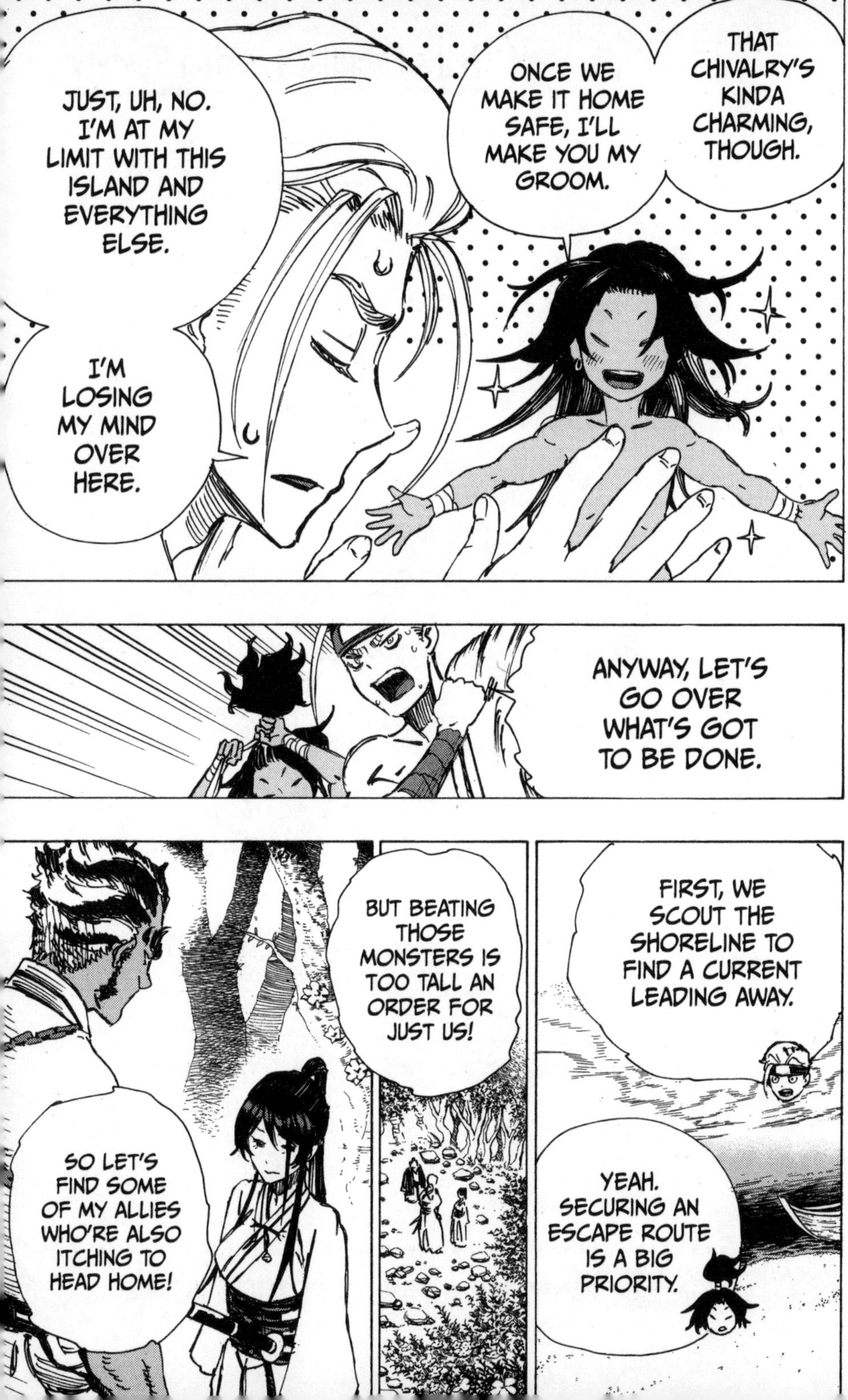
THAT CHIVALRY'S KINDA CHARMING, THOUGH.
ONCE WE MAKE IT HOME SAFE, I'LL MAKE YOU MY GROOM.
JUST, UH, NO. I'M AT MY LIMIT WITH THIS ISLAND AND EVERYTHING ELSE.
I'M LOSING MY MIND OVER HERE.
ANYWAY, LET'S GO OVER WHAT'S GOT TO BE DONE.
FIRST, WE SCOUT THE SHORELINE TO FIND A CURRENT LEADING AWAY.
YEAH. SECURING AN ESCAPE ROUTE IS A BIG PRIORITY.
BUT BEATING THOSE MONSTERS IS TOO TALL AN ORDER FOR JUST US!
SO LET'S FIND SOME OF MY ALLIES WHO'RE ALSO ITCHING TO HEAD HOME!

Hell's Paradise Fashion Review

Sanka Tribe
NURUGAI

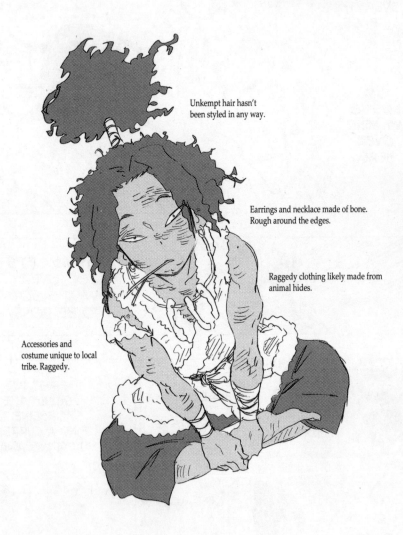

Unkempt hair hasn't been styled in any way.

Earrings and necklace made of bone. Rough around the edges.

Raggedy clothing likely made from animal hides.

Accessories and costume unique to local tribe. Raggedy.

EVALUATION ► WILD CHILD ☆☆☆ LET'S FIND SOME NICER CLOTHES FOR THIS ONE.

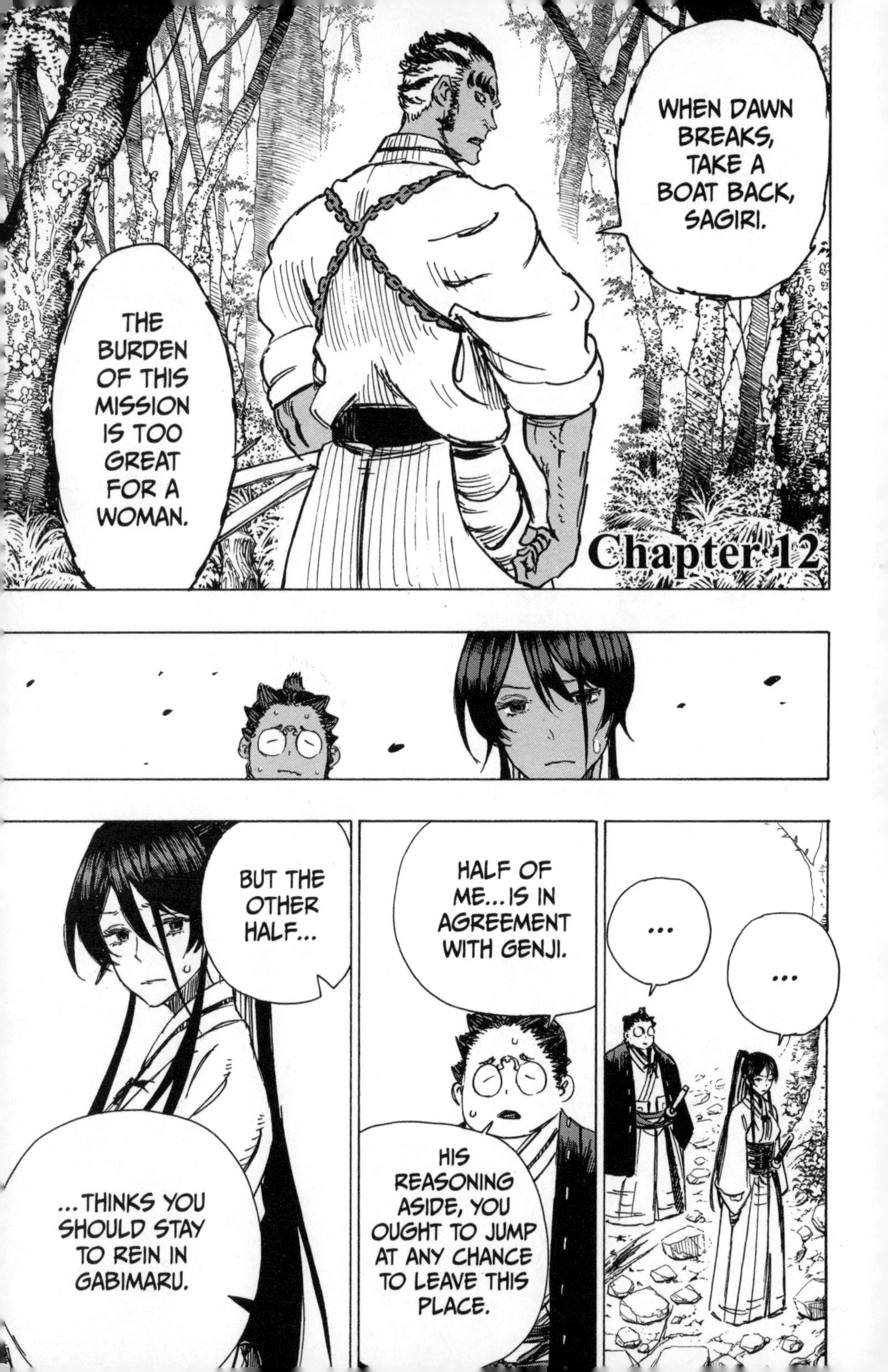
Chapter 12
WHEN DAWN BREAKS, TAKE A BOAT BACK, SAGIRI.
THE BURDEN OF THIS MISSION IS TOO GREAT FOR A WOMAN.
...
...
HALF OF ME...IS IN AGREEMENT WITH GENJI.
HIS REASONING ASIDE, YOU OUGHT TO JUMP AT ANY CHANCE TO LEAVE THIS PLACE.
BUT THE OTHER HALF...
...THINKS YOU SHOULD STAY TO REIN IN GABIMARU.

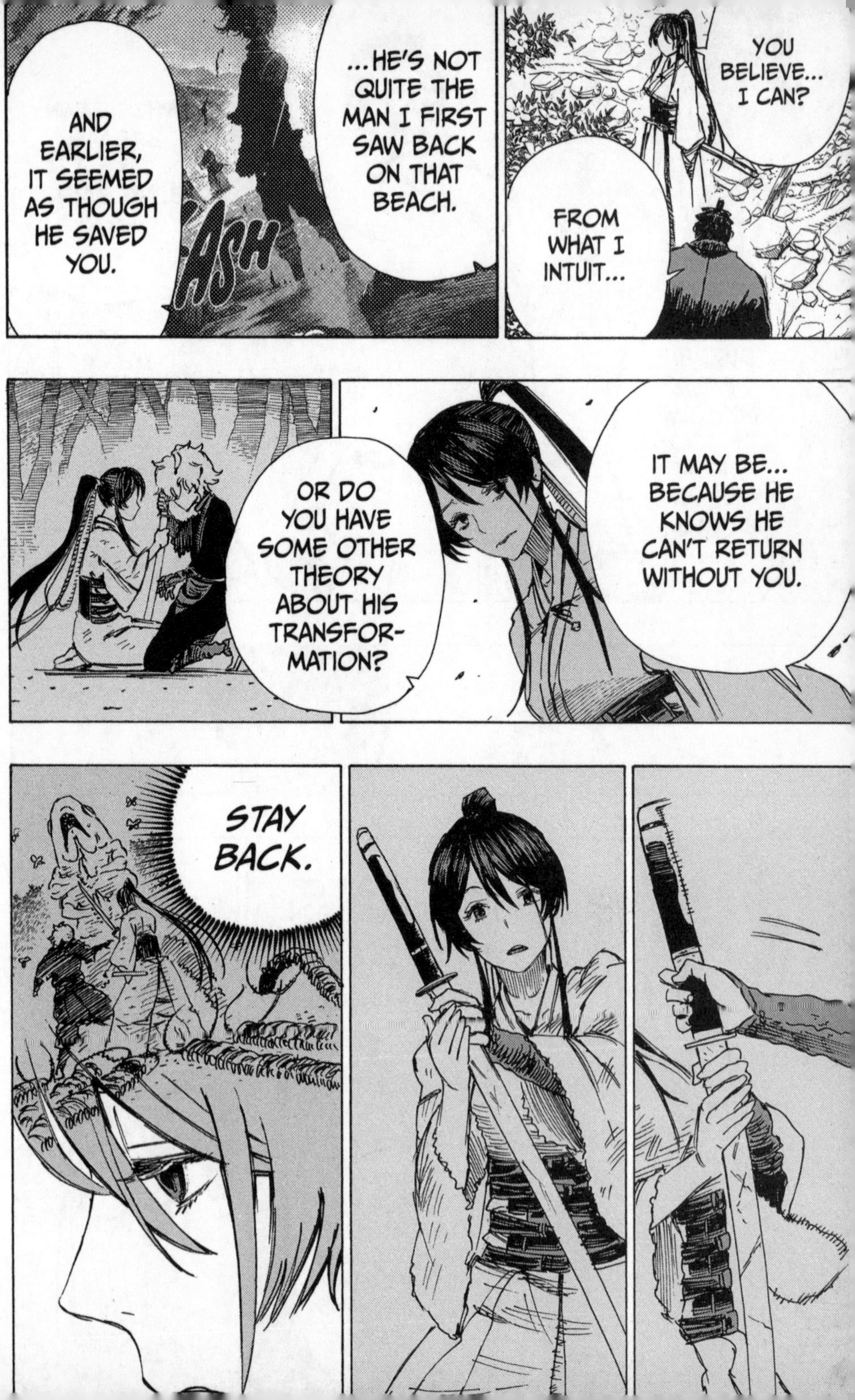
YOU BELIEVE... I CAN?
FROM WHAT I INTUIT...
...HE'S NOT QUITE THE MAN I FIRST SAW BACK ON THAT BEACH.
AND EARLIER, IT SEEMED AS THOUGH HE SAVED YOU.
IT MAY BE... BECAUSE HE KNOWS HE CAN'T RETURN WITHOUT YOU.
OR DO YOU HAVE SOME OTHER THEORY ABOUT HIS TRANSFORMATION?
STAY BACK.

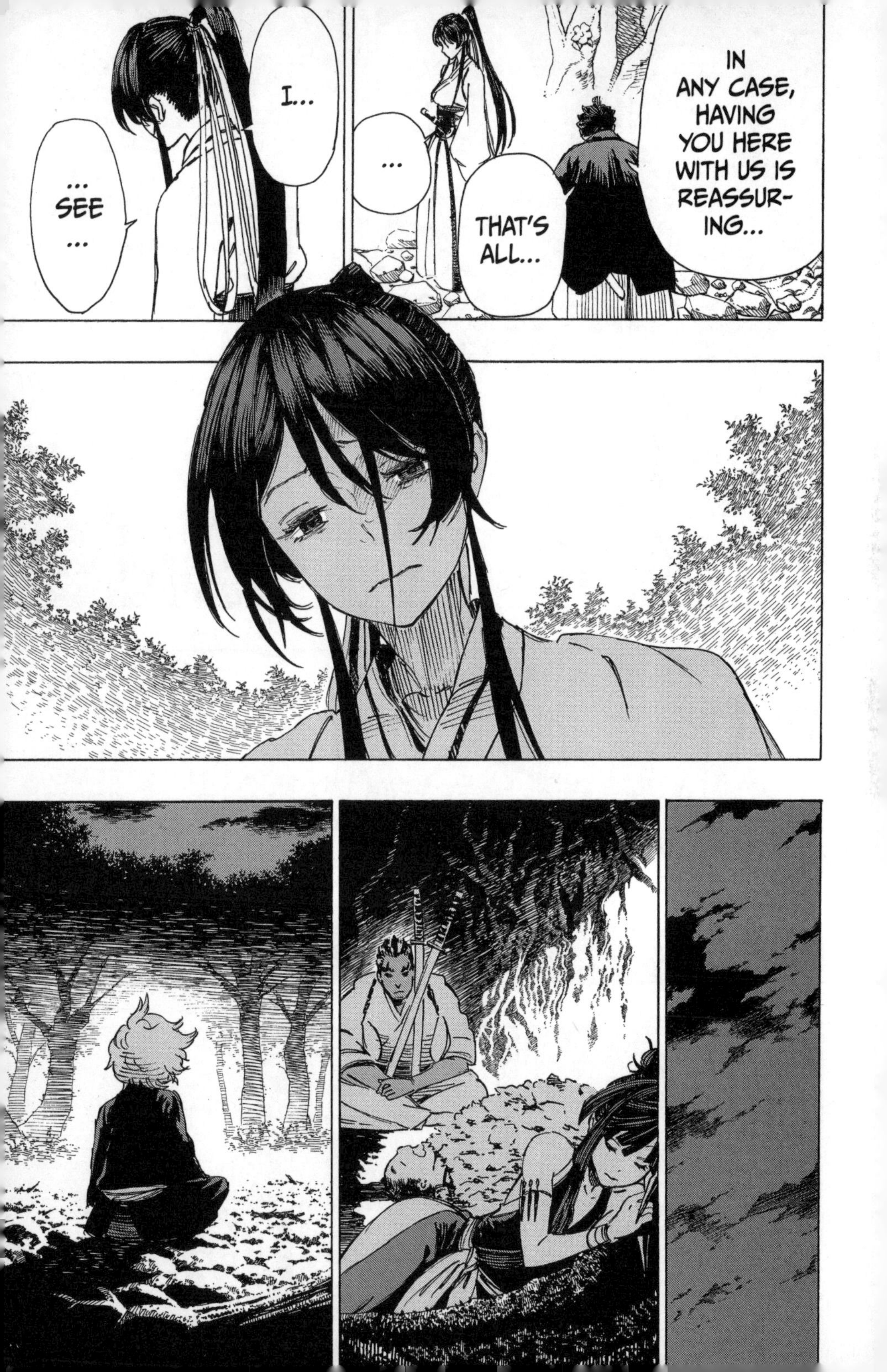
IN ANY CASE, HAVING YOU HERE WITH US IS REASSURING...
THAT'S ALL...
...
I...
... SEE ...

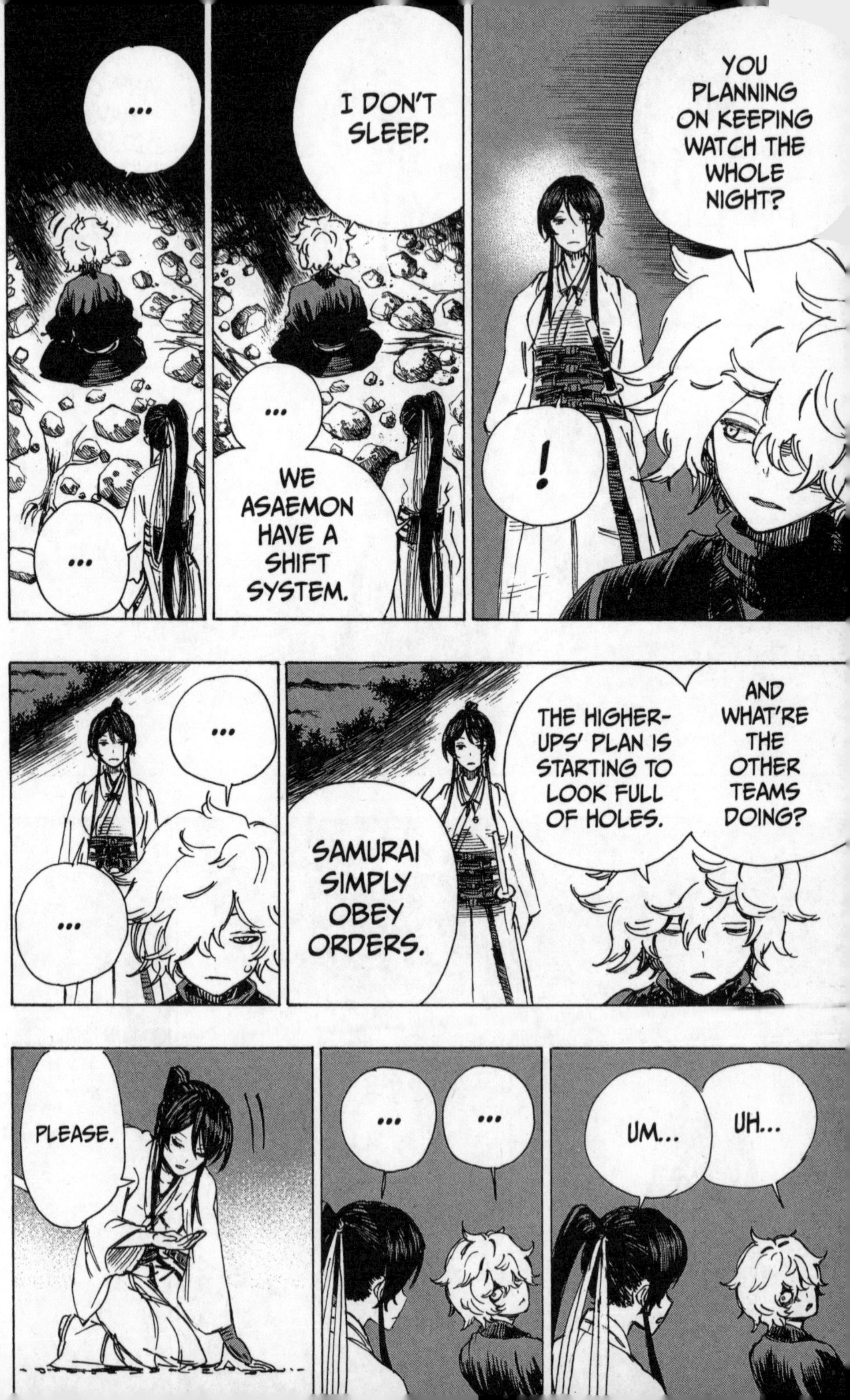
YOU PLANNING ON KEEPING WATCH THE WHOLE NIGHT?
!
I DON'T SLEEP.
...
WE ASAEMON HAVE A SHIFT SYSTEM.
...
...
AND WHAT'RE THE OTHER TEAMS DOING?
THE HIGHER-UPS' PLAN IS STARTING TO LOOK FULL OF HOLES.
SAMURAI SIMPLY OBEY ORDERS.
...
...
UH...
UM...
...
...
PLEASE.

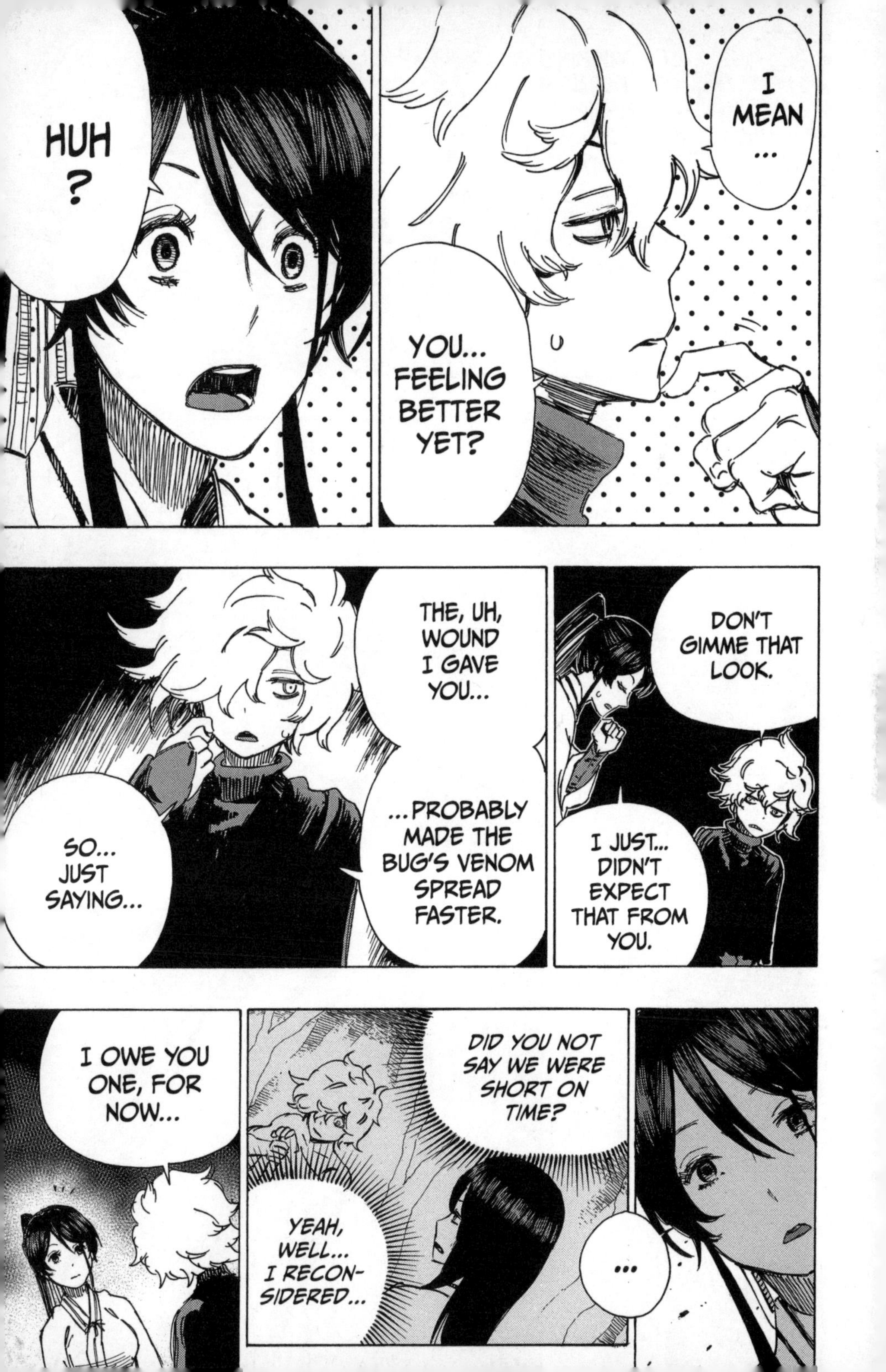
I MEAN ...
YOU... FEELING BETTER YET?
HUH ?
DON'T GIMME THAT LOOK.
I JUST... DIDN'T EXPECT THAT FROM YOU.
THE, UH, WOUND I GAVE YOU...
...PROBABLY MADE THE BUG'S VENOM SPREAD FASTER.
SO... JUST SAYING...
...
DID YOU NOT SAY WE WERE SHORT ON TIME?
YEAH, WELL... I RECON-SIDERED...
I OWE YOU ONE, FOR NOW...

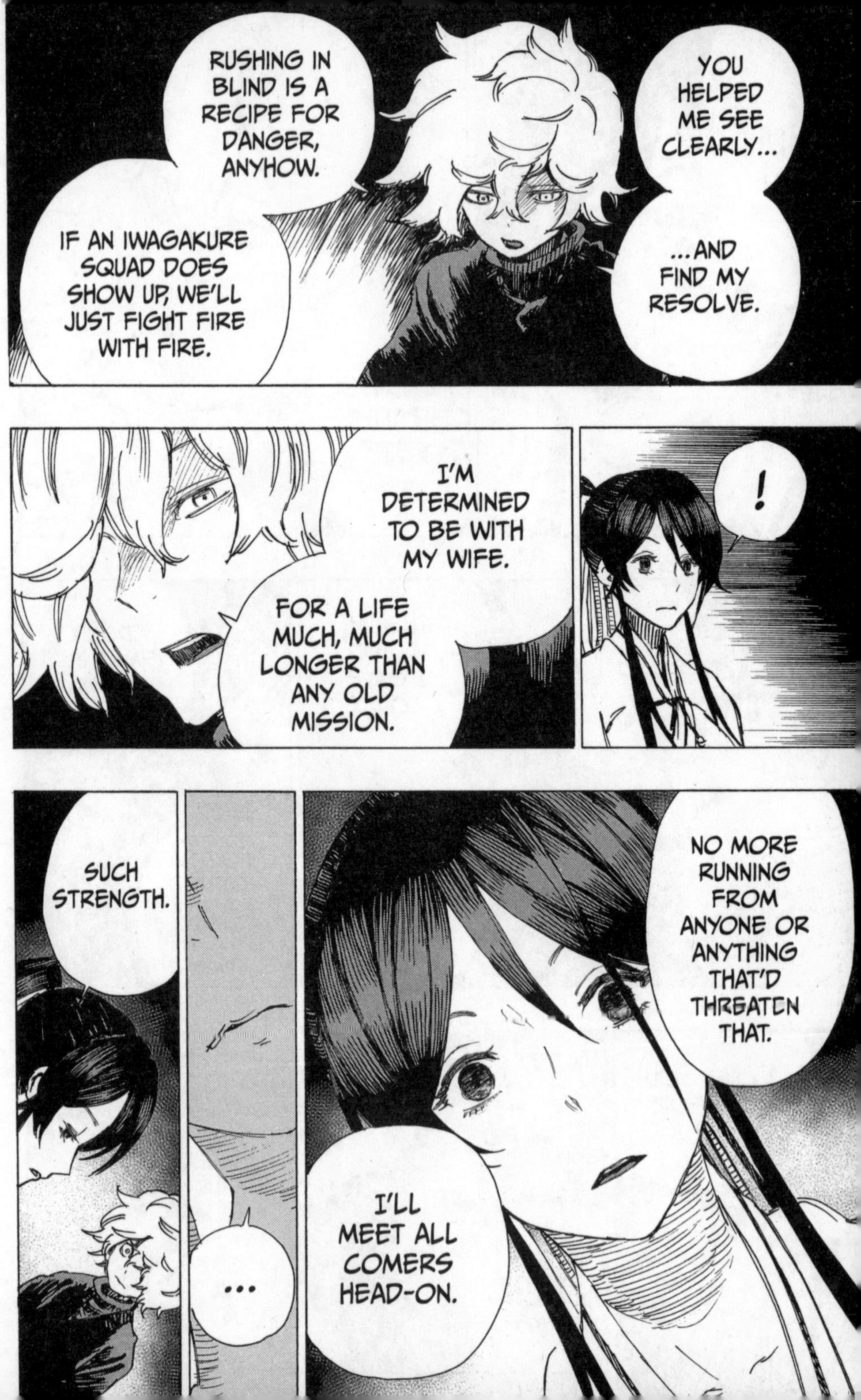
YOU HELPED ME SEE CLEARLY...
...AND FIND MY RESOLVE.
RUSHING IN BLIND IS A RECIPE FOR DANGER, ANYHOW.
IF AN IWAGAKURE SQUAD DOES SHOW UP, WE'LL JUST FIGHT FIRE WITH FIRE.
!
I'M DETERMINED TO BE WITH MY WIFE.
FOR A LIFE MUCH, MUCH LONGER THAN ANY OLD MISSION.
NO MORE RUNNING FROM ANYONE OR ANYTHING THAT'D THREATEN THAT.
I'LL MEET ALL COMERS HEAD-ON.
SUCH STRENGTH.
...

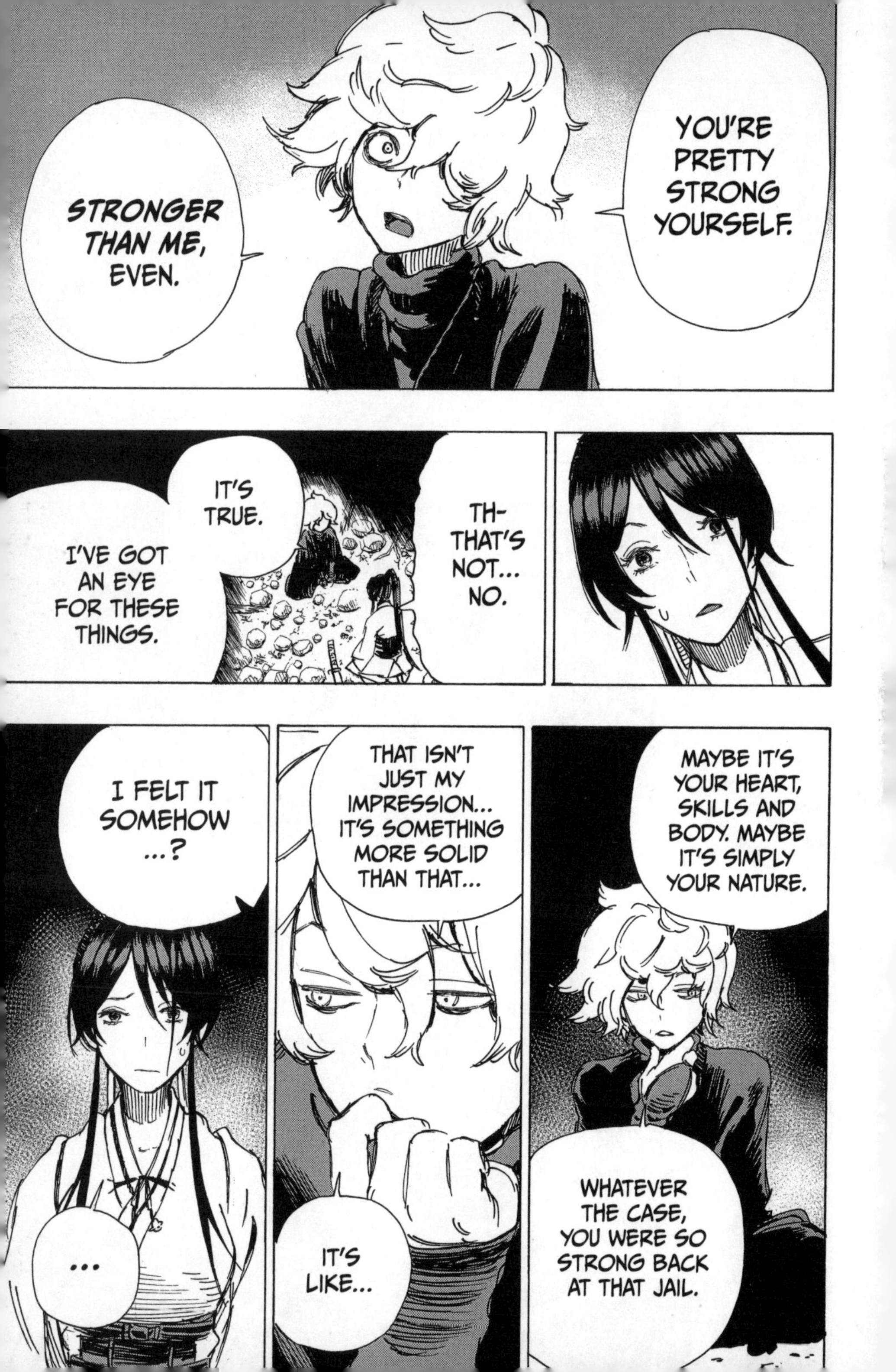

YOU'RE PRETTY STRONG YOURSELF.
STRONGER THAN ME, EVEN.
TH- THAT'S NOT... NO.
IT'S TRUE.
I'VE GOT AN EYE FOR THESE THINGS.
MAYBE IT'S YOUR HEART, SKILLS AND BODY. MAYBE IT'S SIMPLY YOUR NATURE.
WHATEVER THE CASE, YOU WERE SO STRONG BACK AT THAT JAIL.
THAT ISN'T JUST MY IMPRESSION... IT'S SOMETHING MORE SOLID THAN THAT...
IT'S LIKE...
I FELT IT SOMEHOW ...?
...

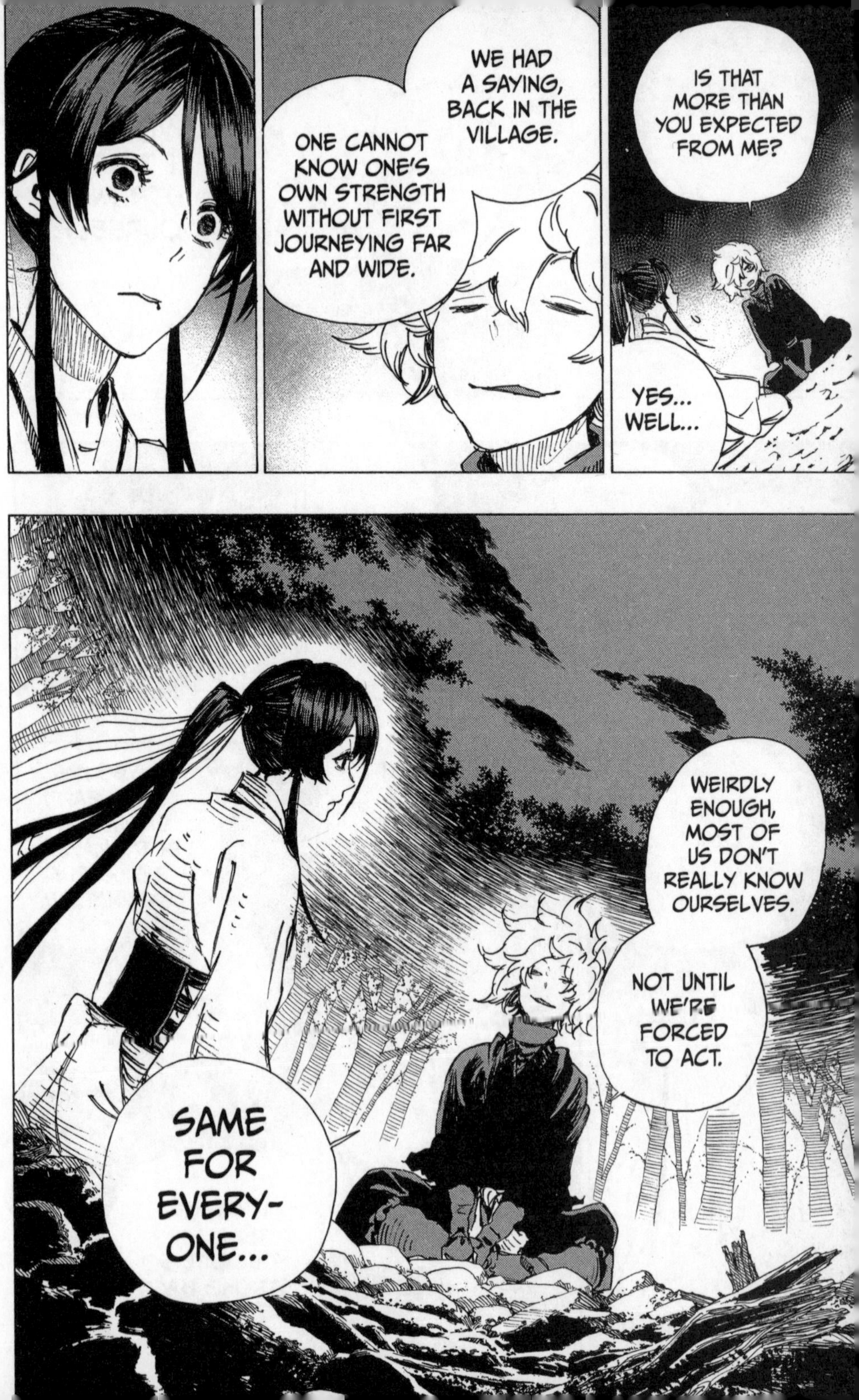
IS THAT MORE THAN YOU EXPECTED FROM ME?
YES... WELL...
WE HAD A SAYING, BACK IN THE VILLAGE.
ONE CANNOT KNOW ONE'S OWN STRENGTH WITHOUT FIRST JOURNEYING FAR AND WIDE.
WEIRDLY ENOUGH, MOST OF US DON'T REALLY KNOW OURSELVES.
NOT UNTIL WE'RE FORCED TO ACT.
SAME FOR EVERY-ONE...

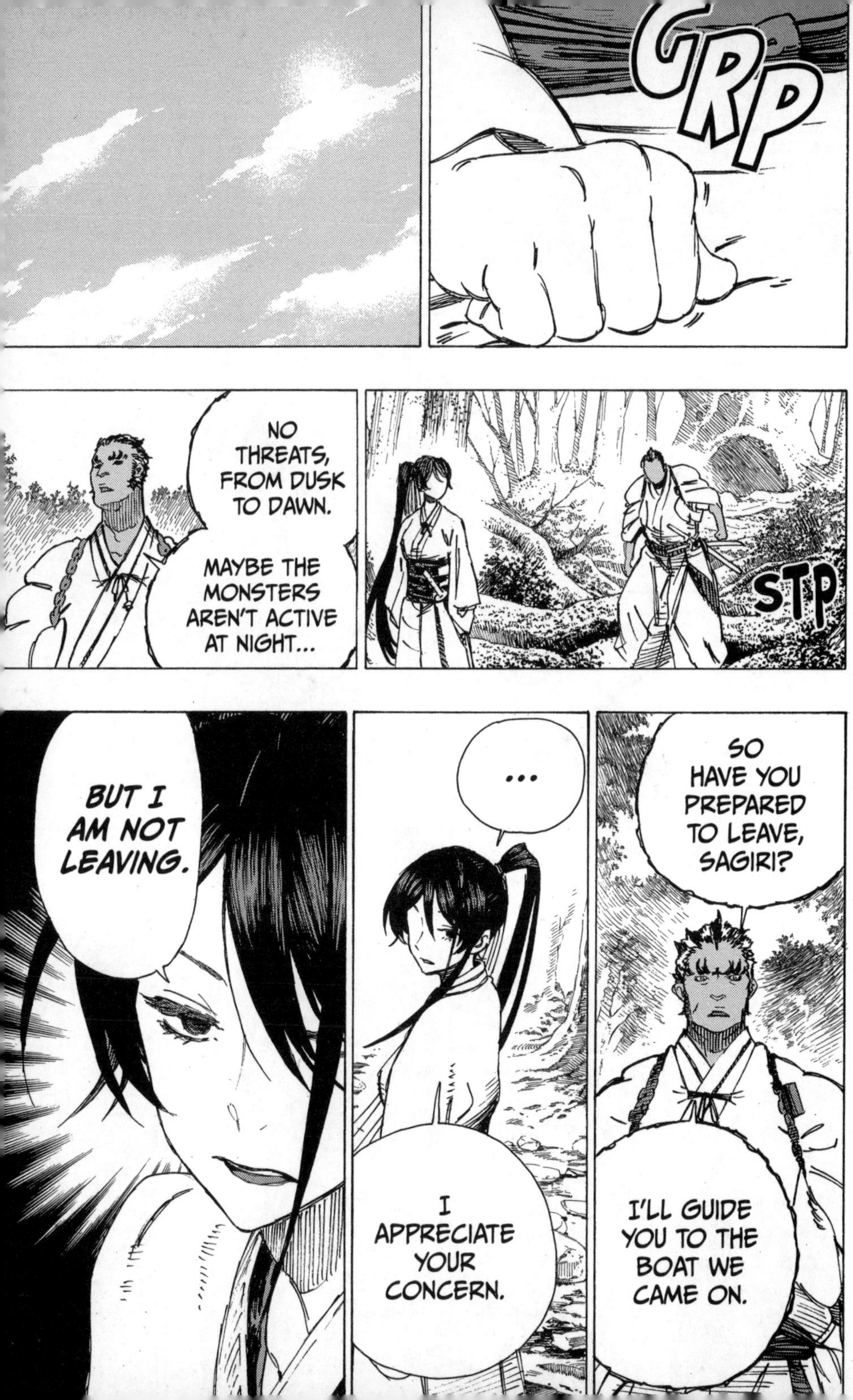
GRP
STP
NO THREATS, FROM DUSK TO DAWN.
MAYBE THE MONSTERS AREN'T ACTIVE AT NIGHT...
SO HAVE YOU PREPARED TO LEAVE, SAGIRI?
I'LL GUIDE YOU TO THE BOAT WE CAME ON.
...
I APPRECIATE YOUR CONCERN.
BUT I AM NOT LEAVING.

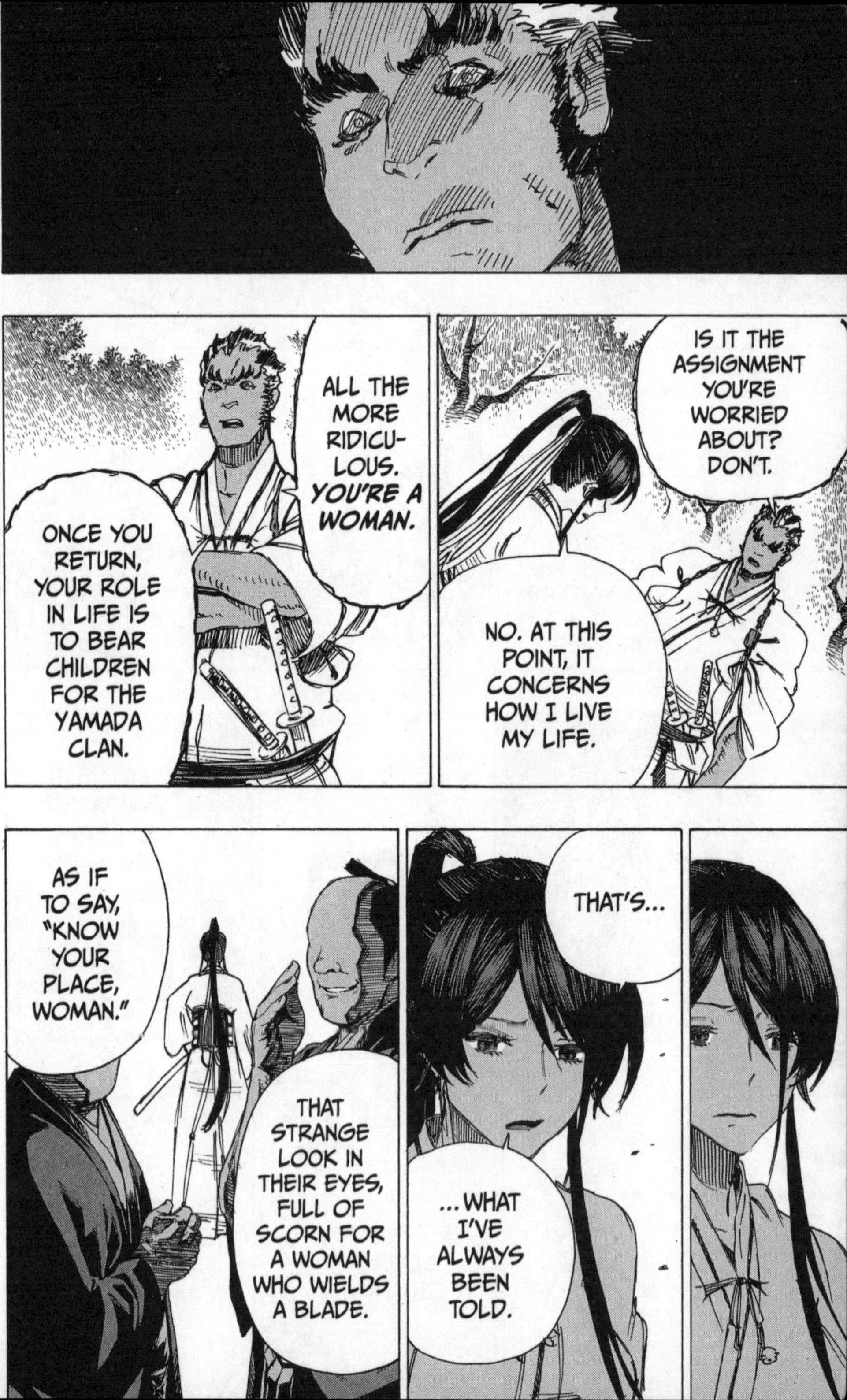
IS IT THE ASSIGNMENT YOU'RE WORRIED ABOUT? DON'T.
NO. AT THIS POINT, IT CONCERNS HOW I LIVE MY LIFE.
ALL THE MORE RIDICULOUS. *YOU'RE A WOMAN.*
ONCE YOU RETURN, YOUR ROLE IN LIFE IS TO BEAR CHILDREN FOR THE YAMADA CLAN.
THAT'S...
...WHAT I'VE ALWAYS BEEN TOLD.
THAT STRANGE LOOK IN THEIR EYES, FULL OF SCORN FOR A WOMAN WHO WIELDS A BLADE.
AS IF TO SAY, "KNOW YOUR PLACE, WOMAN."

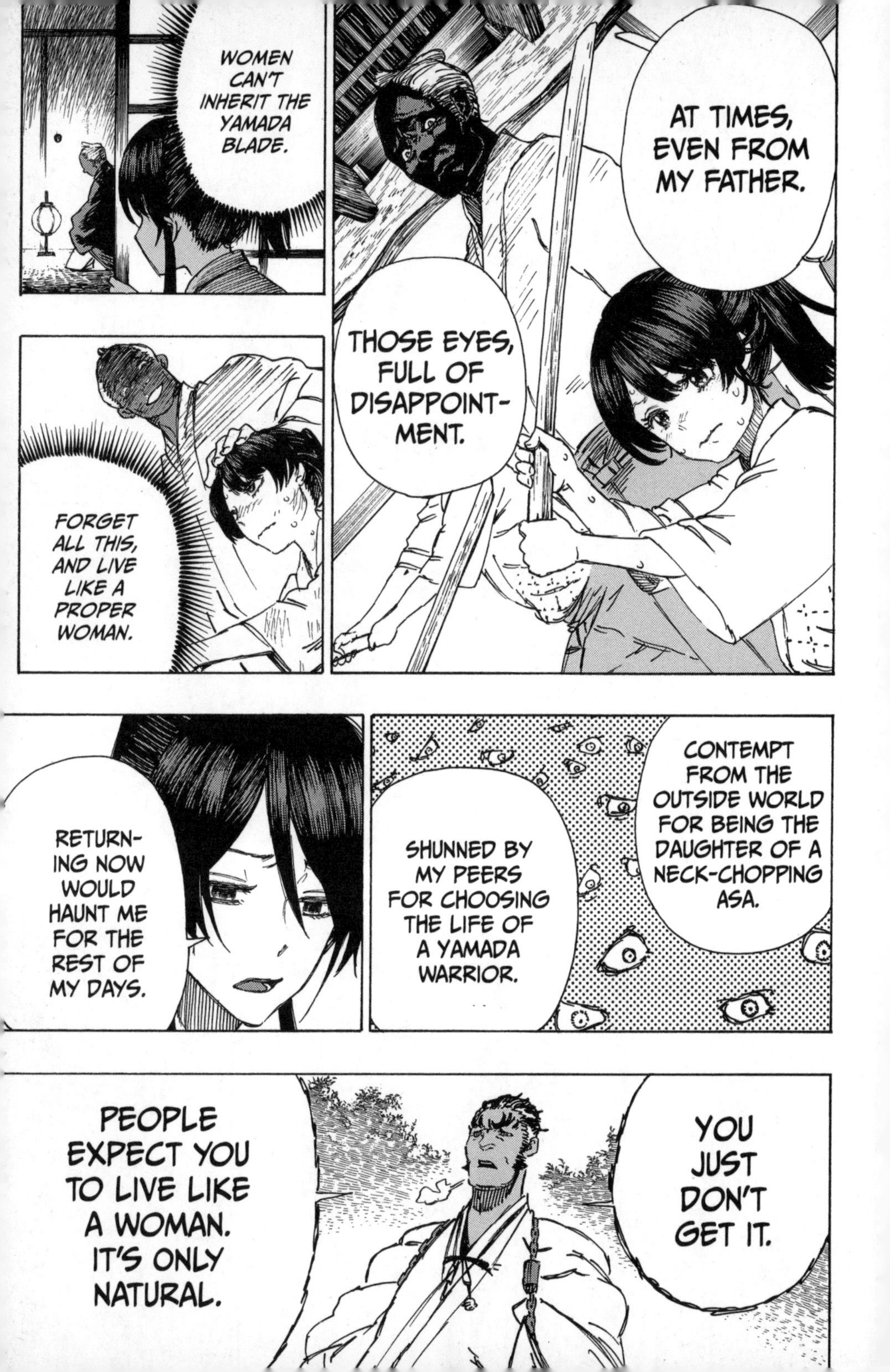
AT TIMES, EVEN FROM MY FATHER.
THOSE EYES, FULL OF DISAPPOINT-MENT.
WOMEN CAN'T INHERIT THE YAMADA BLADE.
FORGET ALL THIS, AND LIVE LIKE A PROPER WOMAN.
CONTEMPT FROM THE OUTSIDE WORLD FOR BEING THE DAUGHTER OF A NECK-CHOPPING ASA.
SHUNNED BY MY PEERS FOR CHOOSING THE LIFE OF A YAMADA WARRIOR.
RETURN-ING NOW WOULD HAUNT ME FOR THE REST OF MY DAYS.
YOU JUST DON'T GET IT.
PEOPLE EXPECT YOU TO LIVE LIKE A WOMAN. IT'S ONLY NATURAL.

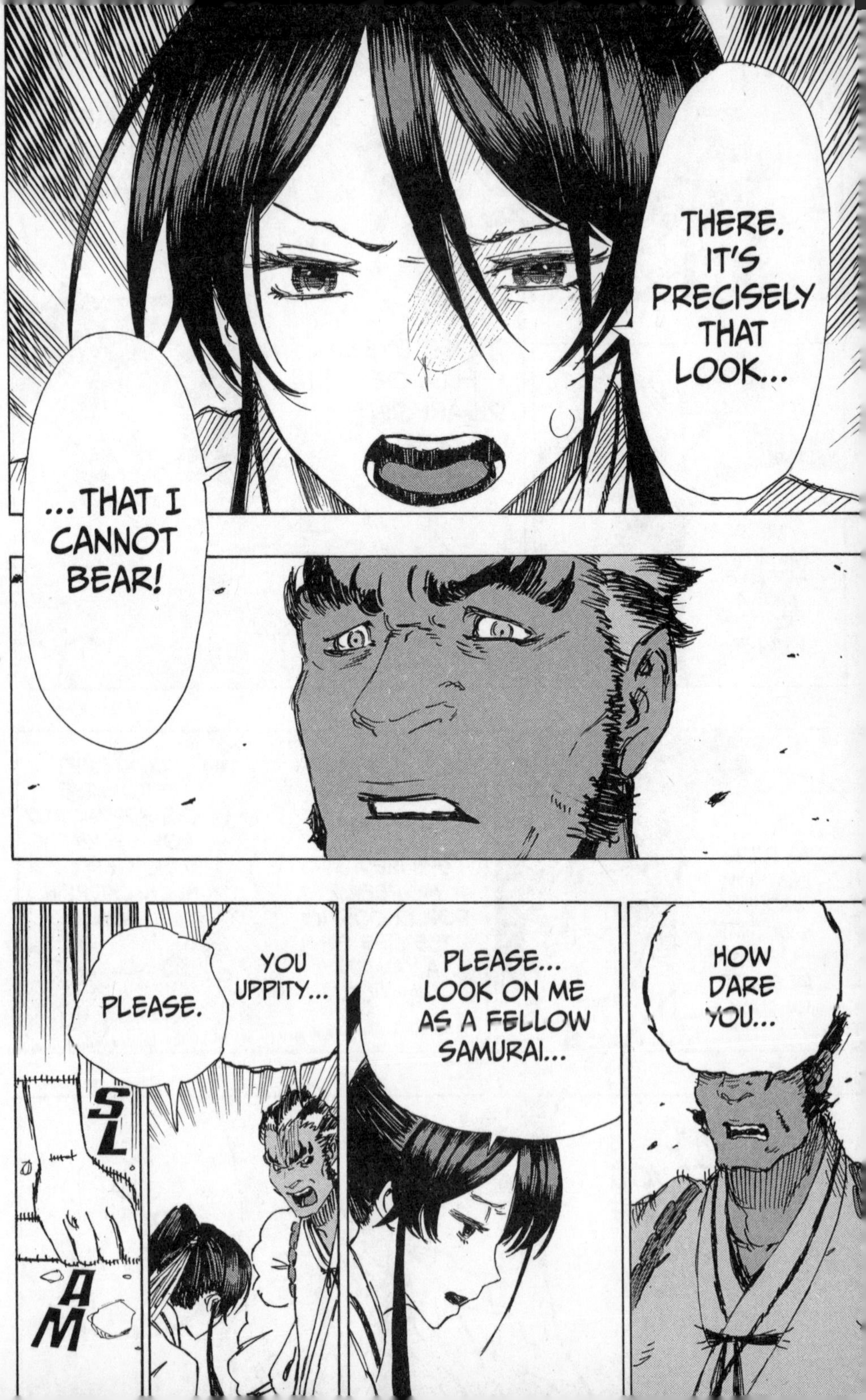
THERE. IT'S PRECISELY THAT LOOK...
...THAT I CANNOT BEAR!
HOW DARE YOU...
PLEASE... LOOK ON ME AS A FELLOW SAMURAI...
YOU UPPITY...
PLEASE.
SLAM

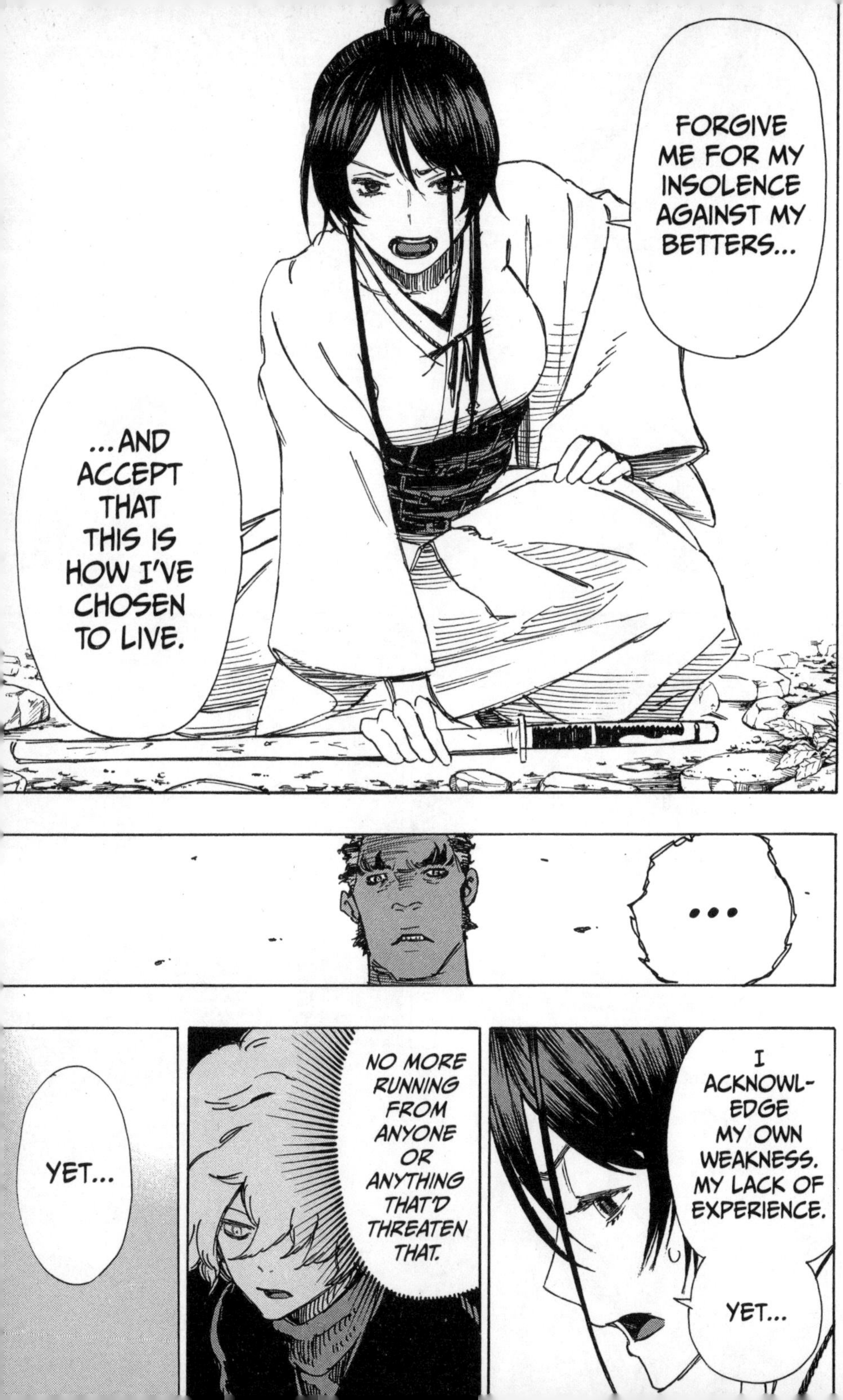
FORGIVE ME FOR MY INSOLENCE AGAINST MY BETTERS...
...AND ACCEPT THAT THIS IS HOW I'VE CHOSEN TO LIVE.
...
I ACKNOWL-EDGE MY OWN WEAKNESS. MY LACK OF EXPERIENCE.
YET...
NO MORE RUNNING FROM ANYONE OR ANYTHING THAT'D THREATEN THAT.
YET...

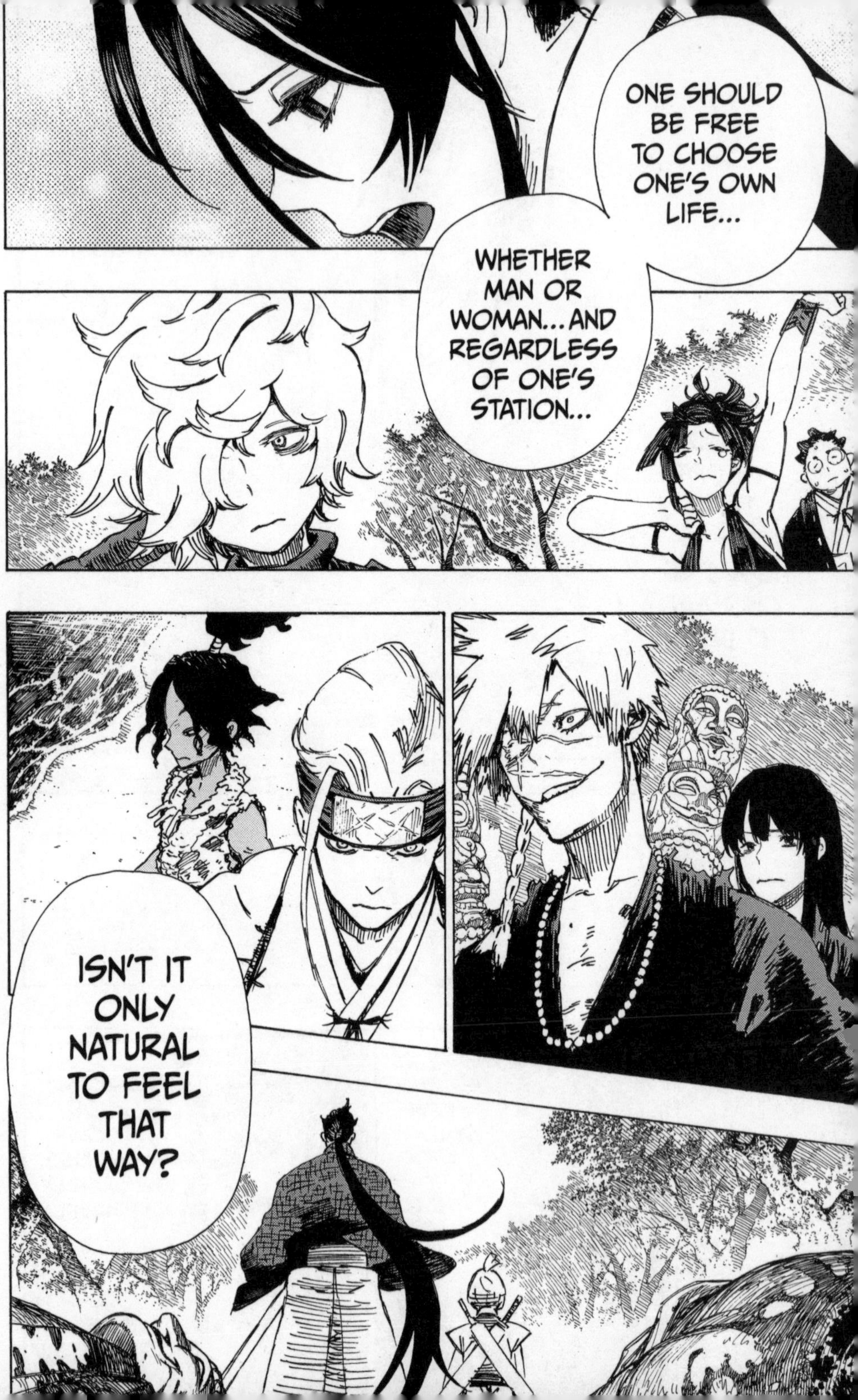
ONE SHOULD BE FREE TO CHOOSE ONE'S OWN LIFE...
WHETHER MAN OR WOMAN...AND REGARDLESS OF ONE'S STATION...
ISN'T IT ONLY NATURAL TO FEEL THAT WAY?

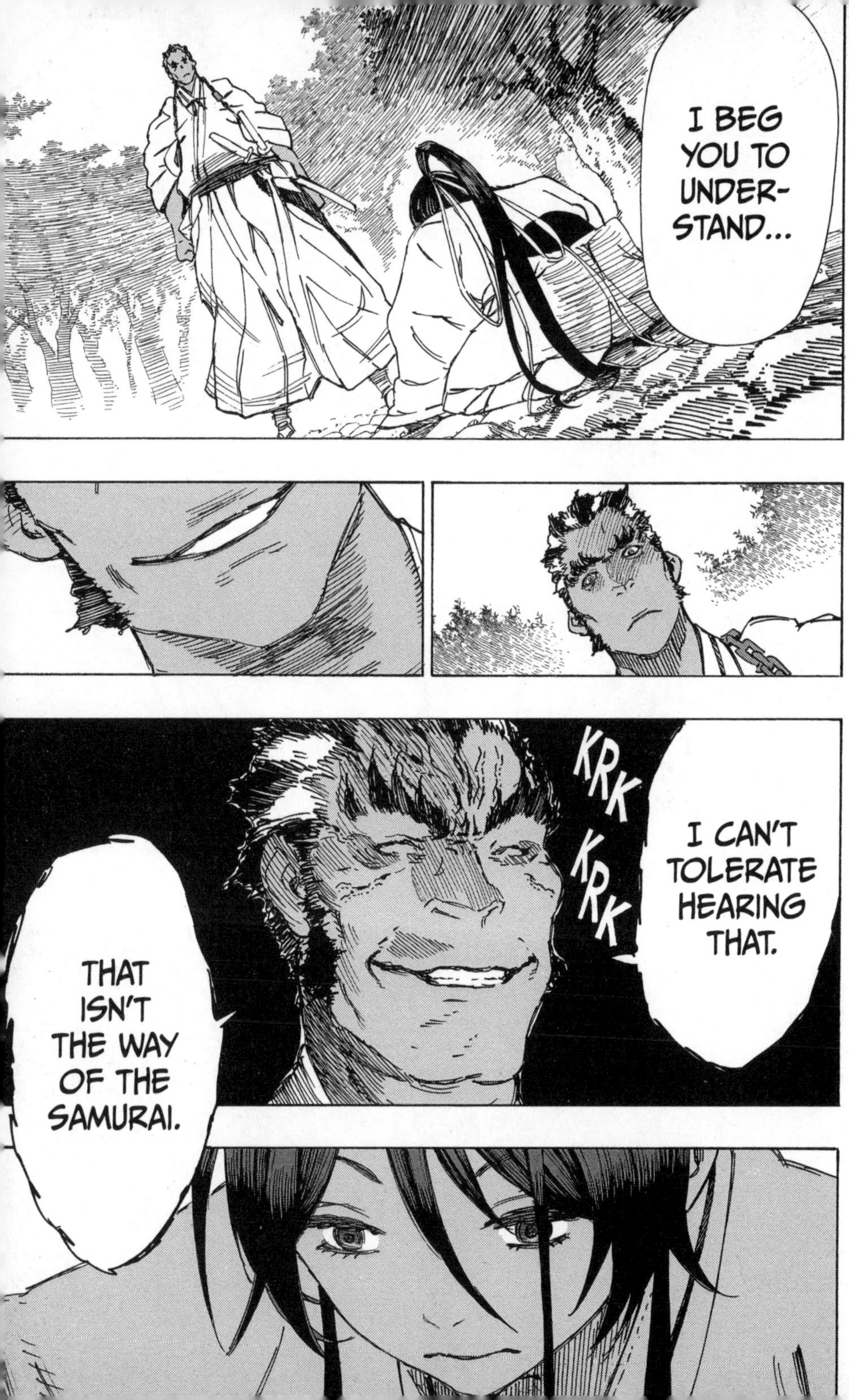
I BEG YOU TO UNDER-STAND...
KRK KRK KRK
I CAN'T TOLERATE HEARING THAT.
THAT ISN'T THE WAY OF THE SAMURAI.

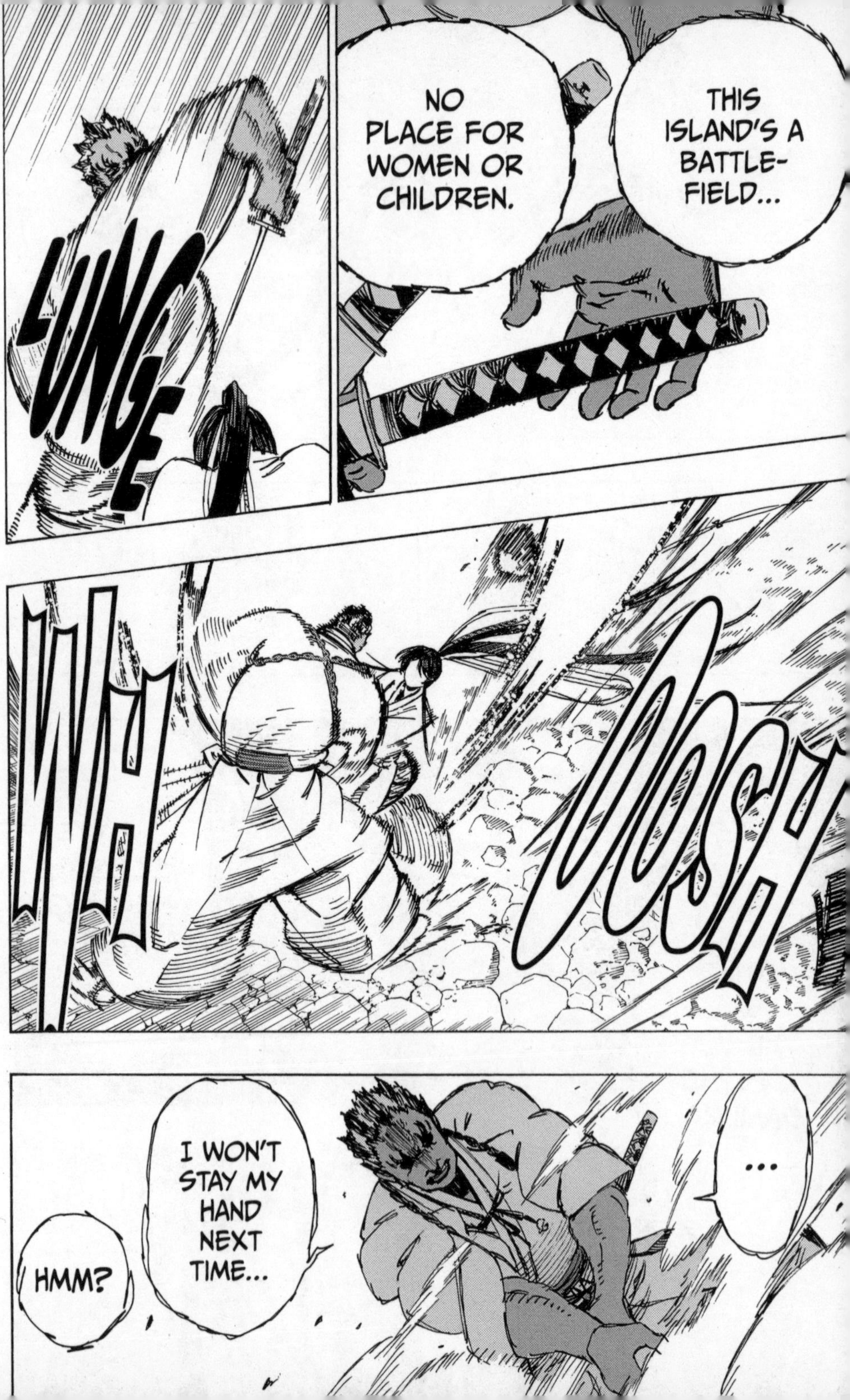
THIS ISLAND'S A BATTLE-FIELD...
NO PLACE FOR WOMEN OR CHILDREN.
LUNGE
WHOOSH
...
I WON'T STAY MY HAND NEXT TIME...
HMM?

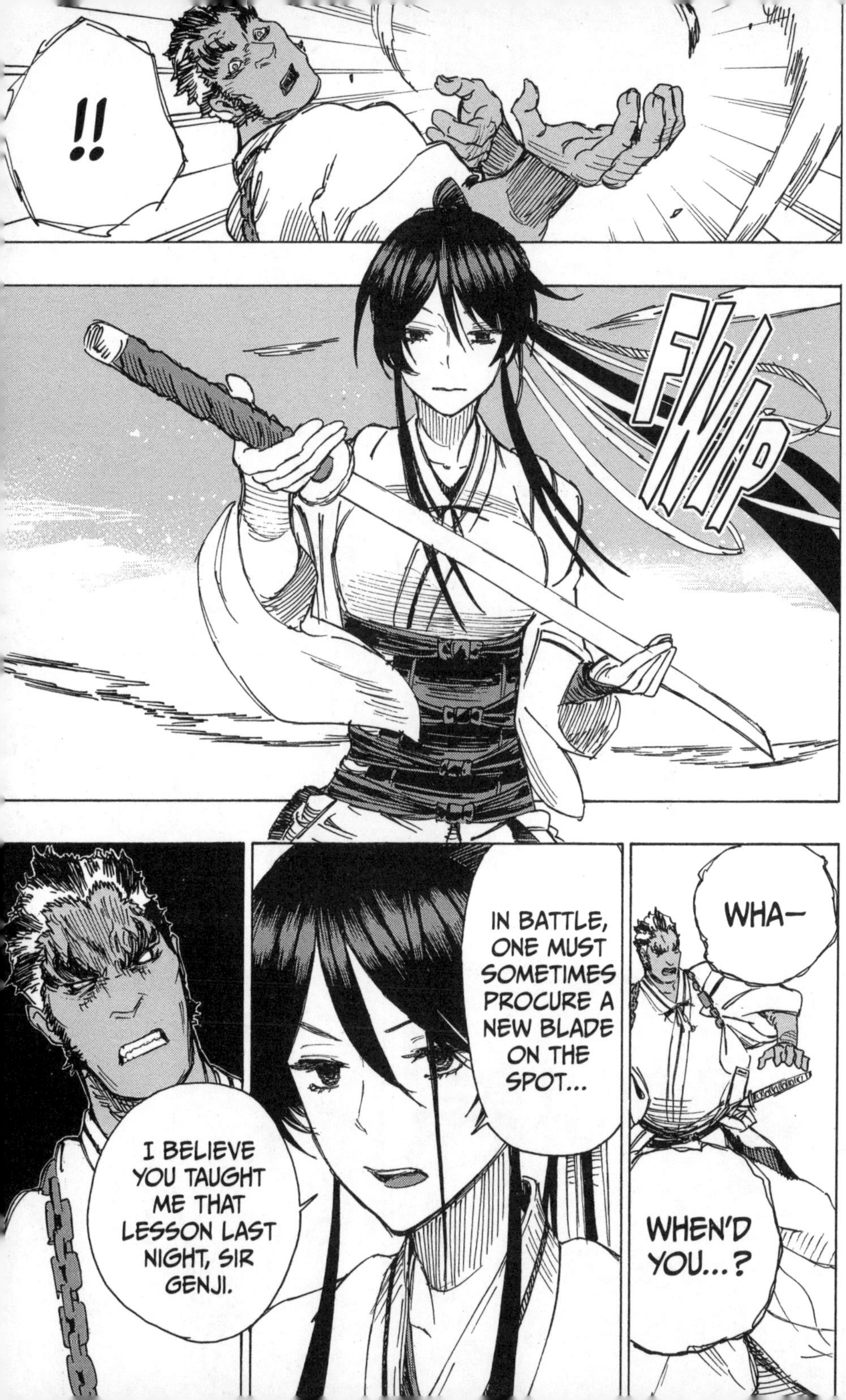
!!
FWIP
WHA—
WHEN'D YOU...?
IN BATTLE, ONE MUST SOMETIMES PROCURE A NEW BLADE ON THE SPOT...
I BELIEVE YOU TAUGHT ME THAT LESSON LAST NIGHT, SIR GENJI.

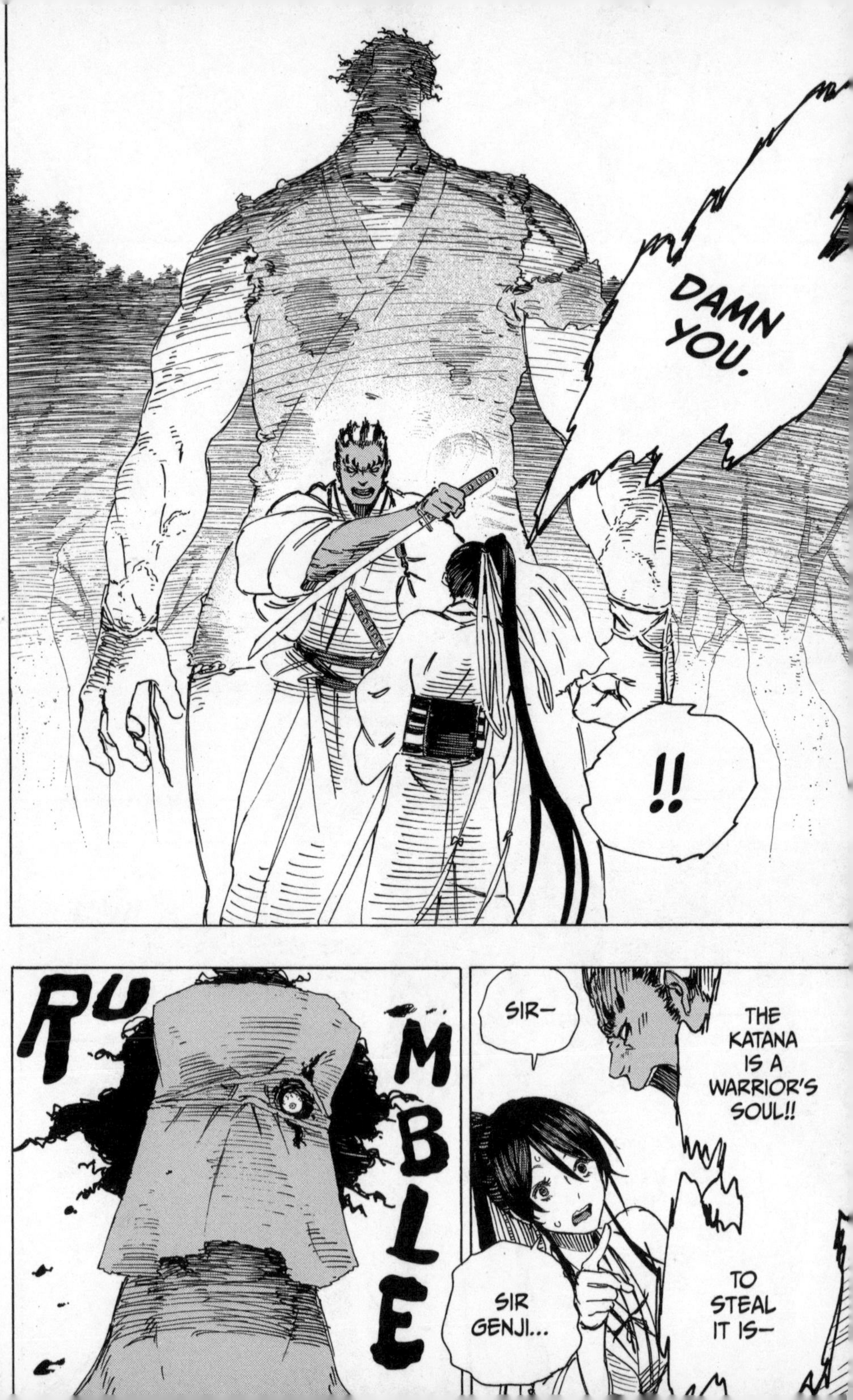
DAMN YOU.
!!
THE KATANA IS A WARRIOR'S SOUL!!
SIR—
TO STEAL IT IS—
SIR GENJI...
RUMBLE

Chapter 13

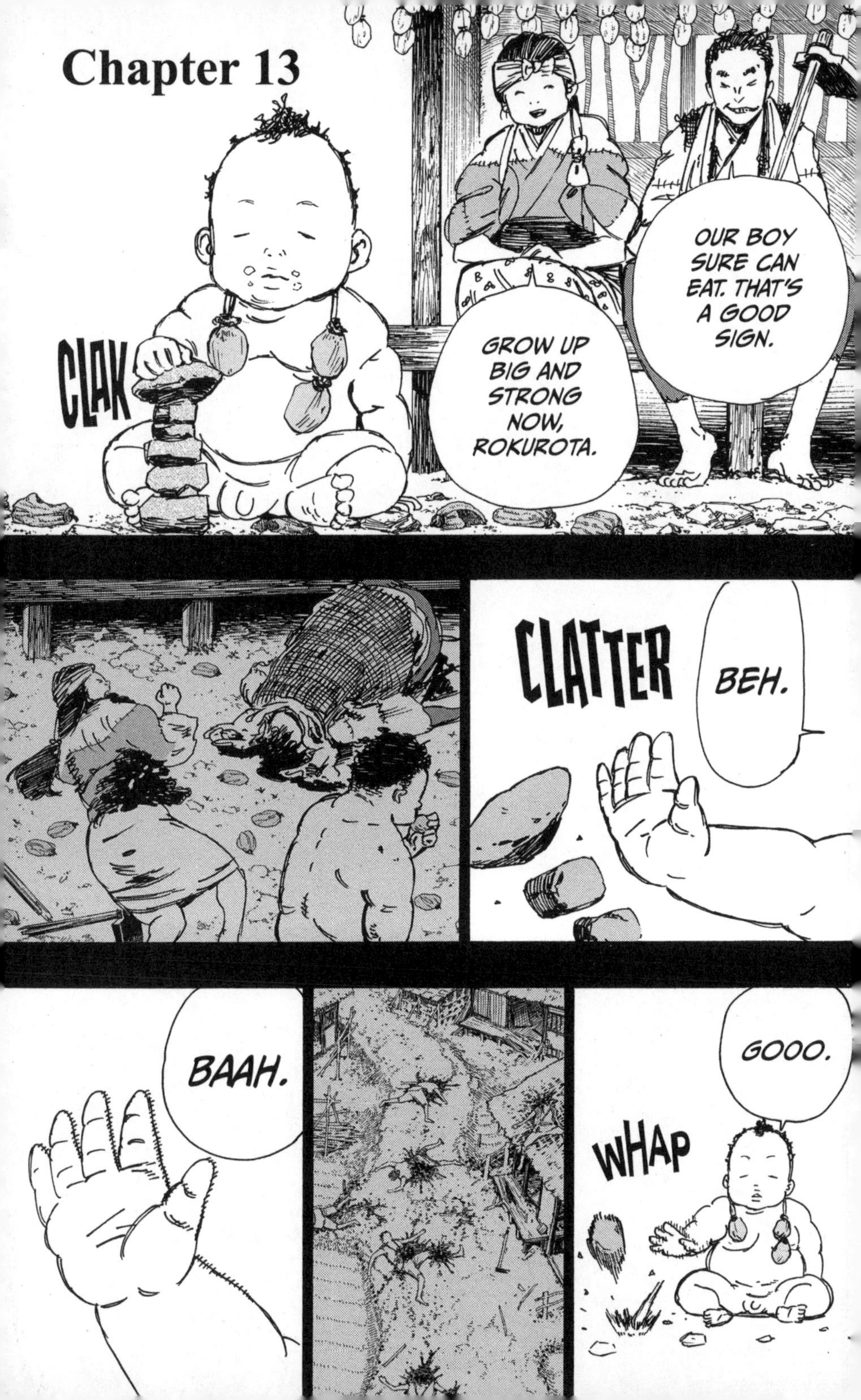
OUR BOY SURE CAN EAT. THAT'S A GOOD SIGN.
GROW UP BIG AND STRONG NOW, ROKUROTA.
CLAK
CLATTER
BEH.
GOOO.
WHAP
BAAH.

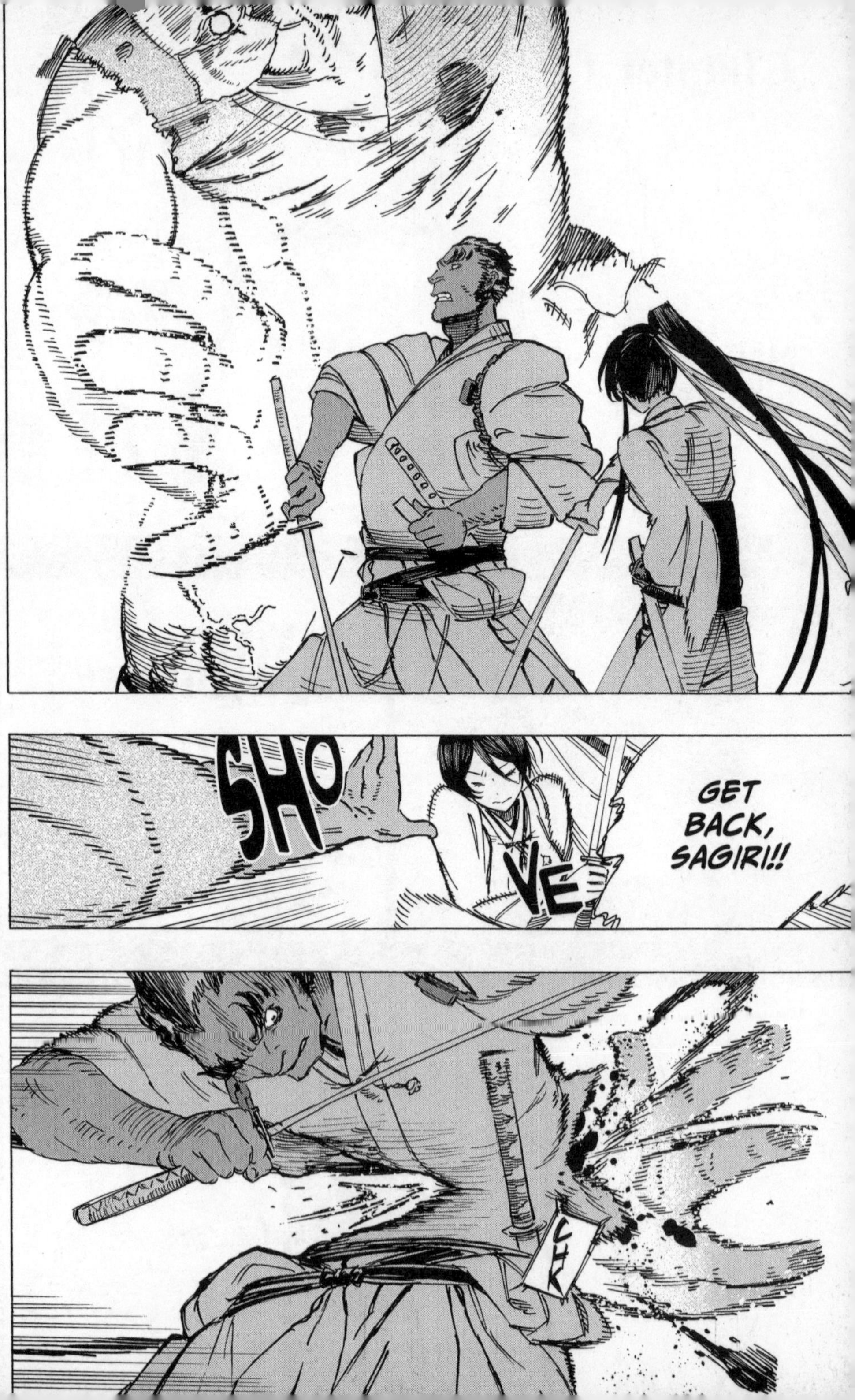
GET BACK, SAGIRI!!
SHOVE
CHK

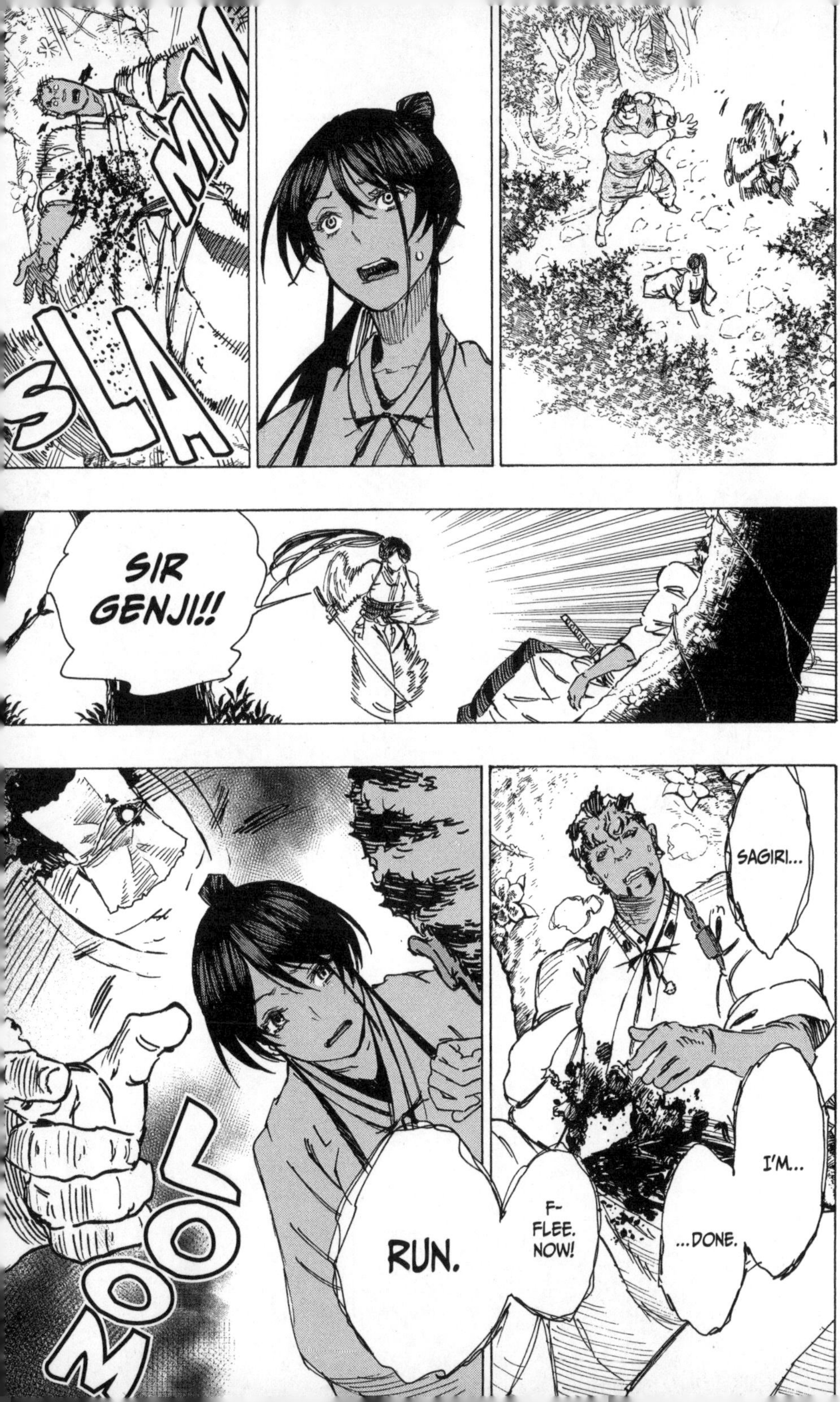
SLAMM
SIR GENJI!!
SAGIRI...
I'M...
...DONE.
F- FLEE. NOW!
RUN.
VOOM

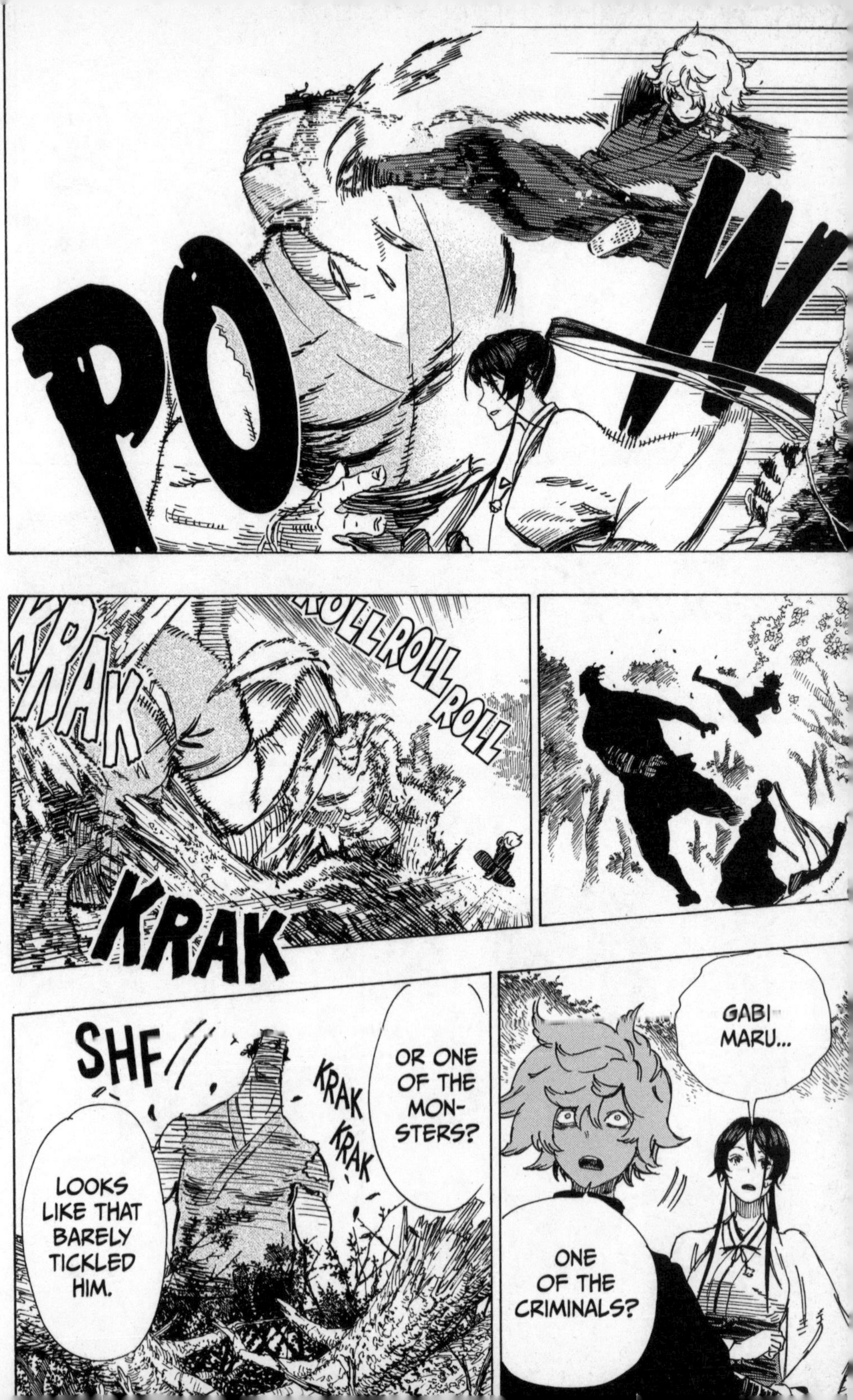
POW
ROLL ROLL ROLL
KRAK
KRAK
GABI-MARU...
ONE OF THE CRIMINALS?
OR ONE OF THE MON-STERS?
KRAK KRAK
SHF
LOOKS LIKE THAT BARELY TICKLED HIM.

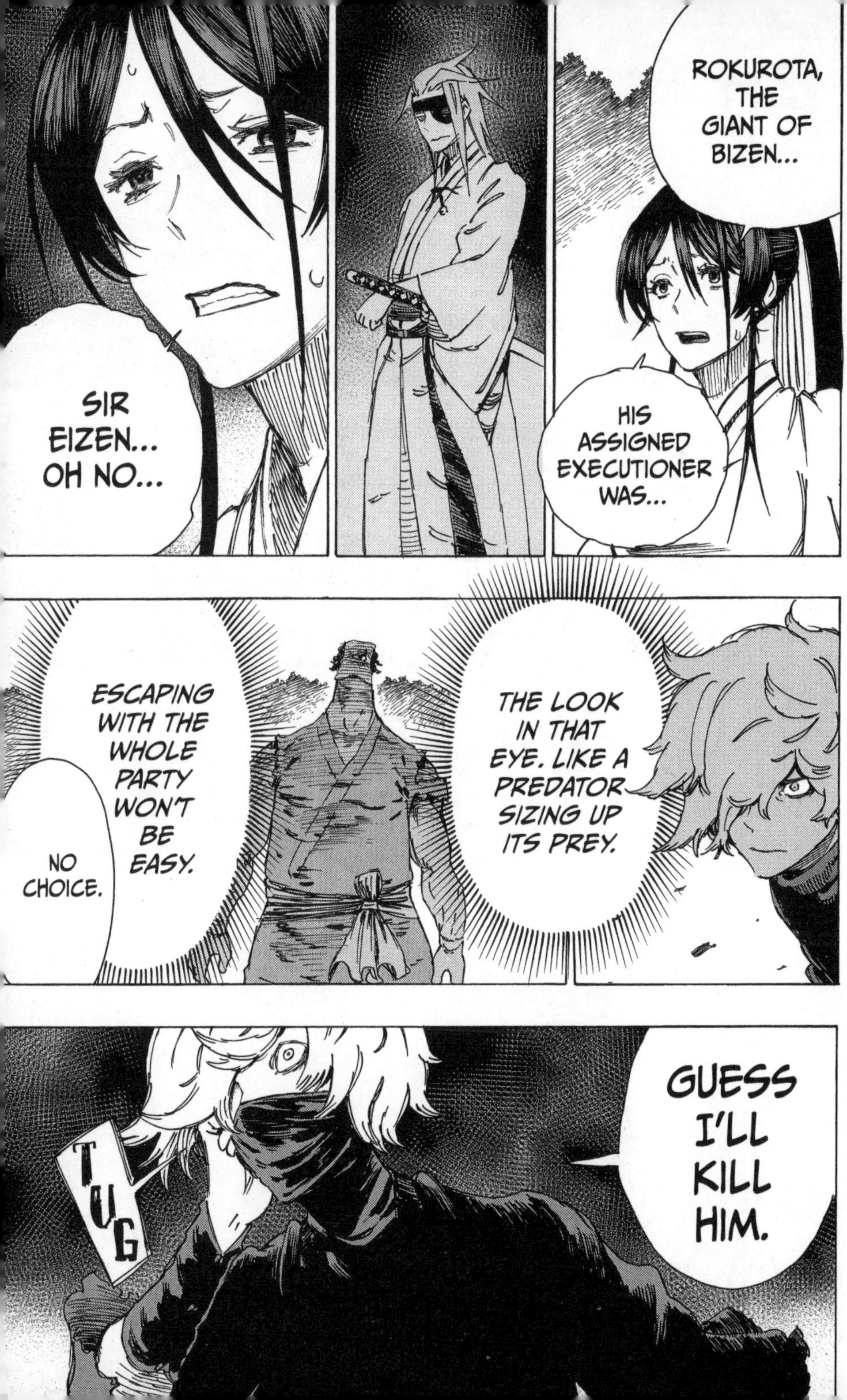
ROKUROTA, THE GIANT OF BIZEN...
HIS ASSIGNED EXECUTIONER WAS...
SIR EIZEN... OH NO...
THE LOOK IN THAT EYE. LIKE A PREDATOR SIZING UP ITS PREY.
ESCAPING WITH THE WHOLE PARTY WON'T BE EASY.
NO CHOICE.
GUESS I'LL KILL HIM.
TUG

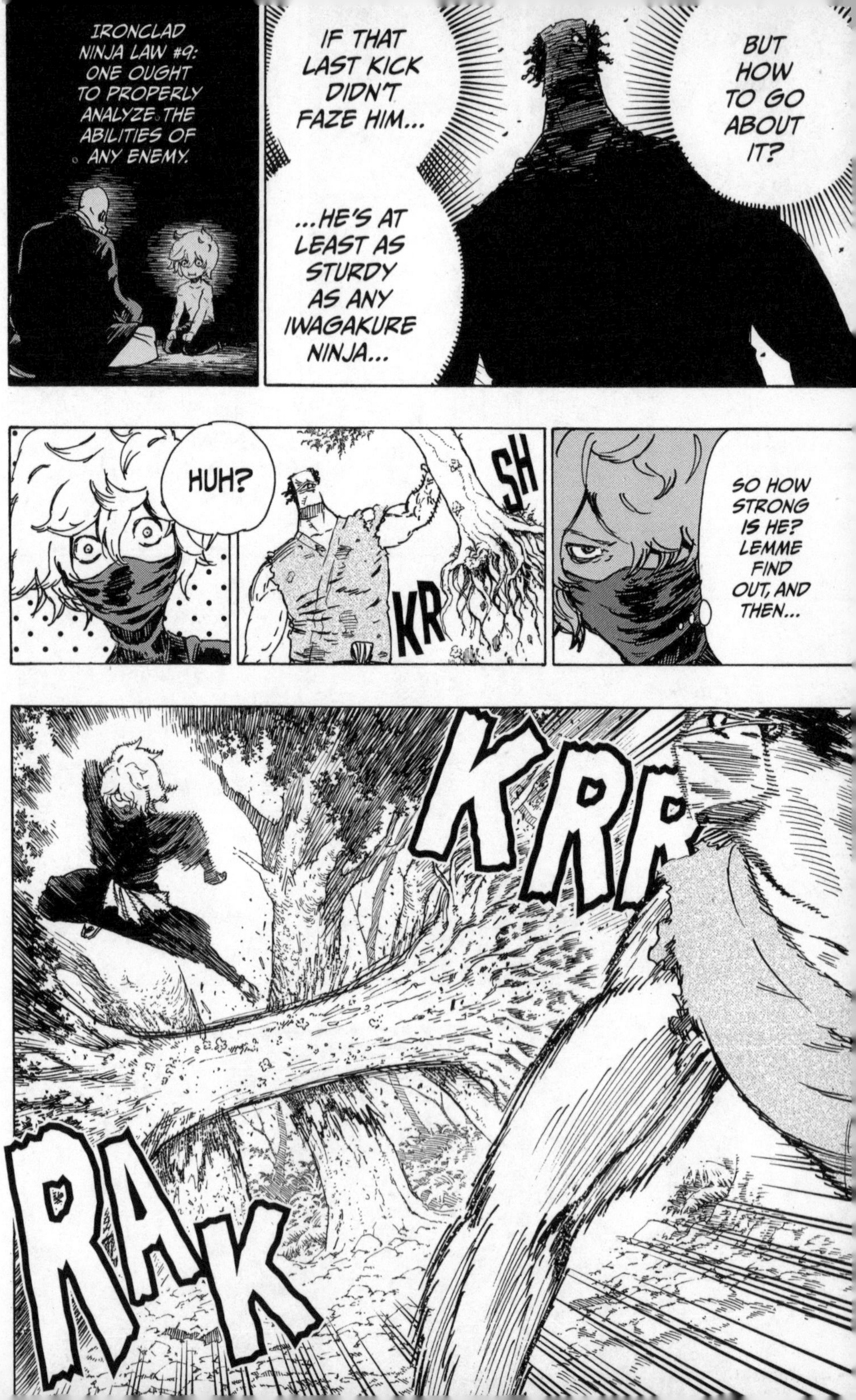
IF THAT LAST KICK DIDN'T FAZE HIM...
...HE'S AT LEAST AS STURDY AS ANY IWAGAKURE NINJA...
BUT HOW TO GO ABOUT IT?
IRONCLAD NINJA LAW #9: ONE OUGHT TO PROPERLY ANALYZE THE ABILITIES OF ANY ENEMY.
SO HOW STRONG IS HE? LEMME FIND OUT, AND THEN...
SH
KR
HUH?
KRRRAK

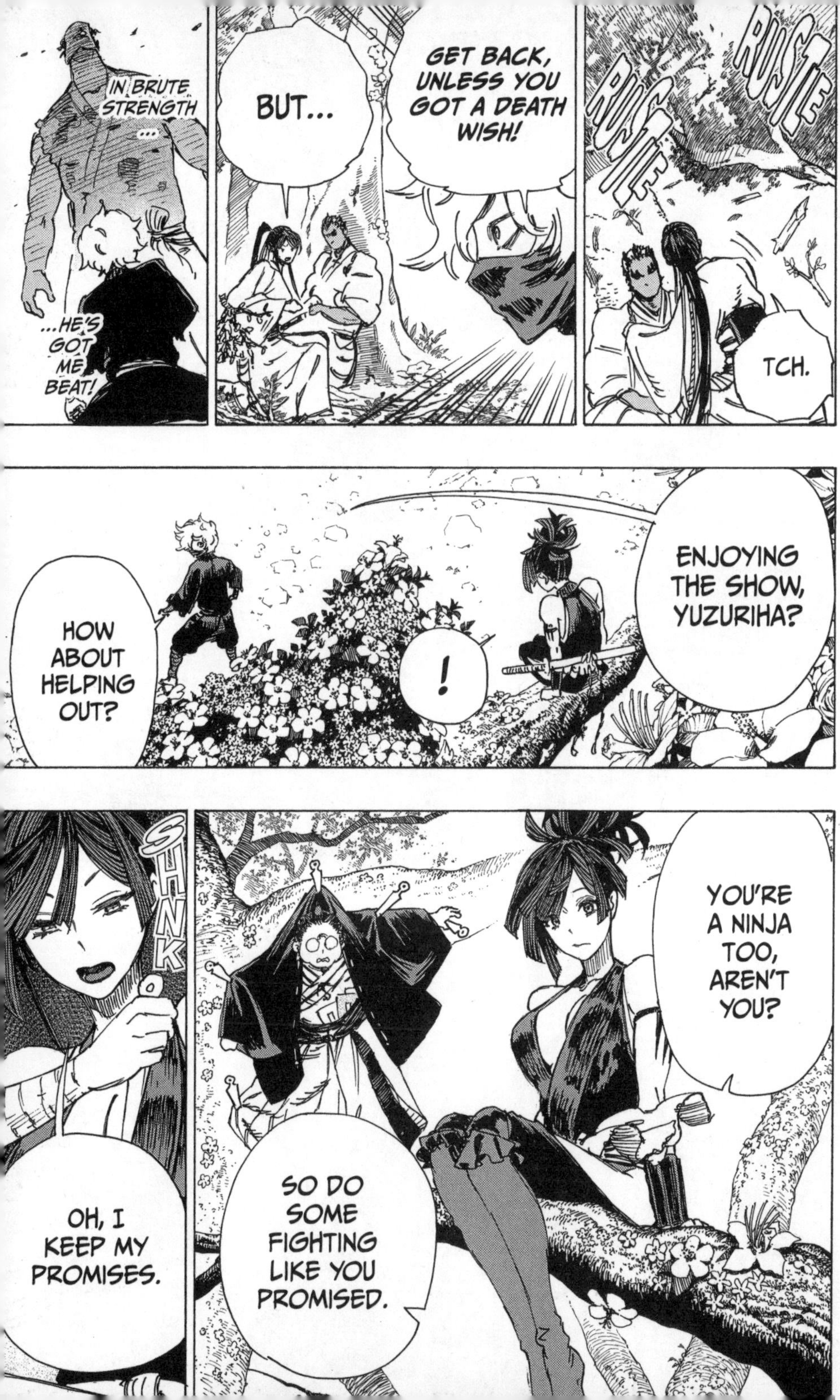
RUSTLE
RUSTLE
TCH.
GET BACK, UNLESS YOU GOT A DEATH WISH!
BUT...
IN BRUTE STRENGTH...
...HE'S GOT ME BEAT!
ENJOYING THE SHOW, YUZURIHA?
!
HOW ABOUT HELPING OUT?
YOU'RE A NINJA TOO, AREN'T YOU?
SO DO SOME FIGHTING LIKE YOU PROMISED.
SHNK
OH, I KEEP MY PROMISES.

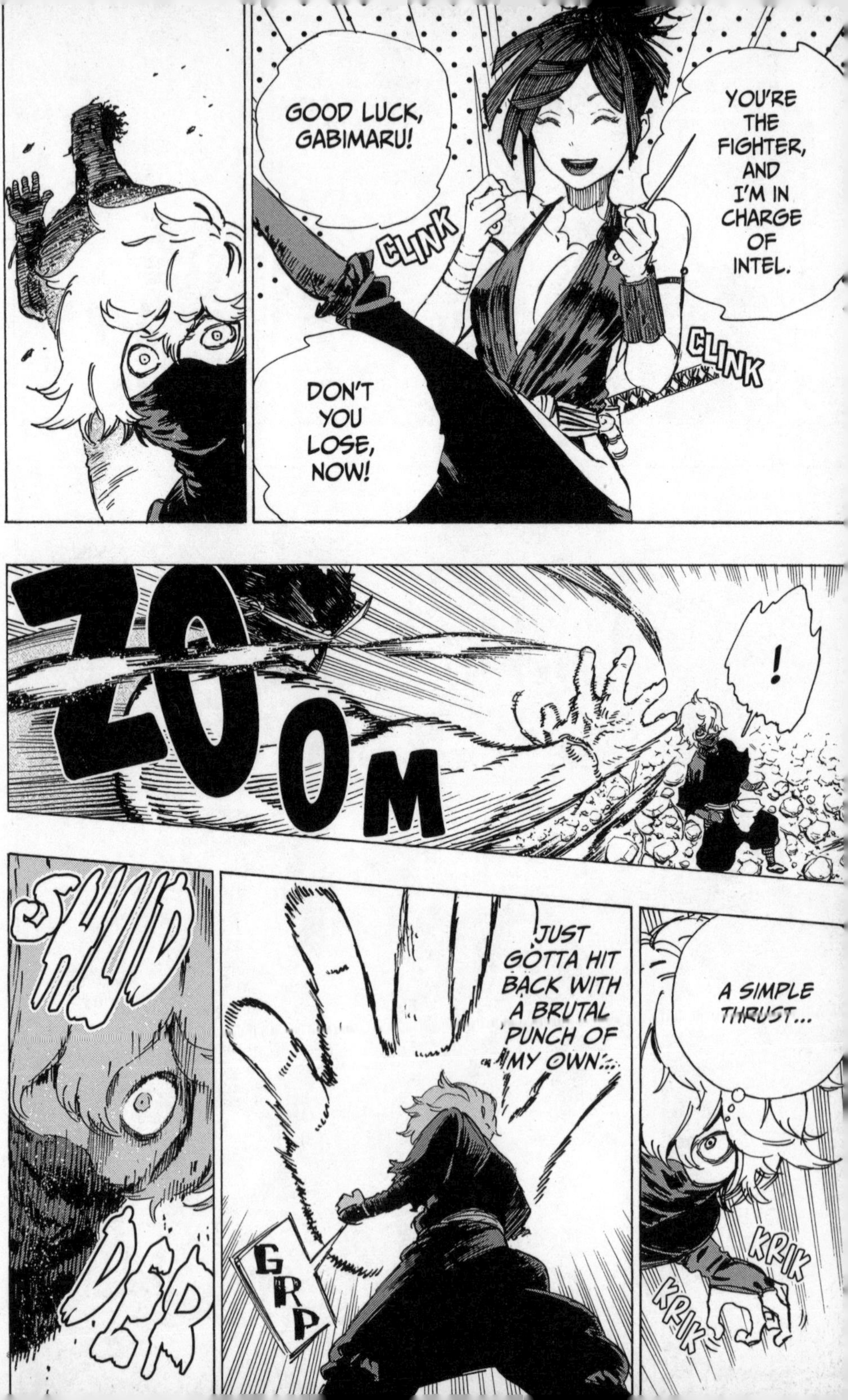
YOU'RE THE FIGHTER, AND I'M IN CHARGE OF INTEL.
GOOD LUCK, GABIMARU!
CLINK
CLINK
DON'T YOU LOSE, NOW!
!
ZOOM
A SIMPLE THRUST...
KRIK
KRIK
JUST GOTTA HIT BACK WITH A BRUTAL PUNCH OF MY OWN...
GRP
SHUD
DER

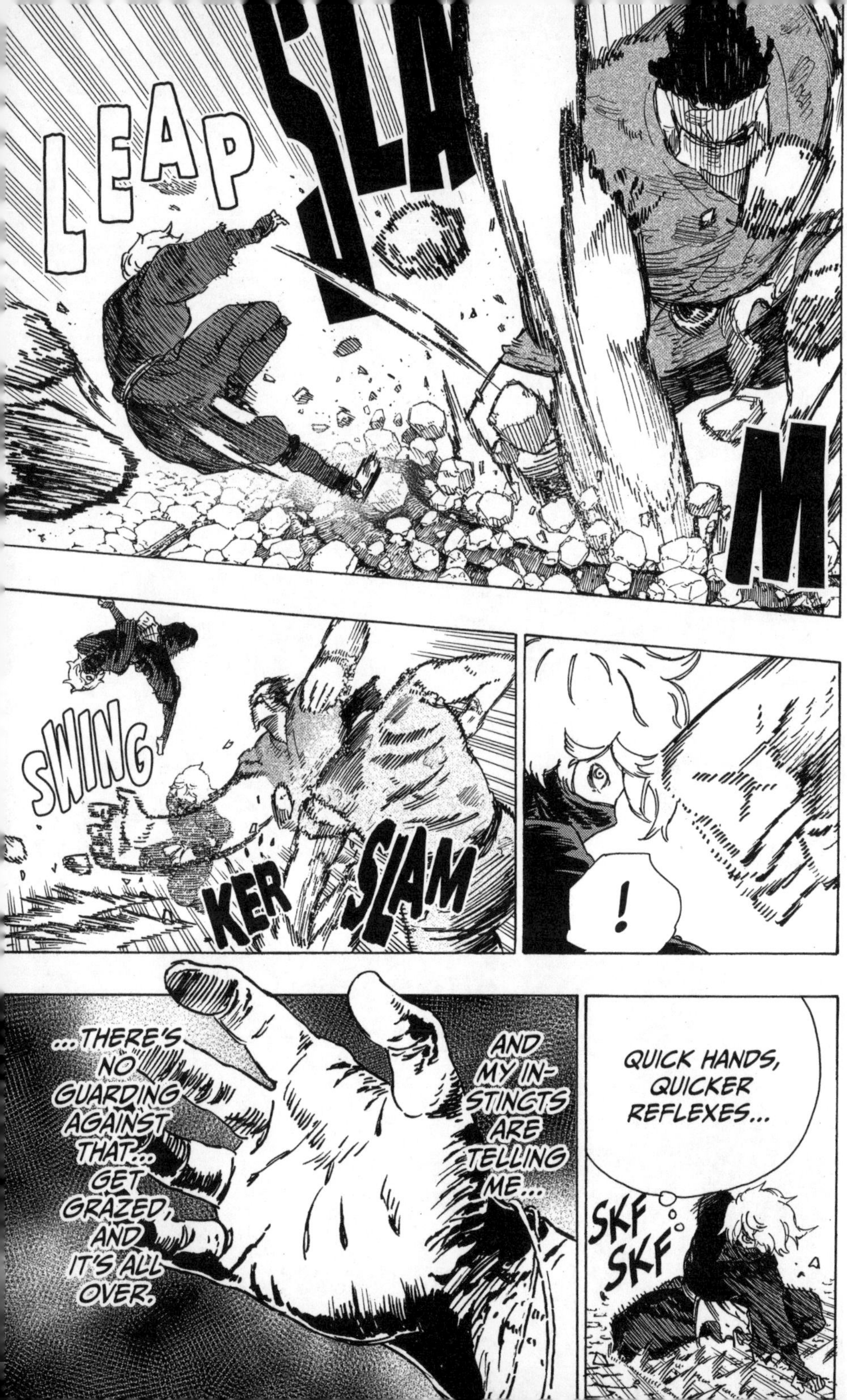
LEAP
SLAM
!
SWING
KER SLAM
QUICK HANDS, QUICKER REFLEXES...
SKF SKF
AND MY IN-STINCTS ARE TELLING ME...
...THERE'S NO GUARDING AGAINST THAT... GET GRAZED, AND IT'S ALL OVER.

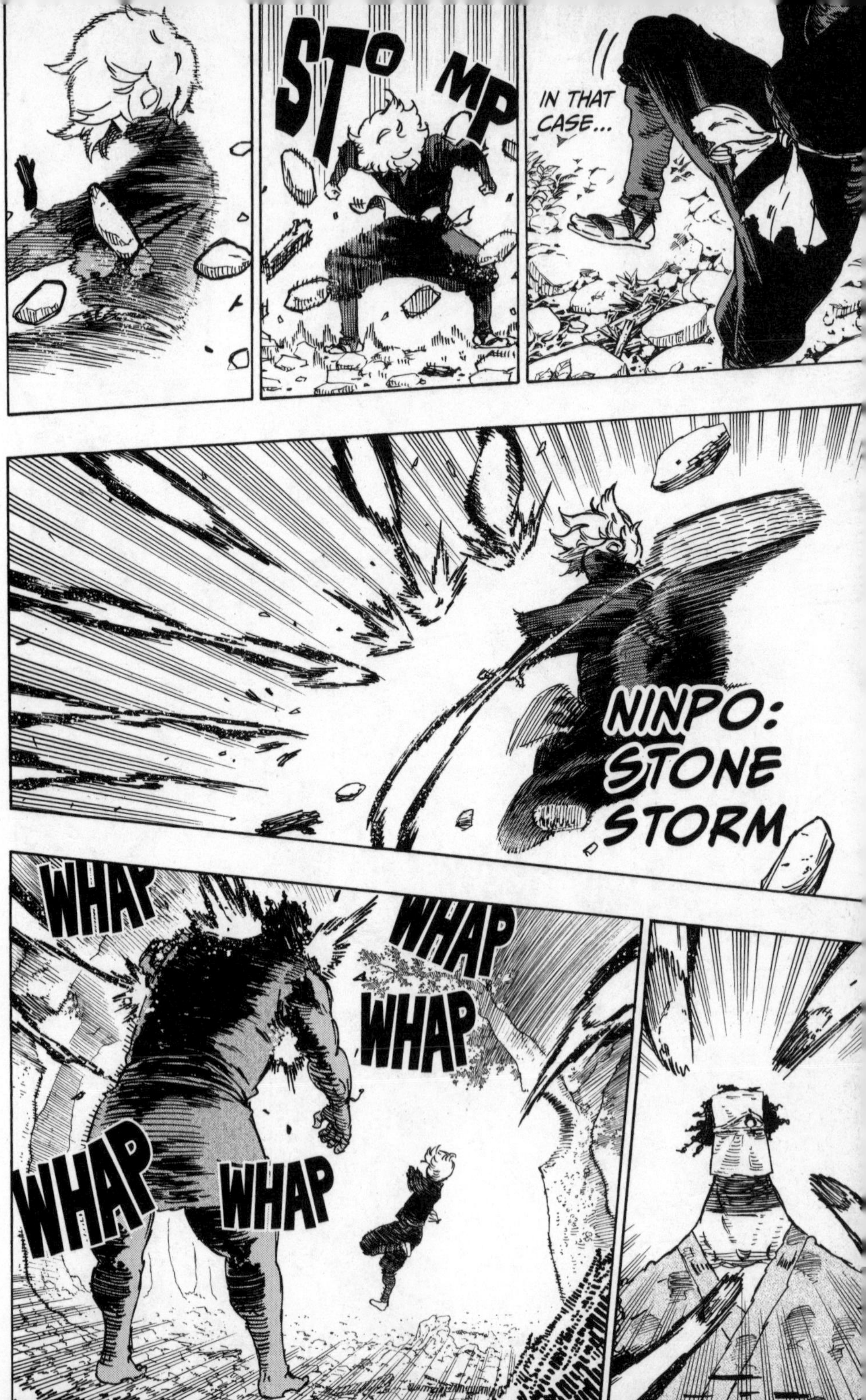
IN THAT CASE...
STOMP
NINPO: STONE STORM
WHAP
WHAP
WHAP
WHAP
WHAP

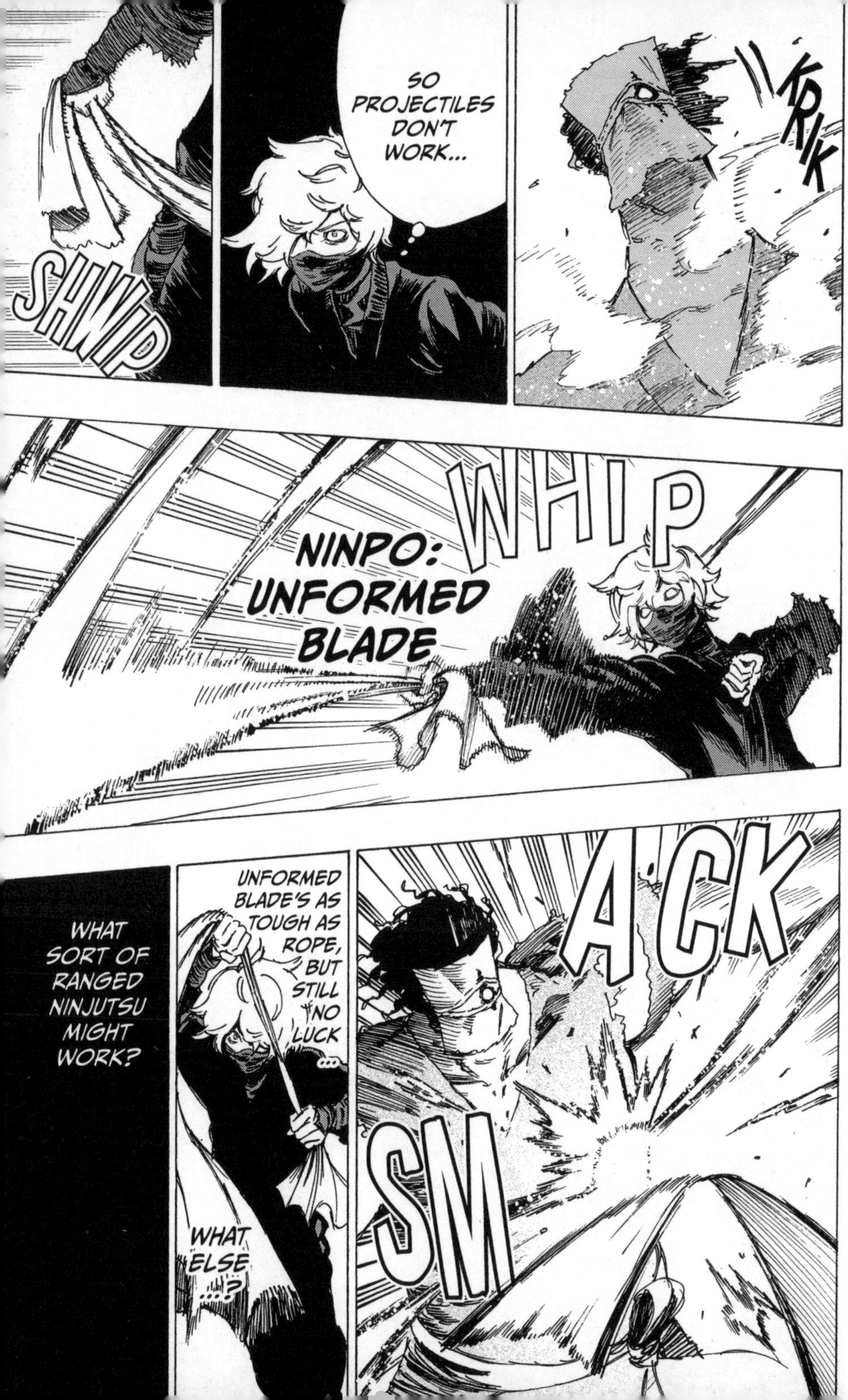

KRIK
SO PROJECTILES DON'T WORK...
SHWIP
WHIP
NINPO: UNFORMED BLADE
SMACK
UNFORMED BLADE'S AS TOUGH AS ROPE, BUT STILL NO LUCK
...
WHAT ELSE ...?
WHAT SORT OF RANGED NINJUTSU MIGHT WORK?

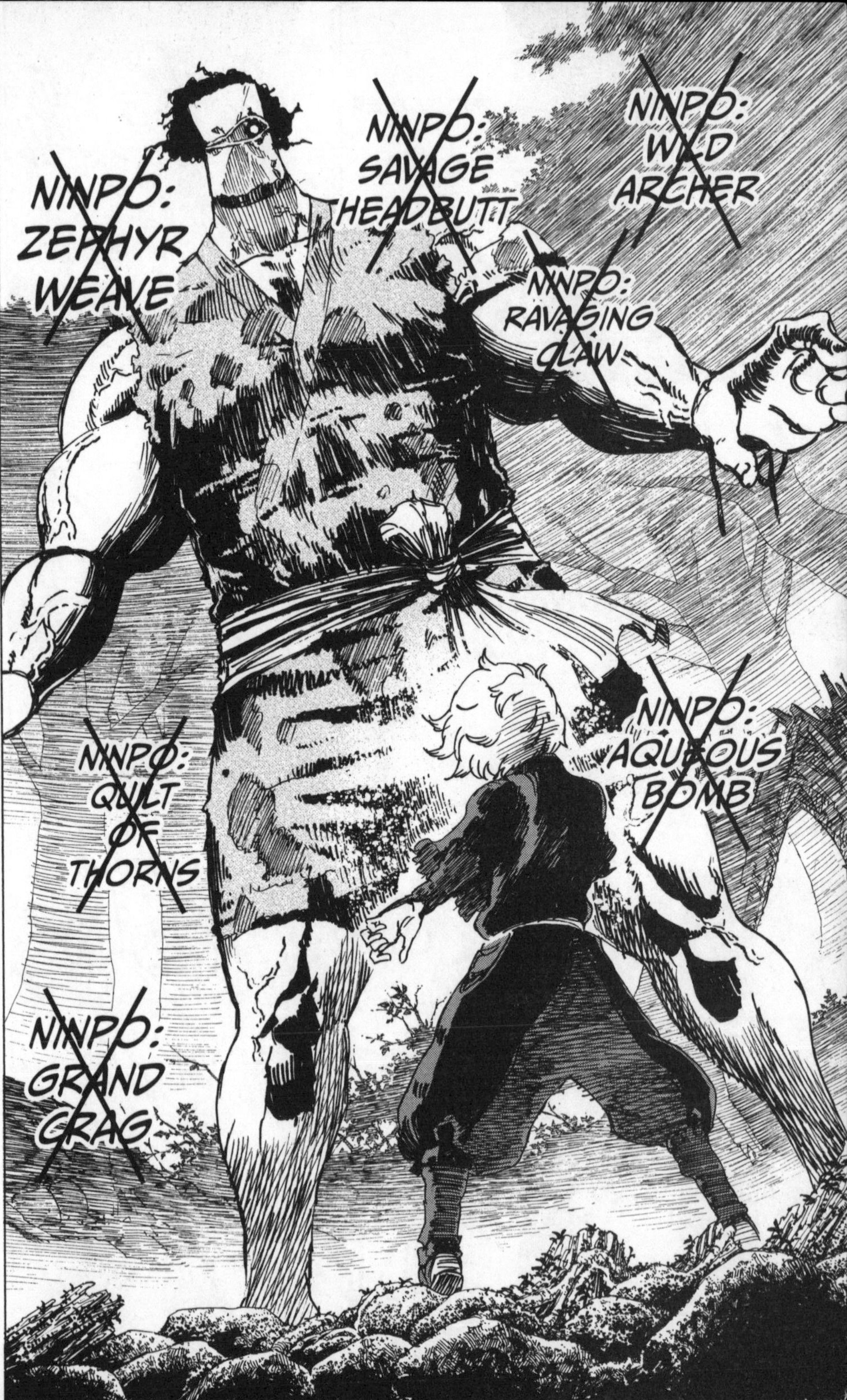
NINPO: WILD ARCHER
NINPO: SAVAGE HEADBUTT
NINPO: ZEPHYR WEAVE
NINPO: RAVAGING CLAW
NINPO: AQUEOUS BOMB
NINPO: QUILT OF THORNS
NINPO: GRAND CRAG

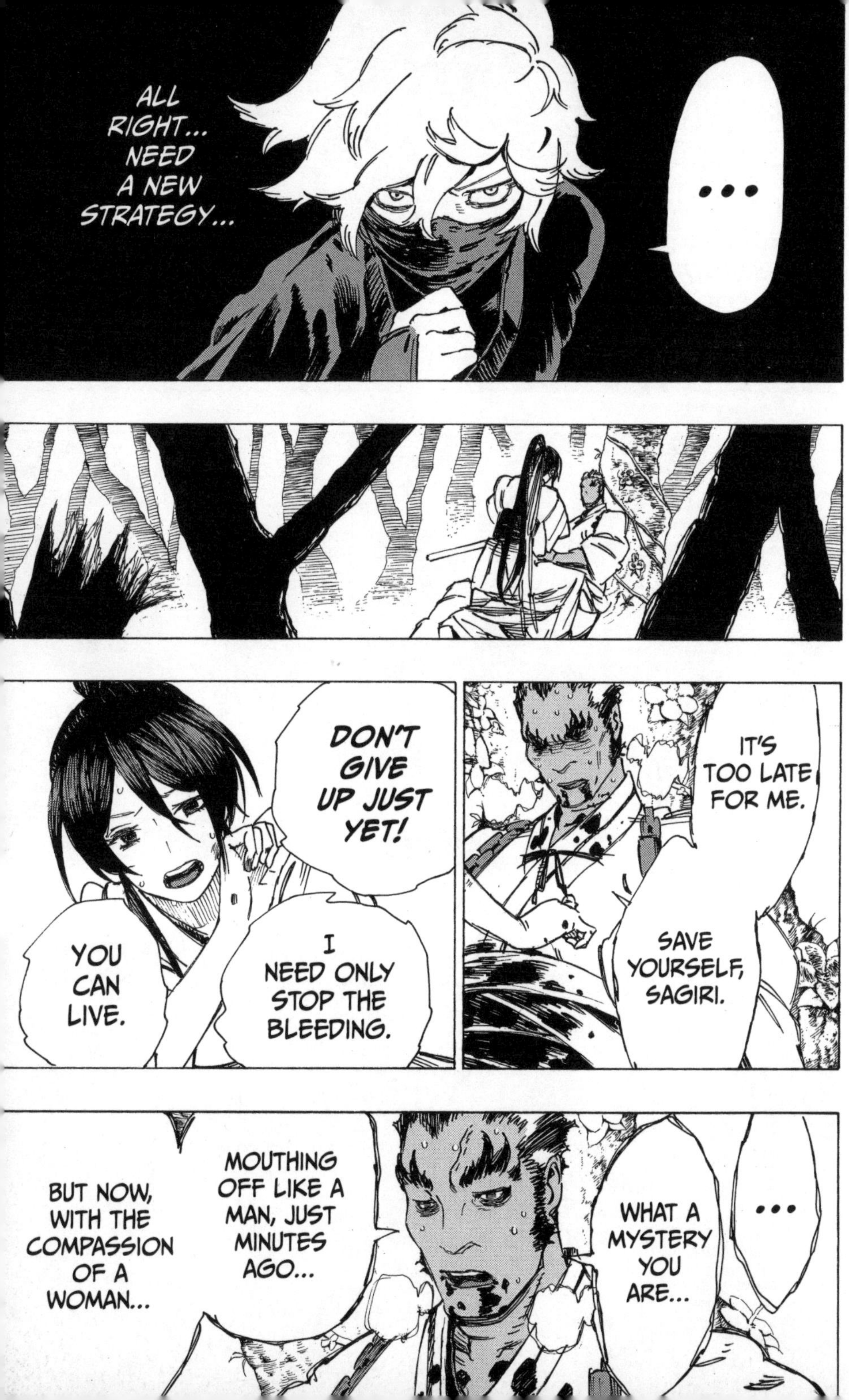
...
ALL RIGHT... NEED A NEW STRATEGY...
IT'S TOO LATE FOR ME.
SAVE YOURSELF, SAGIRI.
DON'T GIVE UP JUST YET!
I NEED ONLY STOP THE BLEEDING.
YOU CAN LIVE.
...
WHAT A MYSTERY YOU ARE...
MOUTHING OFF LIKE A MAN, JUST MINUTES AGO...
BUT NOW, WITH THE COMPASSION OF A WOMAN...

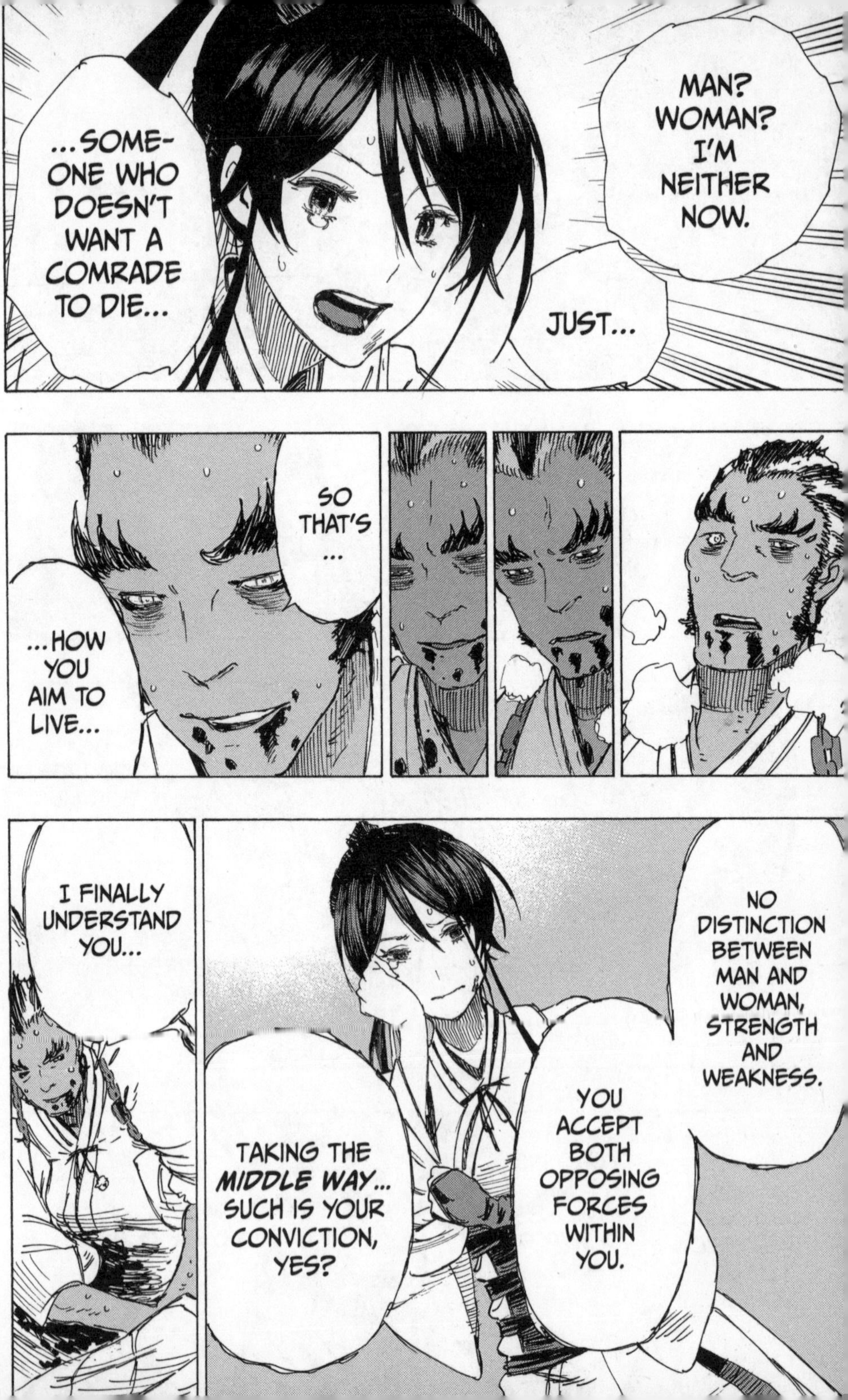
MAN? WOMAN? I'M NEITHER NOW.
JUST...
...SOME-ONE WHO DOESN'T WANT A COMRADE TO DIE...
SO THAT'S ...
...HOW YOU AIM TO LIVE...
NO DISTINCTION BETWEEN MAN AND WOMAN, STRENGTH AND WEAKNESS.
YOU ACCEPT BOTH OPPOSING FORCES WITHIN YOU.
TAKING THE *MIDDLE WAY*... SUCH IS YOUR CONVICTION, YES?
I FINALLY UNDERSTAND YOU...

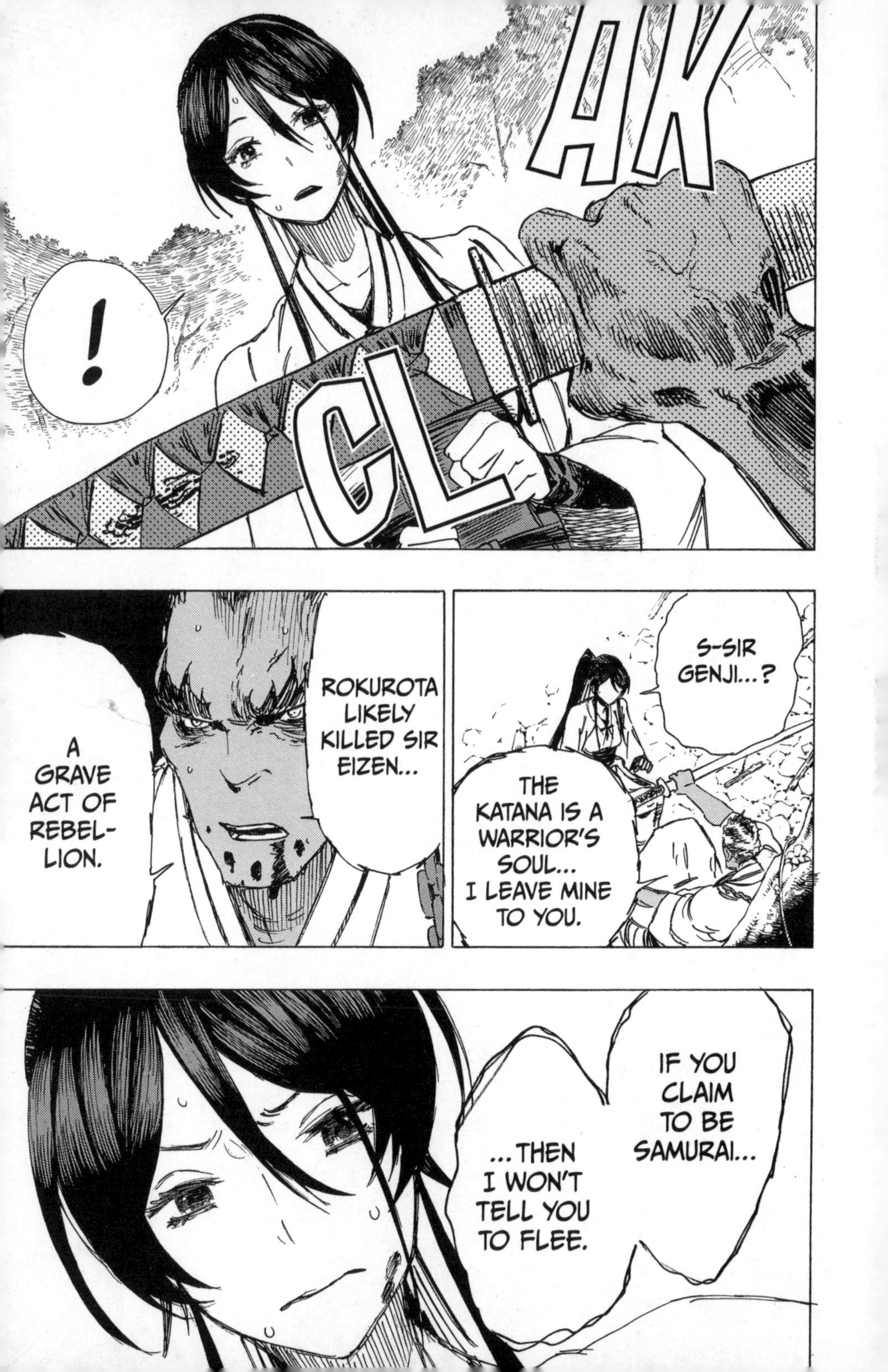
CLAK
!
S-SIR GENJI...?
THE KATANA IS A WARRIOR'S SOUL... I LEAVE MINE TO YOU.
ROKUROTA LIKELY KILLED SIR EIZEN...
A GRAVE ACT OF REBEL-LION.
IF YOU CLAIM TO BE SAMURAI...
...THEN I WON'T TELL YOU TO FLEE.

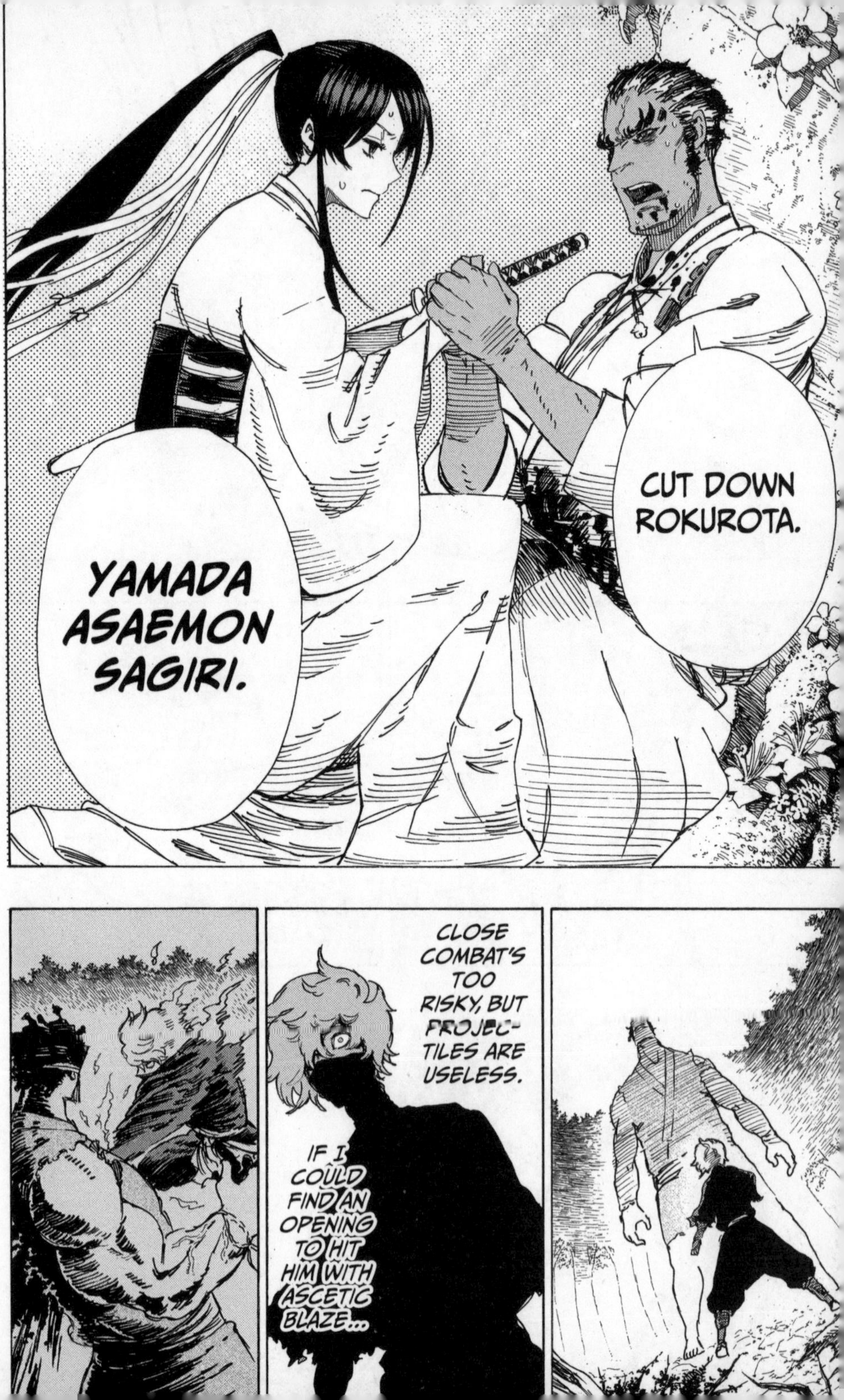
CUT DOWN ROKUROTA.
YAMADA ASAEMON SAGIRI.
CLOSE COMBAT'S TOO RISKY, BUT PROJEC-TILES ARE USELESS.
IF I COULD FIND AN OPENING TO HIT HIM WITH ASCETIC BLAZE...

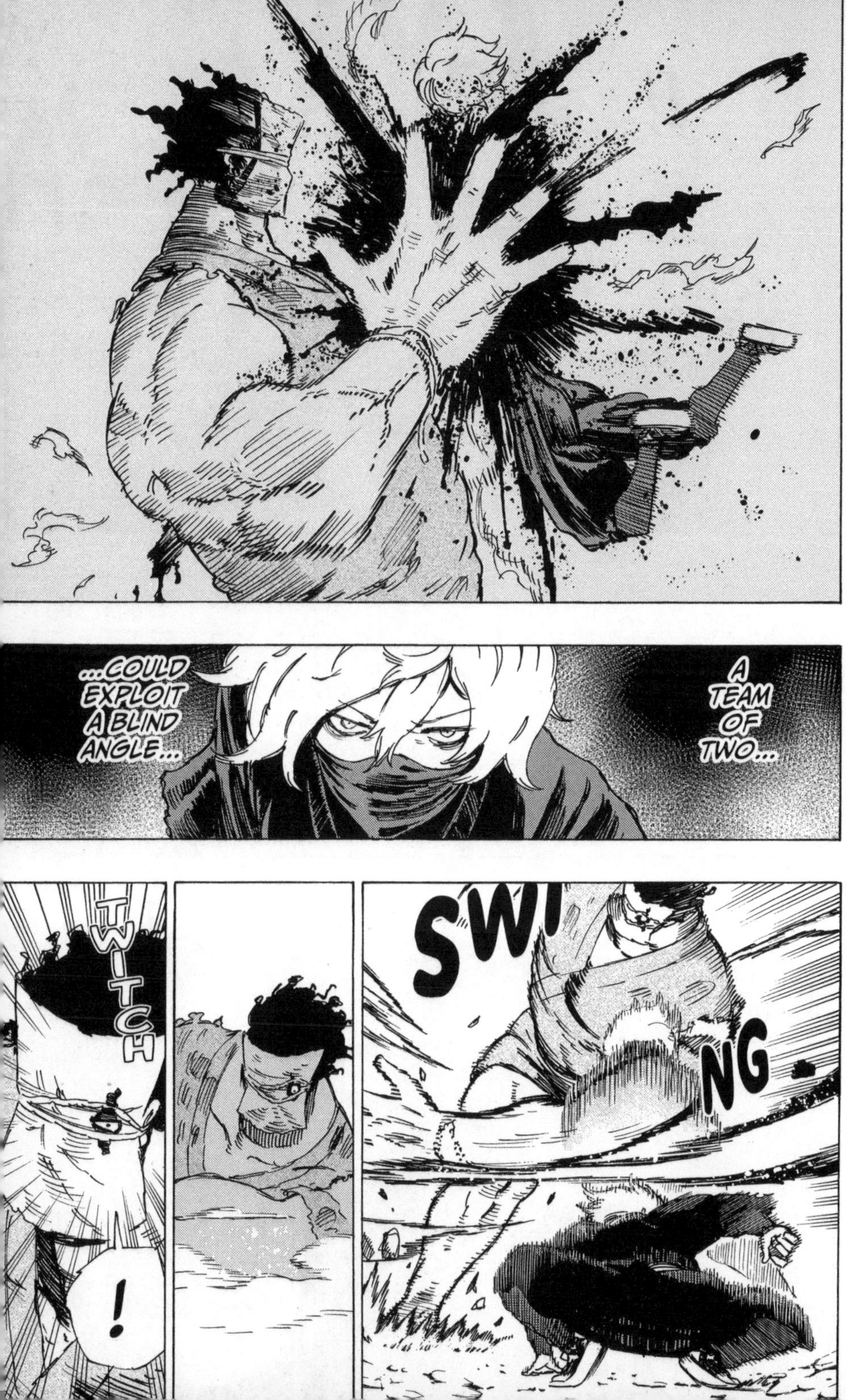
A TEAM OF TWO...
...COULD EXPLOIT A BLIND ANGLE...
SWI
NG
TWITCH
!

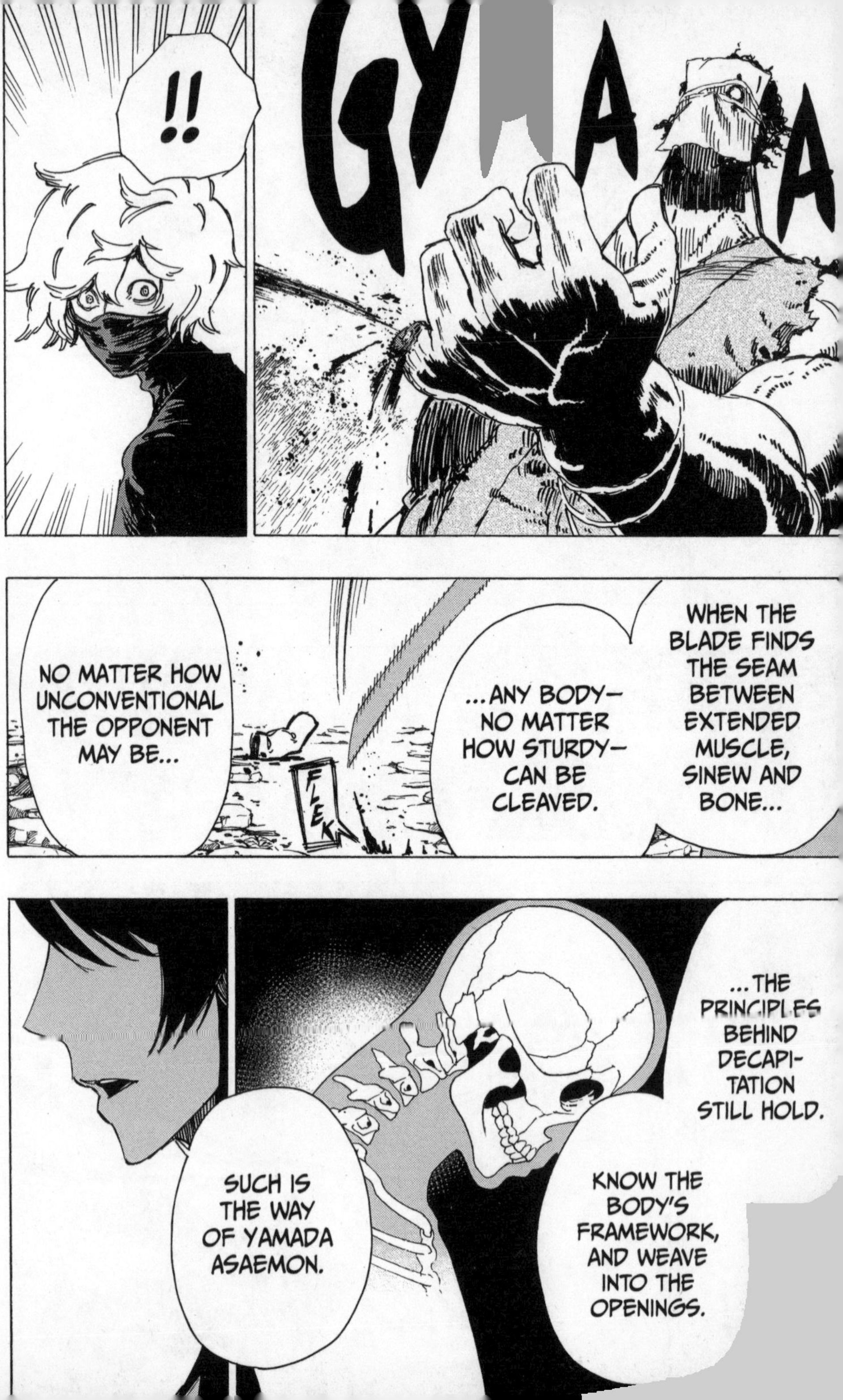
GY A A
!!
WHEN THE BLADE FINDS THE SEAM BETWEEN EXTENDED MUSCLE, SINEW AND BONE...
...ANY BODY—NO MATTER HOW STURDY—CAN BE CLEAVED.
FLEK
NO MATTER HOW UNCONVENTIONAL THE OPPONENT MAY BE...
...THE PRINCIPLES BEHIND DECAPI-TATION STILL HOLD.
KNOW THE BODY'S FRAMEWORK, AND WEAVE INTO THE OPENINGS.
SUCH IS THE WAY OF YAMADA ASAEMON.

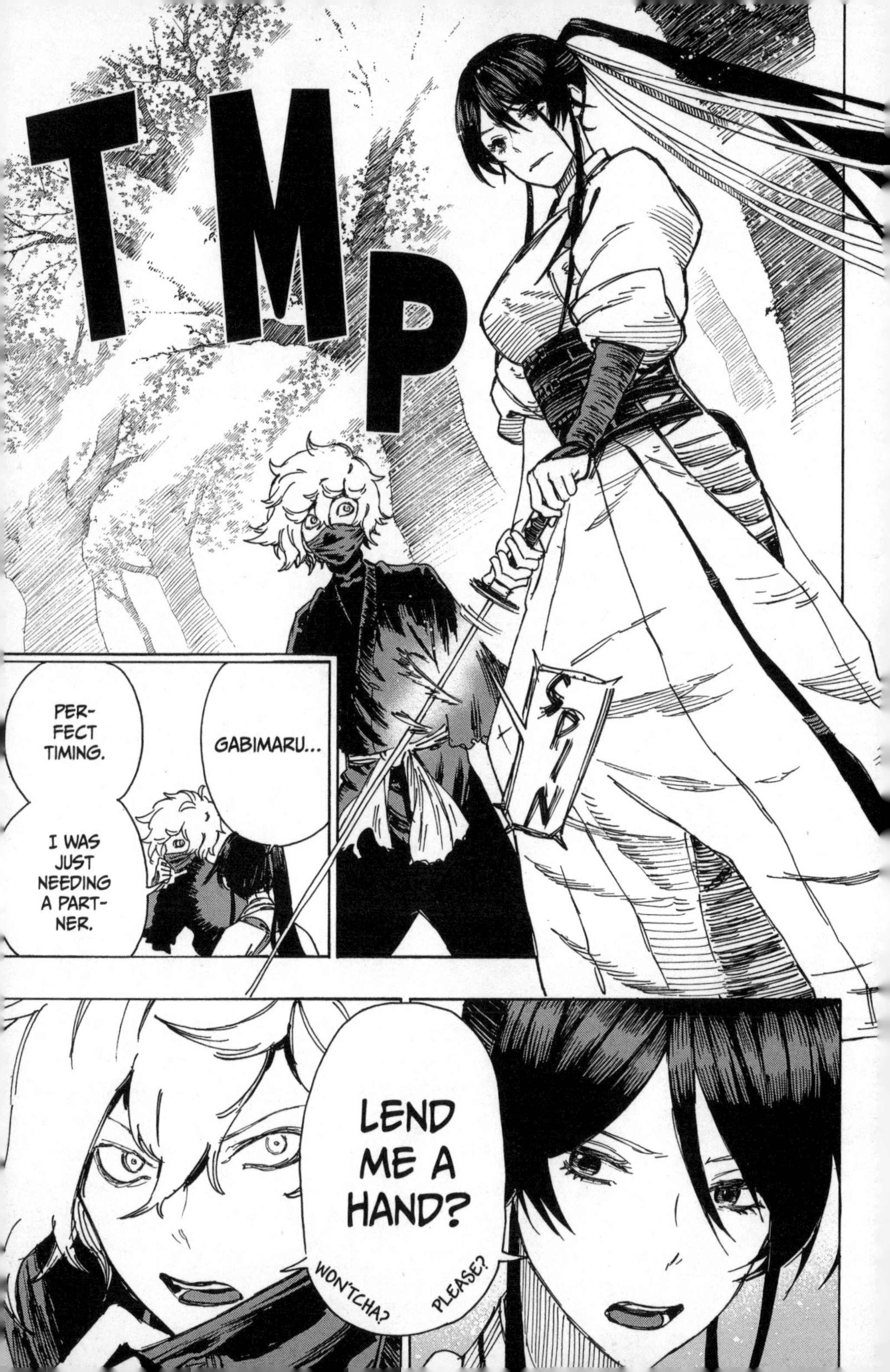
TMP
SPIN
GABIMARU...
PERFECT TIMING.
I WAS JUST NEEDING A PARTNER.
LEND ME A HAND?
PLEASE?
WON'TCHA?

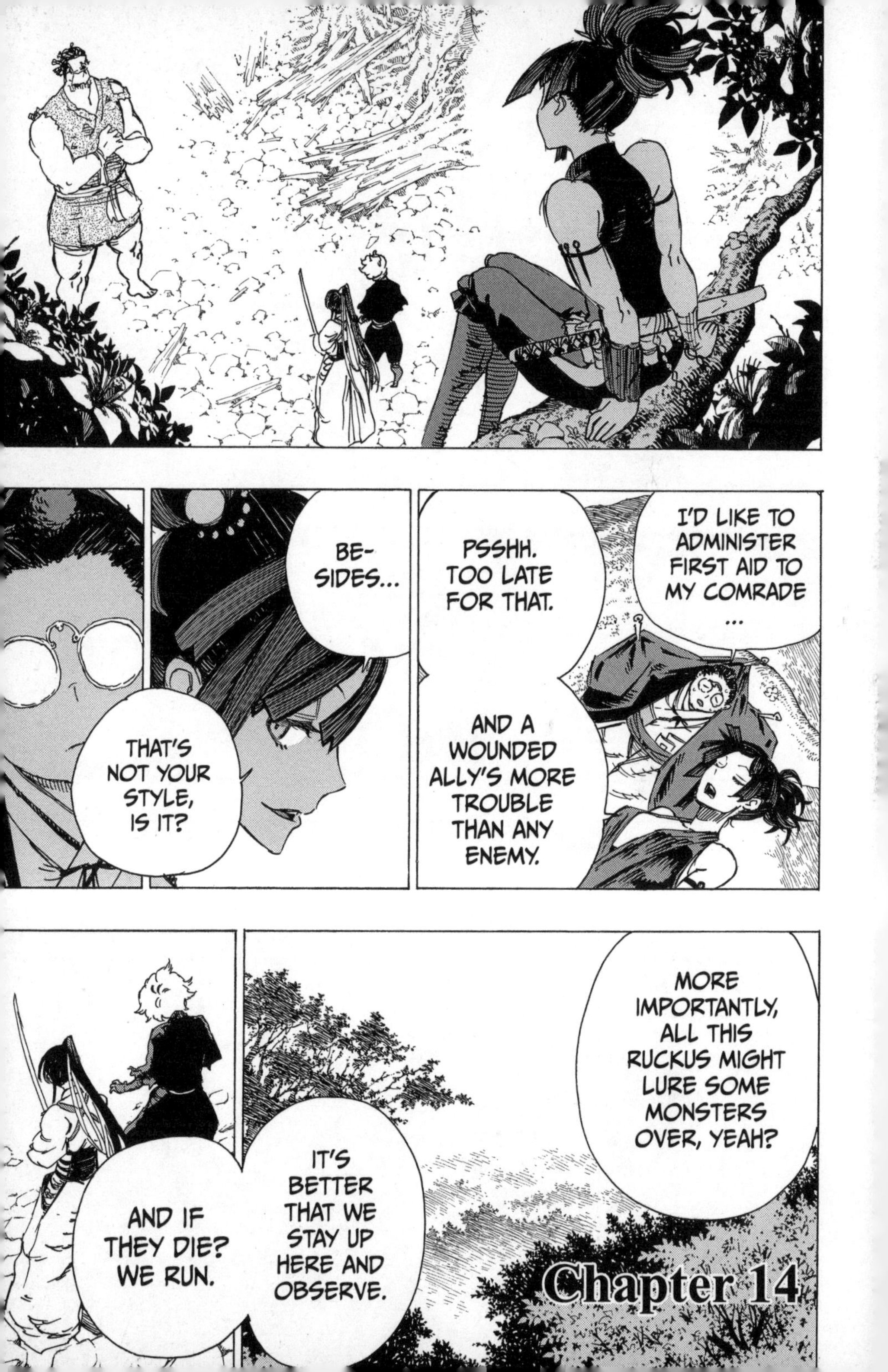
I'D LIKE TO ADMINISTER FIRST AID TO MY COMRADE ...
PSSHH. TOO LATE FOR THAT.
AND A WOUNDED ALLY'S MORE TROUBLE THAN ANY ENEMY.
BE-SIDES...
THAT'S NOT YOUR STYLE, IS IT?
MORE IMPORTANTLY, ALL THIS RUCKUS MIGHT LURE SOME MONSTERS OVER, YEAH?
IT'S BETTER THAT WE STAY UP HERE AND OBSERVE.
AND IF THEY DIE? WE RUN.
Chapter 14

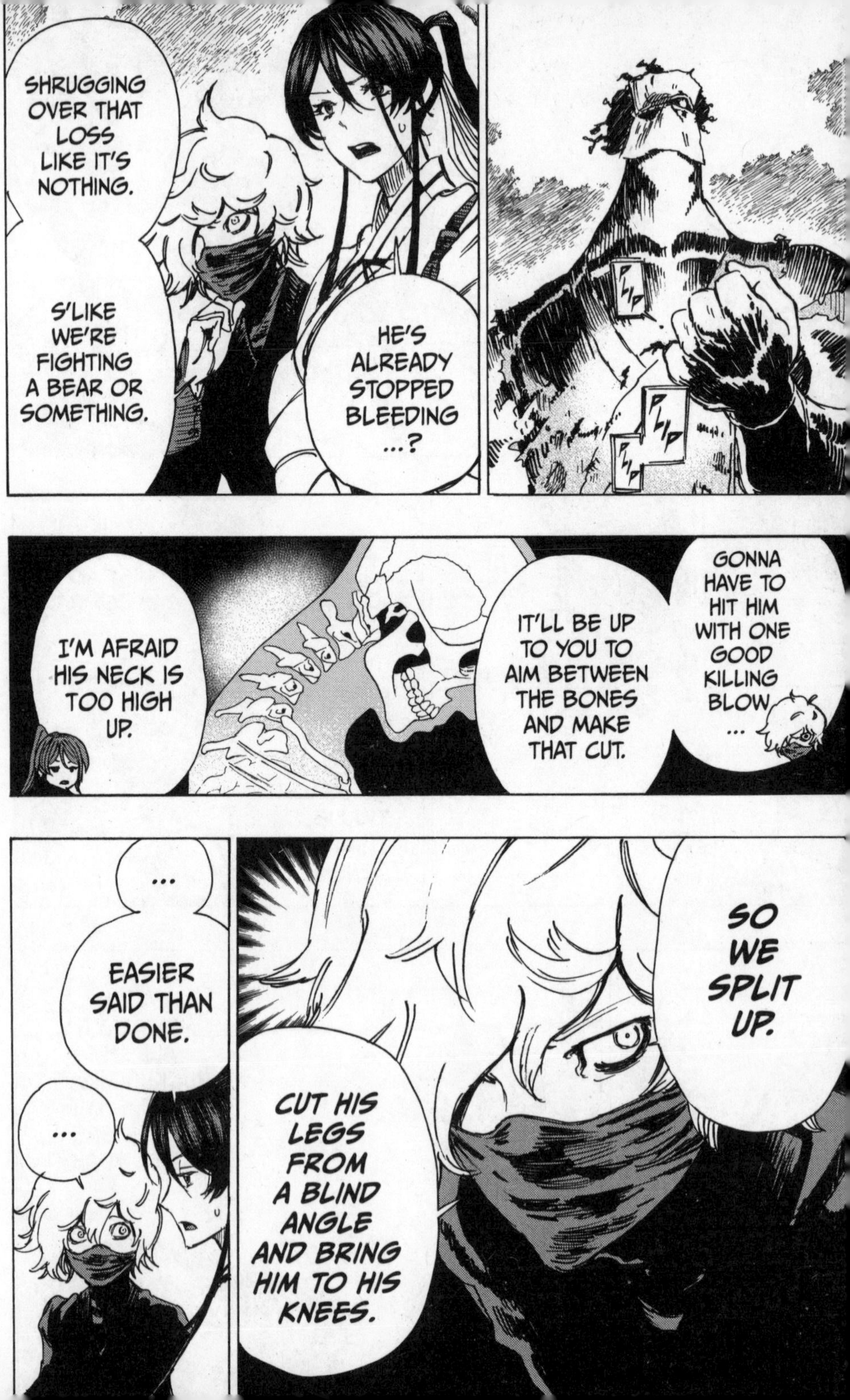
PLIP
PLIP
PLIP
HE'S ALREADY STOPPED BLEEDING ...?
SHRUGGING OVER THAT LOSS LIKE IT'S NOTHING.
S'LIKE WE'RE FIGHTING A BEAR OR SOMETHING.
GONNA HAVE TO HIT HIM WITH ONE GOOD KILLING BLOW ...
IT'LL BE UP TO YOU TO AIM BETWEEN THE BONES AND MAKE THAT CUT.
I'M AFRAID HIS NECK IS TOO HIGH UP.
SO WE SPLIT UP.
CUT HIS LEGS FROM A BLIND ANGLE AND BRING HIM TO HIS KNEES.
...
EASIER SAID THAN DONE.
...

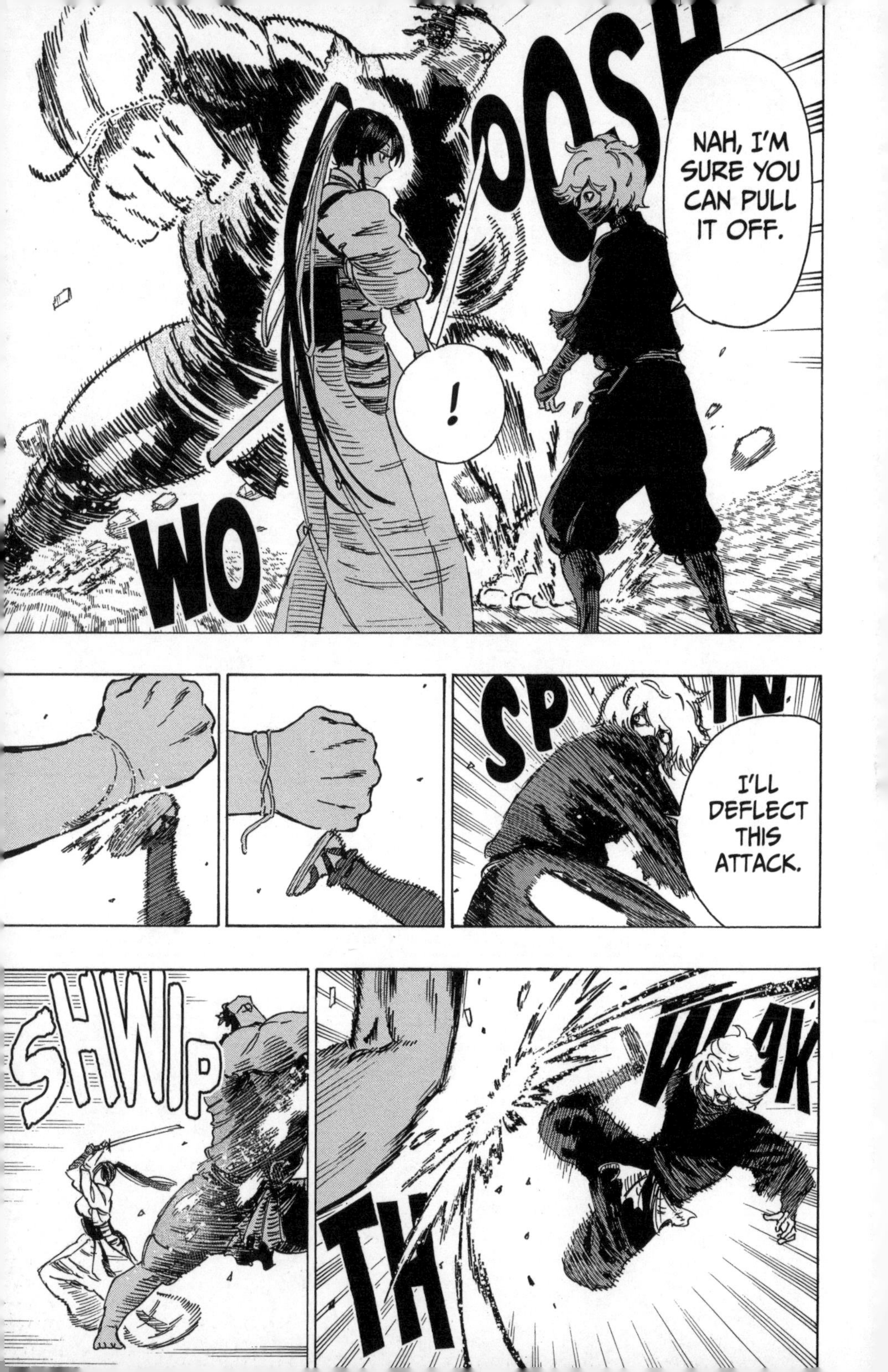
NAH, I'M SURE YOU CAN PULL IT OFF.
!
WO
OOSH
SP
IN
I'LL DEFLECT THIS ATTACK.
TH
WAK
SHWIP

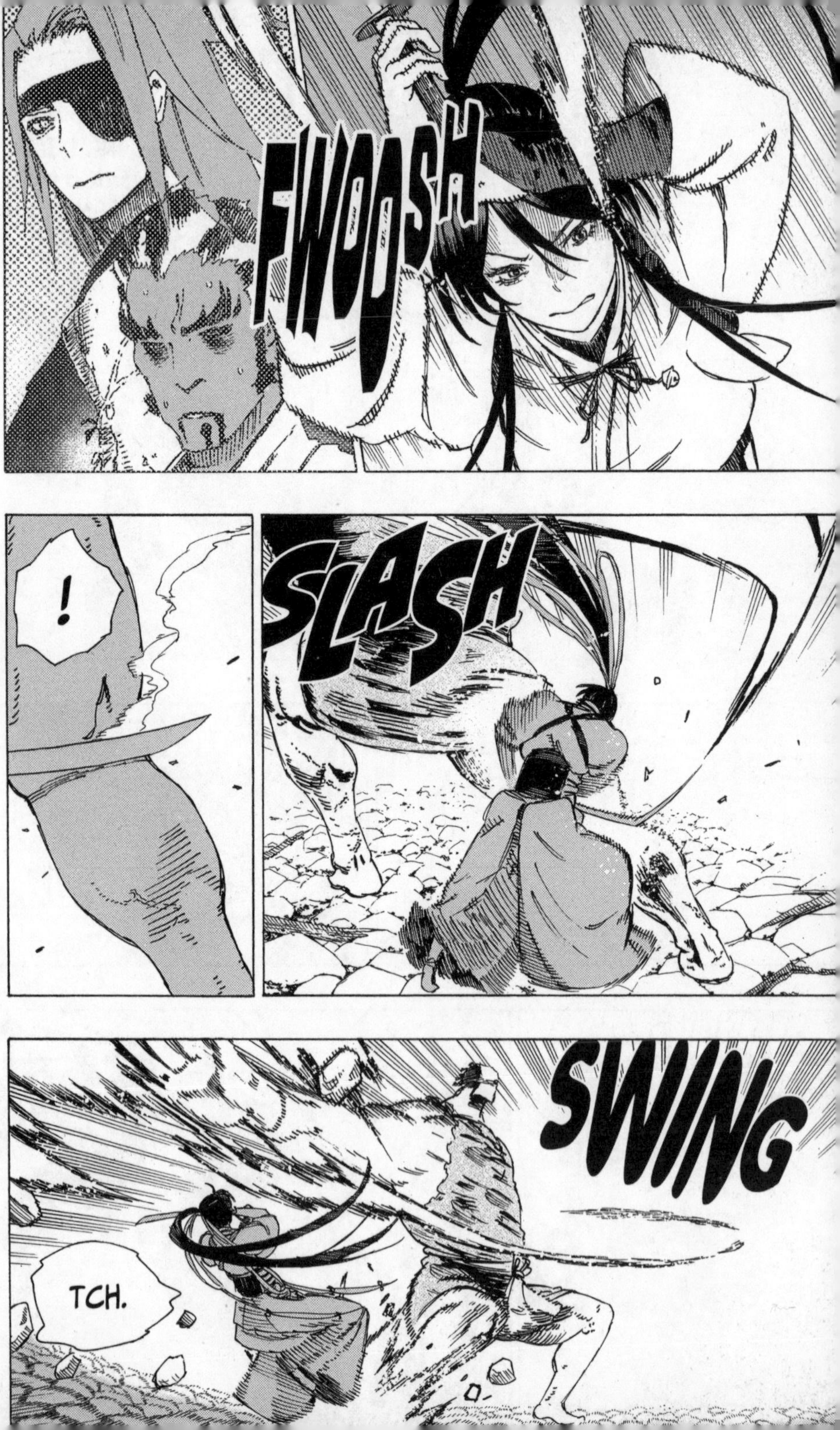
FWOOSH
SLASH
!
SWING
TCH.

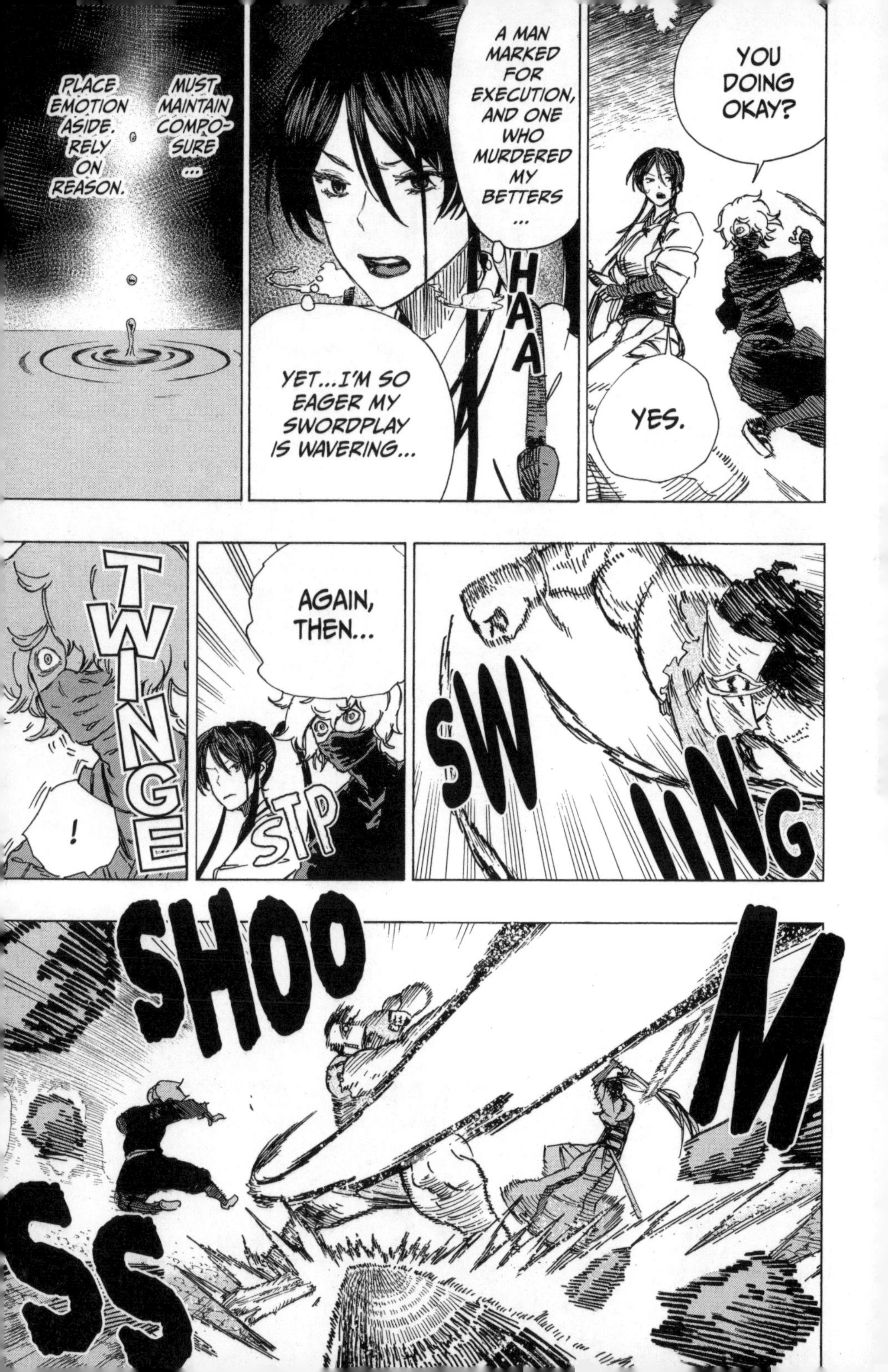
YOU DOING OKAY?
YES.
A MAN MARKED FOR EXECUTION, AND ONE WHO MURDERED MY BETTERS ...
HAA
YET...I'M SO EAGER MY SWORDPLAY IS WAVERING...
MUST MAINTAIN COMPO-SURE ...
PLACE EMOTION ASIDE. RELY ON REASON.
SW IING
AGAIN, THEN...
STP
TWINGE
!
SHOOM
SS

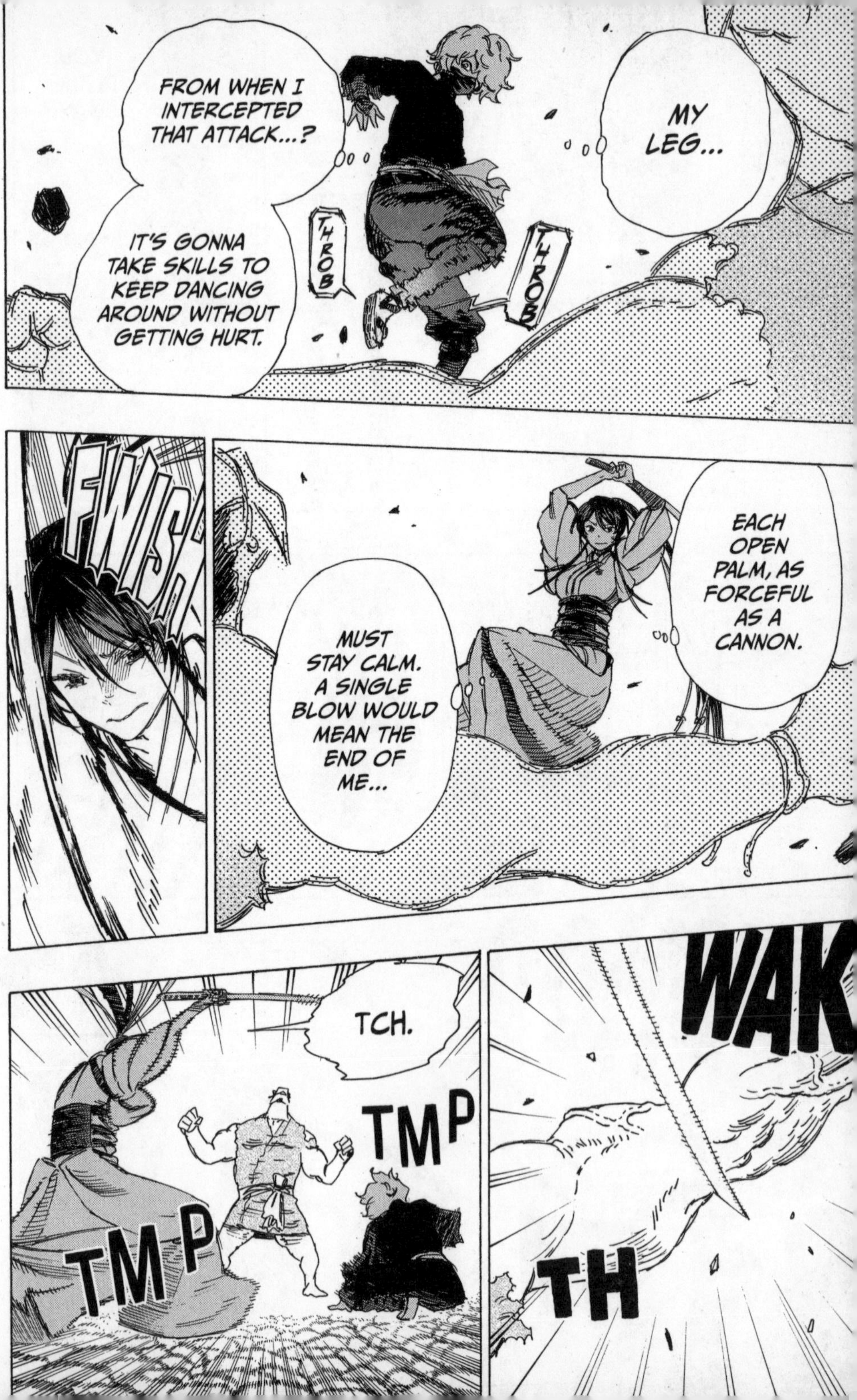
MY LEG...
THROB
THROB
FROM WHEN I INTERCEPTED THAT ATTACK...?
IT'S GONNA TAKE SKILLS TO KEEP DANCING AROUND WITHOUT GETTING HURT.
EACH OPEN PALM, AS FORCEFUL AS A CANNON.
MUST STAY CALM. A SINGLE BLOW WOULD MEAN THE END OF ME...
FWISH
WAK
TH
TCH.
TMP
TMP

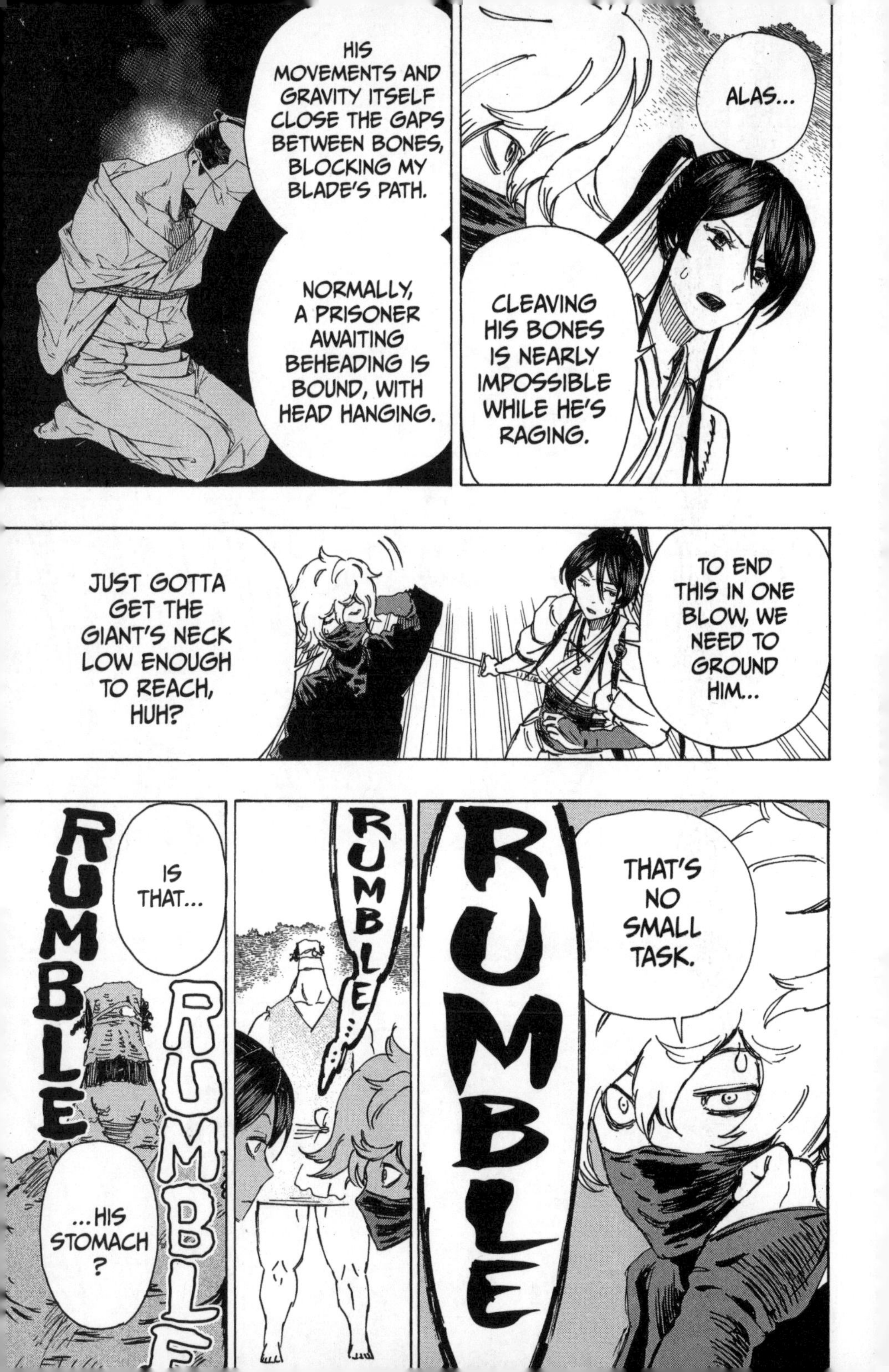
ALAS...
CLEAVING HIS BONES IS NEARLY IMPOSSIBLE WHILE HE'S RAGING.
HIS MOVEMENTS AND GRAVITY ITSELF CLOSE THE GAPS BETWEEN BONES, BLOCKING MY BLADE'S PATH.
NORMALLY, A PRISONER AWAITING BEHEADING IS BOUND, WITH HEAD HANGING.
TO END THIS IN ONE BLOW, WE NEED TO GROUND HIM...
JUST GOTTA GET THE GIANT'S NECK LOW ENOUGH TO REACH, HUH?
THAT'S NO SMALL TASK.
RUMBLE
RUMBLE
RUMBLE
IS THAT...
RUMBLE
...HIS STOMACH?

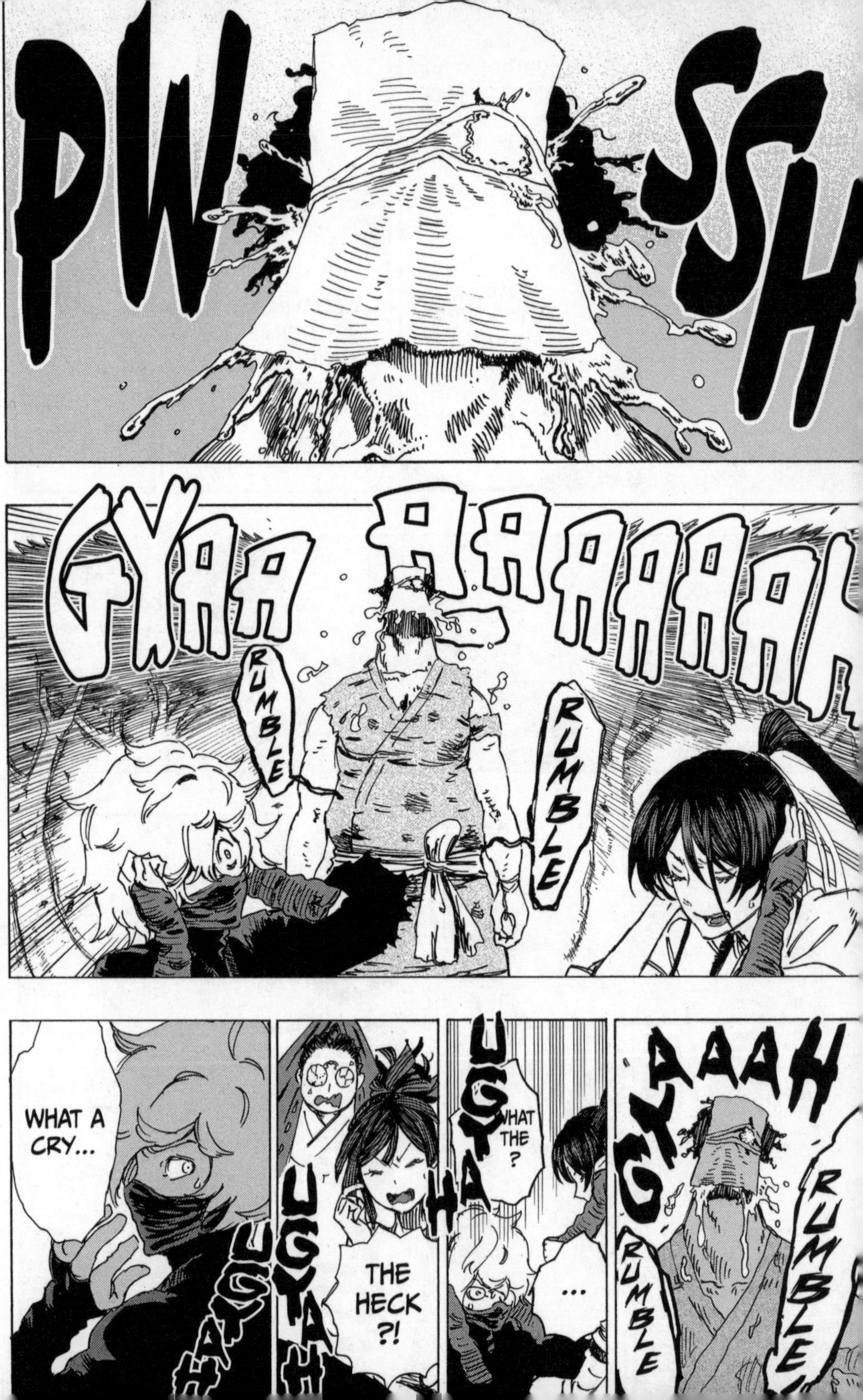
PWSSH
GYAAAAAAAAAH
RUMBLE
RUMBLE
GYAAAH
RUMBLE
RUMBLE
UGYAHA
WHAT THE?
...
UGYAH
THE HECK?!
WHAT A CRY...
UGYAHA

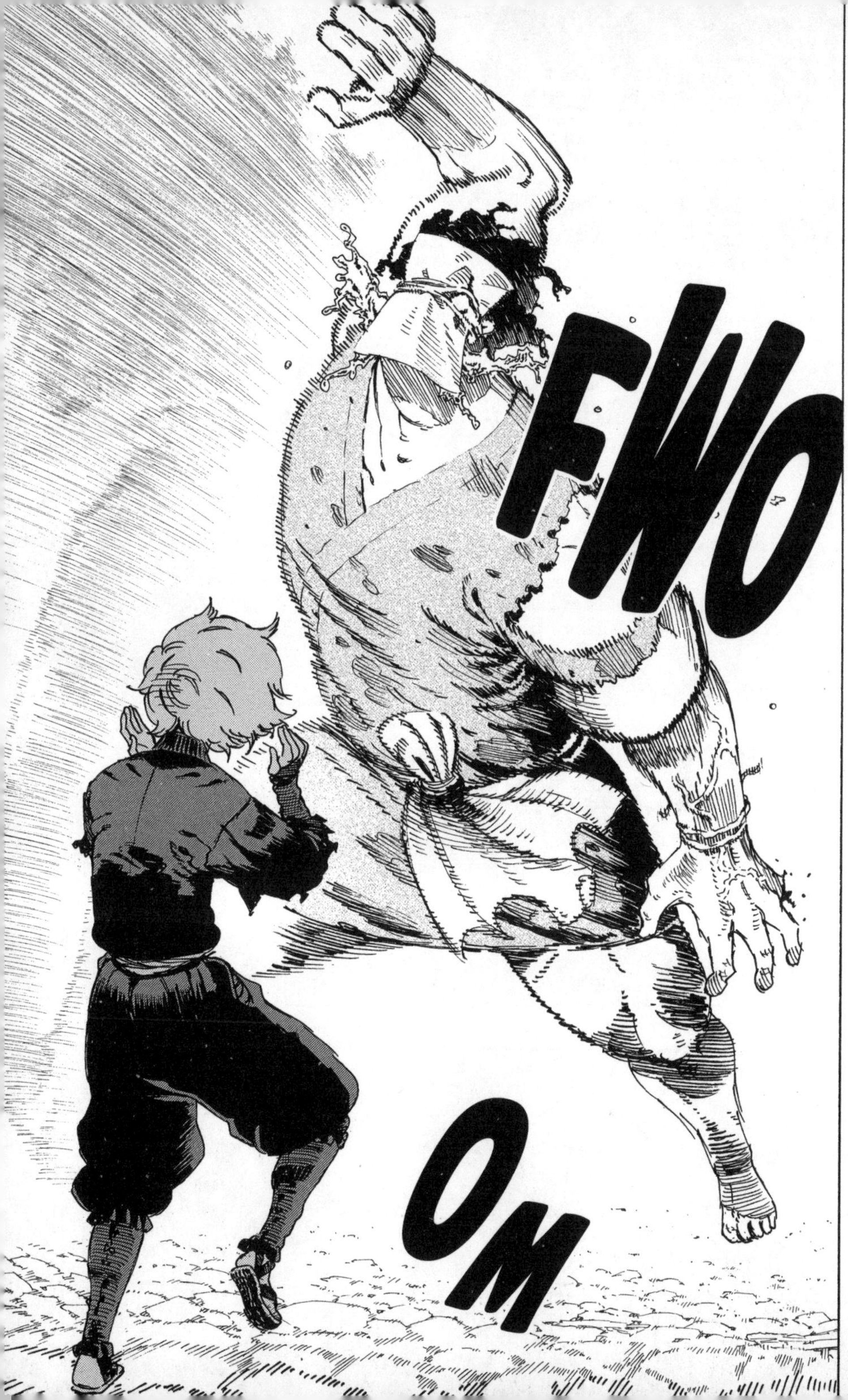
FWO
OM

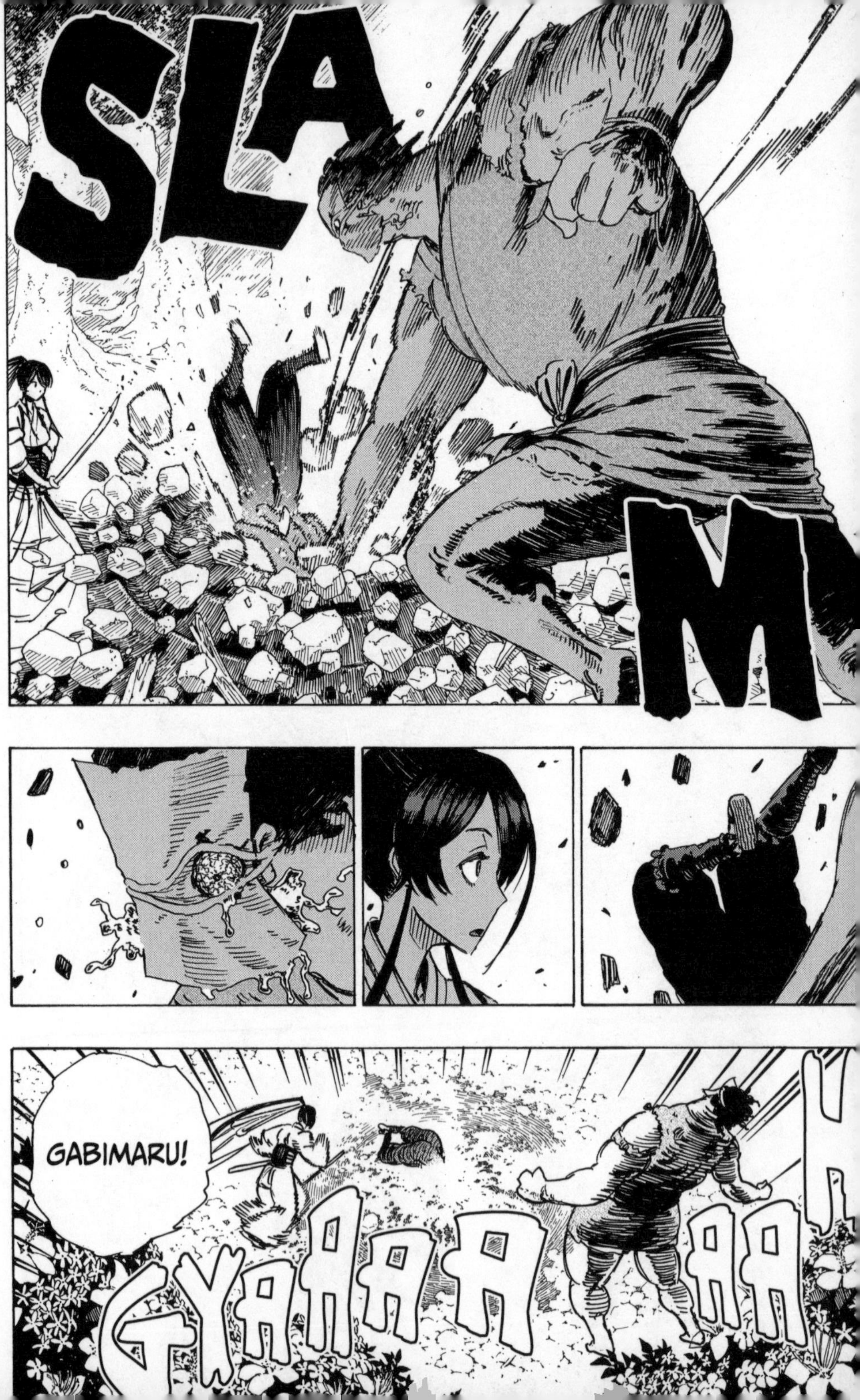
SLA
M
GABIMARU!
GYAARRRR!

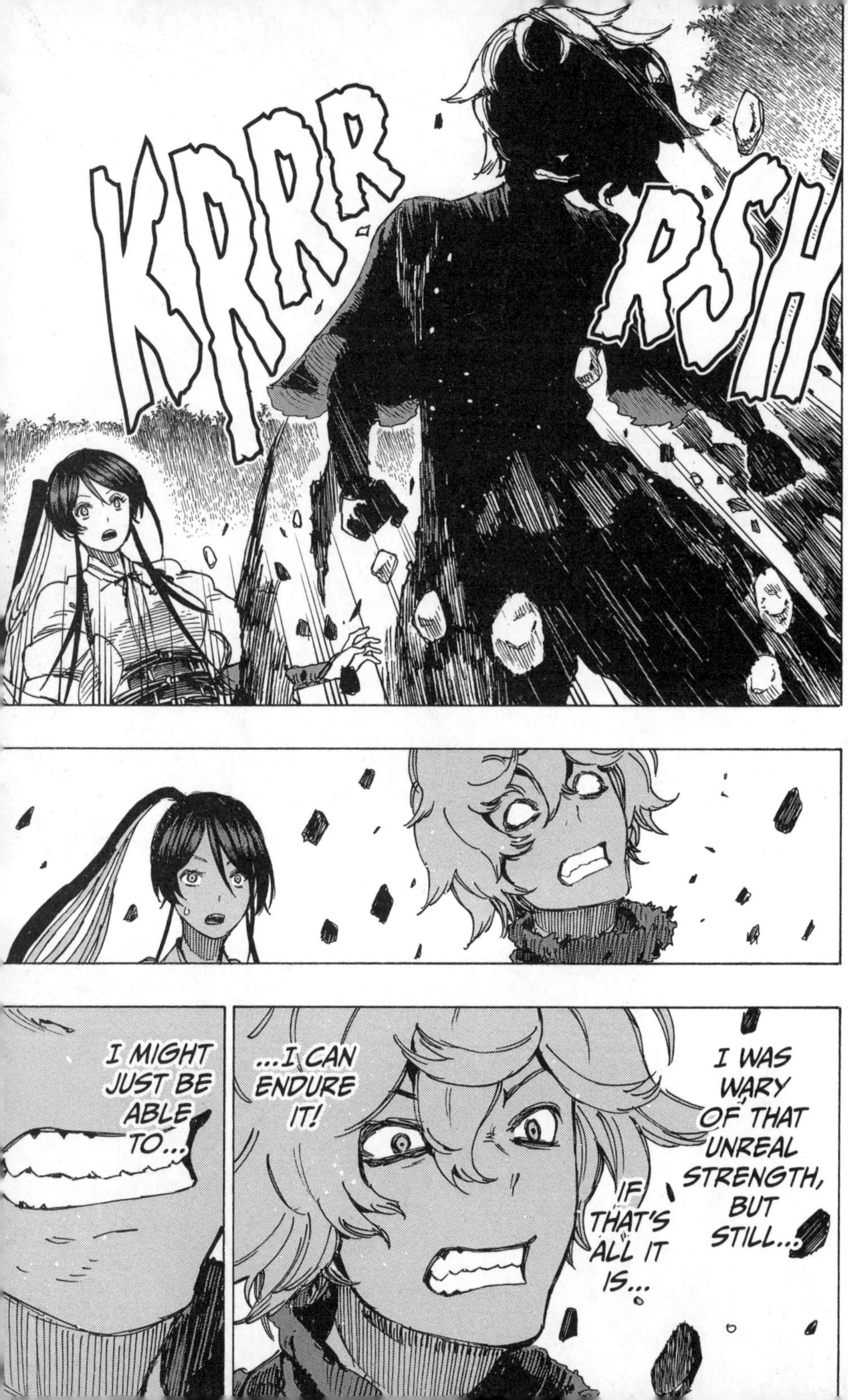
KRRR
RSH
I WAS WARY OF THAT UNREAL STRENGTH, BUT STILL...
IF THAT'S ALL IT IS...
...I CAN ENDURE IT!
I MIGHT JUST BE ABLE TO...

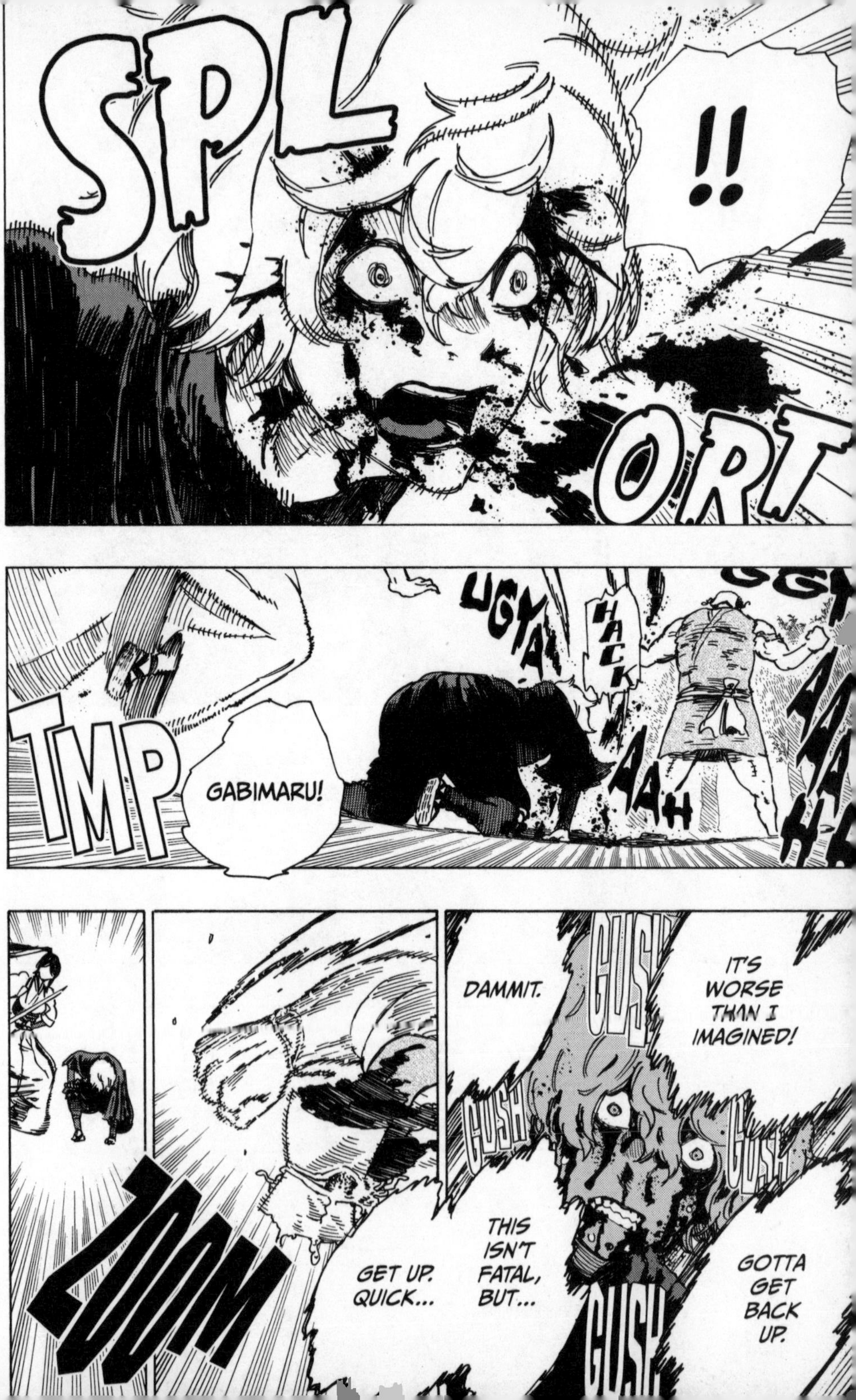
!!
SPL
ORT
HACK
UGYA
AAH
GABIMARU!
TMP
GUSH
IT'S WORSE THAN I IMAGINED!
DAMMIT.
GUSH
GUSH
GOTTA GET BACK UP.
GUSH
THIS ISN'T FATAL, BUT...
GET UP. QUICK...
ZOOM

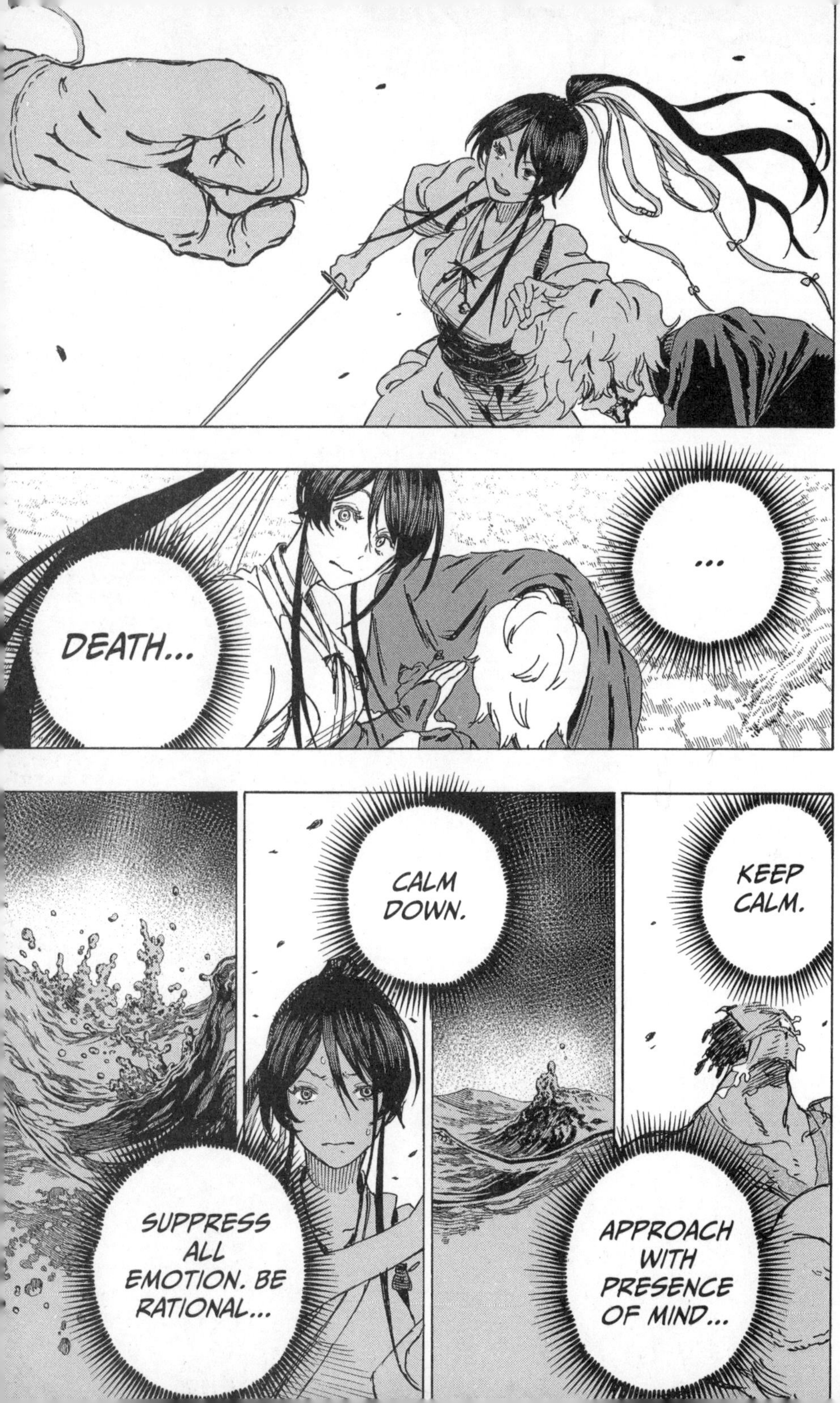
...
DEATH...
KEEP CALM.
APPROACH WITH PRESENCE OF MIND...
CALM DOWN.
SUPPRESS ALL EMOTION. BE RATIONAL...

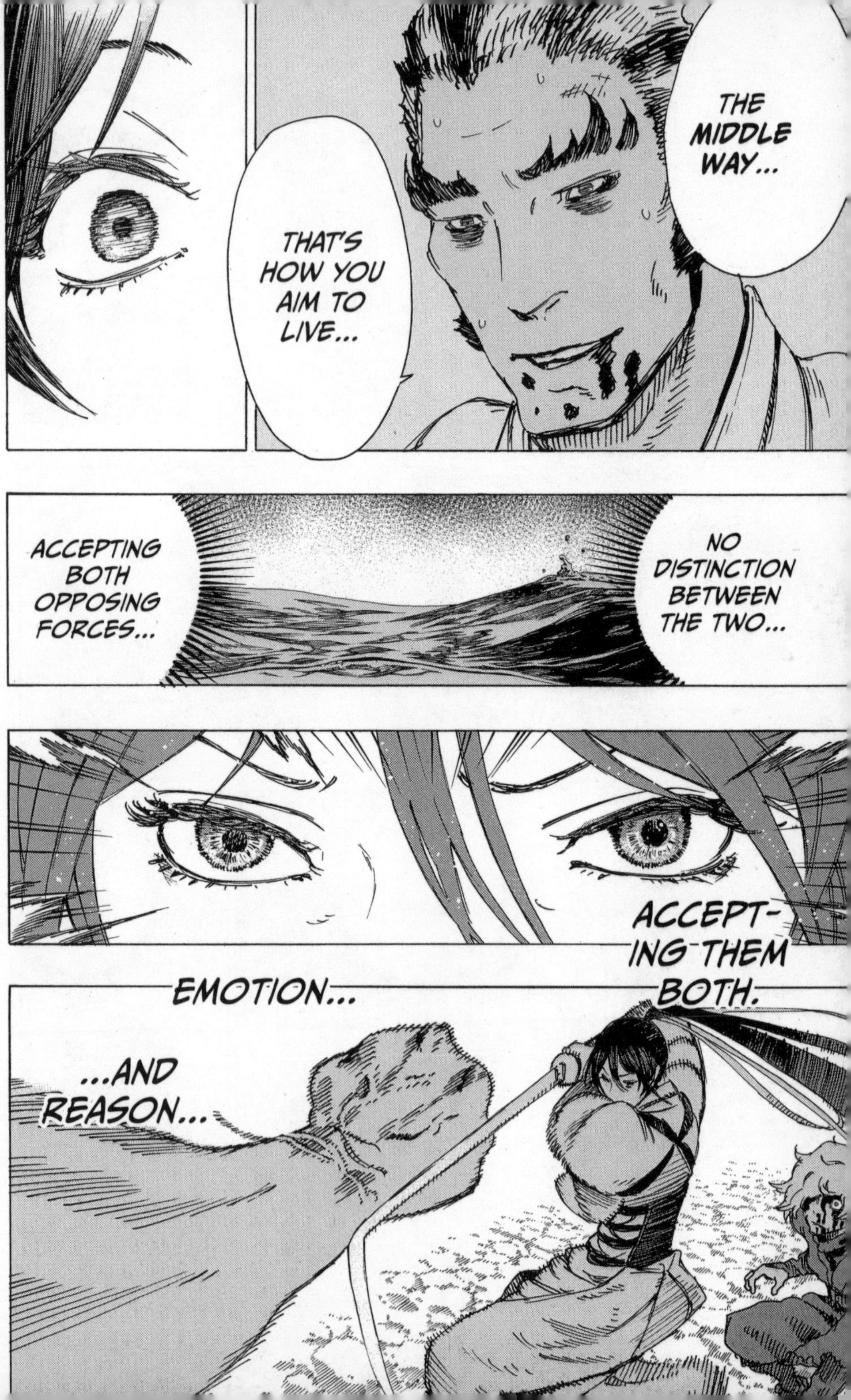
THE MIDDLE WAY...
THAT'S HOW YOU AIM TO LIVE...
NO DISTINCTION BETWEEN THE TWO...
ACCEPTING BOTH OPPOSING FORCES...
ACCEPT-ING THEM BOTH.
EMOTION...
...AND REASON...

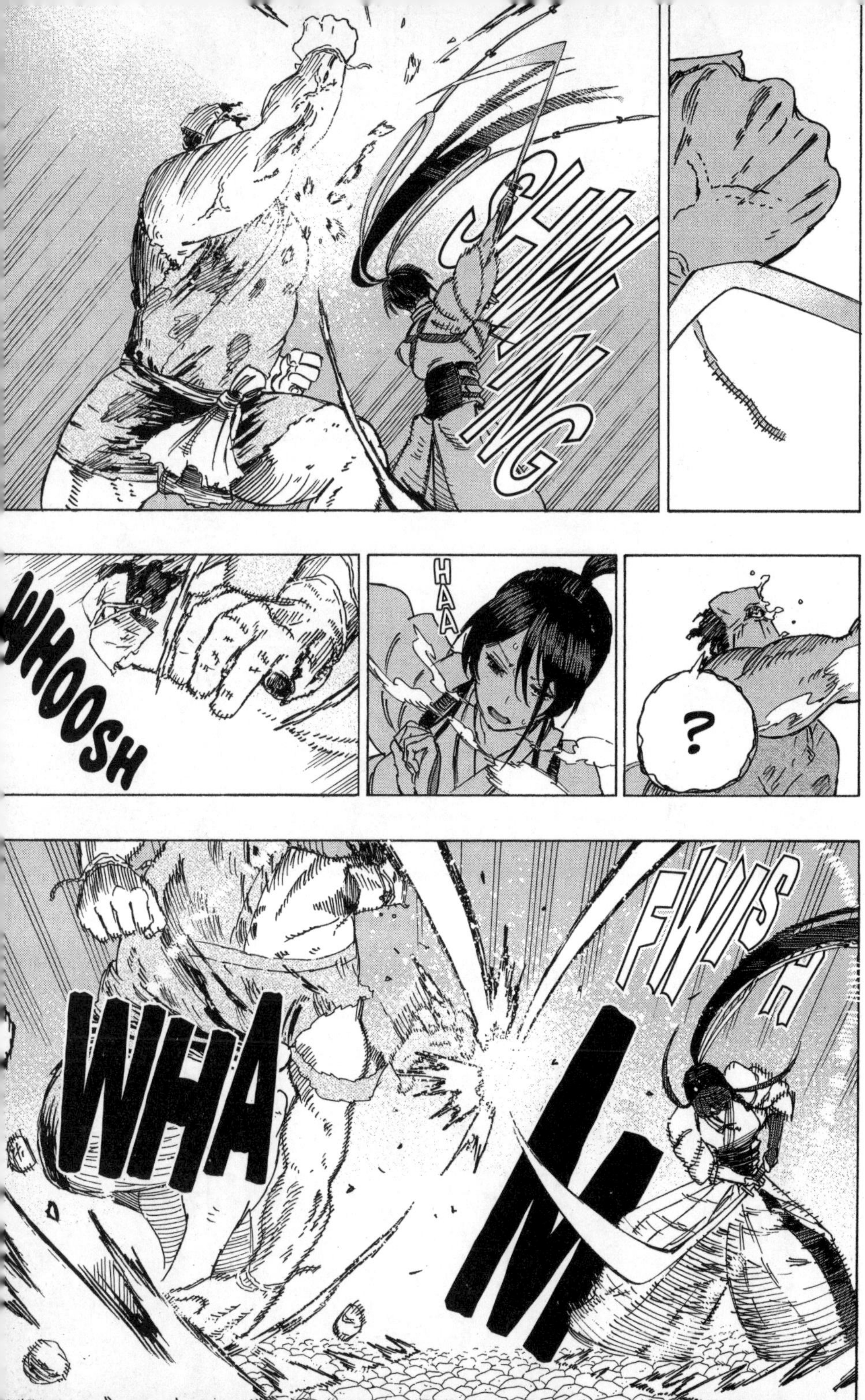
SCHWING
?
HAA
WHOOSH
FWISH
WHAM

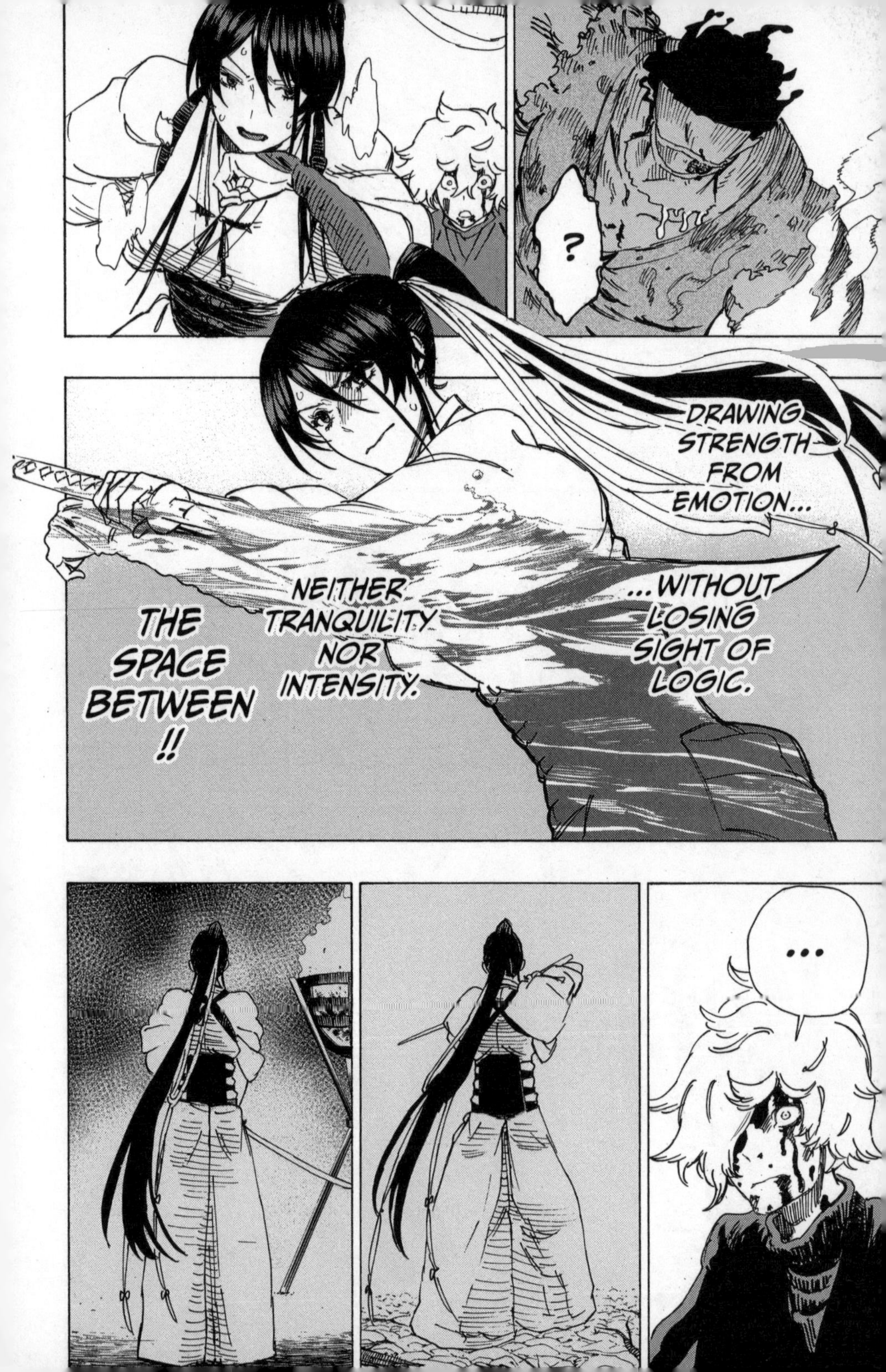
?
DRAWING STRENGTH FROM EMOTION...
...WITHOUT LOSING SIGHT OF LOGIC.
NEITHER TRANQUILITY NOR INTENSITY.
THE SPACE BETWEEN!!
...

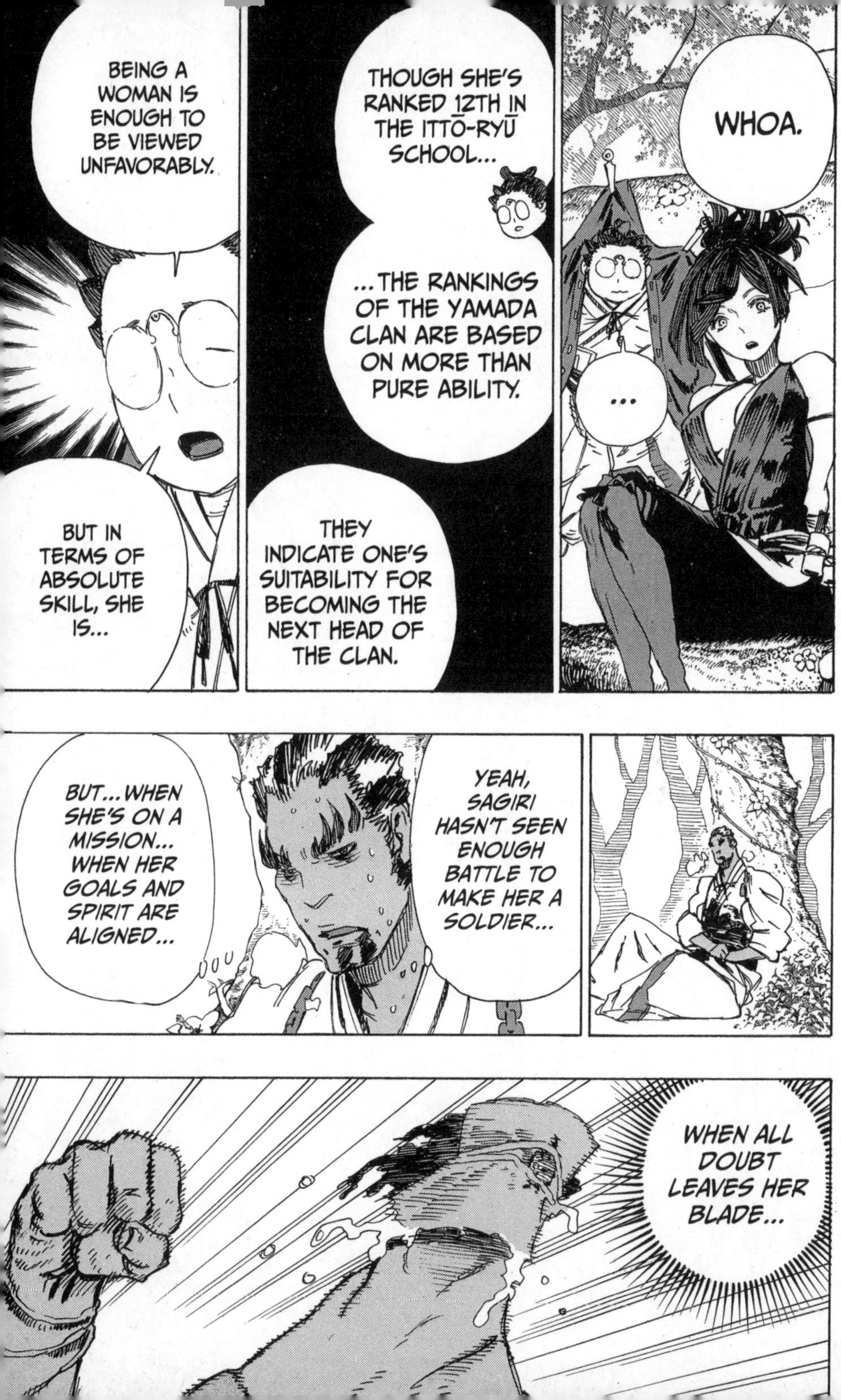
WHOA.
...
THOUGH SHE'S RANKED 12TH IN THE ITTŌ-RYŪ SCHOOL...
...THE RANKINGS OF THE YAMADA CLAN ARE BASED ON MORE THAN PURE ABILITY.
THEY INDICATE ONE'S SUITABILITY FOR BECOMING THE NEXT HEAD OF THE CLAN.
BEING A WOMAN IS ENOUGH TO BE VIEWED UNFAVORABLY.
BUT IN TERMS OF ABSOLUTE SKILL, SHE IS...
YEAH, SAGIRI HASN'T SEEN ENOUGH BATTLE TO MAKE HER A SOLDIER...
BUT...WHEN SHE'S ON A MISSION... WHEN HER GOALS AND SPIRIT ARE ALIGNED...
WHEN ALL DOUBT LEAVES HER BLADE...

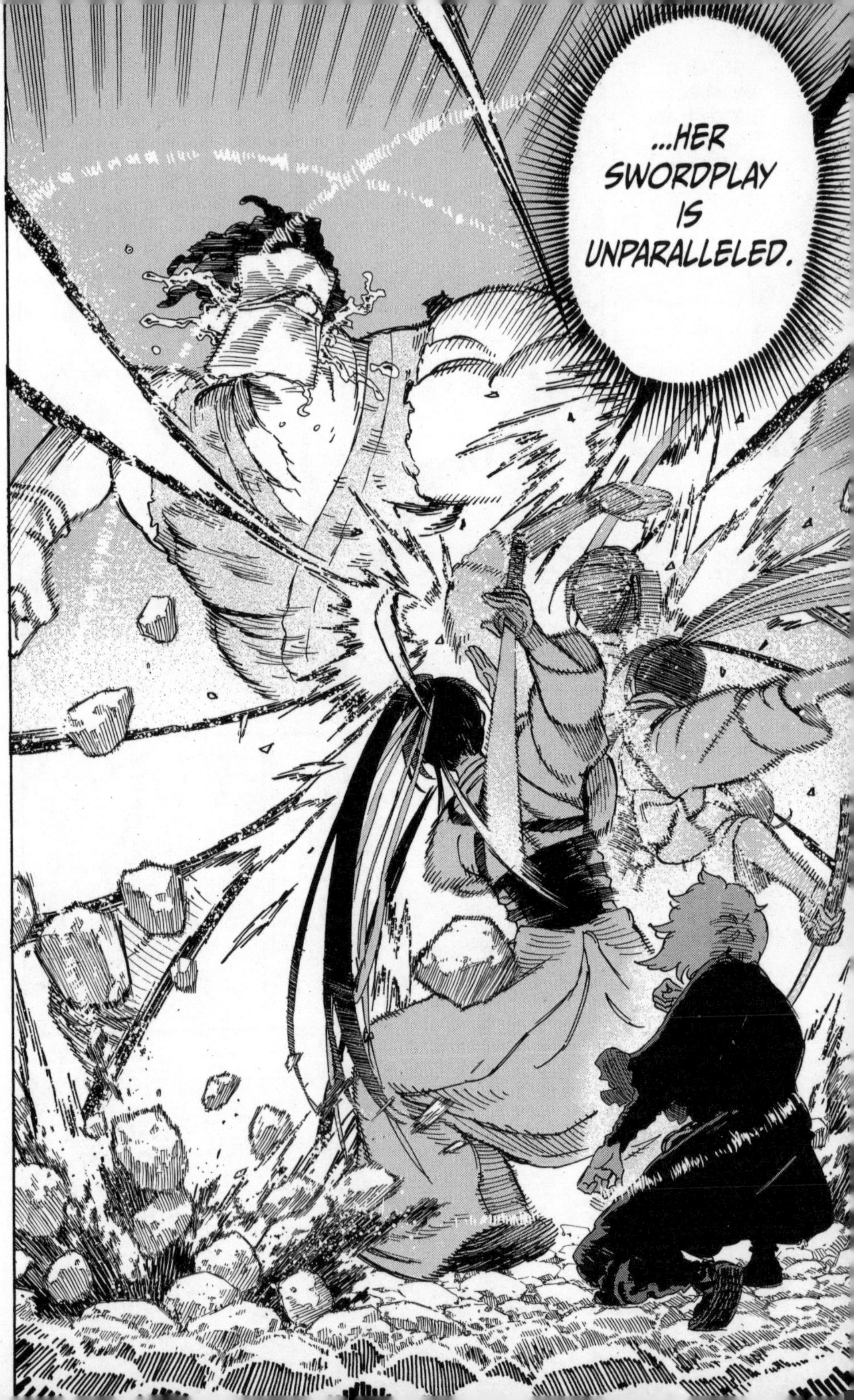
...HER SWORDPLAY IS UNPARALLELED.

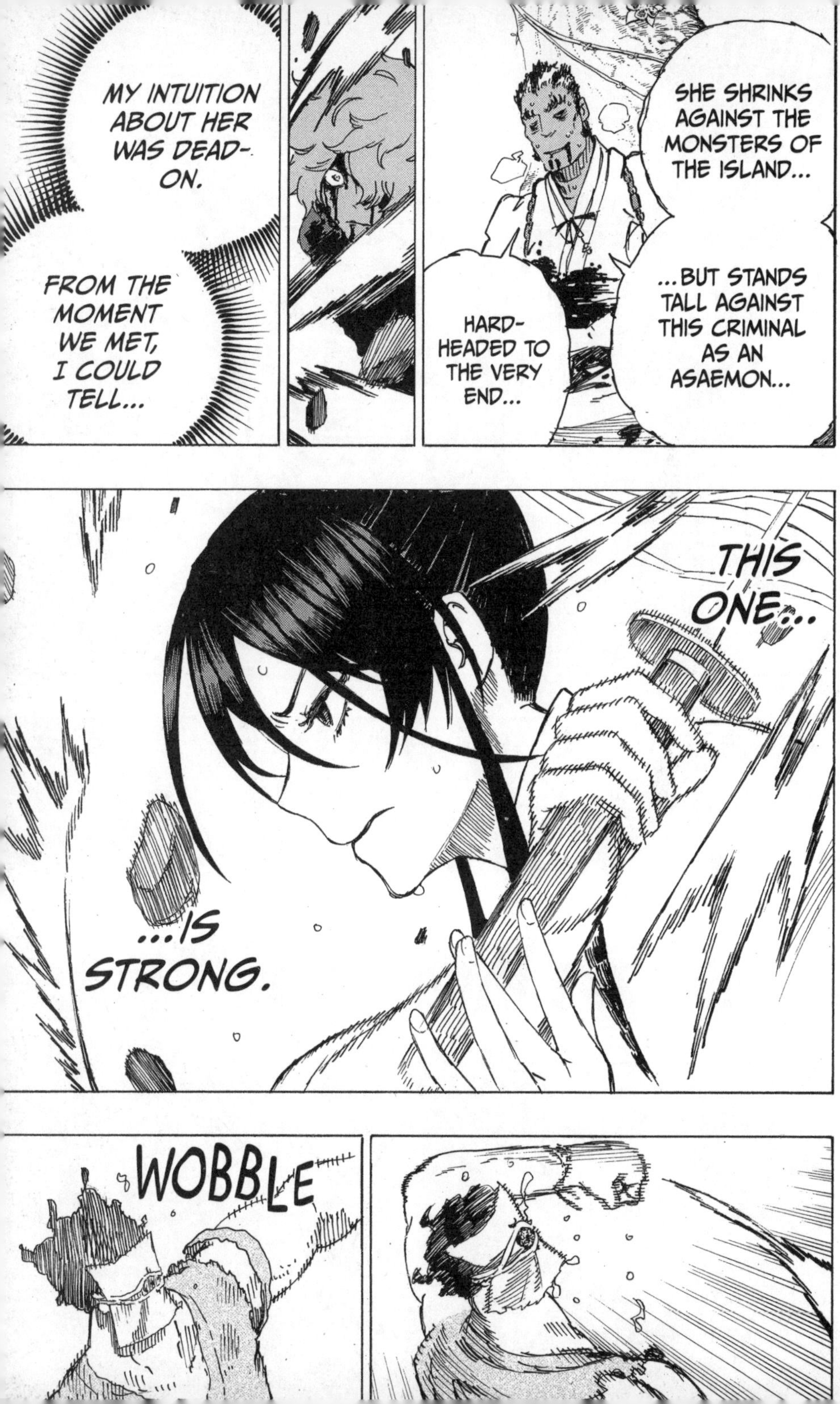
SHE SHRINKS AGAINST THE MONSTERS OF THE ISLAND...
...BUT STANDS TALL AGAINST THIS CRIMINAL AS AN ASAEMON...
HARD-HEADED TO THE VERY END...
MY INTUITION ABOUT HER WAS DEAD-ON.
FROM THE MOMENT WE MET, I COULD TELL...
THIS ONE...
...IS STRONG.
WOBBLE

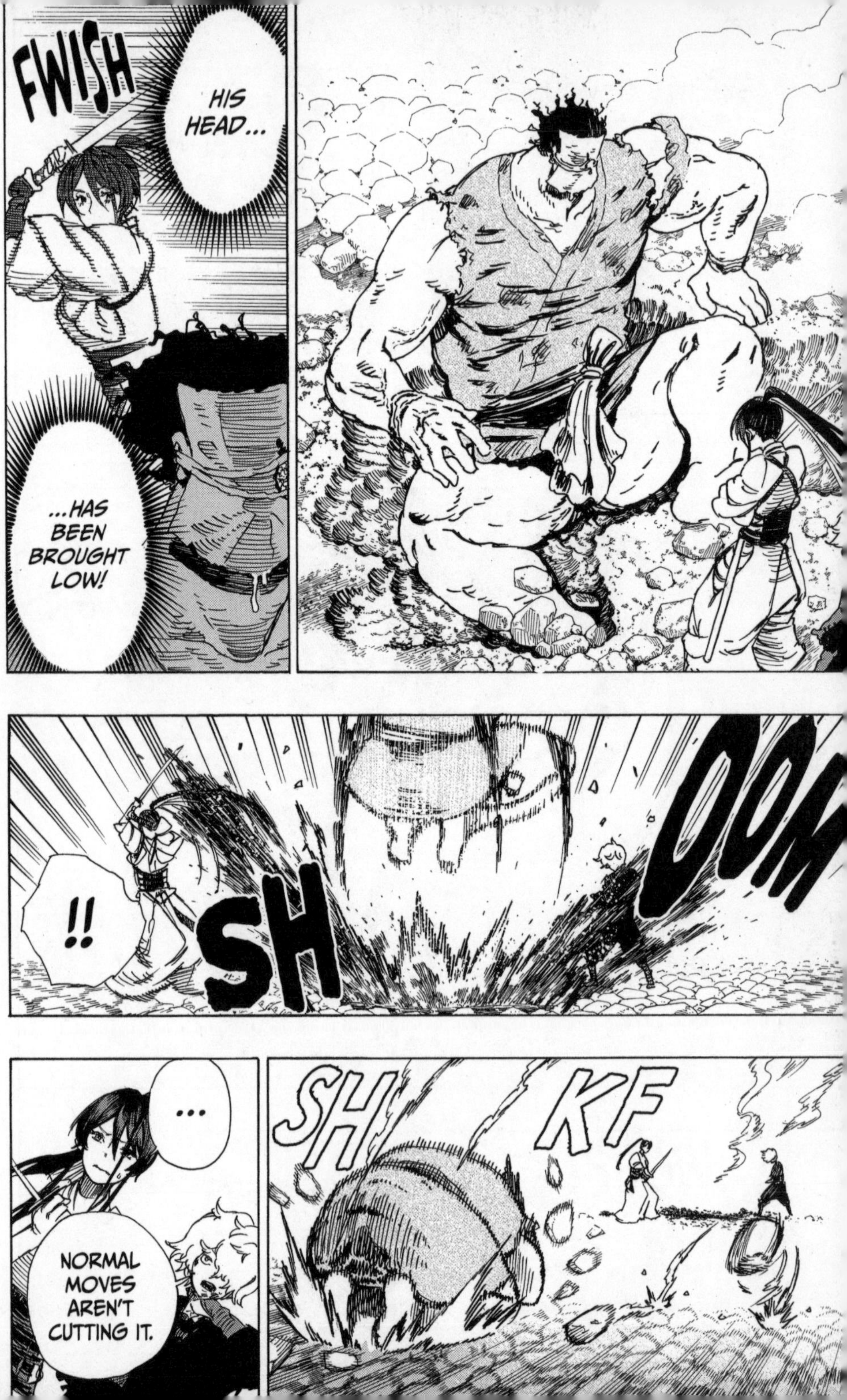
FWISH
HIS HEAD...
...HAS BEEN BROUGHT LOW!
OOM
SH
!!
SH
KF
...
NORMAL MOVES AREN'T CUTTING IT.

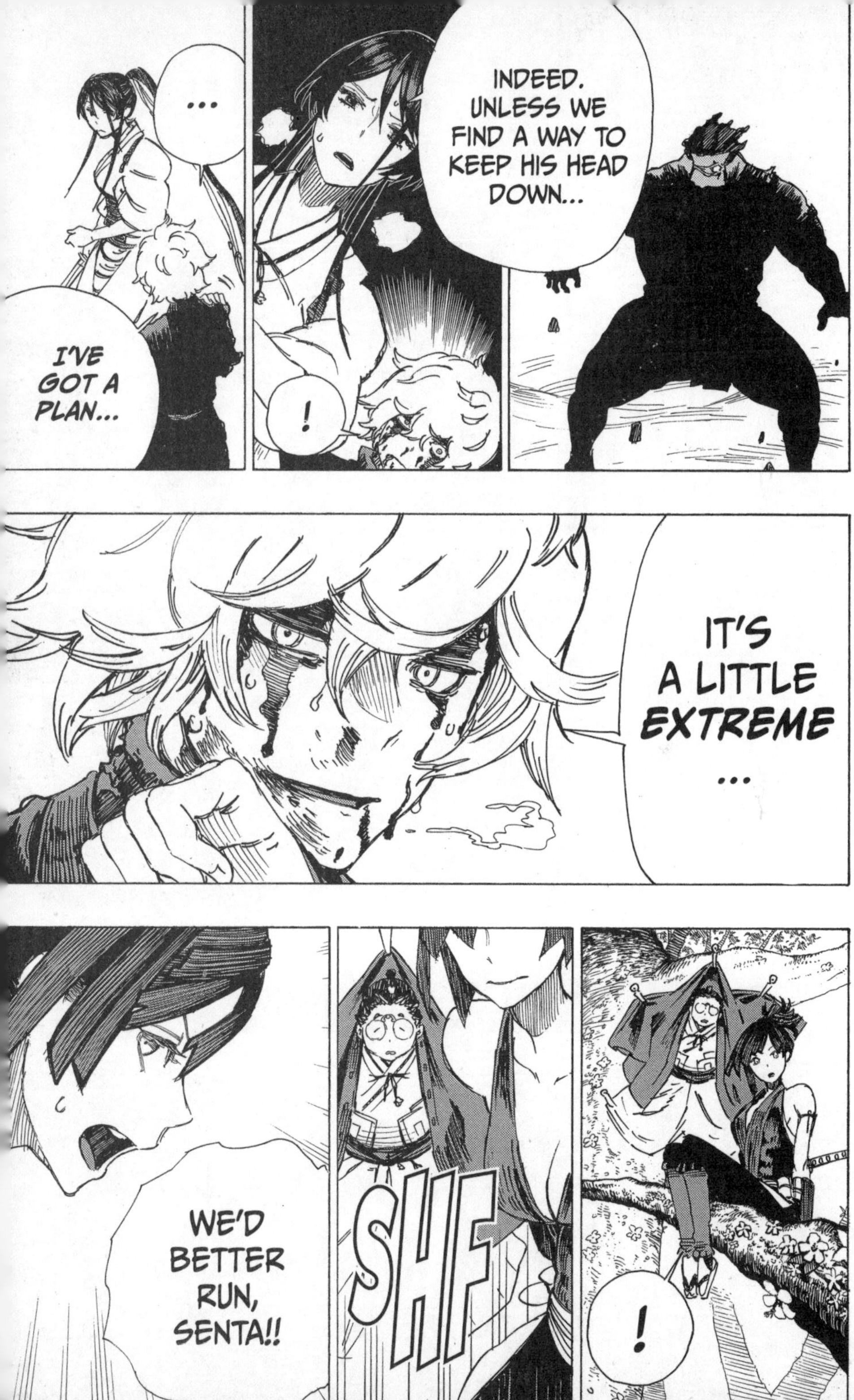
INDEED. UNLESS WE FIND A WAY TO KEEP HIS HEAD DOWN...
!
...
I'VE GOT A PLAN...
IT'S A LITTLE EXTREME...
!
SHF
WE'D BETTER RUN, SENTA!!

Hell's Paradise

JIGOKURAKU

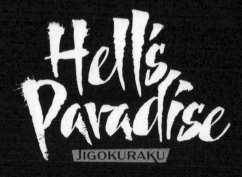

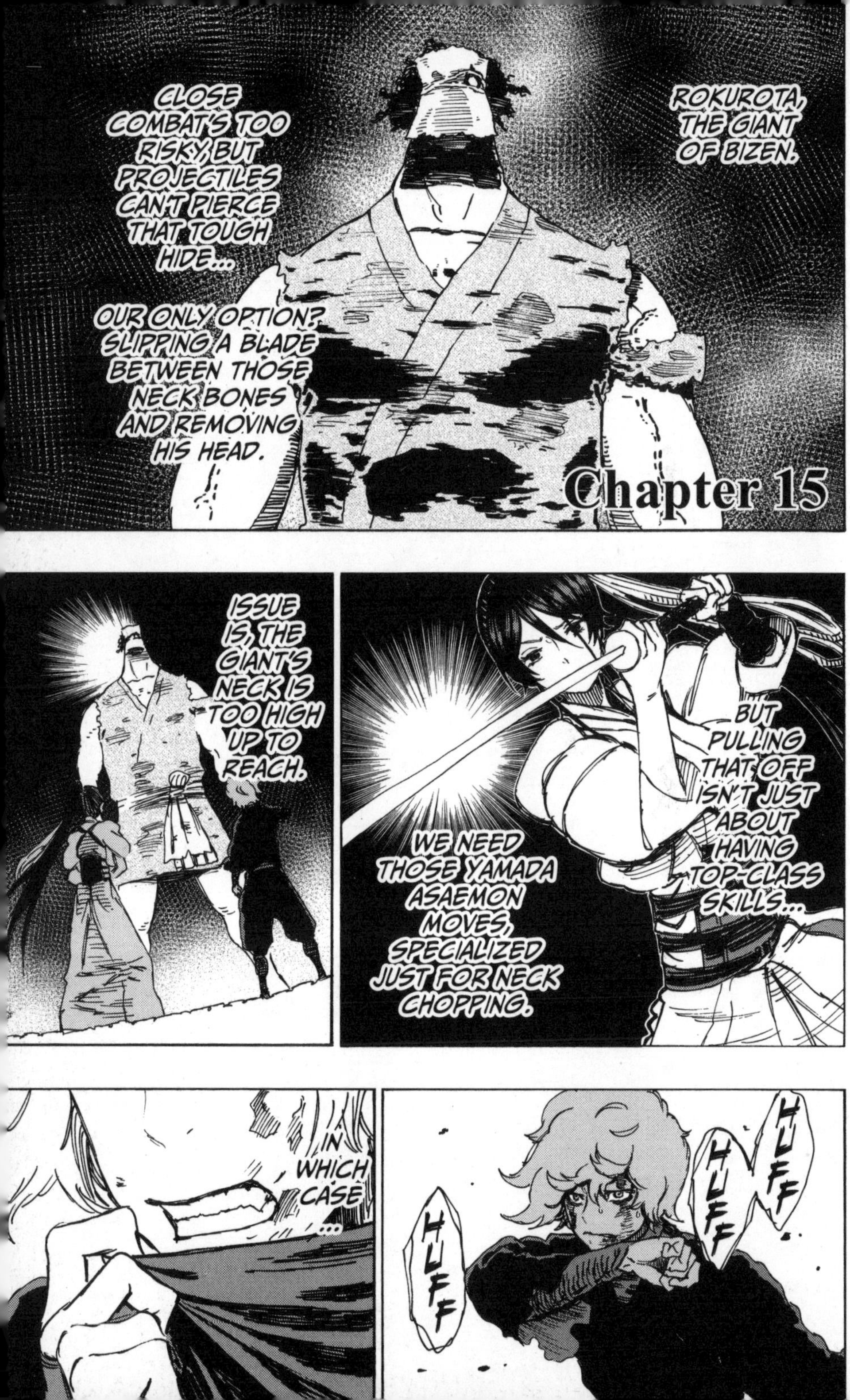
ROKUROTA, THE GIANT OF BIZEN.
CLOSE COMBAT'S TOO RISKY, BUT PROJECTILES CAN'T PIERCE THAT TOUGH HIDE...
OUR ONLY OPTION? SLIPPING A BLADE BETWEEN THOSE NECK BONES AND REMOVING HIS HEAD.
Chapter 15
BUT PULLING THAT OFF ISN'T JUST ABOUT HAVING TOP-CLASS SKILLS...
WE NEED THOSE YAMADA ASAEMON MOVES, SPECIALIZED JUST FOR NECK CHOPPING.
ISSUE IS, THE GIANT'S NECK IS TOO HIGH UP TO REACH.
HUFF
HUFF
HUFF
HUFF
IN WHICH CASE...

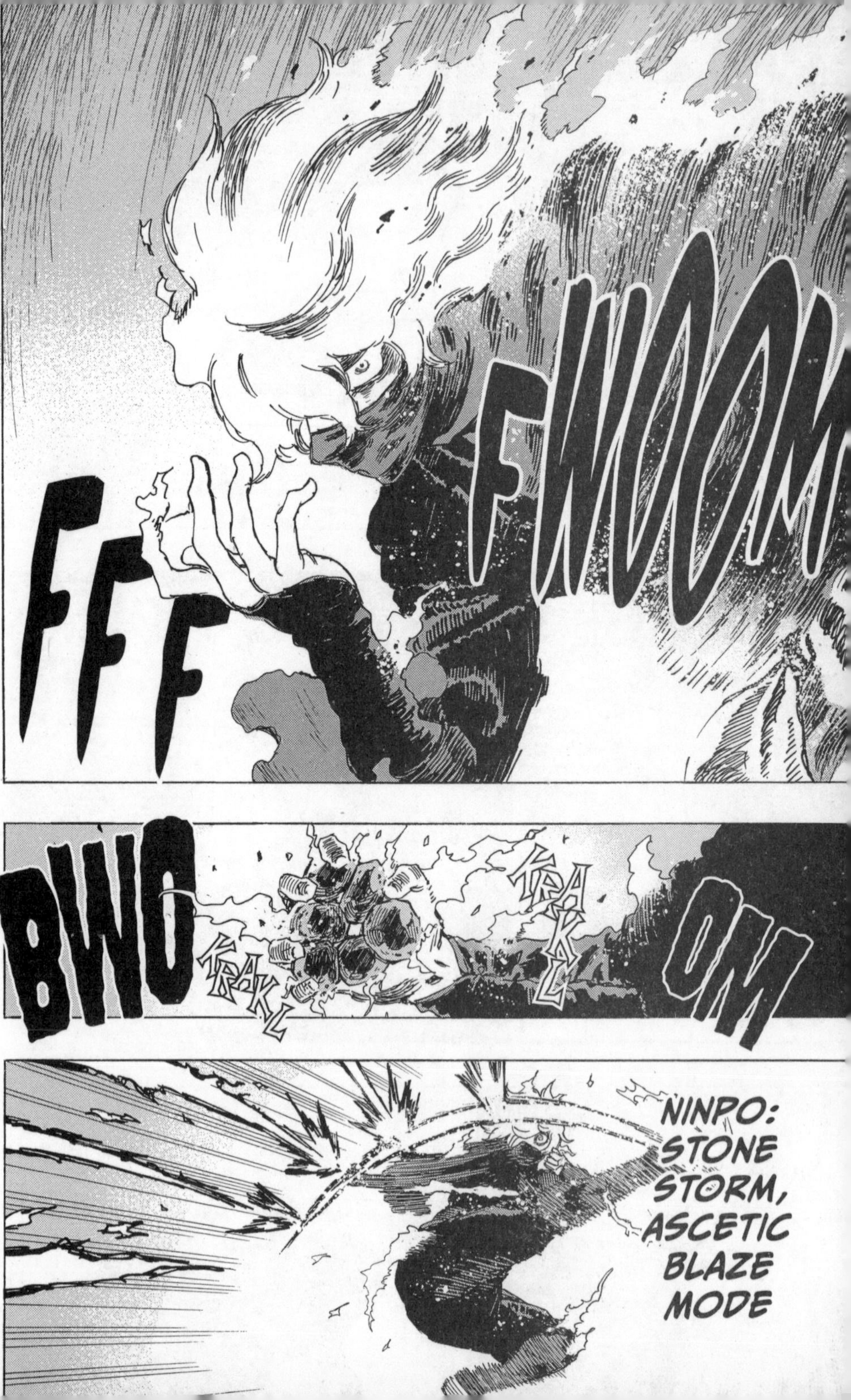
FWOOM
FFF
KRAKL
KRAKL
BWO OM
NINPO: STONE STORM, ASCETIC BLAZE MODE

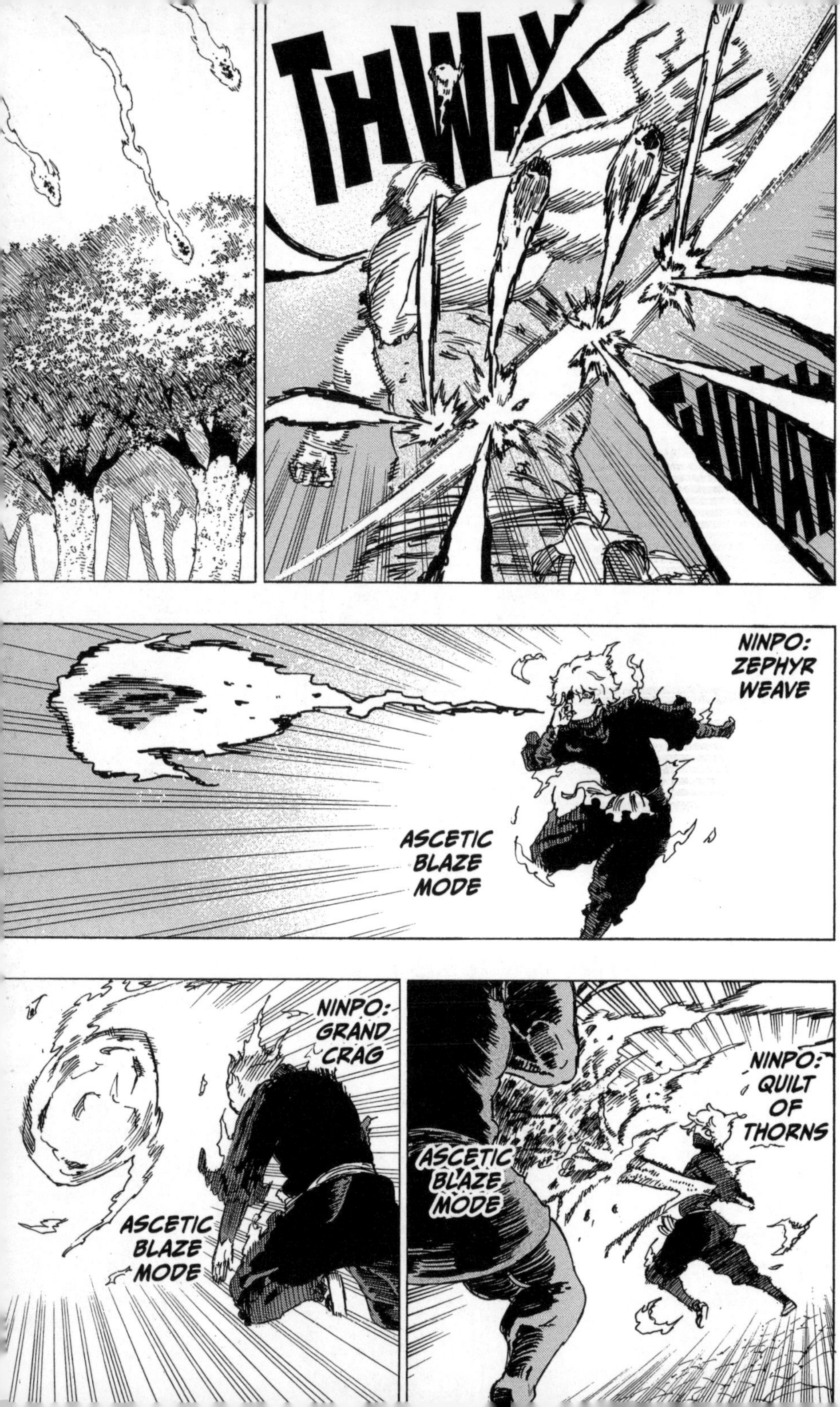
THWAK
THWA
NINPO: ZEPHYR WEAVE
ASCETIC BLAZE MODE
NINPO: QUILT OF THORNS
ASCETIC BLAZE MODE
NINPO: GRAND CRAG
ASCETIC BLAZE MODE

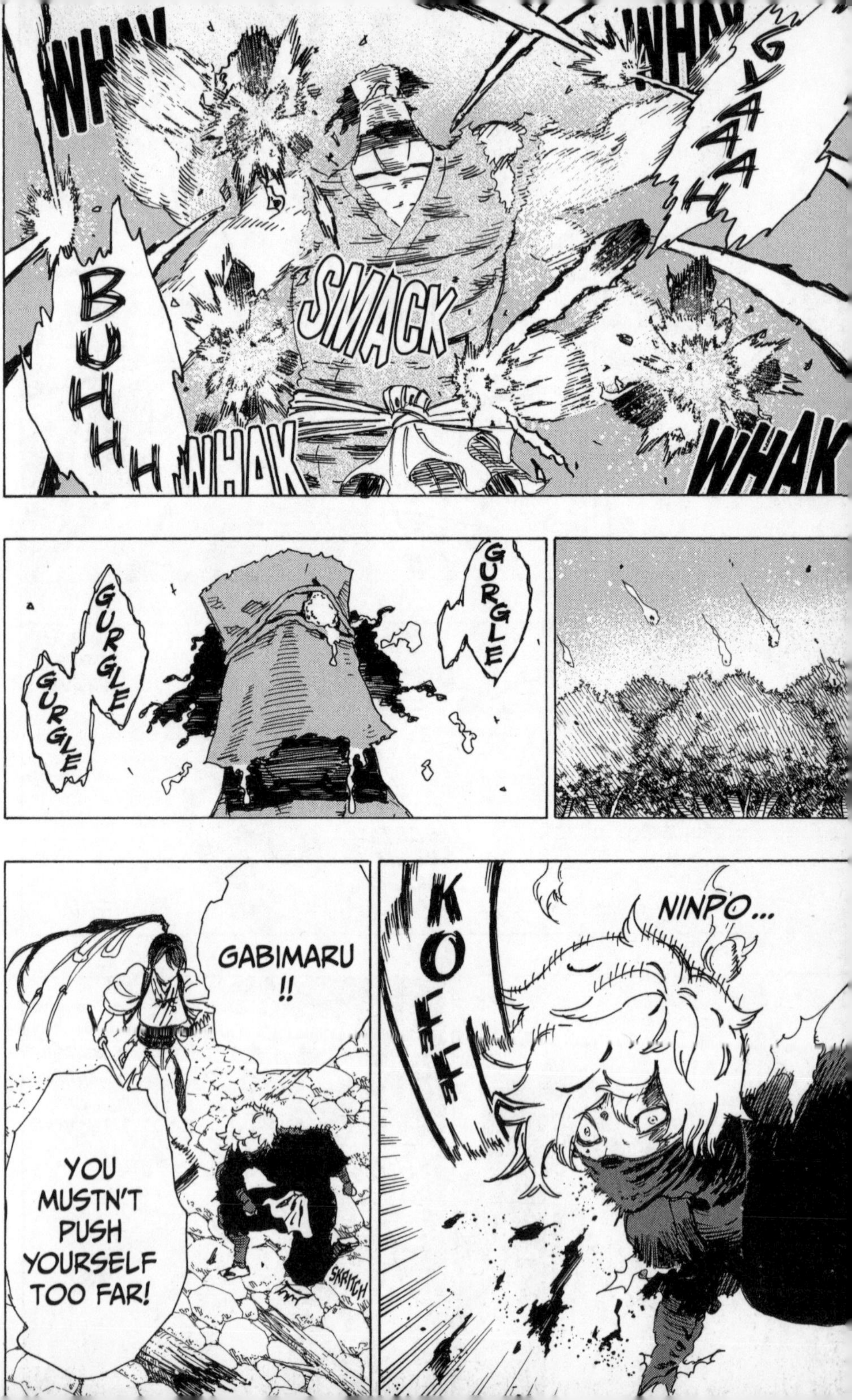

WHAK
GYAAAH
WHAK
SMACK
BUHHHH
WHAK
WHAK
GURGLE
GURGLE GURGLE
NINPO...
KOFF
GABIMARU!!
YOU MUSTN'T PUSH YOURSELF TOO FAR!
SKRITCH

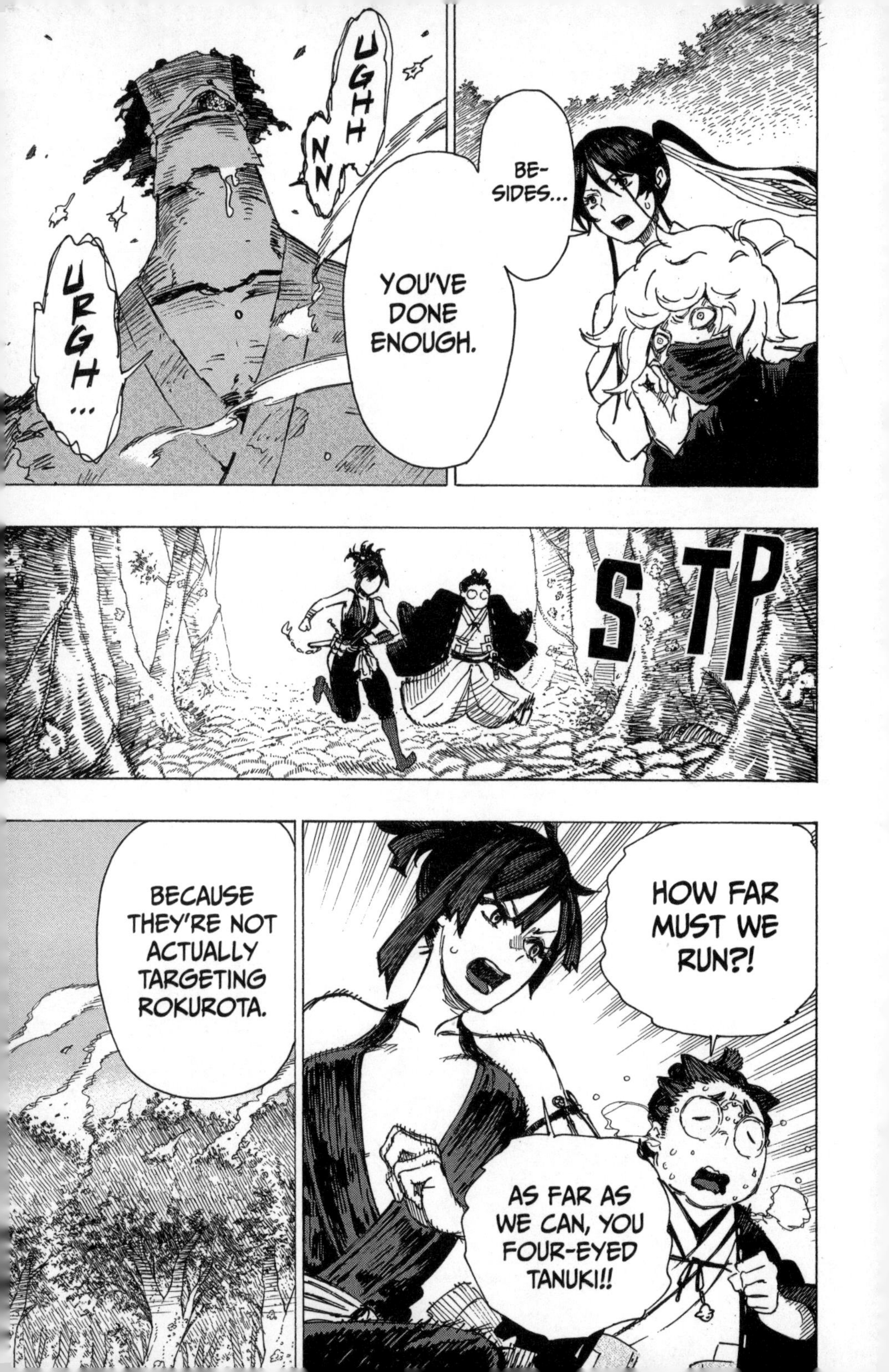
BE-SIDES...
YOU'VE DONE ENOUGH.
UGHH
NN
URGH...
STP
HOW FAR MUST WE RUN?!
AS FAR AS WE CAN, YOU FOUR-EYED TANUKI!!
BECAUSE THEY'RE NOT ACTUALLY TARGETING ROKUROTA.

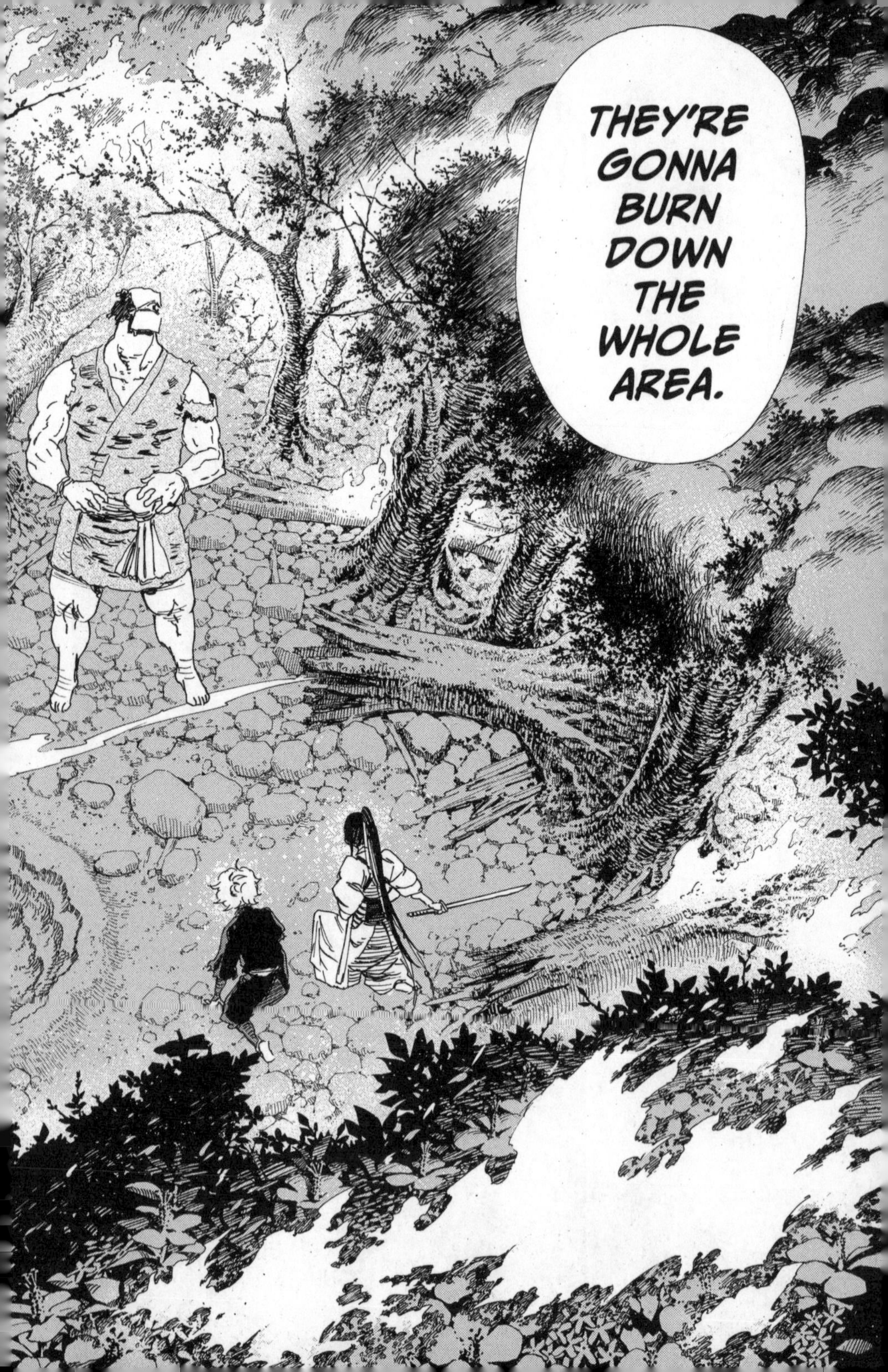
THEY'RE GONNA BURN DOWN THE WHOLE AREA.

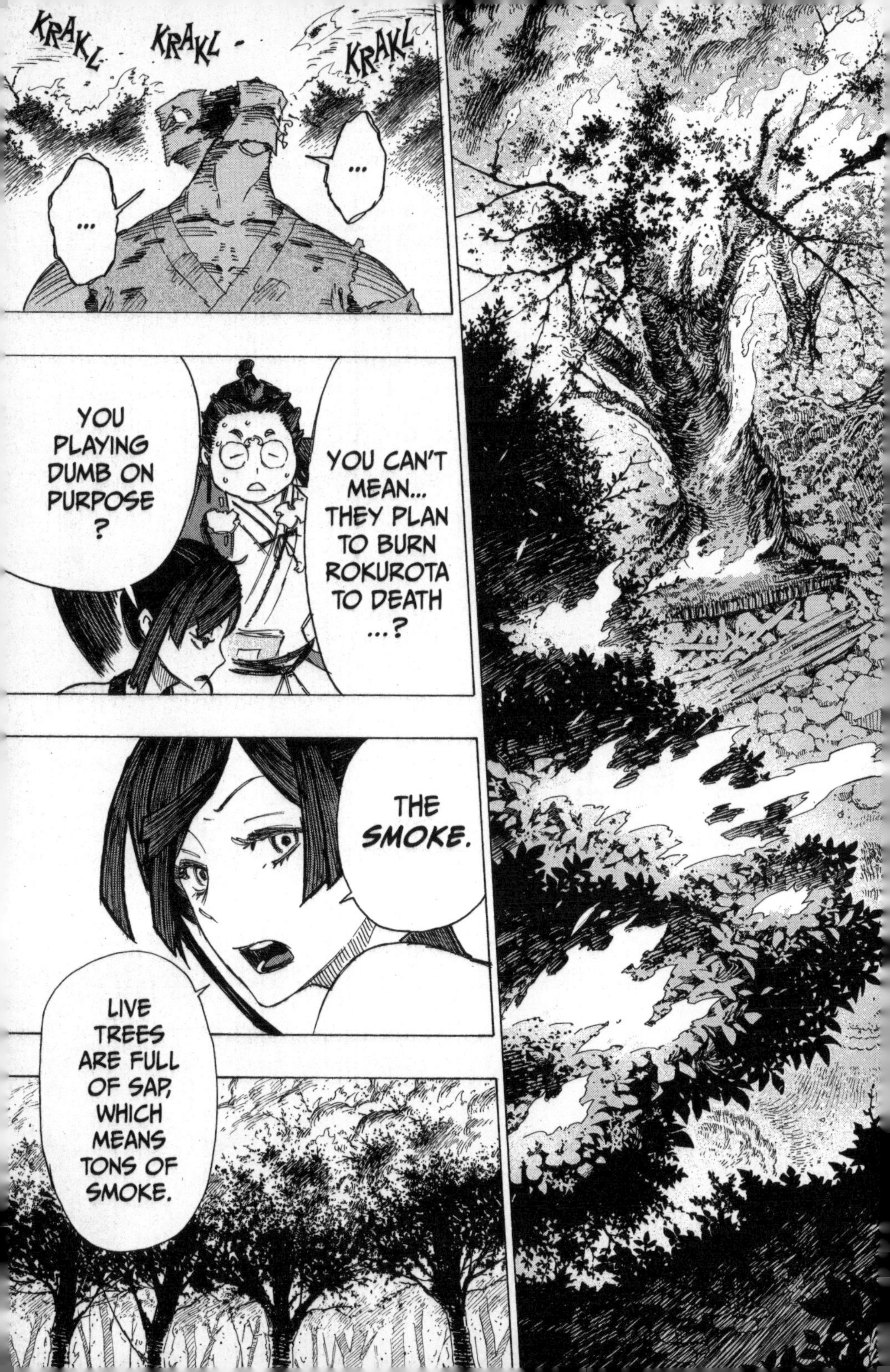
KRAKL
KRAKL
KRAKL
...
...
YOU CAN'T MEAN... THEY PLAN TO BURN ROKUROTA TO DEATH ...?
YOU PLAYING DUMB ON PURPOSE ?
THE SMOKE.
LIVE TREES ARE FULL OF SAP, WHICH MEANS TONS OF SMOKE.

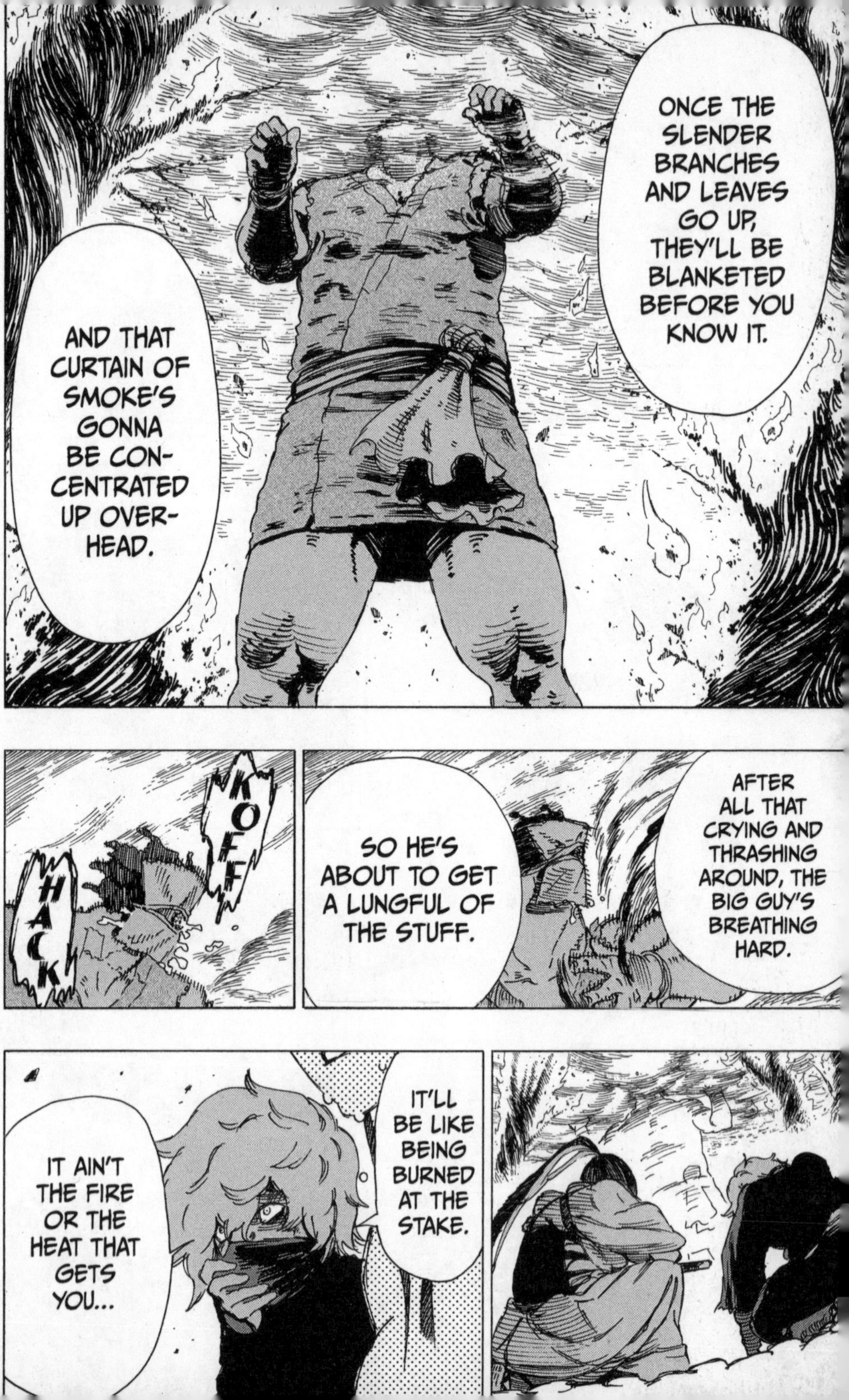
ONCE THE SLENDER BRANCHES AND LEAVES GO UP, THEY'LL BE BLANKETED BEFORE YOU KNOW IT.
AND THAT CURTAIN OF SMOKE'S GONNA BE CON-CENTRATED UP OVER-HEAD.
AFTER ALL THAT CRYING AND THRASHING AROUND, THE BIG GUY'S BREATHING HARD.
SO HE'S ABOUT TO GET A LUNGFUL OF THE STUFF.
KOFF
HACK
IT'LL BE LIKE BEING BURNED AT THE STAKE.
IT AIN'T THE FIRE OR THE HEAT THAT GETS YOU...

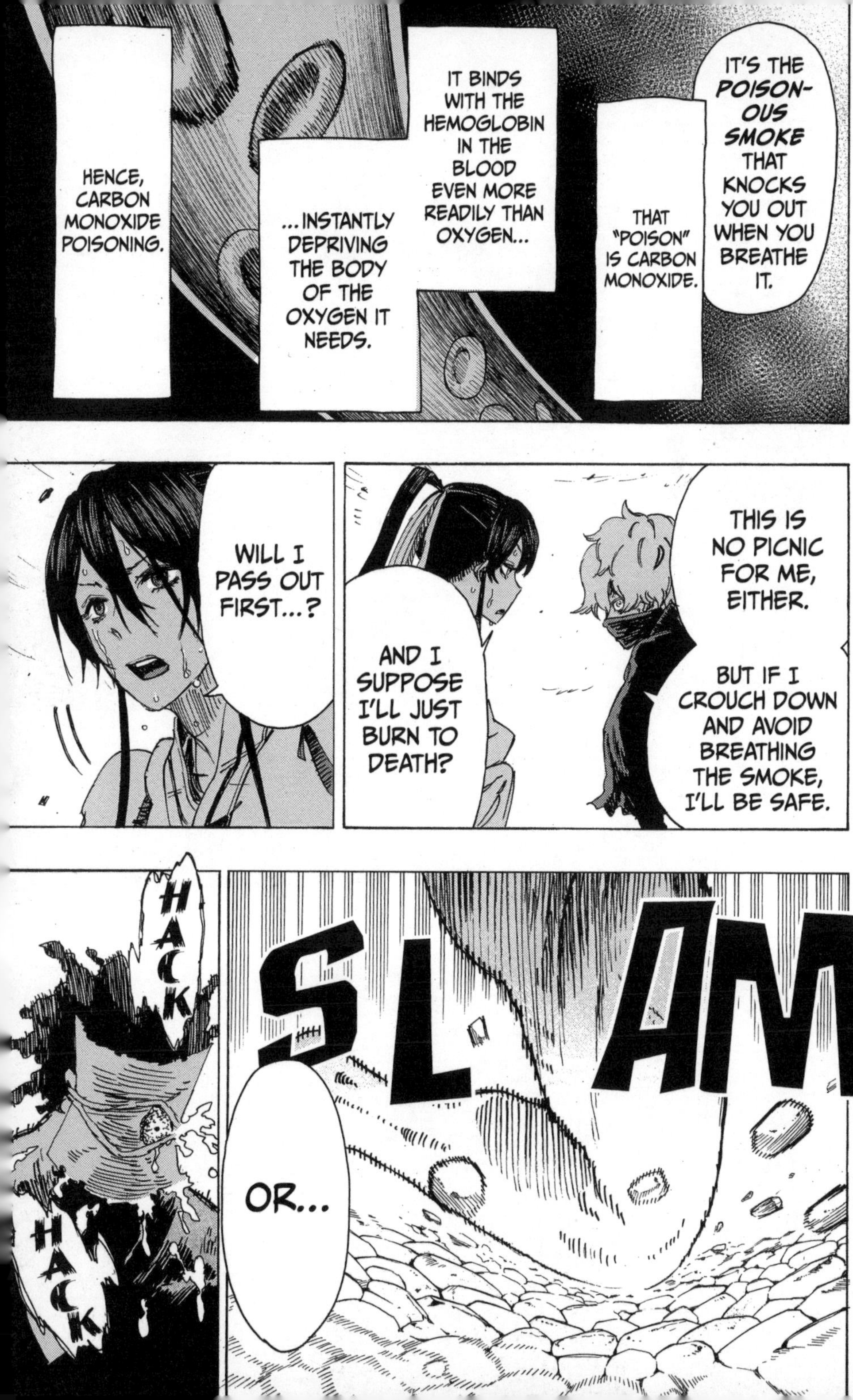
IT'S THE ***POISONOUS SMOKE*** THAT KNOCKS YOU OUT WHEN YOU BREATHE IT.
THAT "POISON" IS CARBON MONOXIDE.
IT BINDS WITH THE HEMOGLOBIN IN THE BLOOD EVEN MORE READILY THAN OXYGEN...
...INSTANTLY DEPRIVING THE BODY OF THE OXYGEN IT NEEDS.
HENCE, CARBON MONOXIDE POISONING.
THIS IS NO PICNIC FOR ME, EITHER.
BUT IF I CROUCH DOWN AND AVOID BREATHING THE SMOKE, I'LL BE SAFE.
AND I SUPPOSE I'LL JUST BURN TO DEATH?
WILL I PASS OUT FIRST...?
SLAM
OR...
HACK
HACK

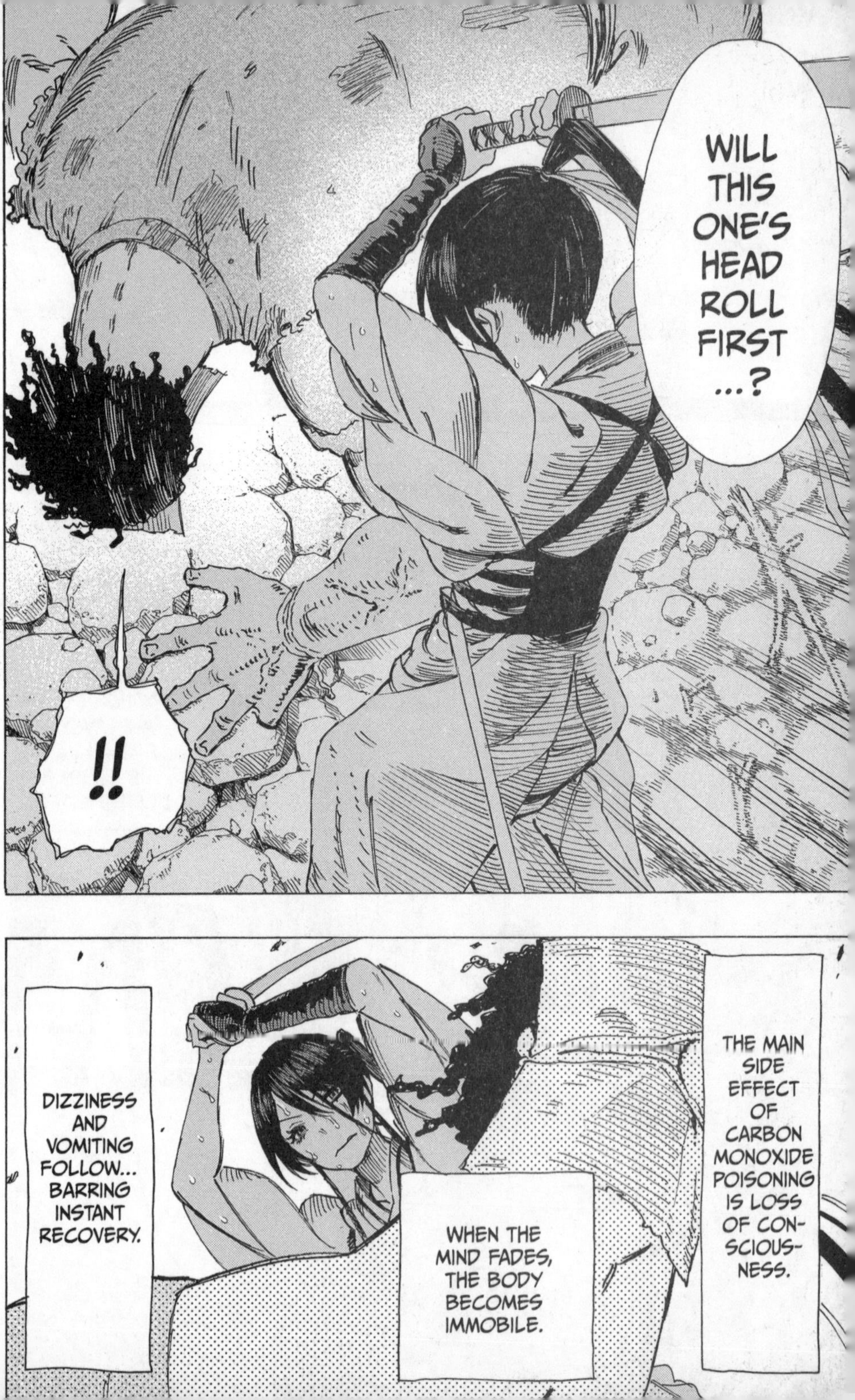
WILL THIS ONE'S HEAD ROLL FIRST ...?
!!
THE MAIN SIDE EFFECT OF CARBON MONOXIDE POISONING IS LOSS OF CON-SCIOUS-NESS.
WHEN THE MIND FADES, THE BODY BECOMES IMMOBILE.
DIZZINESS AND VOMITING FOLLOW... BARRING INSTANT RECOVERY.

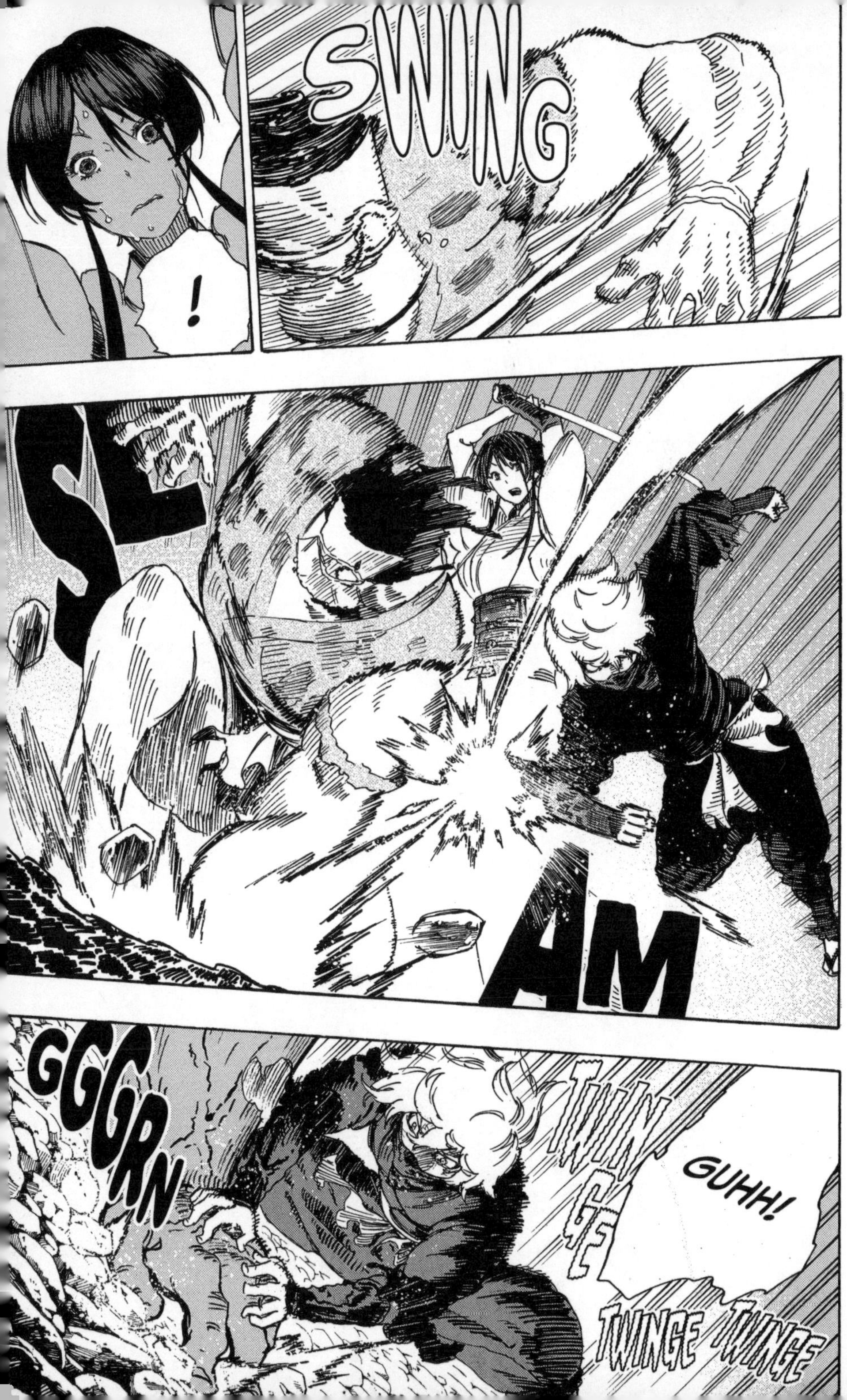
SWING
!
SL
AM
GUHH!
TWINGE
GGGRN
TWINGE TWINGE

GYAAH

HACK

STRAIN

MAKE THE CUT! NOW!

MY MUSCLES CAN'T MATCH HIS FOR LONG!

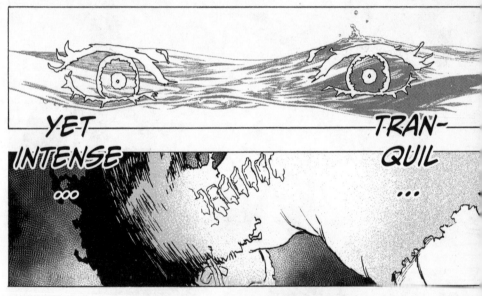

YET INTENSE ...

TRAN-QUIL ...

HA A

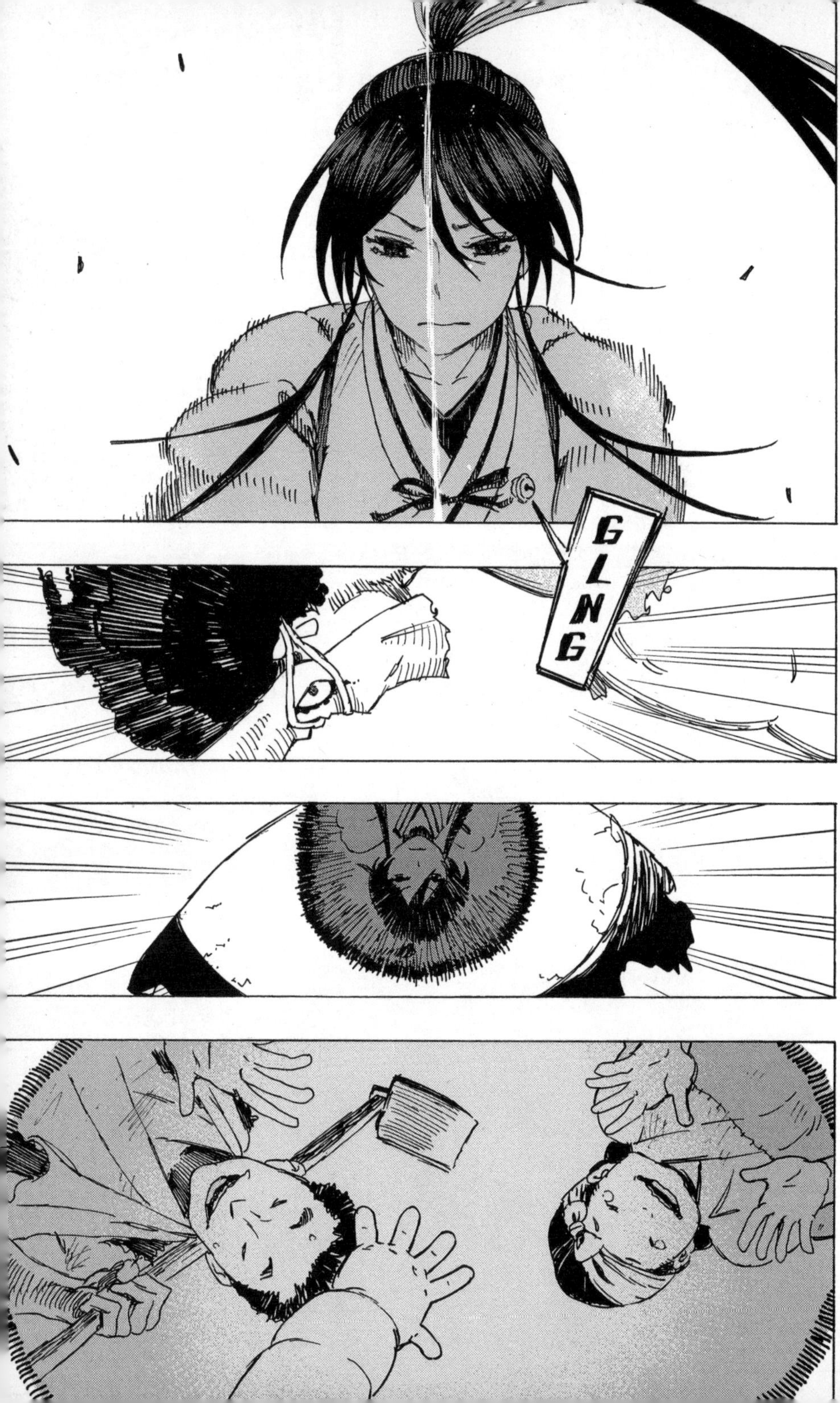
GLING

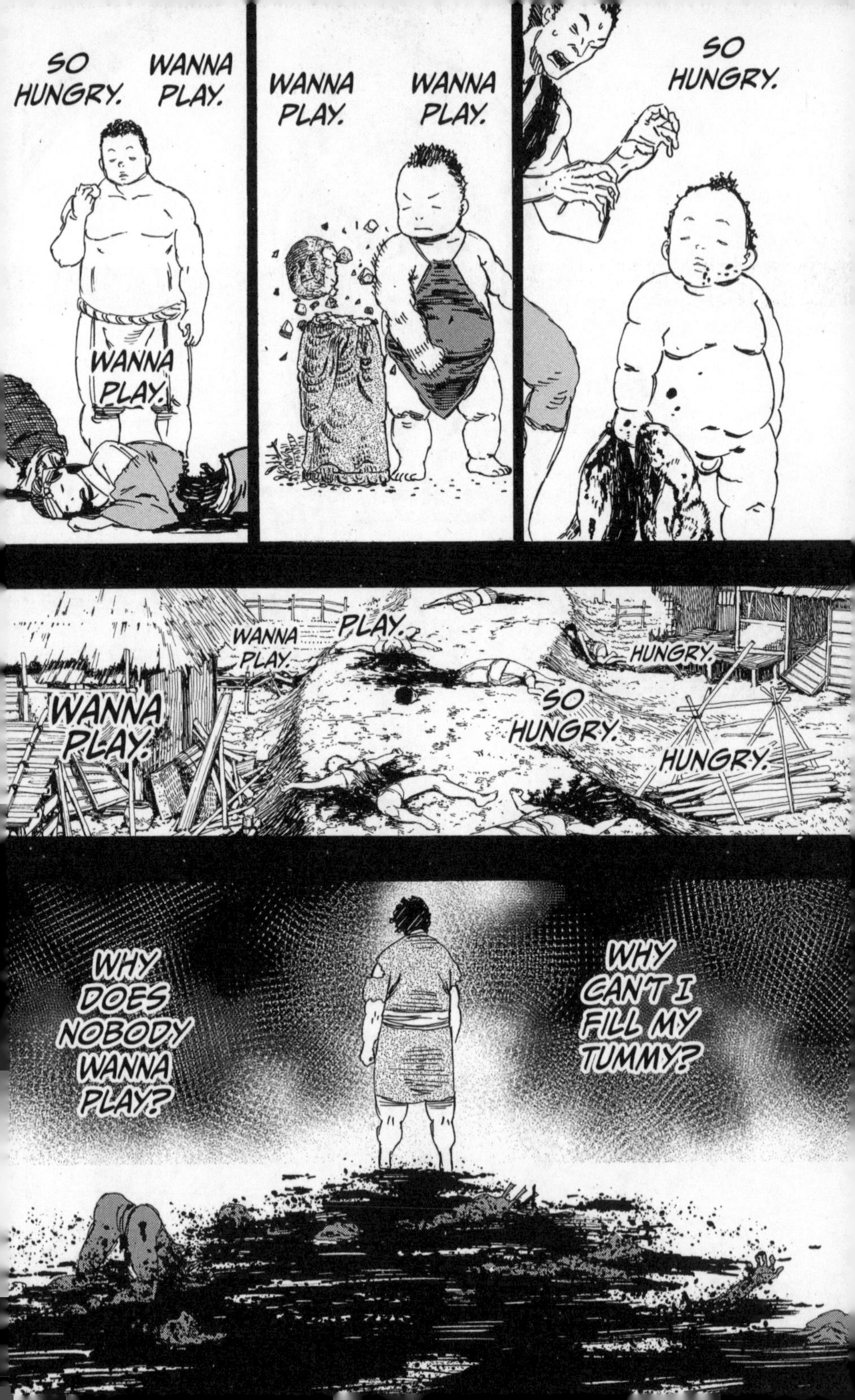
SO HUNGRY.
WANNA PLAY.
WANNA PLAY.
WANNA PLAY.
SO HUNGRY.
WANNA PLAY.
HUNGRY.
PLAY.
WANNA PLAY.
SO HUNGRY.
HUNGRY.
WANNA PLAY.
WHY CAN'T I FILL MY TUMMY?
WHY DOES NOBODY WANNA PLAY?

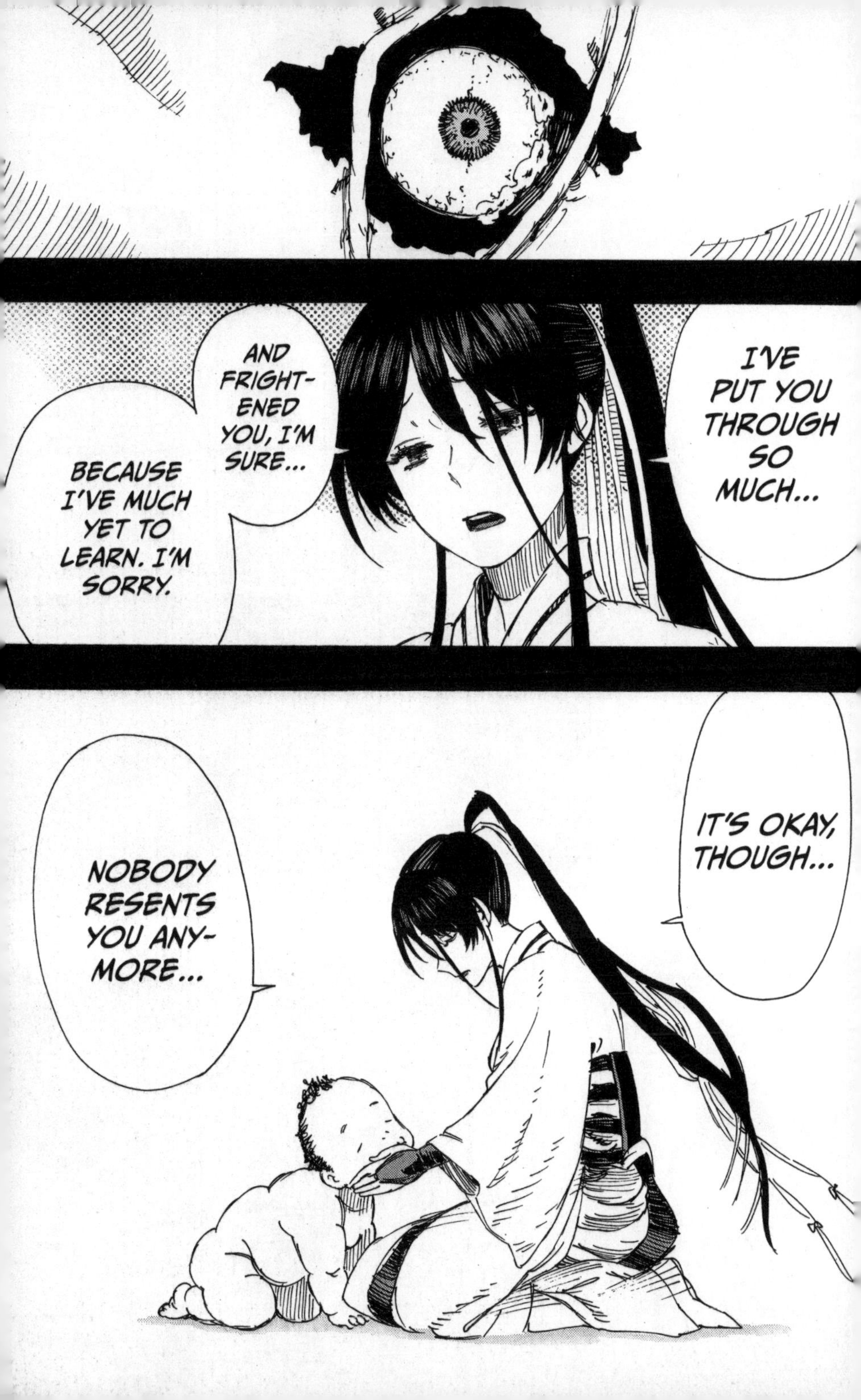
I'VE PUT YOU THROUGH SO MUCH...
AND FRIGHT-ENED YOU, I'M SURE...
BECAUSE I'VE MUCH YET TO LEARN. I'M SORRY.
IT'S OKAY, THOUGH...
NOBODY RESENTS YOU ANY-MORE...

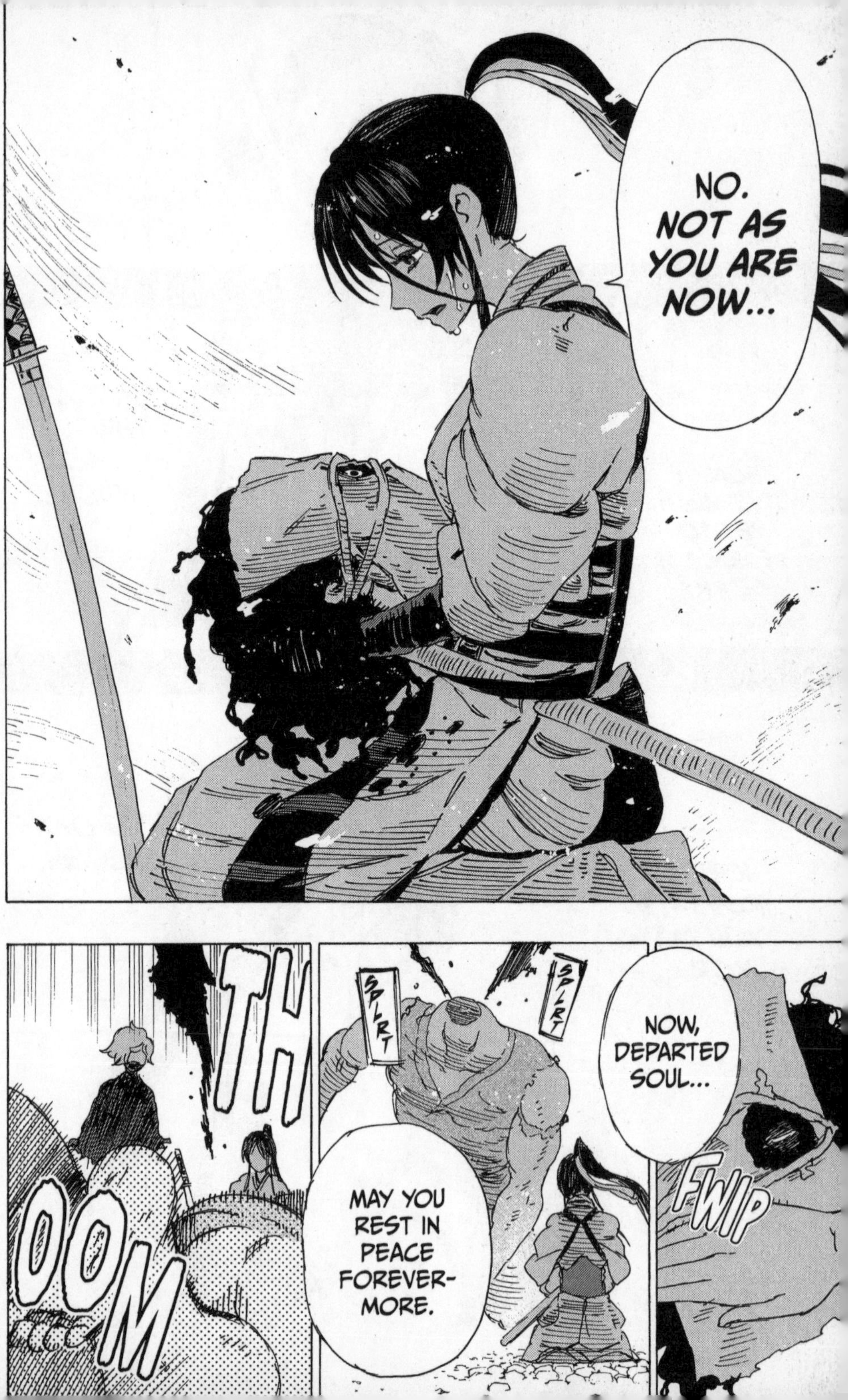
NO. NOT AS YOU ARE NOW...
NOW, DEPARTED SOUL...
FWIP
SPLRT
SPLRT
MAY YOU REST IN PEACE FOREVER-MORE.
THOOM

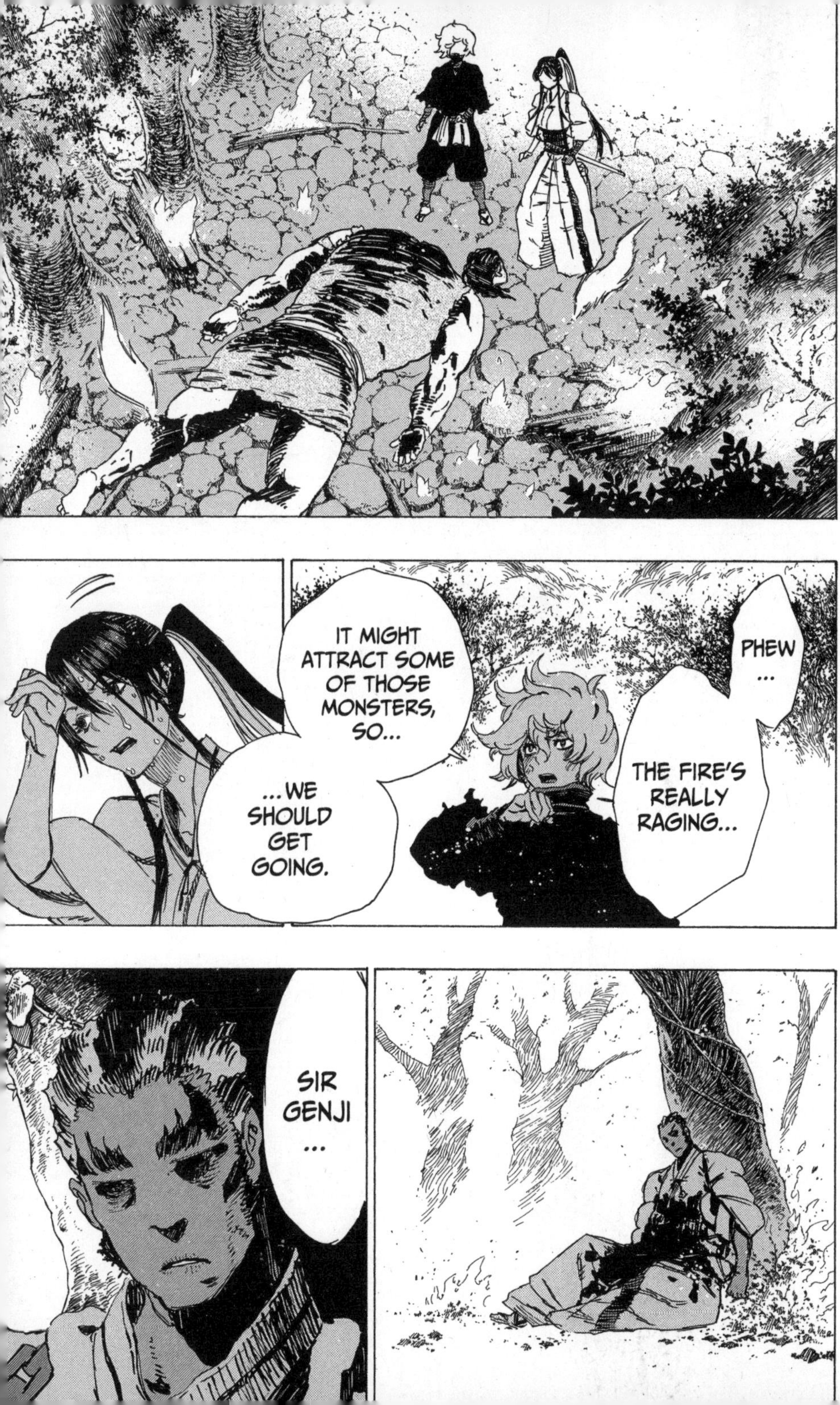
PHEW ...
THE FIRE'S REALLY RAGING...
IT MIGHT ATTRACT SOME OF THOSE MONSTERS, SO...
...WE SHOULD GET GOING.
SIR GENJI ...

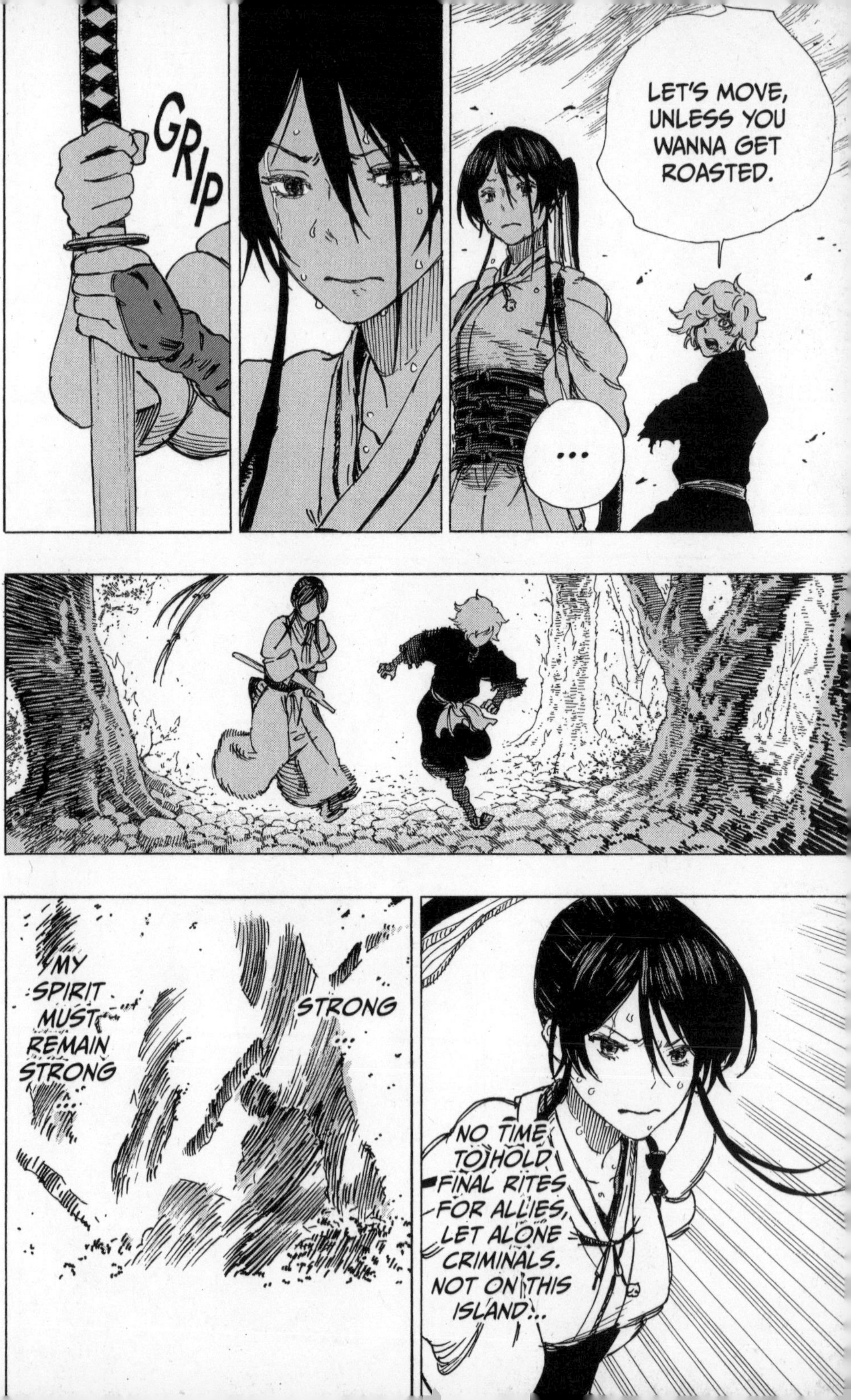
LET'S MOVE, UNLESS YOU WANNA GET ROASTED.
...
GRIP
NO TIME TO HOLD FINAL RITES FOR ALLIES, LET ALONE CRIMINALS. NOT ON THIS ISLAND...
MY SPIRIT MUST REMAIN STRONG...
STRONG...

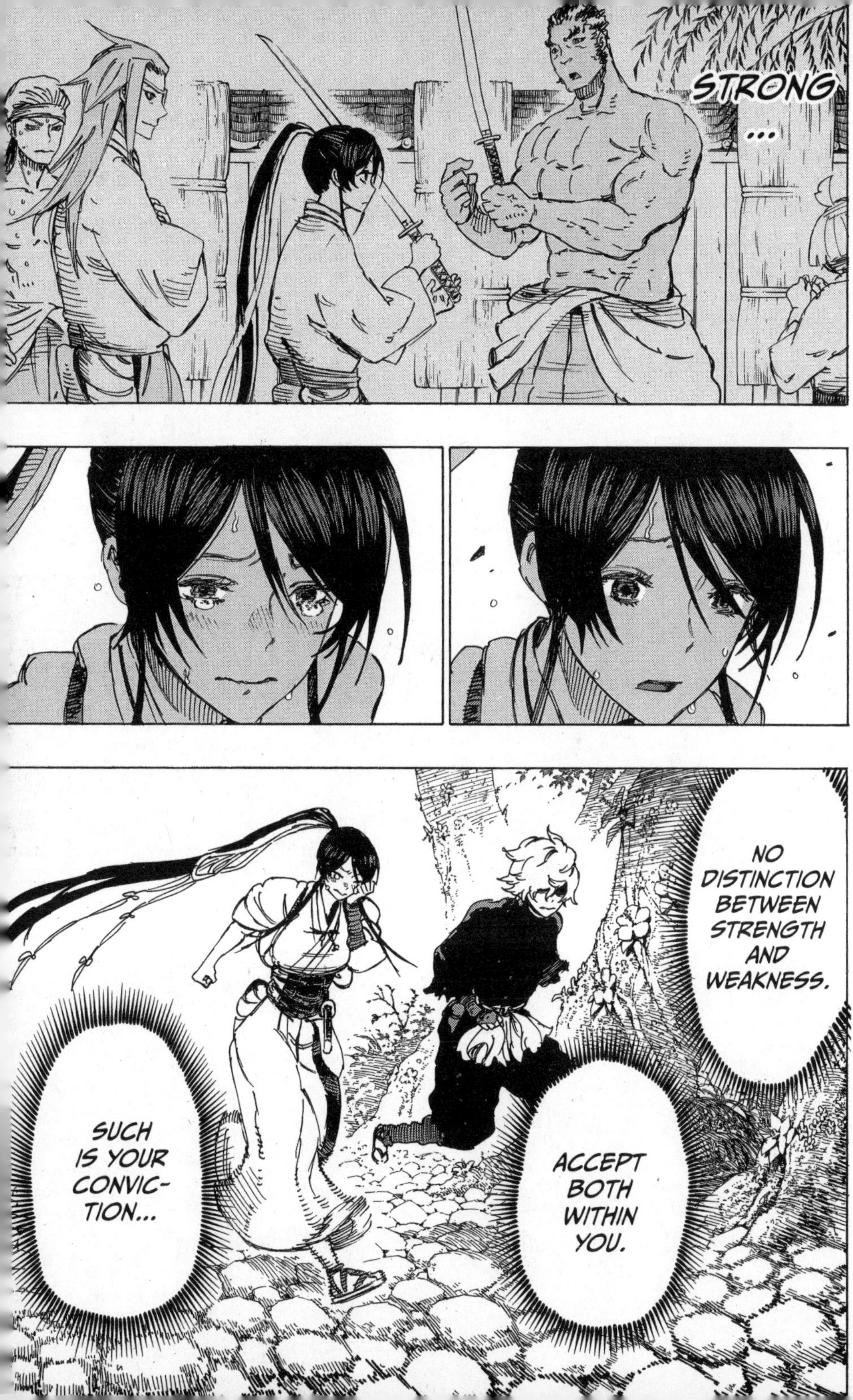
STRONG ...
NO DISTINCTION BETWEEN STRENGTH AND WEAKNESS.
ACCEPT BOTH WITHIN YOU.
SUCH IS YOUR CONVIC-TION...

Hell's Paradise

JIGOKURAKU

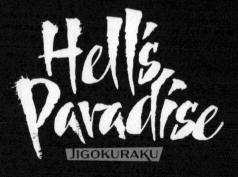

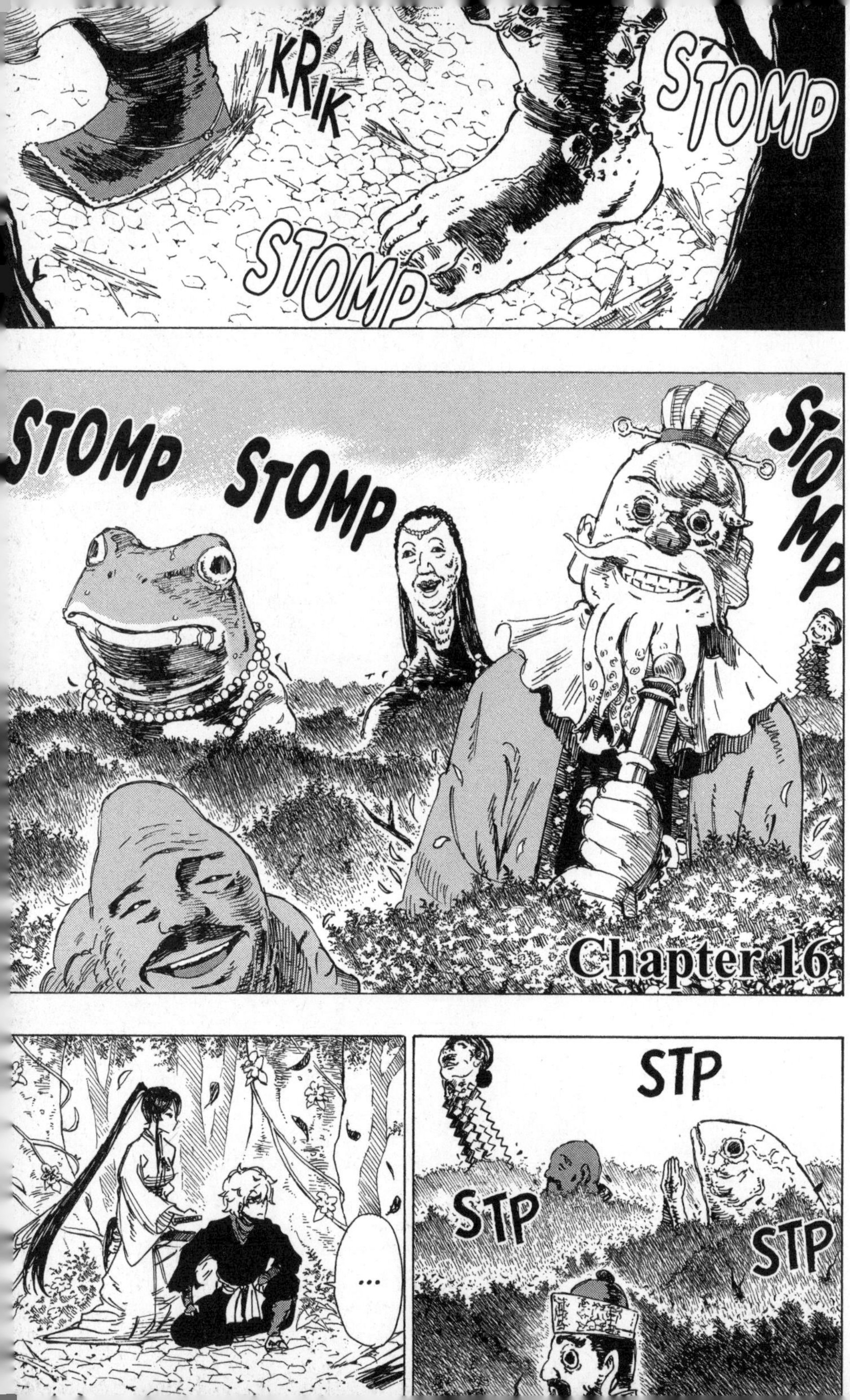
STOMP
KRIK
STOMP
STOMP
STOMP
STOMP
Chapter 16
STP
STP
STP
...

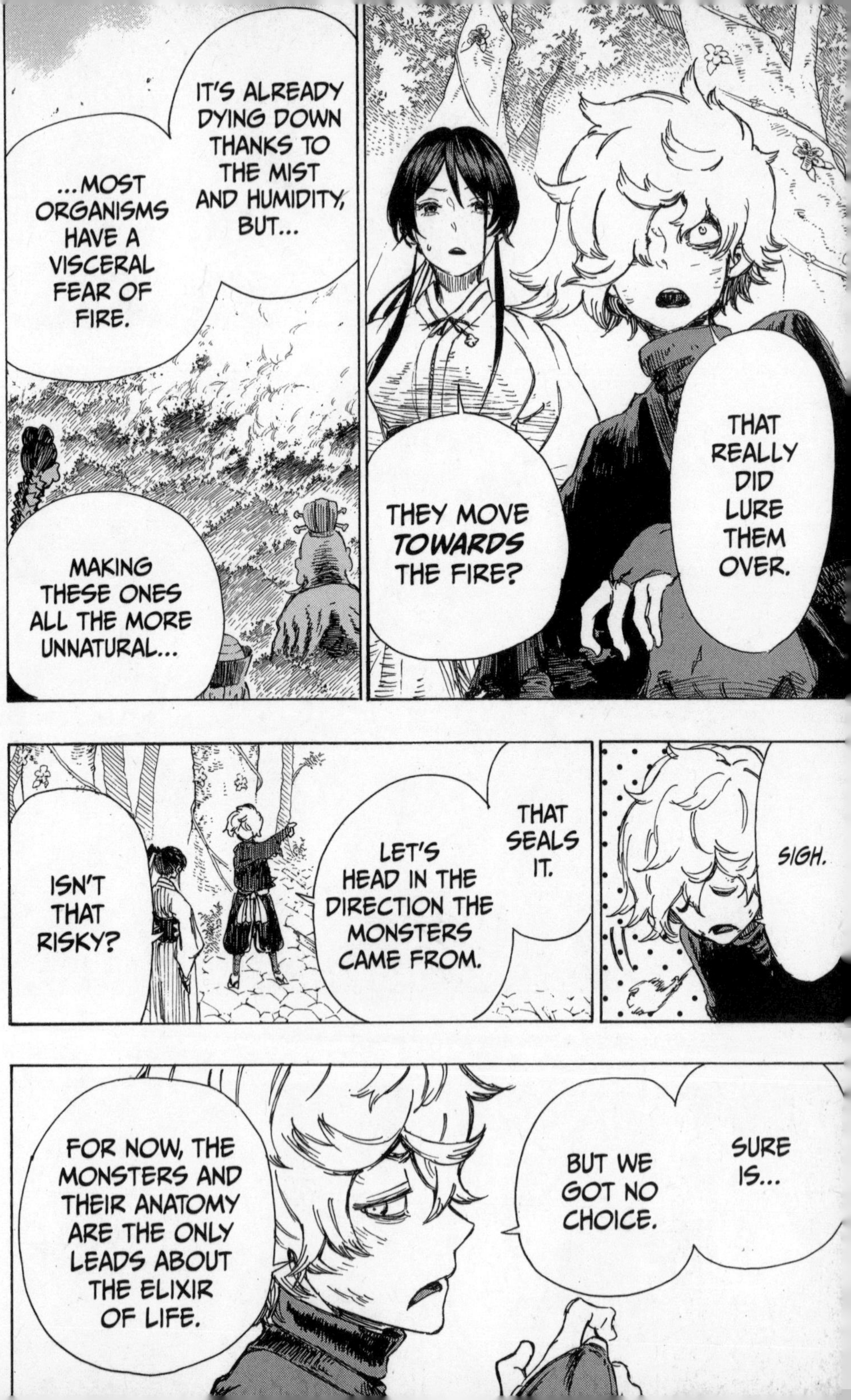
THAT REALLY DID LURE THEM OVER.
THEY MOVE *TOWARDS* THE FIRE?
IT'S ALREADY DYING DOWN THANKS TO THE MIST AND HUMIDITY, BUT...
...MOST ORGANISMS HAVE A VISCERAL FEAR OF FIRE.
MAKING THESE ONES ALL THE MORE UNNATURAL...
SIGH.
THAT SEALS IT.
LET'S HEAD IN THE DIRECTION THE MONSTERS CAME FROM.
ISN'T THAT RISKY?
SURE IS...
BUT WE GOT NO CHOICE.
FOR NOW, THE MONSTERS AND THEIR ANATOMY ARE THE ONLY LEADS ABOUT THE ELIXIR OF LIFE.

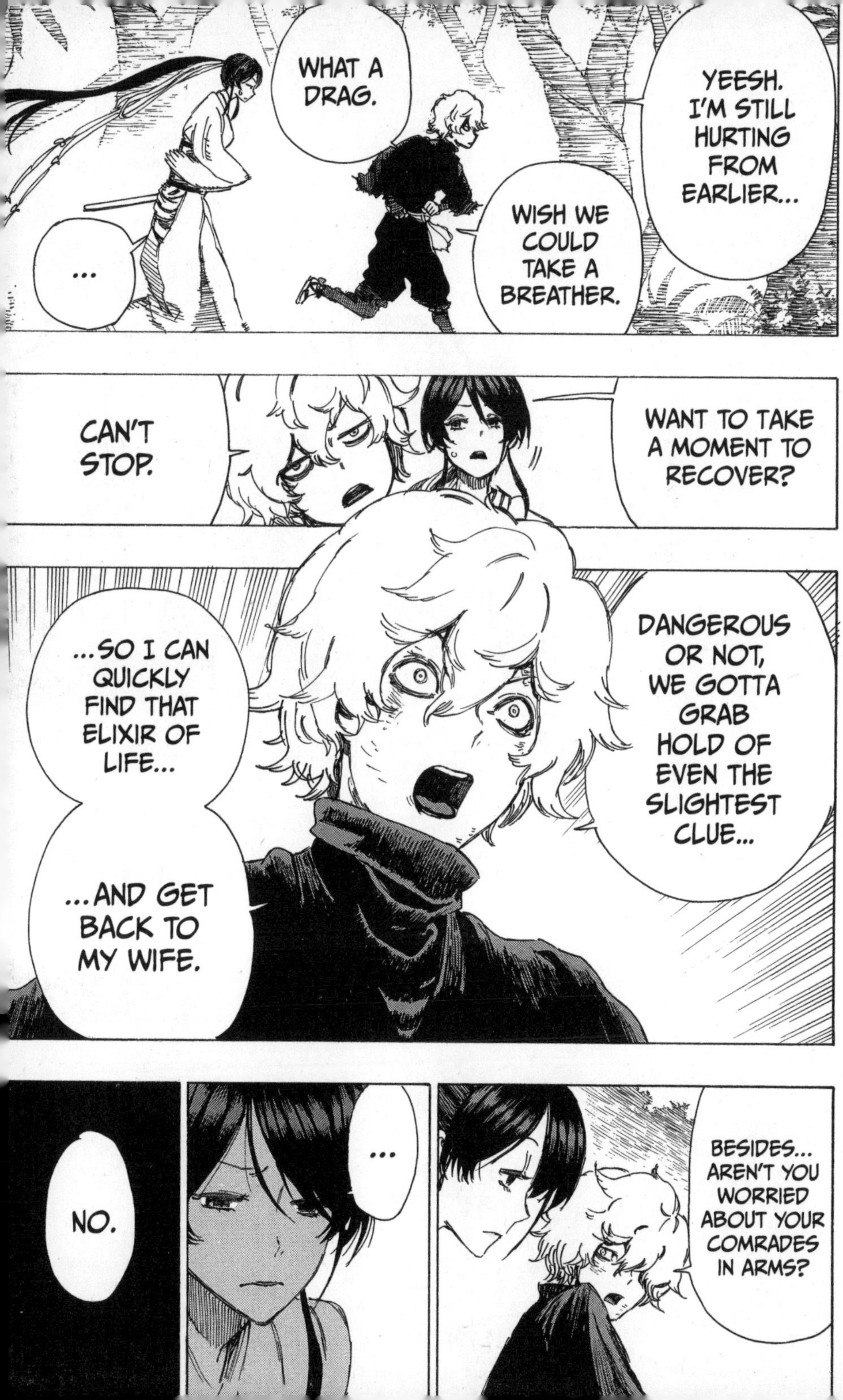
YEESH. I'M STILL HURTING FROM EARLIER...
WISH WE COULD TAKE A BREATHER.
WHAT A DRAG.
...
WANT TO TAKE A MOMENT TO RECOVER?
CAN'T STOP.
DANGEROUS OR NOT, WE GOTTA GRAB HOLD OF EVEN THE SLIGHTEST CLUE...
...SO I CAN QUICKLY FIND THAT ELIXIR OF LIFE...
...AND GET BACK TO MY WIFE.
BESIDES... AREN'T YOU WORRIED ABOUT YOUR COMRADES IN ARMS?
...
NO.

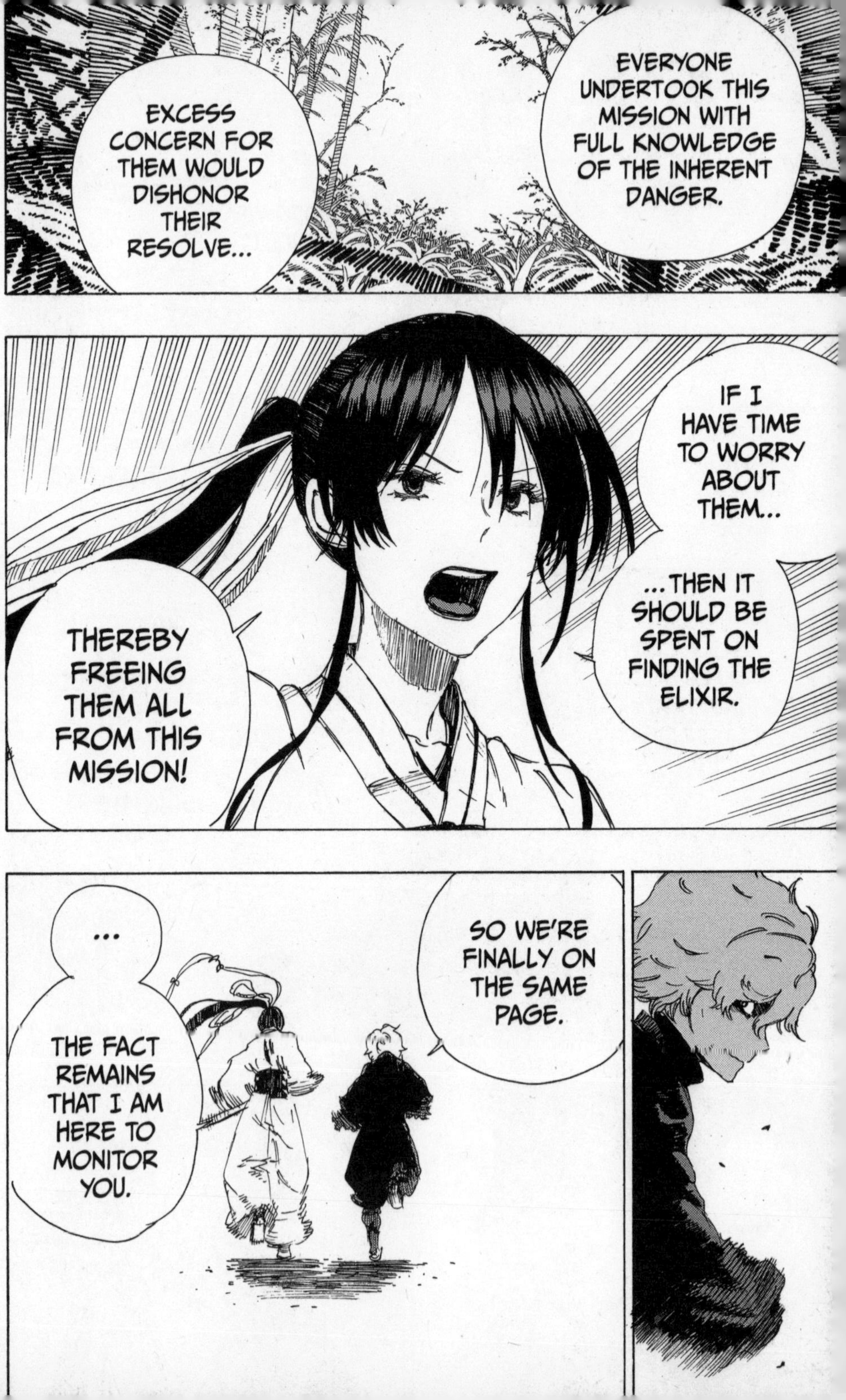
EVERYONE UNDERTOOK THIS MISSION WITH FULL KNOWLEDGE OF THE INHERENT DANGER.
EXCESS CONCERN FOR THEM WOULD DISHONOR THEIR RESOLVE...
IF I HAVE TIME TO WORRY ABOUT THEM...
...THEN IT SHOULD BE SPENT ON FINDING THE ELIXIR.
THEREBY FREEING THEM ALL FROM THIS MISSION!
SO WE'RE FINALLY ON THE SAME PAGE.
...
THE FACT REMAINS THAT I AM HERE TO MONITOR YOU.

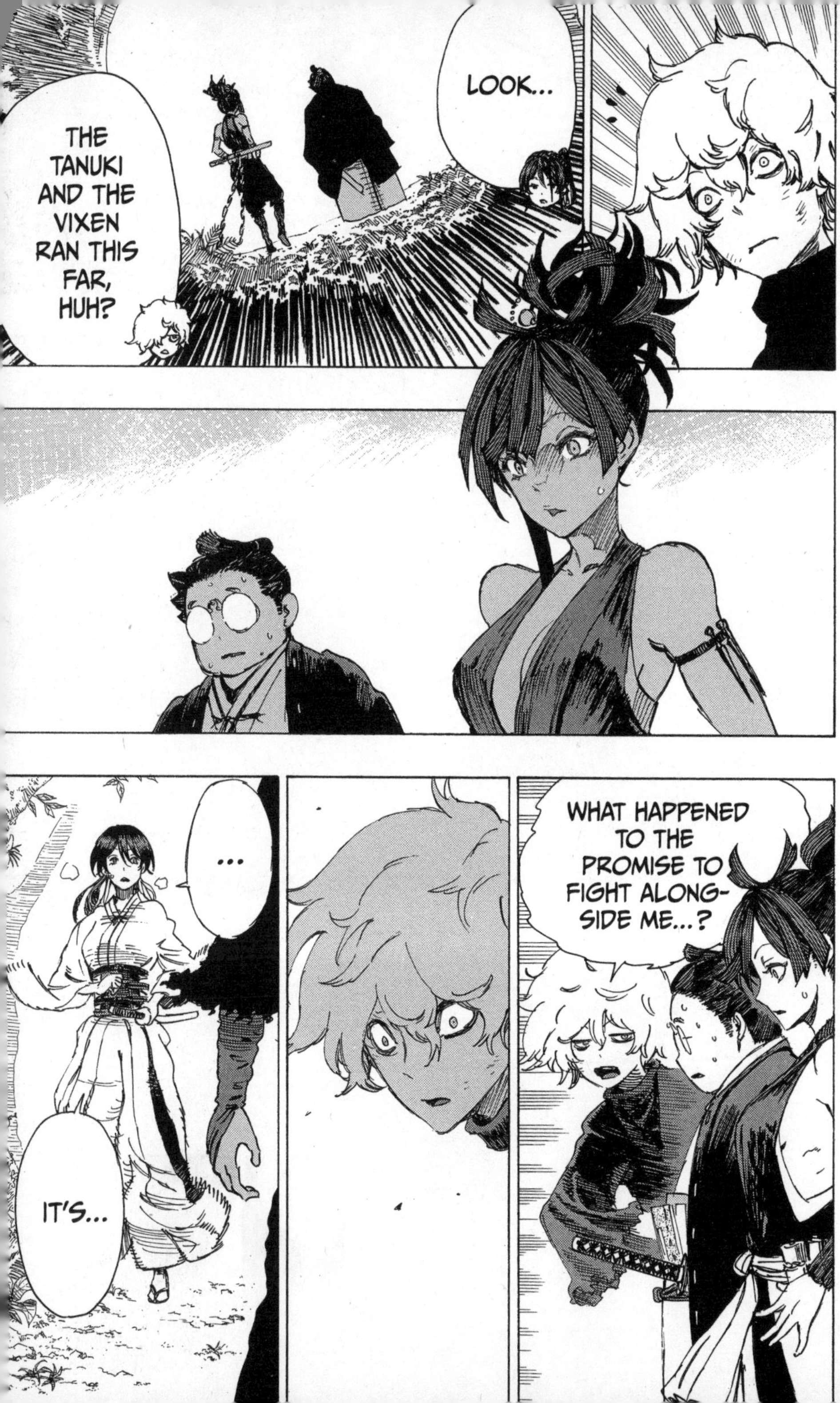
LOOK...
THE TANUKI AND THE VIXEN RAN THIS FAR, HUH?
WHAT HAPPENED TO THE PROMISE TO FIGHT ALONG-SIDE ME...?
...
IT'S...

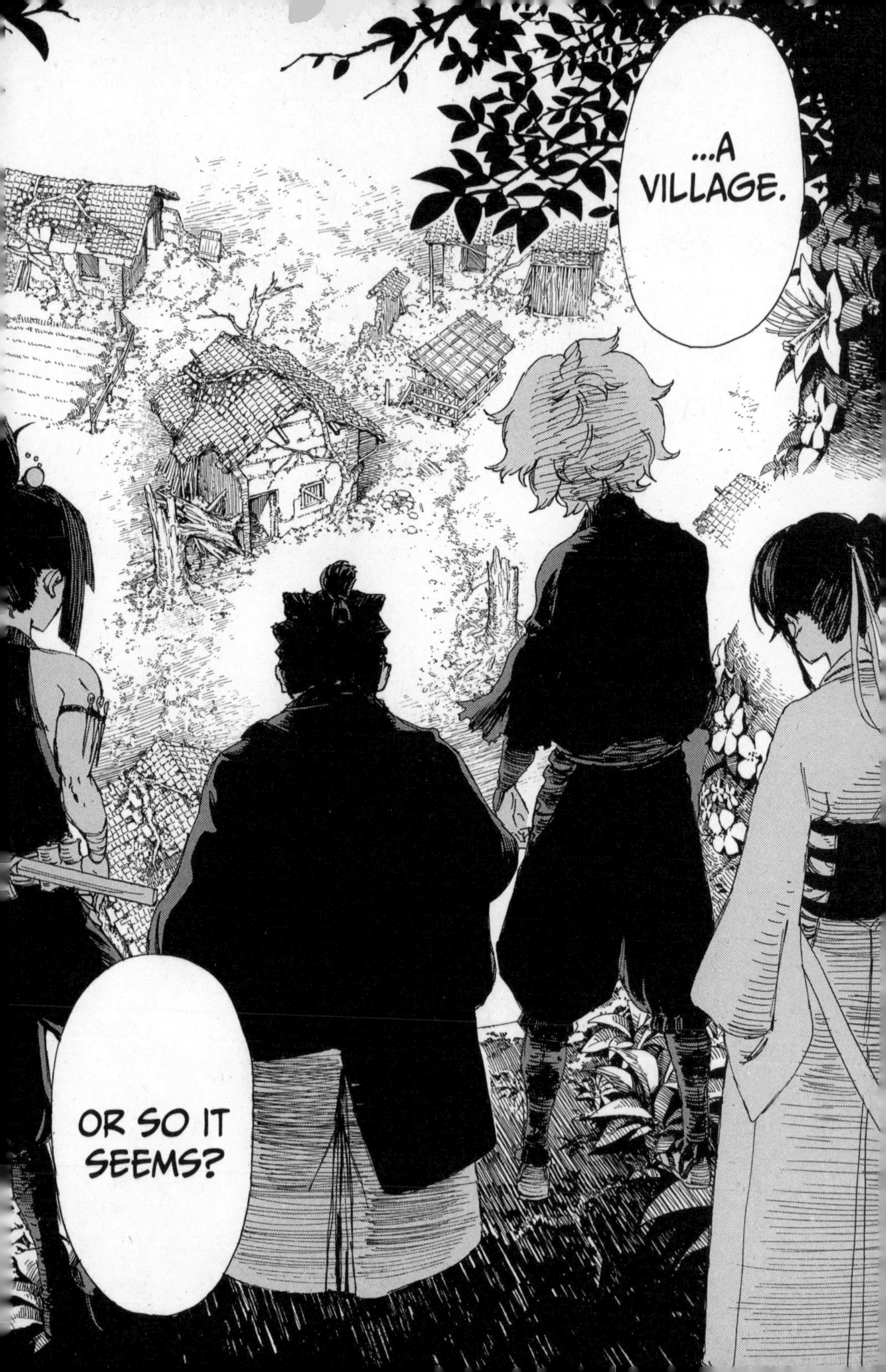
...A VILLAGE.
OR SO IT SEEMS?

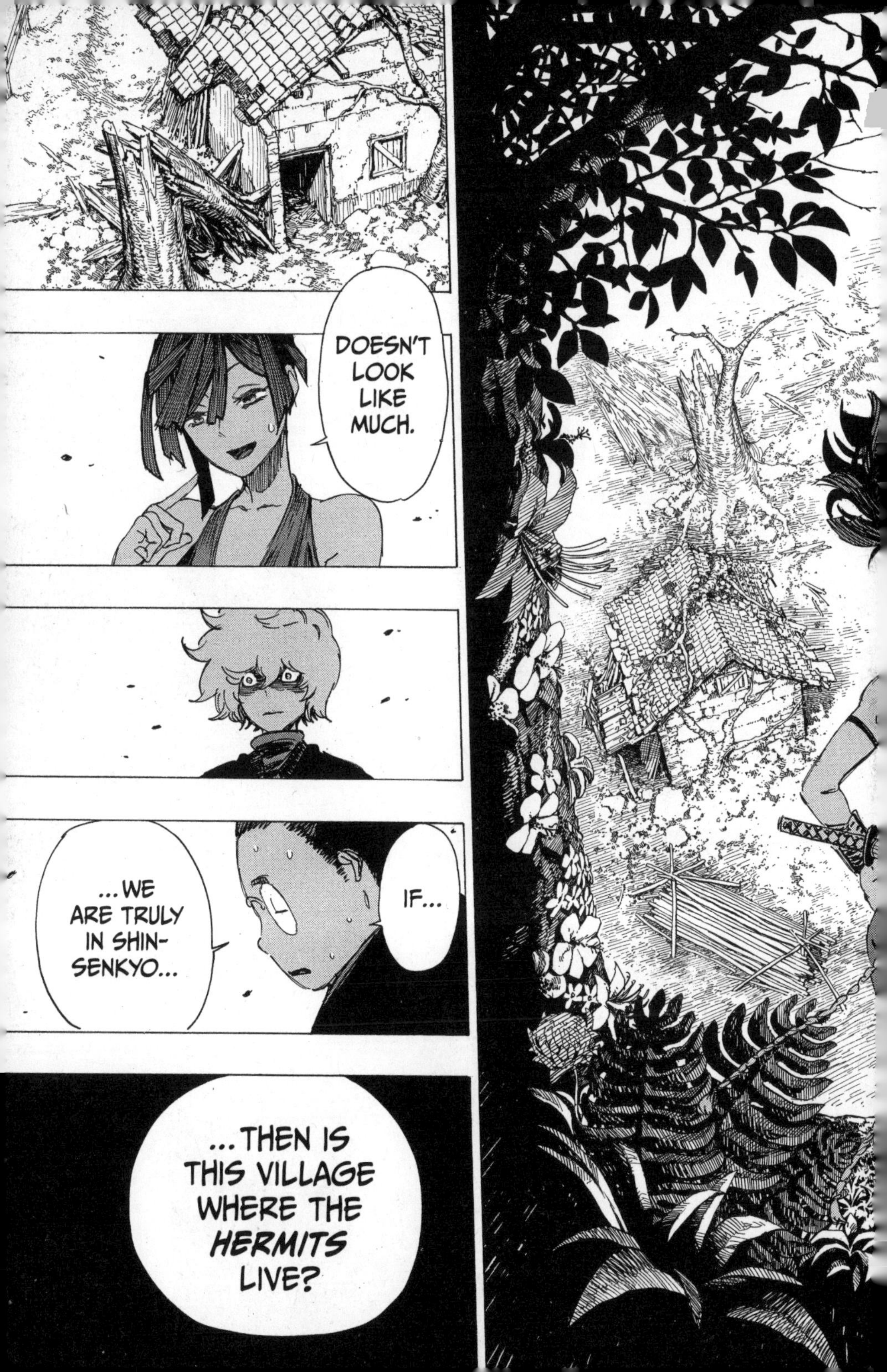
DOESN'T LOOK LIKE MUCH.
IF...
...WE ARE TRULY IN SHIN-SENKYO...
...THEN IS THIS VILLAGE WHERE THE *HERMITS* LIVE?

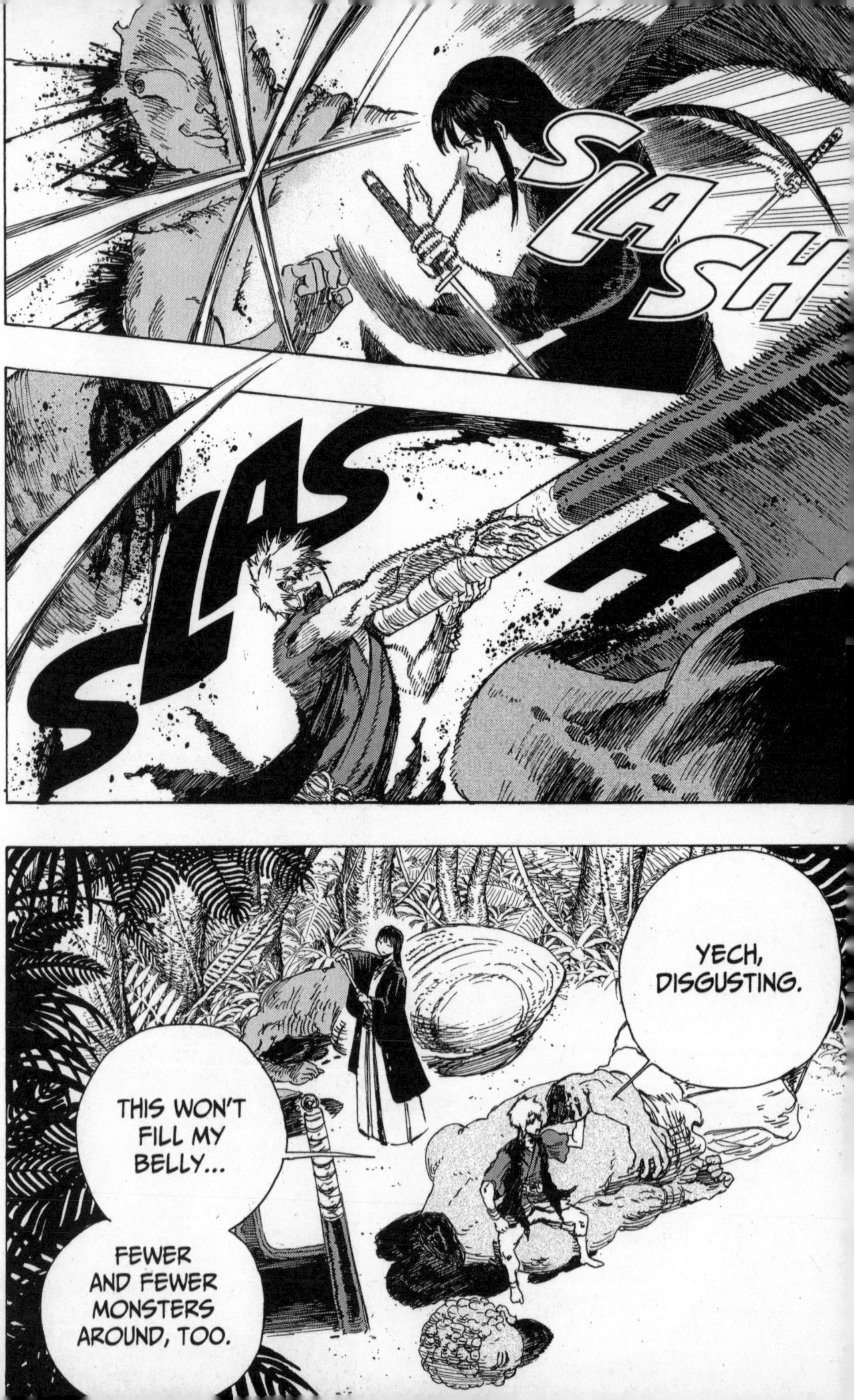
SLASH
SLASH
YECH, DISGUSTING.
THIS WON'T FILL MY BELLY...
FEWER AND FEWER MONSTERS AROUND, TOO.

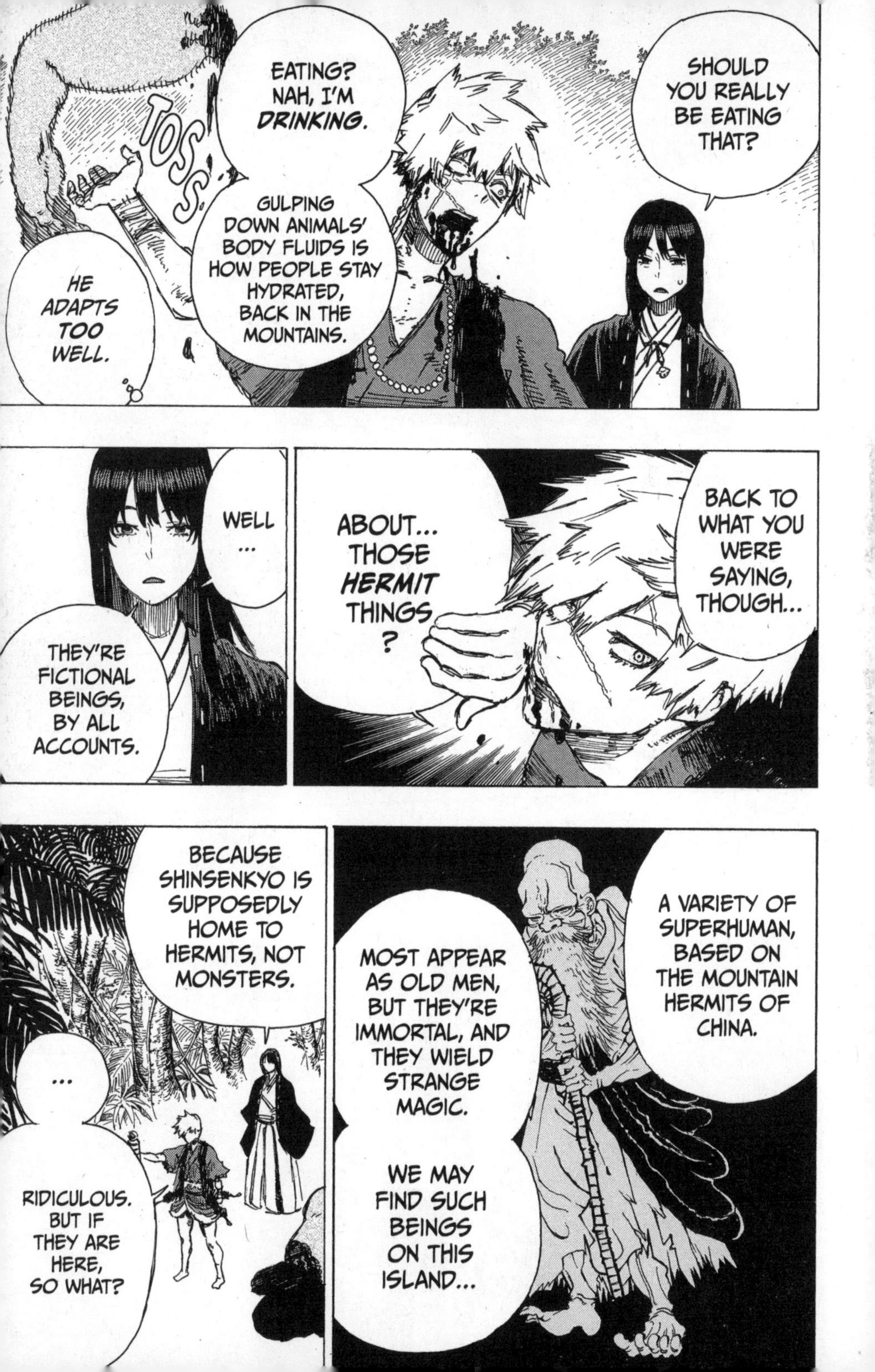
SHOULD YOU REALLY BE EATING THAT?
EATING? NAH, I'M DRINKING.
GULPING DOWN ANIMALS' BODY FLUIDS IS HOW PEOPLE STAY HYDRATED, BACK IN THE MOUNTAINS.
TOSS
HE ADAPTS TOO WELL.
BACK TO WHAT YOU WERE SAYING, THOUGH...
ABOUT... THOSE HERMIT THINGS?
WELL ...
THEY'RE FICTIONAL BEINGS, BY ALL ACCOUNTS.
A VARIETY OF SUPERHUMAN, BASED ON THE MOUNTAIN HERMITS OF CHINA.
MOST APPEAR AS OLD MEN, BUT THEY'RE IMMORTAL, AND THEY WIELD STRANGE MAGIC.
WE MAY FIND SUCH BEINGS ON THIS ISLAND...
BECAUSE SHINSENKYO IS SUPPOSEDLY HOME TO HERMITS, NOT MONSTERS.
...
RIDICULOUS. BUT IF THEY ARE HERE, SO WHAT?

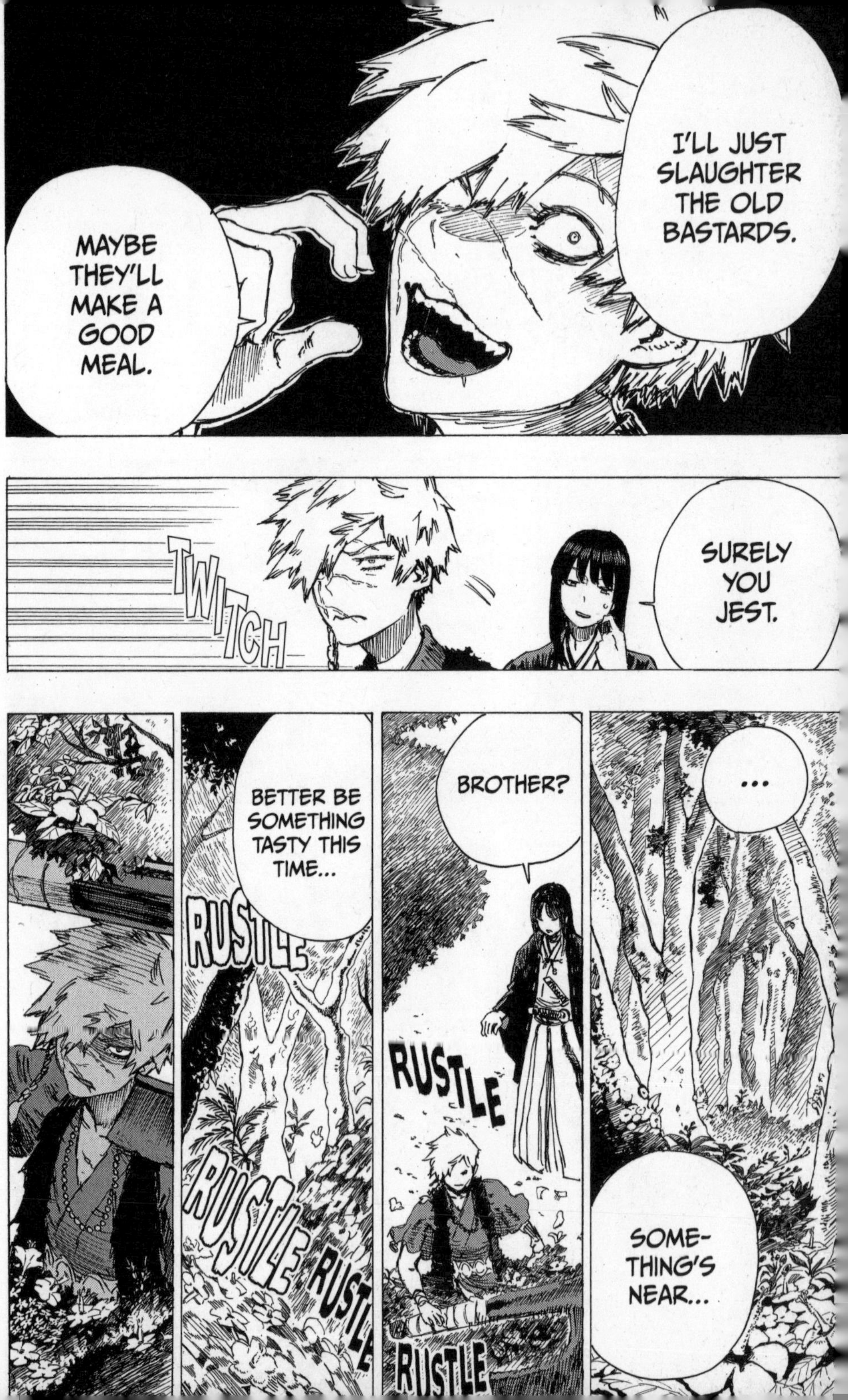
I'LL JUST SLAUGHTER THE OLD BASTARDS.
MAYBE THEY'LL MAKE A GOOD MEAL.
SURELY YOU JEST.
TWITCH
...
SOME-THING'S NEAR...
BROTHER?
RUSTLE
RUSTLE
BETTER BE SOMETHING TASTY THIS TIME...
RUSTLE
RUSTLE
RUSTLE
RUSTLE

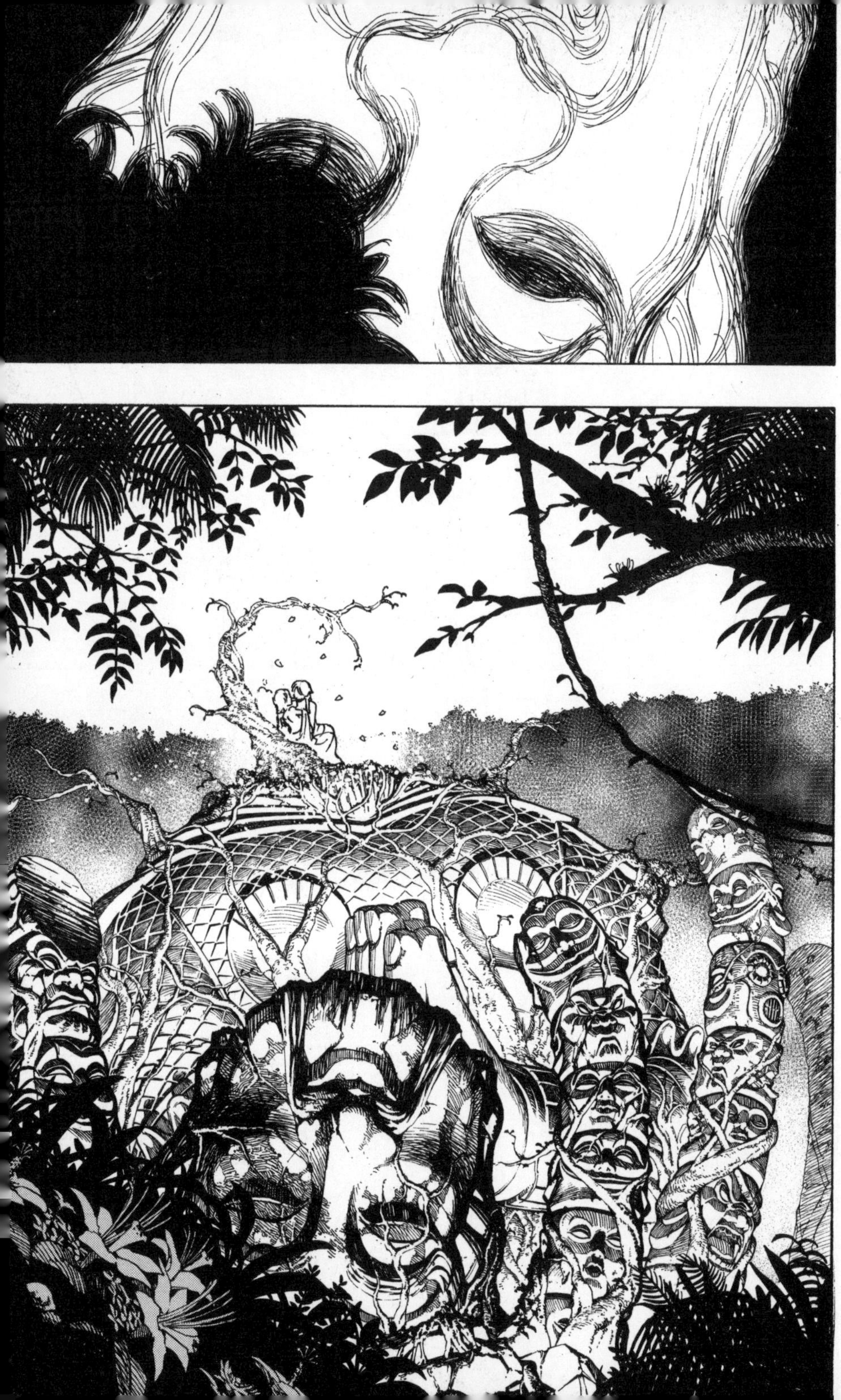

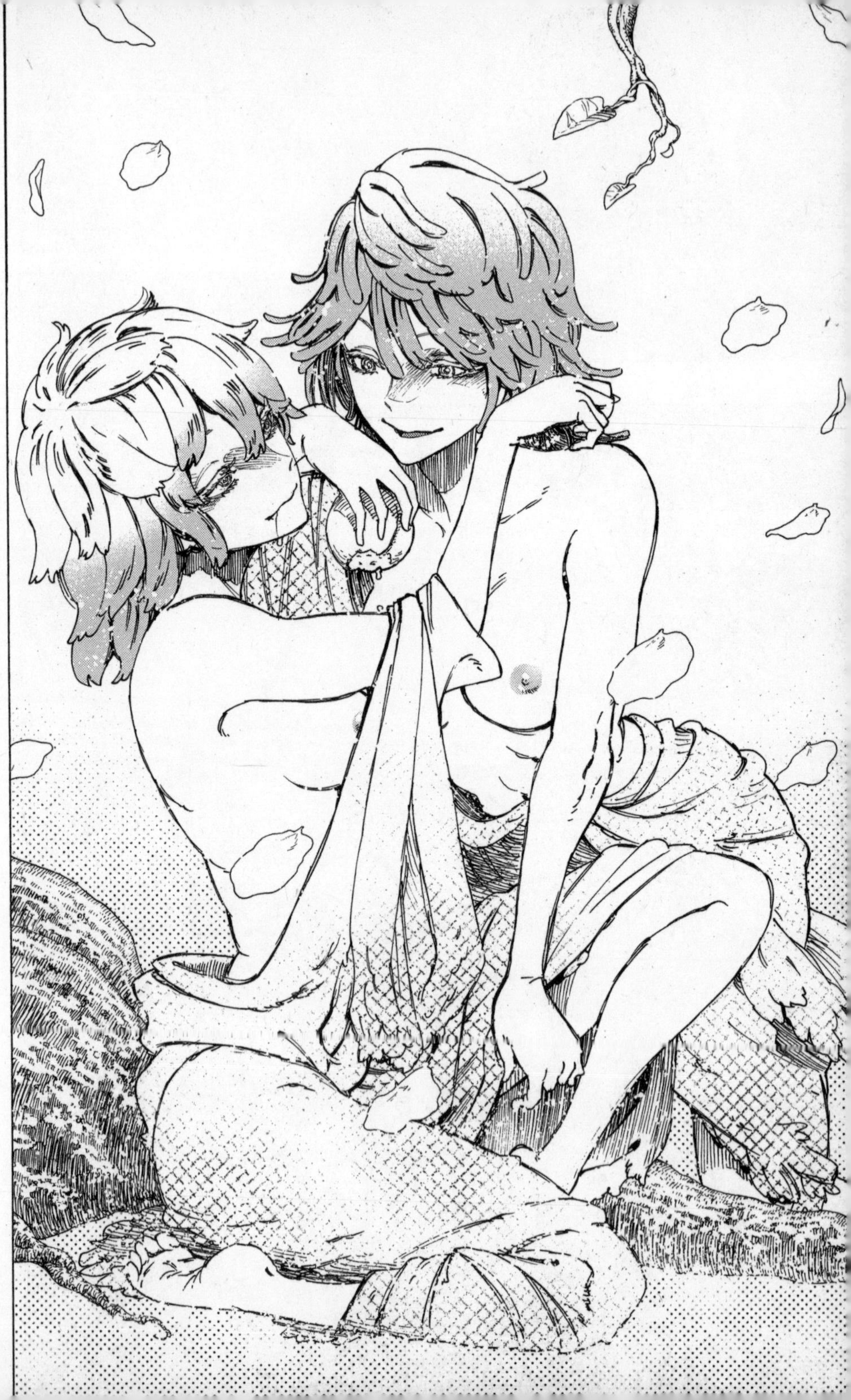

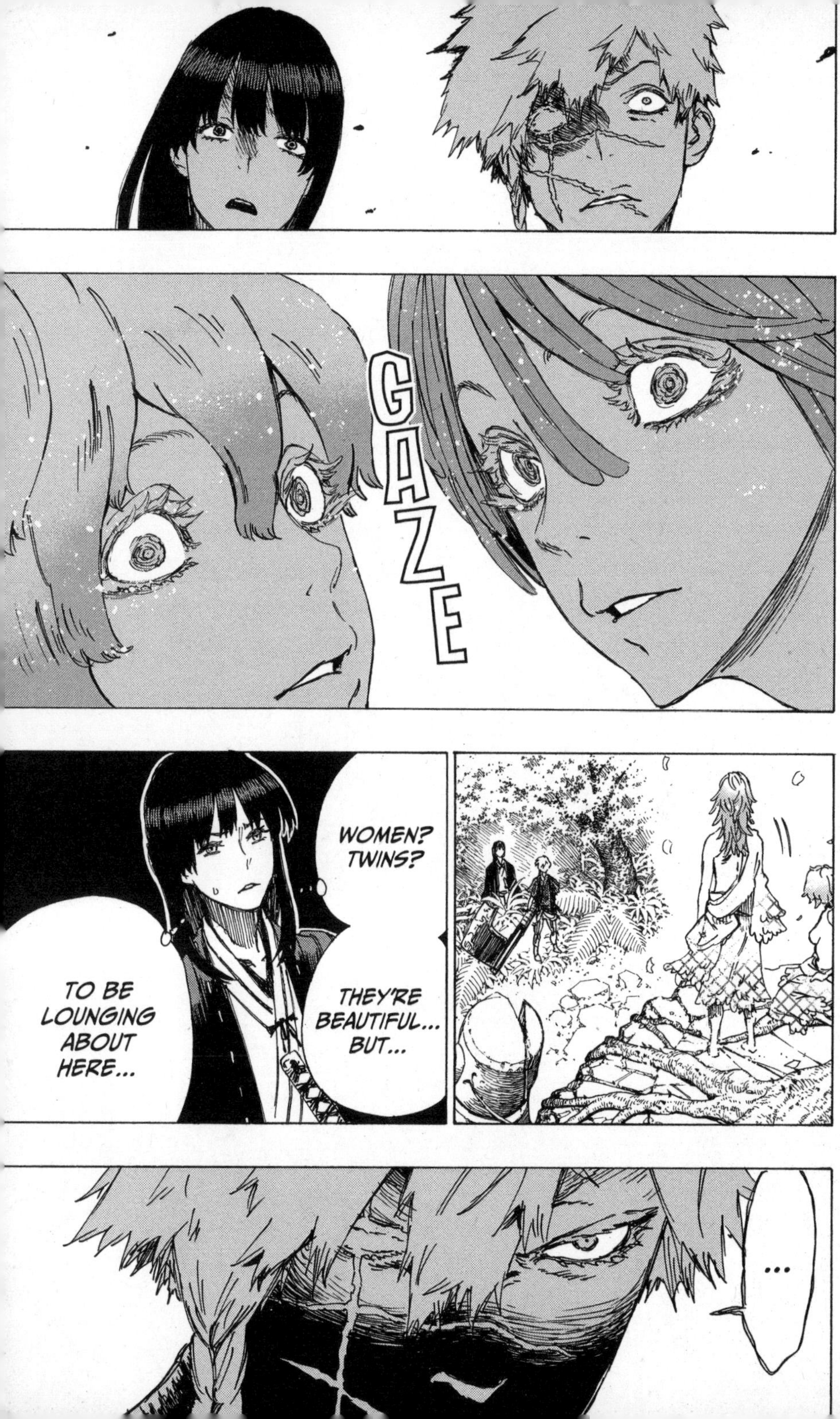
GAZE
WOMEN? TWINS?
THEY'RE BEAUTIFUL... BUT...
TO BE LOUNGING ABOUT HERE...
...

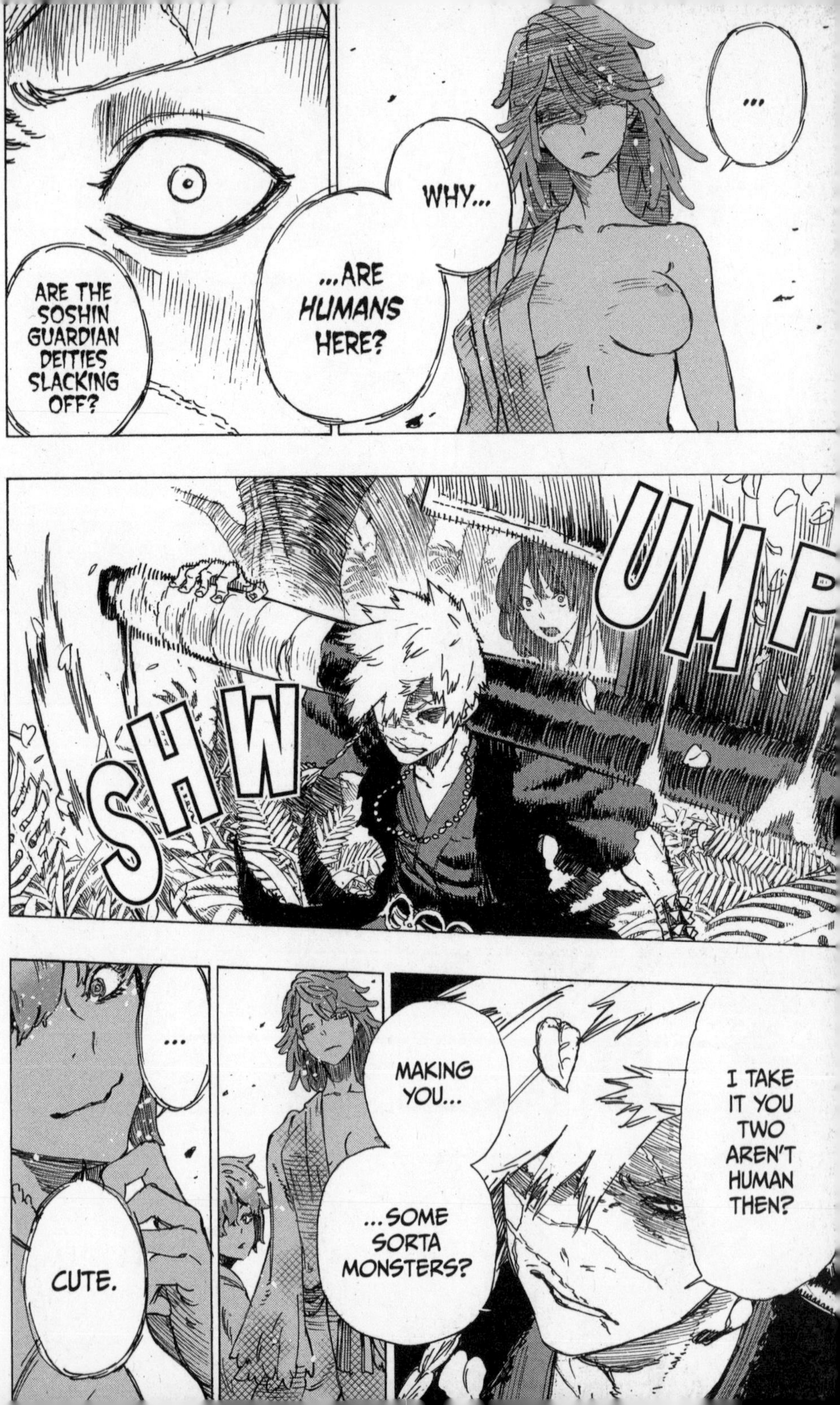
...
WHY...
...ARE HUMANS HERE?
ARE THE SOSHIN GUARDIAN DEITIES SLACKING OFF?
SHW
UMP
I TAKE IT YOU TWO AREN'T HUMAN THEN?
MAKING YOU...
...SOME SORTA MONSTERS?
...
CUTE.

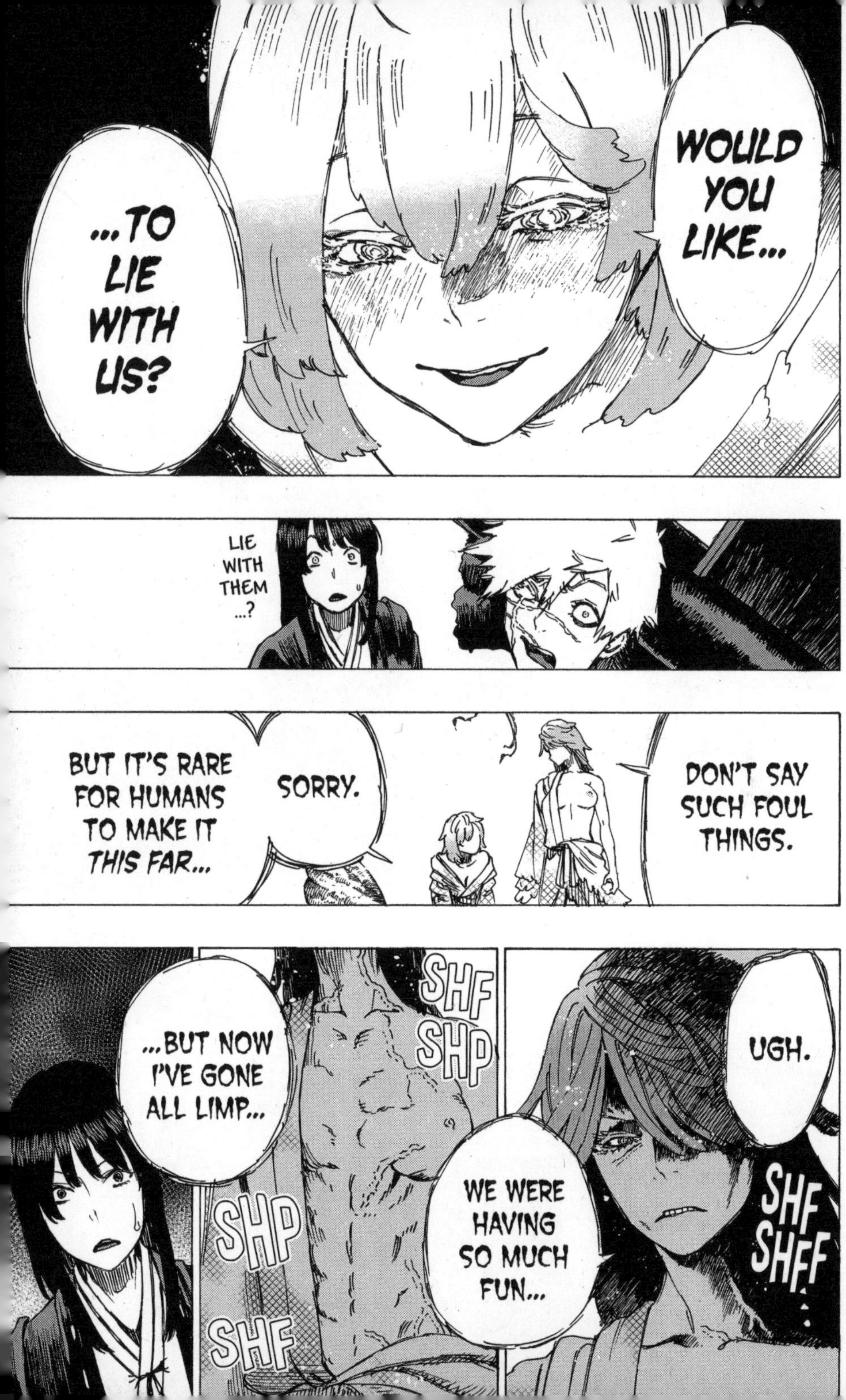
WOULD YOU LIKE...
...TO LIE WITH US?
LIE WITH THEM ...?
DON'T SAY SUCH FOUL THINGS.
SORRY.
BUT IT'S RARE FOR HUMANS TO MAKE IT THIS FAR...
UGH.
WE WERE HAVING SO MUCH FUN...
SHF SHFF
SHF SHP
...BUT NOW I'VE GONE ALL LIMP...
SHP
SHF

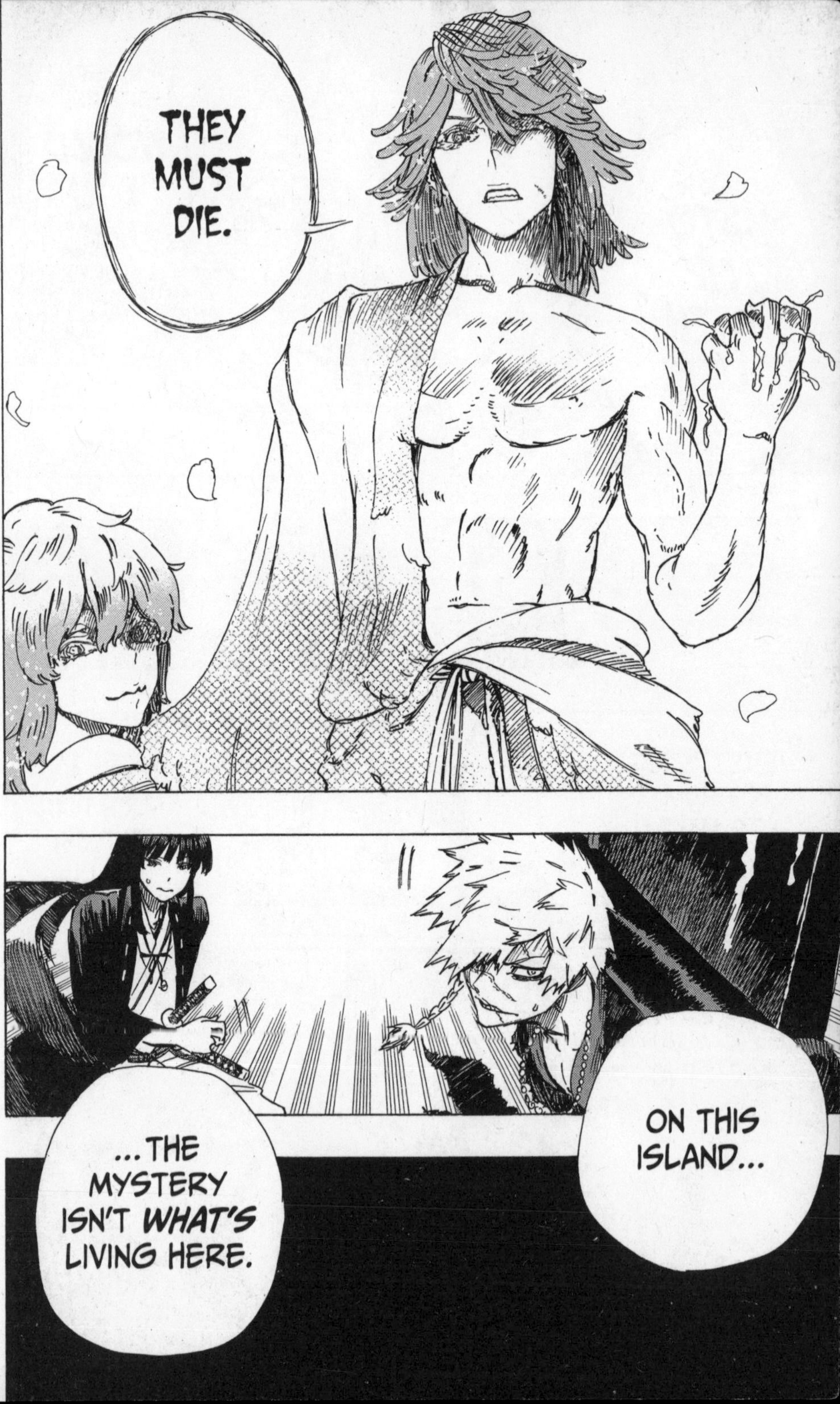
THEY MUST DIE.
ON THIS ISLAND...
...THE MYSTERY ISN'T *WHAT'S* LIVING HERE.

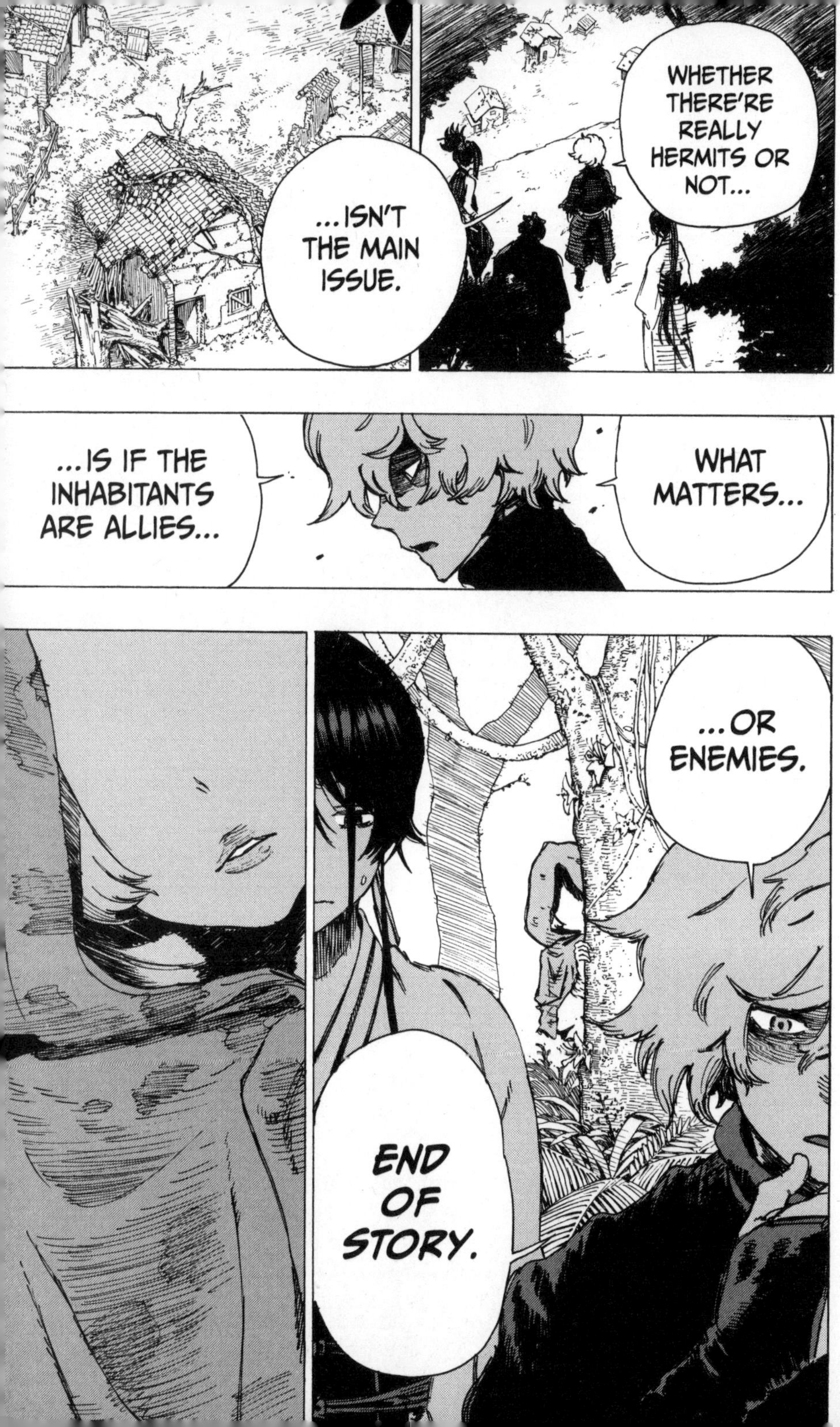
WHETHER THERE'RE REALLY HERMITS OR NOT...
...ISN'T THE MAIN ISSUE.
WHAT MATTERS...
...IS IF THE INHABITANTS ARE ALLIES...
...OR ENEMIES.
END OF STORY.

Hell's Paradise Fashion Review

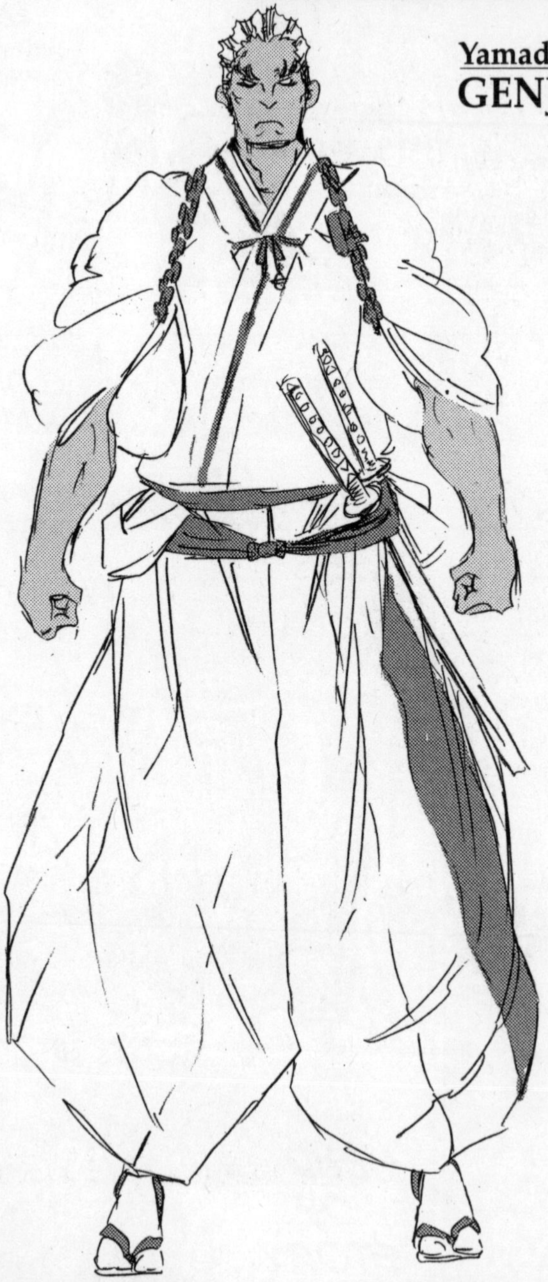

Yamada Asaemon
GENJI

EVALUATION ► FASHION DEITY ★×∞

USING CHAINS AS TASUKI CORDS IS SO TACKY IT COMES OFF AS COOL. ALL HAIL HIS CONFIDENT, UNBRIDLED MACHISMO.

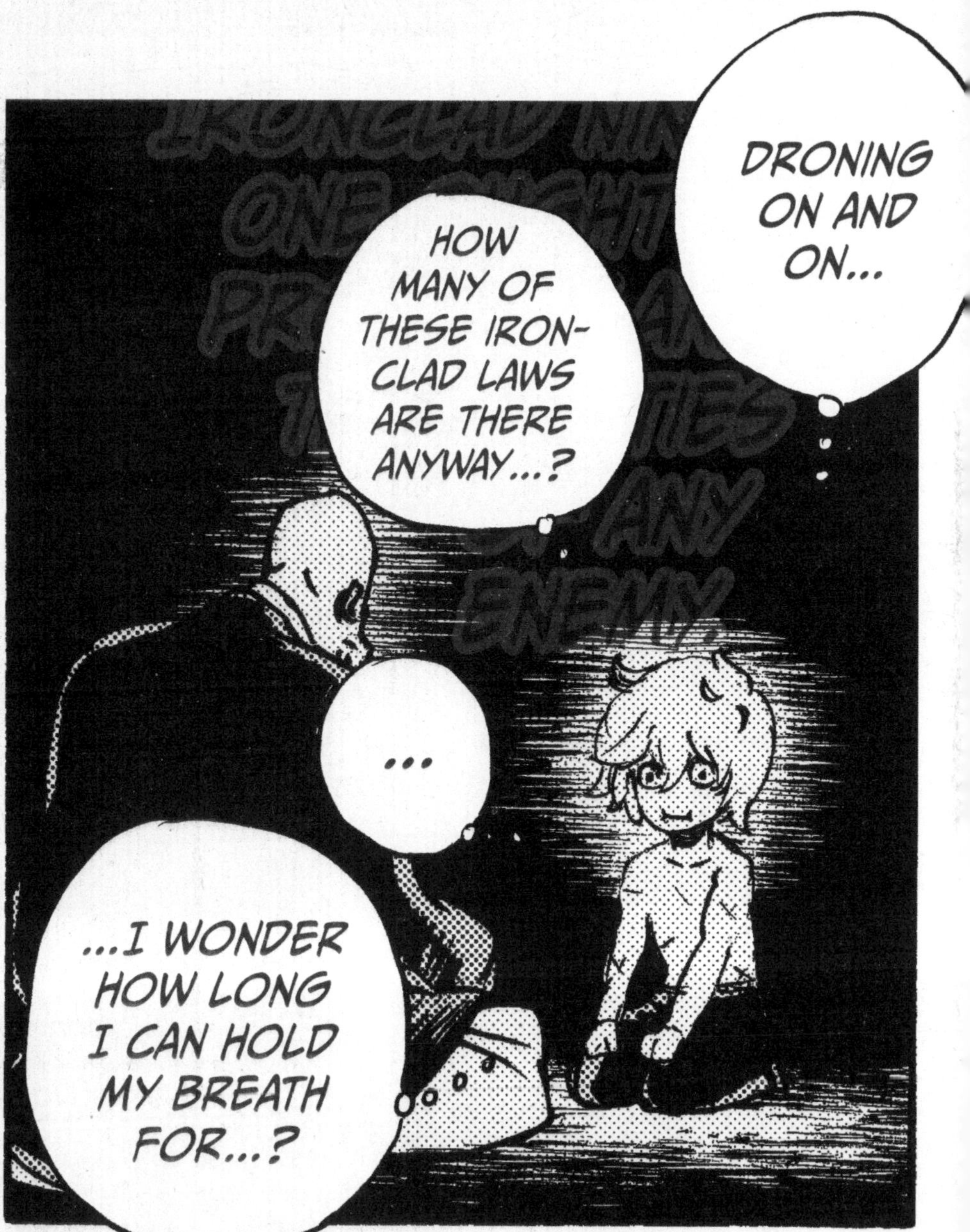
DRONING ON AND ON...
HOW MANY OF THESE IRON-CLAD LAWS ARE THERE ANYWAY...?
...
...I WONDER HOW LONG I CAN HOLD MY BREATH FOR...?

PRODUCED WITH HELP FROM

Akane Arimoto

Megumi Uriu

Chu Kawasaki

Norito Sasaki

Yukinobu Tatsu

EDITOR

Hideaki Sakakibara

DESIGNERS

Hideaki Shimada

Daiki Asami

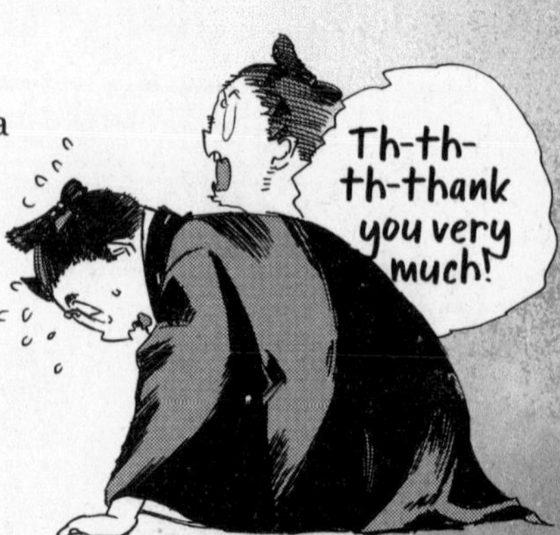
Th-th-th-thank you very much!

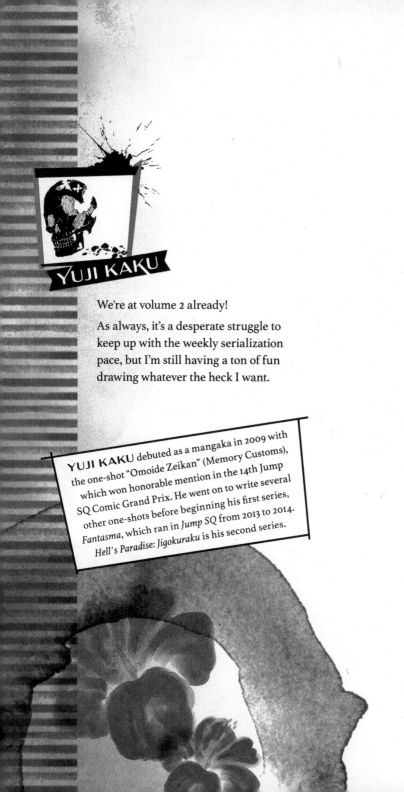

YUJI KAKU

We're at volume 2 already!

As always, it's a desperate struggle to keep up with the weekly serialization pace, but I'm still having a ton of fun drawing whatever the heck I want.

YUJI KAKU debuted as a mangaka in 2009 with the one-shot "Omoide Zeikan" (Memory Customs), which won honorable mention in the 14th Jump SQ Comic Grand Prix. He went on to write several other one-shots before beginning his first series, *Fantasma*, which ran in *Jump SQ* from 2013 to 2014. *Hell's Paradise: Jigokuraku* is his second series.

p.17

SWING
FWSH
TMP

This monster is essentially the stereotypical *oni* found in the classic tale of "Momotaro" (as the inhabitants of Onigashima) and many modern Japanese stories. These oni are visually defined by horns, a spiked metal club and a tiger-skin waistcloth.

The Tao, also known as Taoism, Daoism or "the Way," refers to the traditional Chinese faith and philosophy supposedly founded in the fourth century BCE by Laozi (called "Roshi" in Japanese, whereas Confucius was known as "Koshi"). It promotes ethics based on naturalness and simplicity, rather than dogma and rituals.

MANY OF THE MONSTERS HAVE ATTRIBUTES THAT APPEAR RELIGIOUS IN DESIGN.
THINGS RELATED TO BUDDHISM AND THE TAO.

p.37

p.51

YOU RONIN OF AKO SOUGHT VENGEANCE FOR YOUR MASTER...
AND ALL 47 OF YOU WILL LOSE YOUR HEADS FOR YOUR SINS!
EVEN WHEN FATHER JOINED THE REVENGE SCHEME AND PAID WITH HIS LIFE.

The Aza brothers' backstory references the historical event that the famous tale of the 47 ronin is based on (though the daimyo's name here in *Hell's Paradise: Jigokuraku* was changed from "Naganori" to "Takunori"). It was a popular tale in Bunraku puppet theater and Kabuki plays, though censorship laws meant that the names were usually changed there, too.

UM. KIKATSUGAN, SERIOUSLY ?!
I WAS HOPING FOR SOMETHING AT LEAST A LITTLE APPETIZING.
KIKATSUGAN ?
KIKATSUGAN: RATIONS CARRIED BY NINJA, MADE PRIMARILY OF GRAINS. THE OLD SAYING GOES, "ONE DAY, THREE MOUNDS, KEEPS MIND AND BODY SOUND."
USED WHATEVER I COULD FIND AROUND HERE.
SO I THINK YOU MEANT TO SAY, "WELL DONE, THANK YOU."

p.70

Kikatsugan rations have a basis in reality. The name literally means "starving round," and the corresponding *suikatsugan* means "thirst round." They were usually made of buckwheat flour and *umeboshi* (pickled plums), respectively.

IT'S AS IF WE'VE BEEN TOSSED INTO...
...A POORLY EXECUTED, ILL-CONCEIVED MANDALA.
p.77

Mandala literally means "circle" in Sanskrit, but it's known as a Buddhist and Hindu spiritual symbol that represents the universe with intricate, round geometric designs. Incidentally, mandalas also appear in Japanese Shintoism, though the blended elements on the island come from mainland Asian religions.

p.91

ARE YOU EMISHI?
IF SO, MIGHT WE SOJOURN IN YOUR VILLAGE?
EMISHI? WUZZAT?

The Emishi were a specific ethnic group based in northern Japan with genetic ties to the indigenous Ainu and a history of resisting the rule of Japanese emperors and governments from the south. Sanka, on the other hand, refers to a fringe caste of quasi-nomadic tribes who lived outside of typical governmental jurisdiction, akin to the Romani of Europe. They suffered from discrimination, as do their modern descendants.

TAKE THE CHILD.
WE'LL MAKE THIS ONE POINT OUT OTHER SETTLEMENTS BEFORE THE EXECUTION.
NN!
NNN!!
THAT'LL FINISH OFF THE SANKA IN THIS REGION.
p.92

Hell's Paradise
JIGOKURAKU

VIZ SIGNATURE Edition

STORY AND ART BY **YUJI KAKU**

TRANSLATION **Caleb Cook**
RETOUCH + LETTERING **Mark McMurray**
DESIGN **Shawn Carrico**
EDITOR **David Brothers**

JIGOKURAKU © 2018 by Yuji Kaku
All rights reserved.
First published in Japan in 2018 by SHUEISHA Inc., Tokyo.
English translation rights arranged by SHUEISHA Inc.

The stories, characters and incidents mentioned in
this publication are entirely fictional.

Printed in the U.S.A.

Published by VIZ Media, LLC
P.O. Box 77010
San Francisco, CA 94107

10 9 8 7 6 5 4 3 2 1
First printing, May 2020

VIZ MEDIA
viz.com

VIZ SIGNATURE
vizsignature.com

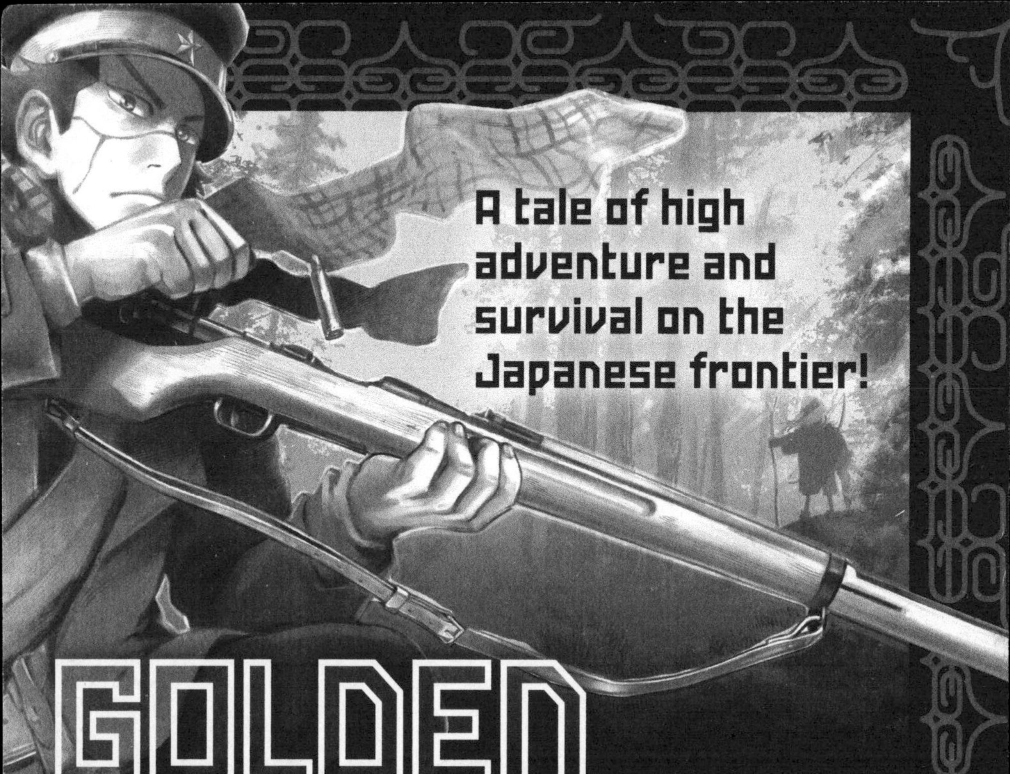

A tale of high adventure and survival on the Japanese frontier!

GOLDEN
KAMUY

In the early twentieth century, Russo-Japanese War veteran Saichi Sugimoto searches the wilderness of the Japanese frontier of Hokkaido for a hoard of hidden gold. With only a cryptic map and a native Ainu girl to help him, Saichi must also deal with every murderous cutthroat, bandit and rogue who knows about the treasure!

Story and Art by **Satoru Noda**

ABARA
COMPLETE DELUXE EDITION
TSUTOMU NIHEI

A visually stunning work of sci-fi horror from the creator of **BIOMEGA** and **BLAME!**

A vast city lies under the shadow of colossal, ancient tombs, the identity of their builders lost to time. In the streets of the city something is preying on the inhabitants, something that moves faster than the human eye can see and leaves unimaginable horror in its wake.

Tsutomu Nihei's dazzling, harrowing dystopian thriller is presented here in a single-volume hardcover edition featuring full-color pages and foldout illustrations. This volume also includes the early short story "Digimortal."

RATED **T** OLDER TEEN

VIZ

TOKYO GHOUL

COMPLETE BOX SET

STORY AND ART BY **SUI ISHIDA**

KEN KANEKI is an ordinary college student until a violent encounter turns him into the first half-human, half-Ghoul hybrid. Trapped between two worlds, he must survive Ghoul turf wars, learn more about Ghoul society and master his new powers.

[
Box set collects all fourteen volumes of the original *Tokyo Ghoul* series. Includes an exclusive double-sided poster.
]

COLLECT THE COMPLETE SERIES

THIS IS THE LAST PAGE.

Hell's Paradise: Jigokuraku reads from right to left, starting in the upper-right corner. Japanese is read from right to left, meaning that action, sound effects and word-balloon order are completely reversed from English order.

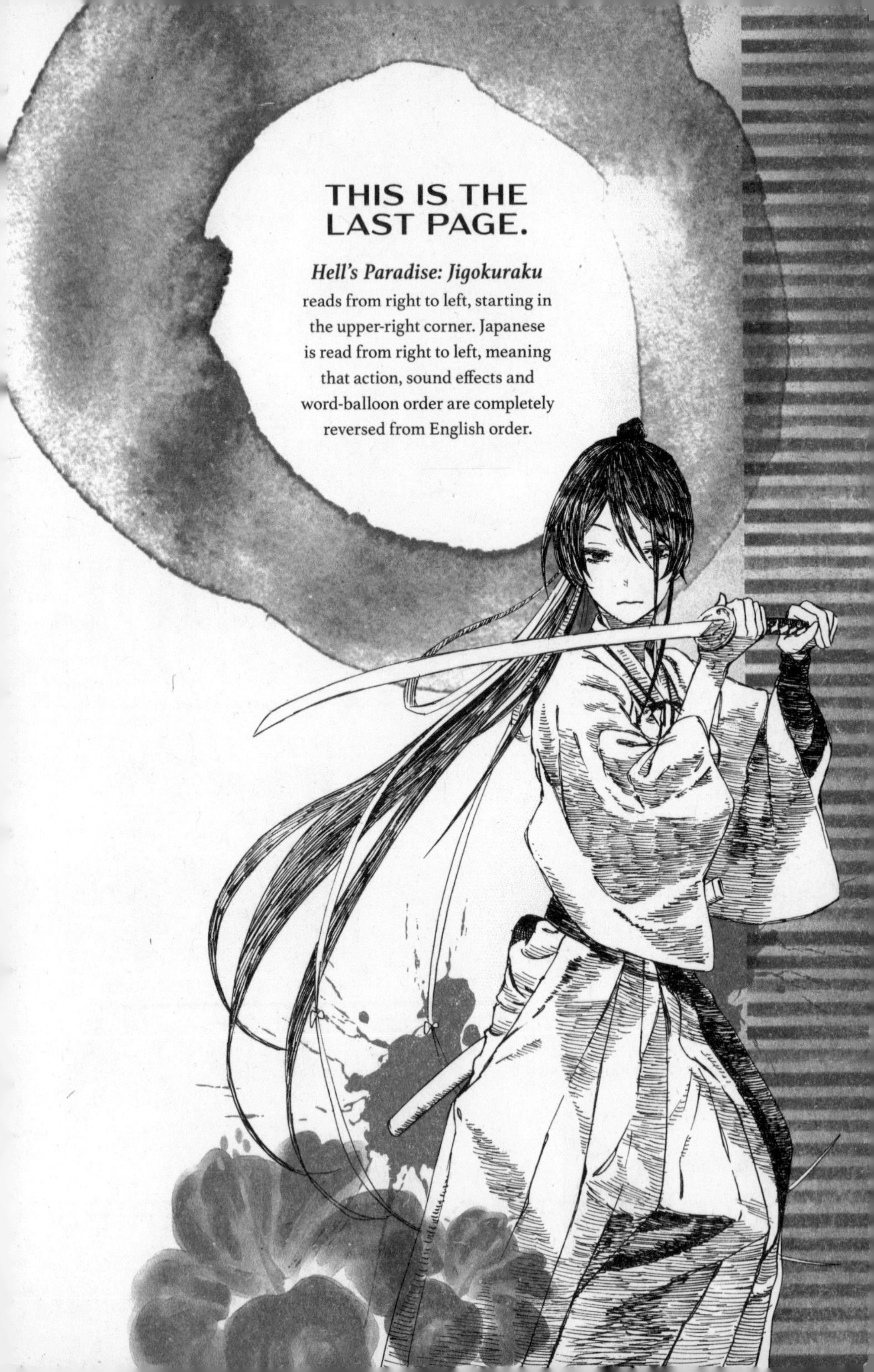